SADDLE BAG AND SPINNING WHEEL

SADDLE BAG AND SPINNING WHEEL

being the Civil War letters of

George W. Peddy, M.D.

Surgeon, 56th Georgia Volunteer Regiment, C.S.A.

and his wife

Kate Featherston Peddy

EDITED BY

George Peddy Cuttino
Charles Howard Candler Professor
of Medieval History
Emory University

MERCER UNIVERSITY PRESS
MACON, GEORGIA

MUP/765

First published in 1981.

Books published by Mercer University Press are printed on acid free paper that meets the requirements of American National Standard for Information Sciences—Permanence of Paper for Printed Library Materials.

Library of Congress Cataloging-in-Publication Data

Peddy, George Washington, 1834–1913.
Saddle Bag and Spinning Wheel

Letters exchanged between Confederate surgeon G. Peddy and his wife, Z. Peddy, 1861–1865.
Includes Index.
1. Peddy, George Washington, 1834–1913. 2. Peddy, Zerlina Catherine, 1838–1927. 3. United States—History—Civil War, 1861–1865—Personal Narratives—Confederated side. 4. Confederate States of America—Army—Surgeons—Correspondence. 5. Heard Co., Ga.—Biography. 6. Surgeons—Southern States—Biography. I. Peddy, Zerlina Catherine, 1838–1927. II Cuttino, George Peddy. III. Title.
E625.P36973.782 [B]
80-83663

978–088146–119–0

In Memoriam
AVI ET AVIAE

Kate Featherston Peddy and Laura

George Washington Peddy, M.D.

Contents

Preface

It may seem strange that a professor of medieval history should venture into the field of The War Between the States or The Civil War (depending on which side one takes) or, as I prefer to call it, The Late Unpleasantness. The explanation is that the letters here edited are family letters. They were kept in my great grandfather's trunk, a receptacle that was always referred to in my youth in terms that might have been applied to the Holy of Holies. But at least the family was historically minded, for practically everything in the trunk has meaning for a historian; and it was all kept. The letters here edited were written by my grandparents during the years 1861-1865, while he was a surgeon in the Confederate forces and she, a housewife in Franklin, Heard County, Georgia. Both the home and the front, then, are represented. Owing to the vicissitudes of an army in the field, understandably more of his letters than of hers survived. But the continuity is still there, so that the letters afford an unusual view of The War, with all the comedy and tragedy, the humor and pathos, of picayune details and world-shaking events. They are the stuff of which history is really made: the chronicle of the unfamous, about whom the historian knows so little and would like to know so much.

I have written an introduction that places the letters in their historical context, but I have deliberately refrained from commenting on the contents of the letters, for they speak for themselves. In editing, I have omitted nothing, but I have refrained from adding an *apparatus criticus* that would be appropriate to medieval documents. Accordingly, I have ignored crossed out, interlineated, or corrected words. I have retained the spelling, which is often quaint, to say the least, but I have sometimes altered or added punctuation, since my grandfather's style especially would today be described as stream of consciousness.

In adding footnotes dealing with military operations and persons, I have drawn extensively on Mark Mayo Boatner III, *The Civil War Dictionary* (New York, 1959).

To Dan T. Carter, James Z. Rabun, the late Bell I. Wiley, and J. Harvey Young, my colleagues in United States history, I am indebted for answers to bothersome questions. My special thanks go to Janet W. Clark for turning some 860 pages of my minuscule into a readable typescript.

G. P. C.

Emory University
St. Frideswide's Day 1980

Introduction

GEORGIA IN 1860 had a population of 1,057,336, of which 591,550 were whites, 462,198, slaves, 3,550, free blacks, and 38, Indians. Heard County, which was the birthplace and residence of the authors of the letters in this volume, is in west central Georgia, bordering on Alabama towards the west, Carroll County to the north, Coweta County to the east, and Troup County to the south. It was, and still is, predominantly agricultural and consequently poor. There is still no railroad running through it, so that the nearest shipping point is, and was, either the small village of Hogansville in Troup County or, more important, Newnan in Coweta County. Coweta County in 1860 had 7,433 whites, 7,248 slaves (607 of them mulattoes), and 22 free blacks (5 of them mulattoes), making a total of 14,703. Newnan, the county seat, had a population of 2,546. Heard was about half the size of Coweta, having a total population of 7,805. Of these, 4,979 were whites (six of them foreign-born), 2,811 slaves (190 mulattoes), and 15 free blacks (11 mulattoes). Franklin, the county seat situated on the Chattahoochee River, was little more than a village. It is little more today, despite some intruding industry, and represents a surviving enclave of the ante-bellum South. The scenery is charming, including a Lovers' Leap of Indian-fable fame. It might be taken from the descriptions of Georgia in Stephen Vincent Benet's *John Brown's Body*. Even some of the ante-bellum homes are still there, although considerably altered and, most of them, in need of repairing and painting.

The population figures bear out the prognostication of James B. McPherson, later to die as a Union general in the battle of Atlanta, when he wrote on 20 April 1861 to a fellow West Pointer and Georgian, E. P. Alexander:

> This war is not going to be the ninety days affair that papers and politicians are predicting. Both sides are in deadly earnest, and it is going to be fought out to the bitter end. . . *It must be lost.* Your whole population is about eight millions, while the North has twenty millions. Of your eight millions, three millions are slaves who may become an element of danger. You have no army, no navy, no treasury, and practically none of the manufactures and machine shops for the support of armies, and for war on a large scale. You are but scattered agricultural communities, and you will be cut off from the rest of the world by blockade. Your cause is foredoomed to failure.[1]

McPherson with uncanny accuracy predicted the course and outcome of the war.

The people living in Heard County in 1860 were young; that is, the peak of what sociologists would call the population-curve was in the age-group 20-29 (both white and black), although there were three people over ninety and two female slaves who could boast a hundred years or more. There were 121 more male whites than females and 20 more female blacks than males.[2]

Curiously, there were few people between the ages of 15 and 19 (both white and black), probably owing to a combination of the Mexican War and the westward movement.

Both the authors of these letters were in the age-group 20-29. George Washington Peddy was born on 10 April 1834, and Zerlina Catherine Featherston, on 26 April 1838, both in Franklin. They were married on 23 June 1859, a little more than two years before the letters begin. Their first child, born on 21 June 1860, was really called Annie Laurie, after the song of that name, but she appears in the letters as Laura, the name that is on her tombstone (she died on 2 May 1941). There was a war baby, Charlie Featherston Peddy, who was born on 18 June 1864 and died on 16 September 1865. The other children, four girls, were all born after the war.[3] All but two of the children later received college educations. Both George Washington and Zerlina Catherine Featherston Peddy died and are buried in Newnan, he on 6 May 1913, and she on 9 July 1927. They had moved to Newnan in 1877, following Mrs. Peddy's father's family by eight years.

---

[1]Quoted in R.S. Henry, *The Story of the Confederacy*, revised edition (New York, c1936), p. 18.

[2]All population figures are from J.C.G. Kennedy, *Population of the United States in 1860; compiled from the original returns of the eighth census, under the direction of the Secretary of the Interior* (Washington, 1864).

[3]See the accompanying genealogical chart. All information about the families comes from family Bibles and papers and word-of-mouth tradition.

This is not the place to record an extensive family genealogy, but something might be said to indicate what social and economic milieu constituted the background of the correspondents. G. W. Peddy was said to have been so eager for an education that he used to run a mile and a half to school, even during winter snows. At any rate, he attended Tulane University, afterwards continuing through the New Orleans School of Medicine, from which he received the degree of Doctor of Medicine on 1 April 1859. He had left home at the age of seventeen and gone to work in a drug store, beginning his study of medicine in the evenings after working hours. After the war he served in the Senate of the State of Georgia and acquired a considerable reputation as a physician whose skill in diagnosis and prognosis is said to have caught the attention of physicians in the East. He was a lover of fine livestock and he owned one of the first automobiles in Coweta County (not to speak of the first Jersey cow). He could not abide organized religion. His father was Alexander George Peddy, also a physician and, unlike the son, something of a tippler. His mother was Celina D. H. Shackleford. His paternal grandfather, Jeremiah, was born in Ireland and served in the American forces during the Revolution.[4] Dr. and Mrs. A. G. Peddy were living in Coosa County, Alabama, during the time of these letters. They had in all four sons, two of whom (William and John T.) are mentioned in the correspondence, and eight daughters.

Zerlina Catherine Featherston was the eldest of the twelve children, all living during the war and many mentioned in the correspondence. Her father was Lucius Horace Featherston, a distinguished lawyer who held the rank of General in the Georgia Militia and who later served as Judge of the Superior Court.[5] Her mother was Maria Ann Tompkins, who came from a family noted for its ability to shoot on sight.

Mrs. Peddy's recollections later in life of her maternal grandparents were both vivid and nostalgic. She wrote:

> Grandpa was Unitarian and liked to argue religion. He was one of the most generous men who ever lived. He met a needy man one day — took off all his clothes, gave them to the man, and went the back way home. One time a circuit rider came along walking. After entertaining him, on the morning when he was ready to leave, grandpa had a negro to bring out a horse. "My friend," he said to the circuit rider, "this is your horse."
>
> He was especially fond of fine fast horses. He had one horse for which he gave $1000. He had 40 or more horses at a time. Every one who was visiting had a horse

[4]*Georgia's Roster of the Revolution*, p. 364. See also *American Biography; a new cyclopedia* (American Historical Society, New York, 1931), xlvi. 237-8.

[5]His papers are deposited in the Emory University Library, along with the letters here edited. Many references to the Peddy and Featherston families may be found in M.G. Jones and L. Reynolds, *Coweta County Chronicles* (Atlanta, 1928).

and went horseback. There was a carriage house across the road. When a horse went out from there he was shined so one could see himself. There was a set of large granite horse blocks from which ladies could mount.

There was a negro called Uncle Jake who did nothing except care for and drive the six mule wagon.

Grandpa was good to his slaves. There were ten negro houses in a row. A walnut tree was in front of each house. There were other houses besides these. The houses were ceiled and comfortable. "I tell you child—your grandpa couldn't have slept if one of his negroes had been cold."

There was a flock of 60 or 75 sheep. After the sheep were sheared the negro women spun thread on rainy days. Poor whites wove a heavy lined overcoat for each negro on grandpa's place.

There was a specially prepared room in Uncle Jake's house for the slaves to dance. Sometimes there were 16 couples of negroes on the floor at one time. The little negroes beat straws.

There were seven negroes to work around the house, four negro men besides the cook, house girl, and milking woman.

Sixteen cows were milked. The dairy had water running through it. (Grandpa owned the first pump in that section.) In this running water were broad deep white bowls for sweet milk — next deep places for jars of buttermilk. A string of negroes came each noon for a share of milk and butter. A small family would get a gallon, large families more.

Aunt Nancy and Uncle Jake had twenty children.

"Uncle Mose" made furniture of lumber from grandpa's saw mill.

The bee house was 8 ft. sq. It slanted to the back. Had openings in 3 sides which could be opened and honey taken out.

The smoke house was about 20 ft. sq. Tiers upon tiers of meat, killed about 125 hogs at one time. Oaken barrels were sunk into the ground. These were used for lard.

The plan of the house at "Hollow Chestnut" was a large, square two story house with a porch all around. There were four large rooms with two wide halls running all the way through and crossing in the center. Back of the house was the kitchen and a store room. There were more dishes in that room than you find in a lot of stores. I'll never forget all those beautiful china dishes. There were seven dozen each of dinner, breakfast, and dessert plates of blue china. You could see through them when held to the light. Had every size dish from one to hold a partridge to one big enough for a shoat.

The silver was made of silver money. When your grandma bought any kind of dress she always bought the whole bolt so nobody could have a dress like it.

In front and to the side of the house was a flower garden with winding walks. Along the road for about 2 miles were walnut trees. Across the road in front of the house was a park with benches, etc. Beyond the flower garden to the back of the house was a fish pond with a cement bottom.

The Featherstons emigrated from England to Virginia before the Revolution and, to the dismay of some of their descendants, were loyalists during the War of Independence. L. H. Featherston owned 22-27 slaves, and G. W. Peddy only one, at the time of these letters.[6] Both families, then, were of Anglo-Saxon and Scotch-Irish stock and belonged to that class that would be described in present-day England as "middle drawer." Despite Dr. Peddy's medical degree, his grammar, syntax, and spelling were far inferior to those of his wife, for she had attended College Temple in Newnan. Mrs. Peddy and Laura remained unreconstructed Rebels to the end. Mrs. Peddy hated Lincoln with a passion; and the surest way to torment her was to stand safely outside the window and whistle "Marching Through Georgia." One of Mrs. Peddy's brothers ("Bud Lou" in the letters), the family firebrand, found it expedient to quit the state of Georgia after the war because of his connection with the Ku Klux Klan. Laura even withdrew from the local Methodist Church in Newnan at the time of the unification of the Northern and Southern Methodist Churches and sent her contributions to a recalcitrant Southern Methodist Church in South Carolina.

---

[6]L.H. Featherston's taxable property in 1860 amounted to $28,940: 640 acres of land ($6,300); 22 slaves ($20,100); 6 mules, 6 horses and colts, 1 yoke of oxen, 14-15 cattle, 50 hogs, 2 waggons, 1 buggy, and furniture ($2,540).

Part I.

COASTAL OPERATIONS IN GEORGIA

28 OCTOBER 1861 - 18 APRIL 1862
1-55

Georgia seceded from the Union on 19 January 1861. Two weeks before, on 3 January, Gov. Joseph E. Brown, evincing the same anxiety towards Ft. Pulaski below Savannah as the South Carolinians were expressing towards Ft. Sumter in Charleston, ordered its occupation. At the time Ft. Pulaski was unoccupied and contained a little ammunition and a few old cannon. The first shot was fired on Ft. Sumter at 4:30 A.M. on 12 April 1861, thus beginning the Civil War. Apprehensive of invasion from the sea, especially after Federal capture of the forts at Port Royal Sound, S. C. on 7 November 1861, Gov. Brown sent state troops to the coast. It was with these troops that Dr. Peddy served, first at Camp Harrison in Screven County, then at Camp Satilla near Brunswick, at Camp Lee outside Savannah, and at Camp Defiance and Camp Brown below Savannah. Ft. Pulaski surrendered to Union forces on 11 April 1862.

1

Head Quarters

Milledgeville, Ga. Oct. 28th 1861

Ordered That you proceed to Camp Harrison located at Initial Point on S. A. & Gulf R. R. and report for duty to the Col. commanding Col. J. J. Neely's Regt. in Genl. Geo. P. Harrison's Brigade of State Troops

By order of Commander-in-chief

H. H. Waters
Aid-de-Camp

To Surgeon
G. W. Peddy

2

Camp Harrison, Ga. Nov. 3rd/61

MY DEAR KITTIE,

I thought I would have written to you ere this, but I thought I would wait until the Regt. got organized and I got properly to discharge the duties of my office. I had to go to Milledgeville to get my commission. I have no news of importance to write, only we are all well with a few exception. Their is a few cases of measles. This is the prettyest country in the world: it is as level as a floor as far as the eye can see; no rocks but plenty of pine timber. I am well s[a]tisfied with my postition. I feel much healtherier here than I did at home. I have not had the headache since I left home. My horse came through safe but looks powerful bad. I have no use for him. I wish he was at home. Lou & Dr. Lane is doing the best in the world. I do not think their is any danger of a fight here, we are thirty miles from the cost. I have lived as well as I want to ever since I left home. I & Col. Nealy are keeping together. Tell Gen. that Capt. Night came down here with his company & got dissatisfied and went back home. Our Regt. is full & organized. We were all mustard in yesterday. We are safe here now. I had rather be here than at home, if I had you & sweet little Laura with me. I want to see you & her so much. I think of you & her all the while. I wish I could get to kiss her once. I do not think I would quit in a week. Kittie, take good care of yourself & little Laura & try not get sick. Tell her Pa will bring you & her a great many pretty things when he comes home. Kittie, rest assured that I love you & Laura better evry day I live, notwithstanding I am away from you. I have not got enough bed cloths. I wrote to you for two blankets & you only sent me one. I wish you have had done so, but I will try to do without it. Tell Gen. that if he comes here, I want him to come prepared to take my horse back home. He can come for half faris if he will get a military ticket, & he can get it if he is on military buisiness. Let me know you are pleased at your old home and how you are getting along evry way. I am anxious to hear from you. Let me have all the news about town. Their is about four thousand troops at this place. It is the grandest scene I ever viewed: the railroad runs right through the encampment. A man in Columbus company cut his own througt here yesterday. My Dear Kittie, let me hear from you twice a week. I will send you some money as soon as I get some so that you can get along more independenly. If a letter comes from Harlan to me, send it to me. You read it first. Let me know what the people have to say about my coming off.

Your true & faithful Husband,
G. W. Peddy

Direct you letter to me Camp Harrison.

3

Camp Harrison, Nov. 6th/61

MY DEAR KITTIE,

I write you a short note per Alo. Williams. I am well & getting along finely. I frequently set dow[n] quietly & try to imagine how you & Laura looks. I can see exacly how you look, but I cannot ixactly comprehend how Little sweet Laura looks. Let me know if you have any letter from Dr. Harlan. I want to know what the people have to say about my leaving home, wheather anything or nothing. Tell your pa if he has a chance to get corn & foddy for any of my debts, to take it & house it up for me until I get home. My horse is falling off since I got here. He does not have much appetite to eat. Corn is worth one dollar 25ct per bushel down here & it is light chaffy stuff that is not fit to feed on. The Government feeds him for me & pays me ten dollars per month for the use of him, & I use him myself & no one else. I may sell him to some one ere long. Let me know how the pigs & evrything is doing at home. Kittie, write me long letters, for I will love to read them from you. Kiss Little Laura for me.

Yours until death,
G. W. Peddy

Direct your letter to me Camp Harrison, Scrivon post office.

4

Camp Harrison, Nov. 9th/861

DEAR KITTIE,

I have written you several letters since I arrived here & not a word have I had from you. I think you ought to write to me, for you & Laura are the pride of my life. Nothing would interest me so much in the way of a letter as one from your dear ha[n]d. I learned that you had gone on a pleasure trip to Caralton from a letter that Dr. Lane has rec'ed. I would be truly happy if you would think of your best friend & most ardent admirer often enough to write to him once & a while. If I was accidentally to get killed without hearing from you, it wold be if possible a sorce of regret after death. You will read in the papers of two Regts. having went from this place to help drive of[f] the fleet, but it is not so. Not a Regt. has moved yet nor will they in a short time, as I know of the fleet has takened the forts bellow Savannah. It, Savannah, is in great danger of being burned up by the fleet. I think we will have a fight or two before we get home. If we do, you need not be uneasy. If I get killed, it will be a glorious death to die in defence of my glorious South. I have read the Gov. message tonight. It is the best production I have seen in some time. Kittie, when I think of you & little Laura, it makes me proud to know that you & her are at home enjoying yourselves. Oh! how I want to see you. It seems to me that I cannot do without seeing you any longer. If it was in my power, I would keep you with me until the last hour of my existence. I can better realize how I love you & little Laura now than I ever could in my life. I am quite healthy here, this climate suits me finely. All that I like of enjoying myself to the brim is not having you & Laura where I can see you evry hour.

Their is but little sickness in our Regt. yet. I have not got my medicine yet. I have done all my practice so far with 1 box Blue mass & a little piece of opium & a little ginger tea. Nov. 10th. My Dear My Dear, I seat myself this Sunday niigh[t] as it to finish my long & wearisom letter to you. It is not wearisom to me, but I fear it might be so to you to read, but I hope not. The arrival of the fleet has created considerable excitement in camps, but I feel no uneasiness as yet. I cannot think we will ever get into a fight, though we may. It makes no difference with me if we do, so I can get to see you & live with again it's all I care for. I often think of the many pleasures we have had together & the many happy moments we have spent in doting on our little sweet child. If I should unfortunately happen to die or get killed, I want you to raise our little girl so that she may [be] an honor to you & her unfortunate father. I wish you would often remind her of me. I love the little darling so well I know not how I can do without seeing her & your own lovly self much longer. Kittie, I have no letter from you yet. I do wish I could. It would allow me the most pleasure in the world. Kittie, I have heard that Dr. Harlan proposes to preach or be chaplain to our Regt. The Legislature at its last session created no such an office as chaplain of a Regt. He proposes to be chaplain any how if he gets no pay if we want him. If Rease of Grantville does not report favorably in a short time, we are going to get Dr. Harlan. I hope he will come. I feel proud of the notion of his coming. Kittie, tell Gen. I hope he will come & carry my horse home. He is the finest horse on the encampment, but from some cause he was appraised about the lowest. He was only appraised at $175. dollars & I am very much dissatisfied about it & want him at home for your use. I believe I can sell him before long for two hundred & fifty dollars, but I will not take it for him. If I had the money, I would send him back tomorrow. I want to keep him as long as he lives just because you like him. If I live to get home I will bring you & your ma a fine silk dress apiece. I will send you some money as soon as I draw some. When we start to meet the enemy I will write to you immediately, & if we get into a fight, I will write to you as soon as it is over. Let me know when you heard from the boys in Virginia & all the news they write. Let me hear also when you hear from Pa's what the news is with them. Billie Lane's son was right sick last night from indegestion & cold, but is up to day. Tell him I will tend to him right. He is a good a boy as their is in camp. Give Mozeley & Brewer my best respects & tell them to come to the defence of our cost. They will be well pleased. My love also to Uncle Jack, Sanders Favor & the ballance of my friends at home. Tell Jonnee, Sis, & Eddy to write to me; your ma & Pa & also all my friends you see. Tell Sallie & Julia if they want me to electioneer with any one in camps for them to send me word & I'll go at it with diligence.

Tell Asbury Copeland to come & have liberty or death. Milt McDonald is getting along finely. His health is improveing & he is well satisfied.

John Winchester is singing beautifully at this moment. Dr. Lane & Lou is well & doing finely.

Kittie, my dear, I would tell you how much I think of you & little Laura if I was not ashamed. You must let no one see all my letter. They might think I was a great simpleton of writing to you in the manner in which I do.

Write soon, my dorlard, for I am anxious to hear from you, you know.

Yours lovingly until death,
G. W. Peddy

Give my love to your Ant Kit.
I hope this will stir you up to write to me.

5

Franklin, Nov. 10th 1861.

MY DARLING HUSBAND,

It is my blessed privilege to seat myself this lovely Sabbath morning to respond to your letters and to tell you the reasons why I have not written before; directly after you left, I had a good opportunity of visiting aunt Sarah and Emily and thought I would get back before your letters reached here, but Pa had to go to Alabama, so he could not send for me sooner; Ma sent Johnny up to uncle Ben's with my letters but I had gone to Carralton and he left them for aunt Dump to send to me, but she did not have and opportunity of sending them. You can't imagine what I suffered up there with no way of getting news from you, I then set down and wrote to Ma to do, pray, send for me, which she did as soon as the buggy came home, so I got here last night at sundown and read your last letter with an aching heart, to think it would be such a long time before I could get you a letter, for the mail don't leave untill Wendsday, but while pondering and thinking I happened to think of Mr. Cones being here, and that I could send your letter by him this evening so that you could get it sooner. Words cannot tell the joy I felt while reading your letter, to know that the worshiping love that fills my heart and envelops my whole being for you finds an echo in your bosome; to say I love you seems like cold and meaningless words when compared to the language of my heart: my love, when you sit by yourself sometimes musing on home, and those that dwel there, think of me affectionately and as one who would feel it the dearest privilege to be by your side to share every privation and hards[h]ip. Without a murmur would I gladly undergo anything to see you once more. You don't know how much I want to see you. I never knew till now how much happiness and pleasure we had together. The days and hours we have spent together are the brightest spots on the desert waste of memory, and if you are only spared to come back, and I should like to see you, certainly no other joy on earth can exceed it. You have been gone three weeks, and what a long time it has seemed to me. You thought I was going round enjoying myself, but you are mistaken, for I never could do that away from you. It is true I try to be satisfied and would to some extend be contentted if I knew you were safte. Don't expose yourself, my dearest husband, if you should get into a fight, for what could I do or how could I live without you. Our little baby is the very image of her noble father and I am so thankful. When I get low spirited about you, it is the sweetest comfort I have to sit and trace your image in every lineament of her baby face. Her bright eyes have the same soul kindling look that beams from her brave father's, and her little rosebud mouth has the velvet tuch and expresses the same firmness as yours. My dear, I would be so glad if you could see her. She will go to any body if they will only tell her they are going to hunt papie. I know she will not forget you, for hardly an hour passes in the day, but I tell her about you. Sometimes she runs to the door and looks for a long time for you, then turns away with a disappointed look on her face. What a lovely child, was the exclamation of every body who saw her while I was gone.

My dear, you are getting tired of hearing about Laura and me. I don't know when to quit writing about how I worship, for love is too meaningless to convey my ideas of how much you are to me. I know you always deserved some one more gifted and beautiful than me, and I never can think of you, my noble and brave husband, without a sigh of regret to think how unworthy I am of so great a prize as your own handsome and brave self. I am affraid from the tenor of your last letter you think I don't want to write you, but I could not get yours, or hear where you were stationed so I could direct my letter so that you would get them. One thing I am very certain: I will never go off that far again while you are gone, for there was no peace for me.

I am very sory to hear Frank was getting on so badly. Perhaps if you could get some Hickory ashes or a little copperas for him, it would give him an appetite; and how he came to be valued at the price you wrote is more than I can tell, for certainly no man in his senses can look at him and say he is worth no more than that. I valued him three hundred dollars and not a dime less. He just suits you. A hansome noble looking man should have a fine horse to show off with, and I should have aded a pretty wife, but I recolected that hansome men invariable take a fancy to very homely women, as in your case, but you have a sweet little cherube to be proud of. Every thing looks dull here, and I intend to work night and day while you are gone to see if I can get rid of the blues.

I quietly established in bud Nick's old room and every thing is very comfortable around me—which reminds me that you said you needed more cover. Ma hunted up a coverlid while I was gone, but could find nothing that would do. I would have sent you those two fine bed blankets that we have when you sent for the others (as I had given the other one like the one you have to bud Lou) but Pa said they would not be thick enough and he thought you would draw some. And I want to know what you done about socks. I could get no wool, and Mr. Grimes said he knew that you would get some of those that was given to uncle Joe's company that was left of Mobry's company. You must be certain to write for I am anxious to hear, so that I will try again to get some wool to knit your socks: and if you want any thing else, if in my power to get, write me word. It will be a pleasure to me to get it for you. I received a letter from brother John yestedy. He had heard of your leaving and regretted not being with you. He sent 80 dollars back, and asked me to keep it for him in your absence. He said I could use it or loand it out as I saw fit. I have no use for money now, nor would I use it if I did, but take pleasure in doing what I can with it. Pa will loand it to some man who is good for him.

You must not send me any money if you need it, for I can't think of your wanting one item that money would buy while away. Ma received a letter also from bud Gily. He was well and getting on finely. Bud Nick was fattening every day and doing finely. There was a talk of their being sent to the co[a]st, but it is doutful. Pa talks of going down to see you, but he is nearly run to death with business.

I must close by asking you to write to me as soon as you can. We all join in love to you. I will write to you by Wendsday's mail and give you all the news. I am as ever your devoted Kittie. Laura sends you a kiss and a hug. good by.

6

Franklin, Nov. 19th/61

MY BEST AND MUCH LOVED ONE,

I wrote to you last Sunday and sent it by the preacher next day to be mailed in Newnan, but I must write again for fear that one may not reach you, and for an other reason. I have a tuch of the blues and must talk to some one and that one I had rather be you than any one else in the world; though you may not like to hear from me when I am afflicted in that manner. I don't know how I can do without seeing you any longer. Every thing looks like the grave to me now. It seems to be continually a black cloud of sorrow hanging over me all the time, and I don't know when it may brake and crush me to the earth. You are in danger every moment, and if any bad should happen to you, I never could get over it. I wish I could [be] by you and share you fate. You and little baby Laura are the only ties that bind me to earth, and I can't give you up. Don't for her sake, if you won't for mine, expose yourself. What would I give to sit by you now, hear again your affectionate tones talking to Laura and I. It does seem like an age since I saw you. I wonder if you ever think of us as often as I do you. I know that you are surrounded by excitement all the time and can't have much leisure time to debate to any thing far away, but would our baby sweet face would be ever present with you to shield and ward off all temptations of evil. I know that you have a good deal of firmness about you, but very few men are prof against the many evils to which they are exposed to in camp life. Don't get angry with me for talking thus. I mean it kindly.

Laura is as fat as a pig; she is very lively to night, laughing and talking about, her merry little face lit up with smiles, and looks more like here dear Poppie now than ever. I know that no other being was ever more blest than I in those I so dearly love, for they are all that is noble great and hansome. I hope, my dear, we will be permitted to raise our little darling so that her mind may be as pretty as her body. I have been down to see the pigs. They are growing and fattening every day. I am going to turn out the little sow; she will be such a nice hog, we can kill her next Winter [if] you like. I hope to get that one Pa gave us in a few days and with the two raise a good number of pigs by next fall. Aunt Kit went down to see them with me. She said she never saw such a change, and advised me to turn the sow out. Ma would like to swap for her, but I am not going to give her up, as she is fine stock. Pa told me tonight Mr. Watts had received a letter from Dr. Harland, and he said he would come back to this county if you would let him practice, but was not willing to take the house and lot back. Now I would not consent to his coming then if I was you, though you know best. I understand Dr. Grimes is coming back to town to practice. He has been trying to get a place up above Carrolton, but was not pleased. Mr. Mathews died last Friday. He was buried in masonic honors. You don't know what taking on the girlds had the morning you left. I believe there was a dozen who came to tell you good by. 2 of them said they had the tooth-ache the night before, and they wanted you to pull them out, but so long as you had gone, the teeth would have to ache the ballence of the Winter, or untill you came home. Old Mrs. Glover brought you some of the nicest fish I ever saw the day you left. She told me to eat them for you and she would bring you some again. She was very sorry she did not get to see you. Billy Mozeley started for Virginia to help bring Wilson Gillespie back. The old man had gone on after him, but could not manage him alone. Wilson has the tyfoid fever. I suppose they are trying to get up an other company for the co[a]st here. Billy and Alec Lane are trying hard. Ma wants you to ask bud Lou if he wants any other coat besides his uniform coat, and if he does, write word. She thinks he will have enough without the other coat; and he must write as soon as he gets this. I don't know what to do about wool to knit your socks. There is none in the country. I can't get any to make Laura cloths. I will make you a comfort and send it in the cloths of uncle Joe's company, and write me word what else. I can't get any envelop here and I will have to close now. I don't like to do without; can't help it. Laura send a kiss. All send their love to you. Write to me soon. Your devoted Kittie. Good by again.

7

Thursday night, Camp Harrison, Scriven Po., Nov. 21st/861

MY DEAR, MY DEAR LITTLE SWEET WIFE KITTIE, never in my life was I so much joyed as when I was reading your lovely letter. Indeed my heart was so affected that in spite of all my efforts I only found relief in tears. Their was a poor sick soldier in my tent waiting on me to get done reading, to get medicine. He ditected my deep consern. I was sad before I got your letter, but now I feel so much relieved to think that one pure heart still beats in sentiments of love for an unworthy soldier. You spoke in yours of not being handsome. You may think so, but oh how beautiful, lovely & grand I think you, and never was their a more angelic woman than your dear self. Kittie, I cannot express my admiration for you & sweet little Laura. Oh how I wish I could see the lovely little bright eyed baby. Poor little Laura, her pa wants to see her so much he is almost dead. Kittie, you don't love little Laura like I do; if you did, I would be afraid you would eat her up. I often think how she used to do when she would see her Pa coming in the buggy with Frank. I have sold Frank to Gen. Coper, the brigadier which we are under. Little sweet Laura will never see Frank any more. I got three hundred dollars for him or am to get it in a few days. He is the finest horse that I have seen here. I am sorry I sold him. I will have no gentle horse for you to ride after when I get home. I will try to get one that will suit you when I get home. Evry time I see Frank I think of you & our sweet little baby. As soon as I get the money for my horse I will send it to you. Capt. Cameron of Troup Co. has let me have a fine horse to ride while I am in the service. He will get here next Monday. It will not cost me any thing to get him here. It did not cost me any thing to get Frank here.

I have written you three letters. This will be the fourth one I have written you. I hope you will get them all. Kittie, your letter was long just such as I like. I hope you will continue to write me long ones. If you will look at the Companion[1] under the head of a communication from Camp Harrison, you will see a pruff of your humble Husband. It is the this week's paper. I have got me a cott & have me some fine sleeping. I like a little more cover. If you get a good chance, I wish you would send me a quilt or something else. Do not send those blankets of hours—some old quilt will suit me better. You need not make me any socks. I have plenty of them. If I get out, I can buy plenty of them in Savannah. Some of our men go up their evry day. We have 86 on our sick list this morning. Nearly all the cases are measles. I have been very hea[l]thy since I have been here. We will move next week down in twenty miles of Brunswick. You may direct your letter to Scriven Po. until I give you father directions. Kittie, I do not think we will get into a fight. If we do, I do not think I will be in any danger unless I go into it beong me duty. Kittie, I wish you to send my Box of Spirits to Redwine & Henry in Newnan so they can send them to me. Tell you[r] Pa if they & my instruments have not been shipped from Newnan, to see that it is done soon. I need they very badly. Lou & Dr. Lane is quite well. Lou is looking for a letter from his ma. Give my love to your Ma & Pa & all the children. Kiss Little Sweet Laura for me & tell her that is for her Pa. Let me hear from you soon, my dear darling. Give my love to Jim & Lelie Turner, Billie Mozeley & Brewer, Judge Grimes &c.

Your true lover & well wishing husband
G. W. Peddy

8

Camp Satilla, Dec. 3rd/861

MY SWEET DEAR KITTIE, With much pleasure I write you a few lines Condy eve. I am will pleased with our new position, which is 17 miles from Brunswick. We have camped near a beautiful river, the Satilla. The boys catch plenty of fish. I have not had time to go fishing since my arrival here. I am quite well & have been since my arrival from home. It seems that it has been two months since I left you. My dear, I wish I had you with m[e]. My only happyness is with you & my dear little babe. I want to see her so much. Kiss the little sweet thing for her pa. I got a letter from Brother John last night; he is well. Lou got one

[1] *The Southern Literary Companion*, a weekly newspaper published in Newnan, Ga., 1859-1865. Only scattered issues have survived, three of which are in the Emory University Library.

from Jillae. Nick was still a[t] Warenton sick. John said their was 60 names on the patition for Nick to resign. I am going to write to him to night & tell him to see them dead first. The patition is gotten up only by those who want to get Office. Those who want the offices, of course, will not sign it, but will encourage others to do it. Wee are all getting along finely. Lou & Dr. Lane are very well. Their are a great many sick in the Regt. with measles. Let me hear from you, my dear, soon. I will be very anxious before I get a letter from you. We have plenty of Oysters to eat here & you know I am quite fond of them. But oh! when I get anything good to eat, I awlways think of you & my dear little Laura. I cannot tell you how much I love you & Laura; I leave you to judge. I hope you think I love you both all I can. I wish the day was nearer at hand when I will be honerabley discharged & be permitted to enjoy the society of my two dear ones. How it is I love noone but you two I cannot tell, but my affection[s] a[re] all concentrated on you & Laura. You must tell Laura how well her Pa loves her & also that he will bring her a great many pretty things when he comes home. Let me hear from you twice a week, my love, if you wish me to enjoy myself occasionally. I have a nice poney to wride evry whare I go. Your true Lover until & after death.

G. W. Peddy

P.S. Direct your letter to me Wayneville, Ga., 4 Regt. 2nd Brigade Ga. S. Tro.

9

Franklin, Dec. [*6, 1861*][2]

MY OWN DEAR HUSBAND,

'Tis ten oclock and all around is quiet, a time when most I love to dwell on our past, a past in which are woven the brightest hours of my exis[t]ence, and painted many beautiful pictures for memory's wall that can never fade, untill time's relentless tread has swep me from the stage of life. Now perhaps your head is pillowed on a hard bed, and you are dreaming of home, of bright eyed Laura, and I dare to think of me too. Would I were with you, my own beloved, to press those lips that ever spoke words of love and affection with kisses that

[2]Postmarked Franklin, 1861 Dec 7 Addressed: Surgeon G.W. Peddy, Waynesville, Wayne County, Geo

can but faintly express my love for you, but how many weary months must follow each other, ere I again am permitted to be near you and perhaps never. I went down home this evening just as the sun set, a time fraught with many fond association, for their we wandered in the garden with Laura, or sit by the fireside in quiet conversation doating on her many childish pranks and mischeif. Oh! how those days come up to mock me in my lonelyness now: one thought like a white dove folds its gentle wings and nestles in my heart, sending glad quaking music through every joy that comes to me, and often drives dul care away, when all other thing fail; and that is where ere you are or no matter what circumstances surround, your heart beats for me. That seems to me rather an assumption on my part which every woman dearly loves to assume. It is only a few days since you went away, but I would give any thing to be with you now, and when you get through these long six months don't never go again. It looks selfish in me to wish you here when you are so well situated and enjoy yourself so well. I did not rent the house to Mr. Tarner. He looked at it and said the place needed too much repareing. I don't know whether he will stay in town next year. I have not heard of any body else wanting the house. I can hire Puss out till you come back to Frank Bevis for six dollars a month, or to Isac Gordan for 75 dollars the whole year. He will not hire for half the time. I can tend the garden myself, or Pa will have it done till you come back. Don't you think I had better try and get some meat somewhere? If we go to housekeeping, you can't get it then without a great change. I don't know what to do; you must tell me. Old man Barker's sale comes off soon and maybe Pa can get you some corn and hogs too. I can fatten them myself and have them killed before you come home. I would have written to you sooner, but we heard by Billy Mozeley when he came home that bud Nick was very sick, and by others writing home that he was sick. Pa has not received a letter from him or bud Gily since a week you came home, and he was on the eve of starting up to see him, but concluded to wait a little while longer. Charlie Tugart wrote back, and they got the letter last Wednesday that he (bud Nick) was sick but not dangerous. Charlie said that about sixty of the company had signed that petition for bud Nick to resign, but he was not going to notice the vile thing. Also John Pendergrass wrote a scorching letter back to his uncle Joe Lane about those who got up this thing, and said those same men did not know anything nor did they want to do right any way or manner. Pa thinks Gartrell is aiding and abetting that club against bud Nick. He thinks it will make him popular here, as some of his friends have written to him from here to that effect. I have been very uneasy about you, knowing you went off sick, and not getting any letter from you Wendsday. Do write often; I am so anxious to hear from you at all times. What do [you] think Pappie? This little kitten is trotting around me calling her mother momma just like a little black negro. She ain't forgot you yet; she remembers the candy and who brought it. The other day she found my satchel lying down and picked it up and looked all through it. She could find no candy and came to me with it quarreling about it. I must close for want of room. Tell uncle Joe to get me some envelops when he comes home. I dislike to write without them. Tell bud Lou all the children and Ma send their love to him and he must write home often. Good by dear. Laura says Papa must kiss himself in the glass for her if he has one. Your wife Kitty.

10

Camp Satilla, Dec. 8th/861

WELL MY DARLING SWEET,

Being as Dr. Lane is going home, I have concluded to write you a few line in advance of a response from my last letter. I know, my dear, that you would have written to your worser half ere this if you had known where to have written too; at lest I have the confidence to think you would. I never have doubted the cincerity you manifest me & God forbid I ever should. My happyness in this life depends upon your true devotion as heretifore to me. My dear, my admiration & love is beond the comprehention of the human mind for you, & my highest ambition is to so live & act in this life that I will never bring dishonor or disgrace upon you & my & your little Sweet Laura. Dear, do try in the absence of you Husband to teach our little one to love & obey her Ma & Pa. Our happiness & pride of her depends upon the manner in which we commence & continue with her. Dear, be positive in your demands of her but be gentle & kind. Donot whip & scold nor get out of humor with her so as to let her detect you iritability. My Dear, I wish I could tell you about what I have heard about some of the ladies in Newnan since I have been here. I will tell you when I get home about how they have been doing for some time. A Gentleman in Camp tells me he has slep frequently with Mrs. Hanvey, Mrs. Steve Smith, & they Taylor's wife (I forget his name) & some others, & he is a man of truth; & he told me that Smith's wife wrote the bucket letters about Mrs. Hanvy. Shame rest upon such characters. I will tell you all about it when I see you. You must not let any one, not even you Ma, know what I have written about those Ladies. You may coppy such a part of this letter as you want to keep & burn the ballance up for fear some one gets to see it. I am well, my dear. I do hope you are & little Laura also. I have a great deal to do at this time: 175. cases of measles in the Regt. this morning. I hope when they get through with the measles their will not be so much sickness & I will have some time to rest. Ambrose Williams is sick at this time with a bilious attack. He is better at this time. I think he will be up in a few days. His negro is also sick. I think he is taking the measles. I was called in the country on yesterday to see a sick child.[3] The child was a son of a rich Rice Planter; they are the real aristocracy. The Lady gave me a great many little pleasant eatible to bring to Camps with me. Kittie, Mrs. Brooks is coming down to Camps about Christmas, if you want to come come along with her, but leave Laura at home. I am afraid she would take the measles if you were to bring her. Write to me what you think about coming. If you donot come, I will try to come home some time in Jan. to see you & my little darling. Let me hear from you often, my sweet darling. Nothing can do me so much good as to hear from one I love so much when I cannot get to see them. Give my love to all & let me know all the news from the boys. Yours ever evene [?]

G. W. Peddy

11

Camp Satilla, Dec. 11th/861

MY PRECIOUS KITTIE, It was with great pleasure, my love that I read your interesting but short letter. When I get a letter from you, I prize it so highly that I read it over time after time. It seems strang to me to think that I have a dear one at home watching over my intrust so closely & carefully, but a noble & generous heart like yours is always looking out in the future for some one's else intrust besides your own. Never was their a man so blessed in a wife as myself. My greatest wish is that our leves will be spared to enjoy the sweetness of each other's society. Kittie, I donot care wheathur you rent the house out or not, but you may let Frank Bevis have Puss until I get home or my time is out by his making a good note for her hire. I would not let Gorden have her. I would rather you would let J. E. Hales have her at the same price if you cannot get more from him, & let it go in the way of what I am oweing him. I had rather do that than risk either of the other two for the money. Any arrangement that you can have made in reference to meet & corn will be satisfactory with me, thouth I donot want any of my patrons pushed to close for fear they fall out with me. I

---

[3]To the Surgeon at Camp at Abrams place — Dear Sir Will you be kind enough to come to my house to see a child attacked with Pneumonia. You will oblige me greatly by coming. I send a buggy for you Respectfully Jas. F. King Dec. 7th 1861

am still in good health. This climate suits me very well. I have an unpleasant cough, but I suppose it is produced by the dust about the camp. Lou also has a bad cough. I guess you had better send per Dr. Lane for him a bottle of Liverwort & Tarr cough mixture, as [it is] hard to get here. I and Col. Brooks sits down evry night to bost of our wives. He saiyt so wrot to his wife that I had the advantage of him in having a nice little Girl to brag off. She in connection with yourself is all I brang of here. Kittie, I cannot hardly keep from shedding tears when I think how we met when I saw you last. My heart was so full, you recollect I only found relief with you in my lap up stairs. Wold that I could see you tonigh[t]. It appears that it has been six months. It is the opinion of many intiligent men in camp that if the Legislature does not alter its corse, that we will be disbanded in two or three weeks. If so, I will come home & remain with you & my Sweet Little Laura. But if we are not disbanded, the time is not very long u[n]til my term of enlistment will expire. Then, my dear, if I live I will come home their to enjoy myself with my little family. That joy cannot be expressed. Col. Brooks got a letter from his wife of ten pages to day. I wish you would write yours that long. I would always write you more if I was interupted evry five minutes by some poor soldier after medicine. I expect you all think their is great confusion in camps about the action of the Legislature, but their is not. Evry soldier seems to be willing to serve out his time or are willing to disband & go home, but if this State Army is let loosd & the co[a]st unprotected, their will be scores of property destroyed, our citizens murdered, & even the chastity of our fair Ladies will be distroyed by the rough Yankee fanattics. If thise desasters befall us & our people, the condemnation of an injured & desgraced peoples will rest on the heads of our Legislators.

I want you to tell Dr. Lane when he starts back to bring my Box of Spirits from Redwine & Henry's Drugstore in Newnan. They are their. I thought they were shiped to me, but they were not. If convient, fix me up a little Box of eatibles & send them per Dr. Lane. I have all my provision to buy, & all that I get from home saves me that much. You may say to Ambrose Williams that his boy Frank has broke out with the measles & is now doing well. I hope he got home safe & is improveing by this time. When you make my shirt that Dr. Lane brings you to make for me, face the Pockets & sleves & collor with cotton velvet. I want you to get me another by the time Dr. Lane comes back. Buy the casamer from Brewer Lane & Mozely. They have a nice piece at $1.75 per yd. Fix it up with velvent. Kittie, I cannot be interested in any thing disconnected with something relating to how I love you. I want to be writing about how I love you & little Laura.

Let me hear from you soon, my love,
I remain yours yours ever true

G W Peddy M.S.

In dorso: Are you all right? You was looking out when I left home

12

Franklin, December the 19./61

MY BEST BELOVED,

I received your very dear letter today and now hasten to reply. You dont know how much joy I experienced while peruseing letters, for I know that you cannot imagine, much less feel, how like my own life you are to me. I often wonder whether every woman loved like me. I know they can't for one of the many reasons, they do not have one as noble brave and, in short, one of nature's nobleman, as I am blest with on which to bestow their love. It does me good, dear, to think of your acting so noble and honerable. You are just acting the part nature intended you to act when she gave you so much of manly beauty; and litle Laura is so much like you. I do hope she will grow up to be as much thought of as you. She has not been well for a day or too. I expect she has taken cold somehow, though I try to be very particular with her for fear she will have an other spell like she did last winter. I carried her down the other day, and she fairly danced she was so glad to get home. It made me feel so sad. I sometimes think I won't go there any more till you come home. I wish you could have seen Laura feeding her pigs. She took some corn and pull off a grain at a time and say pig pig. They would come right up to her feet. When they [got] to close, she would look around at me and say Mamma, pig. They are very gentle, and I never saw any thing grow like they do. I think the largeest will weigh 3 hundred by next fall. I am going to send for that little sow Pa gave Lara soon, and when you come home we will have quite a little stock of hogs. Corn is selling at 4. dollars a barrel now nearly every where, and men are keeping it back that they design selling, thinking they will get 5 dollars. I do hope they can't sell it at all. I will get a barrel or two from Ogelby just to give the hogs some and wait till you come home, and may be if there is a good wheat crop made it will be cheaper. They say polk is down at 8 cents in Atlanta brought from Tennessee.

Mr. Mabry has returned and is a great deal better than was expected from all accounts. His company is sent to the Potomac to prevent the Fedrals from crossing to the right and silencing our batterys. Mat Monk died just a day or two before he left. About 20 of his company was at the hospitals. His first Liutenant McDowd is here also. Pa saw him the other day, and he told Pa that bud Nick was considered as one of the best drill officers in the whole service, and heard him spoken of by the superior as one who would yet win himself a name. He had been very sick but was back in camps. We received a letter from bud Gily yestady. He was coming home. The sergeon had been turned off and a new one appointed and the new one was discharging all that would not do duty. John Hopson and Pitman are discharged and have come home. They say bud

Gily will be here in a few days, as his shoulder is in such a fix he can't do duty, and that bud Nick had come back to camps, but was not well by any means. Pa thinks bud Nick will come home on a furough, and if he does, you must try and come too while he is here. Bud Gily wrote that Brother John was quite sick and affected very much like bud Nick. I am uneasy about him. He is still in camps. The petition had been presented, but bud Nick told them plainly why it was gotten up and he should not resign. I would not have him resign for any thing now if his health will justyfy him in staying. You must write to him often, for he is badly mortified the way his company does.

The gentleman that you bought Frank from came to see Pa the other day to get that money you owed him. He said he was tight pressed for money and would [be] glad if you would pay him. He said it was just fifteen dollars. He seems to be a very clever man and think[s] you could send that amout back to pay him. He will be back in three weeks, and you must send it by the first opportunity so I can pay him when he comes back. He was riding a horse precisely like Frank as near as could be. Ambrose Williams is getting well, so I have heard. He thought he was taking the fever when he first came home, but I recon will not. I heard Sallie Grims say she was going to see him last week. I don't know whether she has been or not. I think her and Tom Cutright have quarreled again. She is claiming a new sweet heart, and knitting him some gloves. I would not be surprised if she is not setting her cap for Ambrose. Julia can't talk of any body but Tom Boddie. He wrote little Mollie a letter by uncle Joe, and I think they forgave him for the other neglect, and said they would send him a box, but they heard he was coming home. Dr. Grimes has moved to town and is living at the place where Asberry Copelan lived. Mr. Houston is going over the river to where Mathews lived. He has rented some of Mr. Miller's land, so the old fellow will have to go to work. Brewer Lane has just returned from Mongomry, and has the tyfoid fever. He could hardly get home. Alec is not gone yet, and is not going soon.

I don't feel very well now nor have not felt well in a week or two. I think it is cold. I have the headache every day, and wake every morning tired almost to death. Laura sucks so much when she is not well, I think helps me to feel bad. I will have to wean her, but it will [be] too bad for the little thing these long nights to take her jug away. Don't be uneasy about us. We will get on very well. I am going to weaving to morrow, and I think exercise will do me good. I had made your shirt before I received your letter, and I do hope you will like it. Laura admires it very much. She troted around and looked at it and turn her little head one side and say pretty, Mamma. I can't get any thing here to make you a shirt. Ambrose got the piece of cloth you mentioned. If you can get any cloth and send it back to me, I will make it and send it to you by Williams. You ought to have an other one any way. Send me some of those sour oranges to me by some one if it is not too much trouble. They make the most delightful pie you ever tasted. I suppose Mr. Wilks has a very poor opinion of you, it seems, for he wrote to his wife that he did not like any of the Drs. down there: they did not do their duty no how. He is not worth noticing any how, for I know better than that.

You say Mrs. Broks writes twelve pages. She must have a good surply of note paper on hand. I can't git any sort here. Pa said he would get me some letter paper in Newnan, but I have no money. I am like you. I love to read long letters from you. I have attempted to tell you how much pleasure I experienced reading your letters, but I think I only drew a faint picture of it. I expect you are tired of the same old story of my love for you, but out out [*sic*] of the abundance of the heart the mouth speaketh, and that is why I am continually writting it. Laura says Papie must not be gone so long. Write to me when you will come home, so I can be here. I have promised Kit to stay with her a good deal after Christmast, and I want to be at home when you get here. I do wish you were here this very moment. I would send you a good many things, but uncle Joe has so much to carry it looks like imposition to ask him to carry it. I must close in haste for uncle Joe is waiting for the things.

Yours ever. Laura sends a kiss.
Kittie Z Peddy.
I am very glad of those envelops.

13

Camp Satilla, Dec. 24th/861[4]

MY DARLIN KITTIE,

You have no Idea how much I enjoyed the reading of your very welcomed letter. It is the second one I have rec'ed from you since I came to this camp. You promised to write to me twice per week. I wish, my darling, that you would do so. If you knew with what intrust I read you handsomely written letters, I know you would do so. I have no news of importance to write you. Evrything is getting along finely here. The Regt. is getting more healthy. I have lost only two cases out of four hundred reported sick. I think that is very good success,

[4]*In pencil at top:* Don't let any one have one *Grain* of medicine out of my Office except your Pa. You have no idea how much it is worth; nether Watkins nor Grimes.

considering the many difficulties patients have to encounter in tents. I was sick a few days back, but have gotten well & am now enjoying fine hea[l]th once more, I have but little to do at this time. I have the more time to think about you & our Sweet Laura. You write to me about her talking. It seems strang[e] to think of her talking. If I was to hear her speek a word, I would eat her up. Dr. Lane arrived safe in camps last night. He lost his boxes, hence has gone after them today. They are somewhere between here & Savannah. I will send this letter to Newnan by Col. Brooks. He will also send some cloth to you to make me another shirt, if he can get the cloth. I am under many obligations to you for the beautiful shirt you sent me. Evry one that sees it [says it] is the pretyest shirt they ever saw. I want you to make my other just like it. You are the best little sweet woman in the world. I have an invitation to a Christmas dinner to morrow at one Mr. King's, a nephew of Thomas Butler King that your Pa knows from character. Enclosed you will find a note his lady sent me when I was sick.[5] I did not accept the invitation, as I was not sick enough. How I became acquainted with them was by their sending for me when their Family was sick.[6] They are very rich & the most aristocratic people I ever saw. I cannot except the invitation to dine because of my uniform not having arrived. I expect you are all greatly joyed at Giles' arrival. I would like very much to see him indeed. I want him to write to me evry week if you cannot. I would be glad to see him or you Pa down here. I have just received a letter from Brother John. He is well & getting along finely. The petitioners for Nick to resign say they are going to publish him. He is not going to resign & I don't blame him. I am going to write to him again ere long. I would not have him to quit now for nothing in the world. Let them publish & give him a chance to reply to them & the bark will fly. I think I will come home by the last of Jan. if not before. I am so anxious to see you & little Laura I do not think I can wait much longer. I will draw my pay on the thirty first, both my wages & pay for my horse, which will be $640.00. I'll be most rich, won't I? I will bring it to you when I come & see if you can keep it. I fear I could not here, Let me hear from you as soon as you can conviently. Kiss little sweet for me. My compliments to all. Your ever true lover

G. W. Peddy

Tell Ambrose that Frank is well.

---

[5]The note is missing.

[6]*Supra*, No. 11.

14

December the 30./861

MY DEAR HUSBAND,

I am now staying out at uncle Levi Pendergrasse's for a few days. I intended to go home this evening and write to you to night, but ma did not send for me, and concluded you would feel somewhat disappointed if you did not get a letter from home this week, and I would write from here. I enjoy myself so well here, it seems like home to me. I know that no body could be better or more kinder treated any where than I am here and I never can forget them for it. I am never satisfied no where when you are absent, for "home is where the heart is" and you know then where mine is now. To night what would I give to be with you and breathe again the atmosphere of love that your presince brings. Surely you don't want to see me as bad as I do or you would come home soon. I think sometimes it would be such a pleasure that I could hardly stand to see you once more, but as you said when you were here, we must learn to stay away from each other. But I can't learn such lessons. They are too hard, and I don't want you to learn to love me less, for in that love rest all my happiness. Oh! I love, I dearly love thee: these will be my last, my dying words upon the earth, ere I bid adiew to all I love. The last of earthly love will be mine for you, and if possible, I would hover around you and my darling babe to shield, if in my power, from the rude storms of life. Oh! what a strange thing is love: its strenght and power cannot be told, it can only be felt. Pappie, you know you would give almost any thing to be waked up every morning with a pair of soft velvet lips being pressed to yours. This morning just about day I waked and Laura was sitting up in bed by me and kissing me every now and then and laughing at me, to get me to wake up. She trys to say a great many words and toddles after some very small pigs aunt Synthia has in the yard nearly all day. I know you would love to see the little sweet thing now. She is very lively. I did not tell you my reasons for not going down with uncle Joe: Laura could not go and it seemed like I could not leave the little thing here by her self, and if I went, we could not have enjoyed ourselves because she was not with us; and I thought if you could come home, there would be no draw back to our pleasure. You don't know how uneasy I was when I heard you was sick. I went down to see Henry Turner, and he said he did not think you was much sick. He is in for you on every occasion, but don't think your assis[t]ant is much. He is of the opinion that nearly every man in the regment thinks you are equal to any immergency. I went to see Alen Pri, the son of the widow Pri over here. He was left at camp Harrison when you moved to Satila, and was discharged. He has typloid fever and diarea. If he does get well, it will be a wonder certainly. He says too that Dr. Nat is not part of a physition;

said the Dr. would come round to see him and curse the boys that staid in the same room with him and not do one thing, give him anything. He thinks if you had been there it would have been different. I know you don't and I do hope you never will, neglect any poor soldier. Ruben Tompson's remains was brought home yestady and buried to day. He was brouught by Tom Watts who went after his son. Wilson went after Almegro, but he would not come home. Bud Gily has been quite sick since he came home. We thought he would have a very hard spell of fever, but he was good deal better yestady. Brewer Lane is very low, and it is doubtful whether he will ever get well. I went down to see him the other day. Grimes came in to see him while I was there. He pronounced him some better. I have not heard from Ambrose Williams since Saturday. It was thought then he could not get well. If he does, it will be a good while first. Your uncle Mort['s] wife is also very sick. They have two Drs. there with her.

I am very glad you liked your shirt. It does me so much good to please you in any thing that way. Col. Brooks did not send me any cloth to make you a shirt. You can get you some cloth as you come home and I can make it for you while you stay. Mrs. Housan Jackson spent the evening with us last Saturday. She said Grimes sent her word, he intended to practice untill you come back, and I recon by that he was asking for her practice. She was very particular in her inquiries about you, but you know self interest governs the humane family. Uncle Joe run off with all the money and aunt Kit is quite rathey about it. Without she gets some salt or money soon, she says you all don't think of us when you get off down there, and declars you will never bring home a cent, but I hope she is mistaken with regard to you. Uncle Levi and aunt Sinthea sends their love and well wishes, and wants you to come to see them when you come home. Dr. Harlan is coming back any how, they say, and will live at John Foster's place though he has not come yet.

I am now at home once more. We passed Alec Lane just now. He says Brewer is just like he has been, says Brewer is a good deal better every morning, but at night gets so he can't move. He told us there was two men stayed at Mr. Bogguses last night who told that the 7 Ga. regment had been sent to the co[a]st, though it may be all rumor. Mr. Grimes told Pa the other day he thought the account of Pleasant Harris was 15 dollars, but Pa could only find 7 on your books. I must close for fear I can't get this in the mail. Be sure to write soon. All send their love. Laura sends all the love in her little sweet heart to Pappie. Do come soon; and then there will be joy.

good by love Katie P.

15

Camp Lee. Four miles above Savannah, Jan 10th/62

MY DEAR, DEVOTED KITTIE, so glad I was to receive you nice letter. Nothing gratifies me so much as reading you[r] letter. I read them over & over & find something new & pleasant evry rereading. We left Camp Satilla on the 8th inst. & arrived here on the night of the ninth. I am very happy of the move. It delights me evry time I start towards where my true love stays. Oh how I wish I was with you & our little sweet Laura to night. I frequently sit down & try to draw you & her in my imagination sitting by the fire at home. What a happy time we could have if we three could be at home toguether. I went down to Savannah today, & evry child I saw I examined it closely to see if it looked like Laura but found none so handsome. I think I will come home before long if the officers will let me off. They do not talk much like it. I cannot think they would be so crewel to me as to deprive me of the joy of seeing me little sweet Laura. If I were at home & Laura was to wake me by kissing me, I could not keep from eating her up. I am afraid she will not know me when I get home, she looked so strange at me when I came home before. I am going to bring you & her a great many nice things when I get to come home. I will send you and her six or seven hundred dollars in a short time if I cannot come & bring it. I want you and her to spend as much of it as you want. I am willing for you & her to have the benefit of it all, as it is for you & her enjoyment that I labor. I am willing to forego the pleasure of using any of it myself in order to let you & her be happy. I want you to keep what you donot spend until I come home. If their is any thing that you want for yourself or Laura that you cannot get at home, write to me & I will try to get it for you, & bring or send it to you. I was glad to hear of your enjoyment at uncle Levi's. That's a good place to be at. I wish I could have been with you. Maybe I could have made it more pleasant. I will go to see them when I come home. Lou & Dr. Lane are well. Lou rec'd Giles letter to day. Say to him that all the places in the Regt. is filled up. We have quit taking in recruits. Say to your Pa now is a good time to come & see us if he has time. I would be very glad to see him down here, but if money matters are tight with him, I can, I recon, forego the pleasure of seeing him until I come home. Kittie, my dear, I expect to try to come home about the first of next month. My time will then be half out. My darling, take good care of yourself & Laura. Donot let any one hurt her nor learn her any bad things. I want us to teach her to get along without any whiping. She is to good to whip, she ought to be worshiped by evry one as I would worship her. I donot recollect how much exactly P. Harris acc't was, but it is more than four dollars. I think there is four in one place & twelve in another, as well as I recollect. Let me hear from you soon, my love. Be shure to give Jim & Lou my love & best

wishes. Yours ever ever more G.W. Peddy
At top of page: Direct you[r] letter to me Savannah 4th
Regt. 2nd Brig. G.S.T.

16

Franklin, Jan. the 14, 1862

MY DARLING HUSBAND,

What can be the matter that you don't write? It has been nearly three weeks since you wrote a single line. I fear my dream is coming true that you have learned to love me less. Surely that is not so, for I can't help jud[g]ing you by myself; and that is that love is the very essence of lif[e's] best charm. I don't reproach you, oh no, but remind you that I am always uneasy about you when I don't hear from you often. You wrote in your last that you would come home soon, and I have looked and fancied I heard you come every night for the last week. I long for the time to come, yet think it must pass away, and I be left alone as before, with only the memory of fond endearing words, which seem to linger around me as a halo of glory, which I often contract with the dulness that sometimes comes over me. You no dout will say, Katies [speak]es out too plain and tells the same old story of which I am heartily tired,

I went down to see aunt Sallie and Susan Lane, but only staid one night. I was sick all night, and to day am up, but have a severe headach. I wish you would come home. I think I would be well; any how just try it.

Bud Gily got well of the spell he had just after he came home and went to St. Cloud to make up a school and rode in very unfavorable weather, which laid him up again. Yestady he was quite sick, to day is some better. Your uncle Jack's family have been sick ever since you left. Aunt Susan says she has quarreled at you just enough to last a good while for going off and leaving no body here. Watkins is traveling all the time, Grimes but seldom. Brewer Lane has not entirely recovered yet. I dout but what he has wished you were here a good many times lately.

Hugh Houston is very sick with typhoid fever, so Jim Brown says. He came home last week, and also Person. I heard you had moved to Savannah, but Pa says it is doutful. I did not want you to go there, for there is danger of a fight there. We have very disagreeable weather now: it rains, and is very cold. Last night it was hot enough for Summer. Such changes will produce sickness. Laura has been sick for the last few days, throwing up and derangement of her bowels. I have her some Vermefuge, but brought no worms. She has fell off considerable. I don't want her to be sick as long as you are away. It will be bad enough any way. She says Papie has gone away.

I want one thing very much, which, if it won't cost too much, I would be so glad if you would get me, and I don't want you to get me any thing else, and that is a bare nice brestpin with your ambrotype in it. You can get it in Savanah and have a good likeness of your self put into it, if it is not too mu[ch] trouble. Don't get me any dressing, for I don't need it. I did want you to get Ma a black silk, not very costly. I would feel like it was paying in polite kind of way for the trouble Laura and I put her too, though I know if she though[t] I was trying to pay her, she would not like it, so you must give it as a present. I did not intend to write you a long letter, but just to remind you that this is the third time I have writte[n] to you since you wrote. I must close, for it is time I sent this to Henry, as he will start soon in the morning.
Your Kittie. Write soon, love.

17

Camp Lee, Jan. 15th 1862

MY DARLING DEVOTED KITTIE,

I received your sweet toned letter on the date of Jan. 5th. With much pleasure I read it. It gives me new life when I hear from you & our darling Laura. When I get the blues the worst kind and receive a letter from you, it drives them away. You need not think I get tired reading you[r] dear letters, nor you need not appolegize for writing such, for you could not please me better than to do so. You cannot imagine how the loveing part of your letters interest me unless you realize the feeling in reading mine. I have written you one letter since I came to this place, but have concluded to write you again tonight before I get a reply to my last as you manifest such anxiety to hear from the opening of the mail. This camp is located, as I said in my last, four miles from Savannah. My precious, I know not hardly how to write you. I have plenty of mater, but cannot get it systematised. I love you, darling, more & more if possible evry day. No one can conceive how much I worship you. Only he that ruleth above, I feel, knows that I have such a noble angel as you are. You & my Little Laura have the love & admiration of my whole heart. I am willing, I love you so well, to lay down my own life for your & little sweet Laura's happyness. The pang of departing this life will be to leave you & sweet Laura. I am so selfish about our enjoyment together that I am vain enough [to] want nature's laws changed so that we could enjoy the time we have been absent from each other. My dear, try and pass the time off pleasantly as you can while I am absent. I want you to let the loom and other work alone. I did not get you to work & get rough: I got you to love and worship. Theirfore do keep from doing anything that fatigues you in the least. Walk about enough to keep your health good, but do not weave any more for my sake, for when you are worne out, my happyness is all gone in this life. I will do the work for you & our little sweet child. Kittie, their has been some order read to day which knocks me out of furlough unless you get very sick & I hope you will not. I intended coming home about the first of Feb., but the way the thing is now, I am deprived the greatest pleasure in life, which is to see you & Laura. It seems to me that I cannot stand to stay away from you three more months. I am going to try to get a furlough in Feb., but I almost know I will fail. I expect you will have to come to see me. If you cannot come, it seems very [wrong] if it's fair for I and you to be so crewally separated so long. Let me know your notions about comeing in your next. If I am not at home by the middle of next month I will give you some information about your coming here whare I am. You will have to l[e]ave our sweet babe at home maybe. I would give almost anything for your & her ambrotypes. I donnot see any chance for a fight here. I think we are here on the co[a]st for a scarecrow for the Yankees. If we were not here they might land & destroy a great amount of property. I have no horse here now. The one that I have had here was sold today for three hundred & fifty dollars & he's nothing but a very small pony worth about one hundred dollars. I have now in my pocket three hundred dollars—a part of my wages. I wish you had. I have no use for it here. I will send it home by some one that I will see passing in a few days. I will get as much more in a few days or weeks & will send it also when I get it so that you & Laura will not be liking for money at present at least. I would freely give it all to be with you & Laura this night. You have my heart & my genuine love. Try to make out with much if you can. Your dreams need not flatter you that I would be cold towards you if it were so, for never do I expect to be cold towards one so pure, so perfect, and so sweet lovly angelic beautiful. When I come home I will bring Laura enough apples for her little sweet life to bite for some time. Tell her Pa will bring her a heep of nice things when he comes home. Show her my ambrotype & tell her whose it is. Let her play with it if she wants to. Tell her to mind her Ma & be a good child & she will not deserve a whipping from her hands & then she will not get any. Pa will not whip here—he loves her to good. I will here close, my darling, as it is getting late. I want you to write soon & much oblige your devoted through all eternity & for ever more. My love to the family

G. W. Peddy M.S. 4th Regt. 2 Brig. G.S.T.

You ought to see me with my uniform on.

I wrote you a letter & finished it. As night has come I have a good opportunity to write. I will make this a continuation of the one I have written this eve. If you cannot send me the scrip I wrote for from Dr. Watkins, I do wish you would come to see me, for I donot know how I can do without seeing you longer. If you come, you must bri[n]g Laura & some one to nurs her. It will cost about sixty dollars for you to come & stay two or three weeks. I donot mind that amount. I would give three times as much to see you, let alone being with you evry day for two weeks. You are at home enjoying the pleasure of being with our little sweet all the while, & I am of here without the presence of ether of my precious jewels. I wish it was so I could go or start to see you in the morning. I would be as happy as I would wish to be. The cars would not take me half swift enough. Oh! what a happy meeting we would have. I would not get done kissing you until you would be tired of me. You must tell Laura about what a pretty chair Pappie is going to buy her. I am going to get her sweet Ma one two so You & her can sit together & rock while Pappie is of[f] from you. For twelve dollors I can get the finest sort of a Chair for you, & for $25.00 I can get as nice a Beaureau as you wont to see with morble tops. You & Laura can then take care of the nice things that you may get. Dr. Lane & Lou is quite well. Their is several cases of Fever in camps at this time. I have but little to do, though, in the way of practice. My tearm of enlistment will run out know in a little more than two months, & then if I am alive, how glad I will be to get home to see my dear beloved little Family. Your Pa said you & Laura had Dysentery. I hope you have go[t] well. You must not think I donot want to see you becaus I don't come home, for I do, my dear. I am satisfied you know I do. Let me hear from you, my sweet Kittie.

Yours ever G. W. Peddy

18

Camp Lee, Jan 17th 1862

MY PRECIOUS ANGELIC KITTIE, I wrote you a letter on the fifteenth inst. I write you again to day to let you know that I have sent to Capt. Sargent in Newnan for you $345.00. Dr. Lane sent in the same pars $100.00 for his wife. He will send it to you by the first one passing, or you may send after it. I will send you more in a short time if I cannot come to bring it myself. If I cannot come to see my two Idols, I shall think it very crewel on the part of the officers.

For it is you & Laura that I live to love. This world would be like a blank sheet to me if [it] were not for you & her. Of all the jewels on earth or sea, I think you & Laura the most precious. No [one] on earth, it seems to me, has tow such noble characters to worship as I have. My heart leeps with joy when I contemplate your supreme greatness & lovliness. I am as well satisfied here as anywhere on earth, that I could not be with you & Laura. I have very little to do now in the way of practice. Our Regt. is very healthy. I hope it will remain so. If I live to get home again, you & Laura will be eat up, I am afraid. I love you well enough. I often think of the many happy moments we ha[ve] spent together. Oh that I could be with you to pass through a similar ordeal. The brightest & happest moments of my life have been spent in your society. Will I not be permitted to realize more of them ere long? I hope to. If I cannot get to see you soon, I want you to think of me often, for you cannot imagine how much pleasure I experience in realizing the fact of a noble one at home thinking about me, unworthy of you as I alwas thought I was and still think so. The weather is quite cold and rainy at the time, the first time if has been so sin[c]e we'v been in camps. I see no chance for a fight here, but we may yet get into one if the Burnsides expedition is destined for Savanah or the co[a]st of Ga. we may get into one. Our time is half out, liking seven days. We have all been paid of up to the 14th Dec. If the Burnsides expedition does not come to the co[a]st of Ga. I will be aped to come home some time in Feb. I have only as yet got fifty dollars of the money due on my horse. I think I will get the remainder on the next payday. I owe Houston twenty or twenty three dollars on a note. I wish you would give the money to him and get my note. You may pay if you want too Mozeley Lane one of the fifty dollar Bills, Grimes & Hales another, & Bunche[?] Levi seventy five dollars. You will then have left $145.00, or a little more, & I recon you had as well take up a little note of ten dollars that I owe Sam Boggus. Consult you[r] Pa about paying the above amts. out if he recomends it do so. The Yankees might take Savannah. Then the money on the Savannah Banks would be no accou[n]t. If I was at home, I would speculate on it and make it pay more than to pay debts with it. If you[r] Pa could buy Grimes' fine horse for two hundred dollars, I could sell him here for three or four hundre[d]. Tell him to try to buy him any how or get some one else to do it, & if he does not send him here, I will take him at two hundred cash and keep him for my own use when I get home. Tell him to find out the lest that the could be bough[t] for. Tell you[r] Pa to try to rent for me the Patches & garden about the hotel. Wilkerson in Newnan owns these. Let me hear from you often, my dear; as I cannot get to see you, it will afford me great pleasure to read the lines that you write with your lovely hands. Your as true & devoted as can be. Kiss Laura for me & tell her Pappie wants to see her so much.

G W Peddy

19

Franklin, Jan. the [17th] 1862.[7]

MY DEAREST HUSBAND,

To night is one of the loveliest I ever saw. The silver moon in all her radient splendor rides queen of the starry host of heaven, shedding her quitet holy light on many different scenes; and, alas, not on many glad happy hearts on this continent. How many noble brave hearts are trobing for the last time, and bidding adiew to loved ones. Hearts almost bursting with angush as they behold the fondly loved one [s]trugling with the last foe fighting his last battle. God grant that may never be my fate, but I fear it may be so. I am sad to night from all the reports in the papers confirm the [news] that you will be attacted by a land force. They are determined to take Savanah, and I fear it will cost the life of some of our brave men. Don't, my heart's best beloved, run into danger, for how could we live without you? Pa thinks you have not forces enough nor are prepared to meet the enemy advantageously. He don't have much confidence in the skill and good generalship of your commanders. All except Lee are inferior in maneuvering so as to gain a victory with as little loss as possible. I would be glad if you would write to me all about what you think will be done and also what if any artilery you have. I don't know much about it. Pa says you all are mistaken about thinking the Yankees will not leave the co[a]st. He is affraid you don't know any thing about it and sleep in blind security, but I can't think so. You don't know how very uneasy about you I am. I do wish you would come home. I have rested contented untill now thinking you was safte, but now I can't tell why, but I think different. Bud Gily is very sick now. When he first came home he was sick but got well as he thought and got out too soon, and now is thrown back again. He has typhoid fever, and I am affraid he will have a very tight spell. I received a letter from brother John. He was well, and saide they would soon have their winter quarters done and would be more comfortably situated. He said you owed him a letter. He said the chain he gave you was a *present*, and if any body had to pay for it, he would do it.

A letter came from old Nelson Carter the other day duning you for the money you owe him. If you can't pay all, he is anxious to get a part. I thought I would tell you so you could do what is for the best. I paid to the man you brought Frank from the money he wanted. You did not say what to do, and I did what I thought was right, considering how much you sold the horse for, and besides, the man said he lost so much by the trade. If you don't come home soon, don't you think I had better have the garden and yard fixt up with new

[7]Postmarked Jan. 18. Address: Dr. G.W. Peddy. 4h Reg. 2.d G.S.T., Savannah. Gea.

pailings? I don't think we can get along an other year without having something done. You can attend to that if you come home, which I am in hopes you will. Sallie Grimes was here this evening. She was very lively and talked a good deal about Tom. I don't think they liked it about Tom Boddie not coming up to see them. They and uncle Doer's family are getting as friendly as ever. Mrs. Dr. Grimes is very sick, she said. I went out to see Lu Hales yestady. She is fat as a guinea shoat. I don't think she will be down before you come back. She said she was mad with you for going off, and if she did get sick she would not send for no other Dr. I could hardly get off from her. She was anxious for me to stay several days. Jim saide he was going to write to you soon.

I did not finish my letter last night, and this morning I asked Laura who she loved. She said Papie and Manna. She is the sweetest little fat baby living. I know you would be glad to see her, and I don't think she will forget you any more. Ma says she has Laura now, for she will never be satisfied at home any more, but when here Papie comes home she will stay any where he does.

Pa says money is too scare and hard to get for him to take such a tripe, says nothing would be more pleasant than to go down to see you. He says if he knew when the fight would come off he would go down any how, but I am in hopes he is mistaken in thinking there will be a fight down there. Aunt Kit will be over to day and stay untill tomorrow. I will go home with her if bud Gily gets better. She is very uneasy also. Ambrose Williams is nearly well. He thinks he will be able to go back to camps in a few days. I have never been down there yet. I will look so anxiously for the time to come for you to come back, but then you will have to leave again and that will be bad again. The time will be half out shortly, but it seems to be it is six months now. I must close, as Pa will start downtown directly. Get Laura some shoes in Savanah and send them. She has worn out the pair she has. Don't get fine ones. Don't forget my *brestpin.* All send their love to you. Write as soon as you get this. Yours forever. Kate.

20

Franklin, Jan. the 18./62[8]

MY OWN DEAR HUSBAND,

This letter will be very unexpected to you I know, but I was anxious to write on something particular. Aunt Kit received a letter from uncle Joe today. His

[8]Postmarked Jan. 22; addressed: Surgn G.W. Peddy, Col J.J. Nealy's Reg., Savannah, Ga. 4 Reg. 2d Brig. Ga. S.T.

feelings, I am affraid, are hurt with aunt Kit, about what you laught at him about his not sending the salt, or some money to her. Now I am the cause of it, for I had no business to write to you any thing about it, but I always tell you every thing that occurs when you are here, so I try to write the same. Aunt Kit was not made, she says, with uncle Joe, only distressed to know how she could get any salt, for she was affraid uncle Joe could not get an opportunity of sending the money home soon enough; but as soon as Pa loaned her some, she was not pestered. I want to tell uncle Joe how it was, for I know it would nearly kill me for you to think hard of me, and I would not be the cause of such a thing; and you know amongst strangers he hated to be told of it. Aunt Kit says she knows you did it in a joeking way, and she is not mad with you, and uncle Joe told her not to tell me any thing about it; but it hurt her so bad to think uncle Joe was hurt about it, she could not help it. I never was sorry for any body as I was for her, and to think I am the cause of it. Do for my sake streten it up. I know you think a great deal of uncle Joe and aunt Kit too, but such things are calculated to make men think less of him where he is not known. You can tell him twas all a joeke, for I would not have him think hard of me in the lest. You must not think uncle Joe is mad with you, for I don't think he is, but be certain to tell him better, for you know his family has as much as any, and aunt Kit is one of the best of wives. I have said enough, I know, for you will do what is best. Write back to me immediately, for I am so hurt to think I am the cause of any disturbance. I did not think you would ever mention it to him. Don't be mad with me.

Bud Gily is very sick. His fever came back to day. Pa sent for the Dr. this evening. He said bud Gily has typhoid fever. I would not be surprised if he did not have a severe time of it. I heard this evening The. Person was dead. He died in Richmond. I was sorry to hear it. Hamp Cocran that boarded at mr. Watts and went to school is dead also. He was a fine looking boy. I saw Mrs. Hendric to day. She looks as well as ever. She inquired very particular about you, and insisted on my coming to see her.

I laide down my letter last night intending to finish it this morning, but some bad child came and scribled all over it, and I have not time to write over again. This morning is very warm and showery. I am affraid it will produce sickness. How do you get along now about cooking? Do you stay by yourself, or do you mess with Col. Neely? Maybe you think I am very inquisitive, but curiosity is the predominant trait in woman's caracter. I will close, for I have written all the news. Don't forget to do what I have requested. Come home soon. Laura sends the sweetes kisses from her little lips to you. Write soon. All send their love to you.

Kate Z Peddy

21

Camp Lee, Jan 19th 1862[9]

MY DEAREST TWO, I wrote to you day before yesterday; I write to you again today, as John Winchester is going home on furlough. He will bring you the money that I sent Capt. Sargent, Newnan, Ga. If you had rather keep the money, do it than pay out the amts. I wrote to you to do. Be shure, my dear, to keep enough to render yourself & Laura plesant & comfortable. I will buy you the pin you spoke off & send or bring it to you if it cost fifty dollars. I have never bought you any thing nice since you were mine, but will from now on get you anything you write for if it can be had for money in this market. Mrs. Brooks is going to pick out the pin for you. She is in Savannah & has been there for some days. I intend by writing so often that you shall not complain any more. I am going to buy you[r] Ma a nice silk dress if I can find one before long & make a present of it to her. I am quite well today & doing nothing. This is Sunday. I feel well satisfied when I have plenty to do, but when I have not, I am all the time thinking about you & our dear little sweet Laura. You must keep these letters to show to Laura after she gets large enough to read them. They will show her how much we love & care for her & may serve to make her love us more. We expect a big day tomorrow. The Gov. is going to review the troups of this post. I have a nice uniform coat. I expect to be out & look knowing, but how such things sink into insignificance befor me when contrasted with the pleasure of being with you & Laura. You can imagine by consulting your feeling, if you worship I & Laura as we do you. I know she loves you but is to little to love you as I do. Tell Laura that her Pa never expect to act in any way that would bring reproach upo[n] her & her mother. Nothing would serve to make me seek eminence, only the though[t] of reflecting credit upon you & our darling child. I have sent you all the money I had excep one dollar. I will draw on the fifteenth of next month I guess about $324.00 & I expect to get then the ballance on that due, which is $250.00. I will send all the above to you for safe keeping when I get it. If I get home safe, we will have money enough to pay nearly all our debts & to buy something good for us three to live upon until I can make more. I have to pay sixty cts. a lb. for coffee here. I think I will not use any more & save my money for you. I think if I can get through here safe we will be able to get along the ballance of the time easy if I can get any practice, & I hope my friends will not think any less of me when I get back home. I hope you will not, if they do. My darling, write to me twice a week so that I may spend a few bright moments as often as I read your letters.

---

[9]Envelope addressed: Mrs. Z.C. Peddy, Franklin, Ga. Per the Politeness of J.P. Winchester

Lou sent $20.00 in my pocket book to his Pa. Dr. Lane sent $100.00 to his wife. They are both very well. Lou rec'ed your letter. Henry Turner brought me one from you sweet hand. I will write to you again in reference to sending me a horse by A. K. Williams. Let me hear from you soon, my ever dear & lovely one,

G. W. Peddy

22

Camp Lee Jan 21st/62[10]

MY DEVOTED KITTIE, I rec'ed your letter with no date this eve.[11] I was truly glad, my dear, to hear from you, but sorry to learn that you are so uneasy about me. As to getting into a fight, you can tell as well as I can. I cannot tell what the notions of our enemy are. I cannot think we will get into a fight, although we are making preparations for one if the Yankees come. I think your Pa's notions about our Gens. is without foundation. He seems to have confidence in one (Gen. Lee). I have less in him than nearly any of them notwithstanding his high military position. Savannah is well defended. All the entrances to the City are well fortified & we have plenty of large Guns, but few rifled cannon that I know off. I supposed you Pa has no idea of the number of troops around Savannah. I think we have enough to expell any Yankee force that that Sherman & Burnsides may bring on their Fleet, though if they do come & whip us & I am killed, my greatest grief will be that I have not left enough for you & our little sweet Laura to get along through this cold & disconsolate world, & the though[t] of not seeing you again on earth is something that I will not think off. To leave you two, I will not write more about it. I think even if we were to get into a fight I will not be in danger of being killed. I will be in the rear of the line out of the way of danger. It seems to me that I write to you evry day. I hope you are like I am, wish that I could get a letter from you evry hour. I could read one if it were long enough from the beginning of one month to another. Their was but little of the soft felesent words in your last. I know, my dear, you love me, but I like for you to tell me of it often. A simple notion I recon you may think, but yet true. The rain is droping gently on my tent. It makes me think of you all

---

[10]Envelope addressed: Mrs. Z.C. Peddy. Franklin, Ga. To be mailed in Newnan

[11]*Supra*, No. 19

the while I recollect how glad you used to be when it would commence raining about the time we would go to bed. Oh that I could be with you again tonight to hear you talk about it. I think when I get home I will not sleep any for sometime. I must sit up & look at you & Laura. My dear Kittie, consider that I love you above all thing under my consideration & circumstance in life. In my hours of sadness or glee my heart reverts to you as the cheif of all earth's jewels & more dear that any object could possibly be to any one. I think when the excitement blows ove[r] about the fleet coming here I can get a furlough to come to see the dearest idol on earth. If I cannot I will let you know so that you may come to see me. I expect ere this that J. P. Winchester has arrived in Franklin with my money for you. I will get more in a short time to send or come & bring. You shall, as I said in my last, have your brespin. I do not know what size shoe would fit that sweet little foot of Laura's. If I did, I would get her a pair of shoes. Send the measure of her foot in your next letter. My love to all & compliments to Miss S. Grimes. I want you to write often to me if you can, my darling. I make it as a request of you, my dear, that you donot weave any more. I donot know what to say about the pailings. Do just as you see fit to do about them. If your Pa will let Peter put them up nicely while Puss works in his place I believe I would have it done. Tell your Pa to have nice pailings put around the yard. I donot care if them around the Garden are corse and rough if the post will be of good material. If your Pa think plank the cheepest, he can use his own pleasure which he puts around. We must try to keep out of debt as much as we can for that was my greatest trouble when at home. If you Pa wants to send me Nell by Ambrose & he will bring her & get transportation from Gen. Foster in Atlanta, the[n] I will keep her here to ride if she is large enough. I have no horse now nor donot need one very bad but would like to have one. Tell your Pa to keep a sharp lookout & try to get Dr. Grimes' horse for me. Your ever loveding G. W. Peddy

P.S. You can buy envelops from Mozeley & Lane.

Tell your Pa to try to get my money due on the Thompkin's account.

23

Camp Lee, Jan. 25th 1862

MY DEAR SWEET KITTIE,

I recived you letter of the 18th inst.[12] I was glad to hear from you. My antisipation of reading a sweet tenored letter from you was the highest pitch,

[12]*Supra*, No. 20

but behold, when I opened it, I kept thinking at the end of evry line that the subject you commenced with would be dismissed. But to my great dissatisfaction it was continued for over a page & a half. It give me the blews all the evning to think you had become so cold towards me. You shurely from the way you wrote that letter have become tired of writing to me. I was sadly disappointed when I found no sweet consoleing sentances for me. It appears that I have a hard enough time anyhow here in the woods, but when I get such letters from you my task appears double. If you are tired of writing & thinking about me, all I wish is to see you & our dear little child once more. Then I am willing to come back & die if need be in defence of my native state. I hope this sad view of the letter is rong. I will dismiss the letter. Its contents are being read by Dr. Lane. I know it's all right with him, but if you are to blame about it, let it fall on me. I am able to bear anything. I care not what it is. If they want to get mad about as small a thing as that, they can go. I am eating to myself. Ambrose's boy is kooking for me. I sent by J. P. Winchester for a box of something to eat. I hope you are at home so that you could send it, if you have anything to send. If you have not, I will have some more money the first of next month & will buy. I will try to send you more money by the first one that goes home from here. I will draw the 1st day of Feb. $253.00 more & get the ballance due on my horse. I will send nearly all to you. I want you to take care of it. It's for you & Laura. I only want enough of it to buy Beef & Bread with as that is what I have been living on for sometime. I have to pay nine cts. for it. I have bought your pin & have my ambrotype in it. I[t] cost sixteen dollars. It's a very nice one. I wish you had it at home, so that you might be wearing it. I am going to try & get a furlough sometime in Feb. I donot know wheather I will succeed. If I donot, I will not come until my tearm of enlistment expires. If I think I cannot get out of debt when I get home with about twelve hundred dollars & what I have owing to me their, I will go in again & risk getting killed to render you & our dear darling Laura comfortable & happy. If this republic is overrun by the enemy now, all lost & me with some of the ballance that have fallen. No more credit could I reflect upon you & our little Laura than ocupy a soldier's grave. The wages I am getting is, it['s] true, an object, for without it at this time you & Laura might eventually get into a bad fix, a thing I never want you & her to get into, at least if my efforts will avail anything. Kittie, I hope that you will write to me oftener if it does not bore you so much. If it does, tell Laura she must get big enough to write to her Pa. The little thing is unconcious of how well I love her, & her Ma is also in the same situation. You spoke in your one before the last about having the garden & yard pailed in. I expect you had better have it done. Our time it just half out to day. I wish it was out so that I could come to see you & our little Darling Laura. My hart will leep with joy if I am spaired to live through the campiagin so that I can get back home to see my two could not get her any in town. I am now knitting her some, and going to sew bottoms to them. You must get her a pair, and send by the first one passing; 6 or 7 will fit her of children shoes.

I received the money safte that you sent. I felt very rich indeed, but the feeling did not last long, for I had the money only a half day when Sam Boggus sent up a *dun*. I went down and paid him and Billy Mozely. The amount was 80 dollars for articles sold on cash, and he had 80 for his account before him and Brewer commenced selling together, and he said there was a small amount on Wood & Mozeley's books due, but I only paid 50 dollars. Grimes was out of town, but will pay him soon. Dr. Grimes sent word that you owed him 80 or 85 dollars and you promised to pay him some as soon as you drew any, but I never knew you owed him any thing. I did not pay him any thing, for you did not direct me to do so. He says he will not take a dime less than 200 and 50 dollars for his horse. He is not near as fat as he was when you were here. He has been riding him and driving him a good deal lately. Pa says he would not risk having him shiped for the chance of making fifty dollars. He thinks it is a bad trade, but you can do as you please.

I commenced writting this letter when Ma sent Amanda to the post office. I did not expect I would be as fortunate as to get one again from you, but there it lay filled with glowing words, which make me indescribably happy. I am now filled to overflowing with happiness. Honey, I do wish I could find language to tell you how happy I am, how much I love you. It seems to me now it would be almost too much joy if I could be with you once more, for I am only happy when by your side. Dear, can't you come? Do try. You said I did not write much of loving words to you in my last. If you could have lifted the vail of my heart and looked in, you would have seen painted there in characters of living light the idolitrous worship that are written there. It is the only thought that fills my whole being with joy. Shurely, my darling, you cannot love me as well, for I am affraid sometimes I do love you too well, something bad may happen to you. I am very much relieved about your being in danger if you should get into a fight. I do want you to be careful of yourself, for as you know, there is as much danger from disease as from the enemy's bullets. Bud Nick telegraphed to Atlanta and they wrote from there that Tom Brown of Corrinth was dead, also Hearn. Brown's father has gone on for his body. Pearson is dead also. I have hired out Puss, so that she can't work in Peter's place, and he has never got well since he came back from Va. I don't want to be at much expence, but I don't think we possibly go through another year without having something done, but I expect I had better wait till you come home to do it. Pa has not said any thing about giving you Nell. She plows well now; and one of his mules has been hurt so he can't plow her, and I expect he will need all the stock he has. He is trying to make a big crop this year. I have not said nothing about it to him, for I know he jewels. I expect you think from this letter that I am hurt with you, but I am not nor never expect to have my feelings with you. I will love & adore you if you hate me. My heart, my hole heart, and all its good feeling is your[s] forevermore. I will try after this to write you better letters than I have ever done if I can. I will write to you oftener if I can spare the time, but if I do, I will write evry day, for I have written to you almost evry other day. Let me hear from you as soon as possible, for I want to hear from you evryday. Nothing short of seeing you affords me so much pleasure as reading all your letter[s] except your last, which I [have] no objection to, only the length of the first not interesting subject. Your ever true & devoted lover, G. W. Peddy

24

Saturday Jan 25 1862[13]

MY EVER LOVED HUSBAND,

I wrote to you by the box, but having an opportunity of sending a letter by *mr.* Williams, I thought you are like myself, fond of letters when they come from loved ones. I have been depressed in spirits for several days as if some evil was going to befall those I love or that you was in danger some way. I do dislike to have so much anxiety for it is truely painful. Last night I dreamed you had come home, which I nearly always dream, but I was so happy in my dreams, but when daylight dawned, it put all those happy blisful dreams away: the cold reality again was present. I would give any thing in my power to be with you now, for all goes well when you are here, but some how I can't do as well when you are gone. I know it is selfish in me to want you here when you are where you can do your country and fellow men so much good, but I am only a woman and a very ordinary one too, not competent or worthy to be your companion in the brigh[t] and glorious highths in world's opinion one which you should have been placed at first; but no other woman so truely and devotedly loves as I. It is my life's life, and without you all earth would be a desert waste with not one green oasis excep Little Laura's love. Papie, she is not well yet, but is better than she was when I last wrote. She has the yellow thrash. Sometimes it hurts her so bad she will put her little hand over her mouth and come to me saying, mamie, Oh! Oh! I know it is bad: she caught cold from not having on good shoes, but I

[13]Enveloped addressed: *Dr.* G.W. Peddy, Savanah. Ga. politeness of Mr. Williams

would feel bad to refuse, and I don't think he can spare her. He said if he could find time he would go down and look at that horse for you at Liberty Hill. Nell is not in very good order now: they can't fatten her and ride and work her too.

I think I have written all that will interest you. Laura says she loves her papie and wants him to come home. I will go out to aunt Kit's tomorrow if the day is good. Billy Mozeley says he would come down if he could find time and any business to attend to. He was very proud of his money, for hard times are here, I can tell you. I must close, for Ambrose will be on directly to take this letter to you. Remember, dear, I love you no matter what fate befalls you. Yours ever. Kitty

---

25

Camp Lee, Jan. 29th, 1862

MY DEAR DARLING KITTIE, The first request I wish to make of you in this letter is for you to burn up the one I wrote you last. I beg your pardon, my dear bloved K. I will write you never again one like it. I was bothered nearly to death or I would not have done so. Ambrose came safe to camps today with a sweet letter from you. I would give all I'm worth to be with you this night. My heart is with you always, but I am not satisfied with that; I want those dear lips of yours and our little sweet Laura. Kittie, do not mention the last I wrote to you in your next nor let's never think of it again if you please, my darling Kittie. I have the headache to night. I do wish you were with me to rub my head. I think that would cure it. I remember with fondness how kind you were to treat me when I was sick. I am not sick to night but have the headache—not bad like I used to have it at home. Kittie, I rec'ed a letter from Dr. Watkins asking me to let you pay him some money. I donot want you to pay out to no one only the amts. I wrote to you to pay out. After that's done, keep the ballance that I sent you, all that I may send you in the future. I will pay it out when I get home, & if I donot live to get home, you will have enough to last you & Laura sometime. The Devels just want the money to speculate on. They shall not have it. They might come to the war & suffer some privations as well as myself. I will draw again day after tomorrow. I will send or come & bring it to you. I am going to try to get a furlough the last of next week. If their is not much prospect of a fight I think I will get off. If their is a fight I want to be in it. It would be disgraceful for me to go off on the approach of a battle. If I see their is no chance for me to get off, I will express the money to you as far as Newnan in care of J. E. Dent so that he may send it you per first passing. We may get into a fight in a short time.

I cannot tell. I believe now if the Yankees[k]new it they might take Savannah, if their war vessels will stand 48 lbs. Balls. Their is three or four vessels in four or five miles of the City now. They will have to do some hard fighting if they get the City. Their is a great many troops about the City. You will have the news from the papers more at length than I have space to write. Consult them often & you will see all the news about how we are coming on. I am truely sorry to hear of the death of Thomas Brown. He was a fine young man. If I cen just get to home home next week, what a happy time we will have. I fear I will be overcome with joy at the sign of my two dear darling ones. I love you so well I donot know what to think of but you & Laura. Do you not want something else besides the pin? I am going to buy you a nice cloak if I can find one, & I think I can. You need one, I know, & must have it. If I find one that suits me I will send it to you by express also. You wrot something about a horse. I donot want one now. I find I can do as well without as with one. I have no use for one in the world. I thought at the time I wrote I would want one just to appear important, but I will forego that appearance of importance. Our Surgeon Gen. has no horse, & if he can do without, I think I ought. I think when I get back Grimes will let me have his for two hundred. If he does not, I can get one cheaper that will do as well. My darling, if I donot come I want you to know that wherever I am I love you more than can be though[t], let alone speaking and telling. You & Laura have all my affection; no others do I love one hundreth part as well. Wilks wrote he did not like the Drs. in the Regt. I donot want his friendship. Anyone that stays all the time with Wores that he can get leave of absence for, I donot want to like me. He can be found at an[y]time when away from camp & at Savannah in one of them bad house. He ought to be ashamed of himself, having a wife & children at home. Let me hear from you soon. My love forever,
Peddy

26

Thursday, Jan the 30. 1862

MY OWN DEVOTED HUSBAND,

I was truely glad to receive your letter, but somehow my pleasure was tinged with regret, for I could not divest myself of the idea that you was displeased with me on some thing I had done. You seemed to doubt my love for you. It would be a greater pain to my heart than any dager could inflict if I thought you did not love me or I did not return that love fourfould. Whenever you think of me, allways think and believe that you have one heart whose every throb is yours, whose only happiness lies centered and bound up in your love for me. My darling, I have tried ever since we have been married to tell you how much I love you and how inestamable is your love to me, but I have only given you a faint idea. I have often been a wayward wife and caused you, no doubt, a great many unhappy moments, yet with all my faults I loved you well and I never can look back on our past lives since we have loved each other. But I sigh to think those joys are gone perhaps forever and I may not have the chance to prove to you how fondly I love you. Yet I do trust that these dark days that "try men's souls" will yet pass away, and the sun light of happiness dawn in all its deliciousness yet: when we can sit by our cheerful fireside and weave bright dreams of the future, when our cherub baby will be old enough to return some of the love which we now lavishly bestow on her. She, bless her baby heart, is all unconcious how well we love her, but she will one day find it out. I do wish more than ever now you could come home. How I would love to pillow my head on your bosome, and feel like all was safte now. I could not have the ills of life surrounding me, for your arm would encircle and shield me from all evil. How I wish I could be with you at all times to cheer sad hours and if render you happy.

I have grieved for fear you did not keep enough money to buy all that would render you comfortable. I do wish you had kept a plenty. I did not know you had to live so hard, for I supposed you lived so near the city that you could buy any thing in the line of eatables. John Winchester did not tell me you wanted a box. I sent one, but it did not hold much, and I thought you had every thing anyhow: it would only be a treat from home. I will try and buy some nice hams and dry them and send to you. If you think a box could go through safte shiped to Savanah, write to me and I will send it, if no one passes so I can send by them. Mr. Williams got off so soon I did not have time to fix up any thing when I found he would soon start. I suppose he has got there by now and given you all the news that his county affords, and I will not trouble you enumerate any. Your uncle Tom received a letter from Dr. Harland. He is very anxious to come back, but said he could not come to preach alone, and you would not release him from his obligation not to practice unless he took the house back. He said he sold you the house in prosperous times, and he could not take it back at the same price. He did not know you proposed to pay any rent, so Pa thought when he read the letter, and your uncle Tom too. I think it would be a good plan to write to him and try to get him to take it again even if you have to give a good price for rent. You will then be nearly out of debt, and it will not be such a weight on your mind. I do not care for my self, for I feel like I could do any way, or live any way [if] you could only be with me, but I don't want you to toil so hard, and I do nothing. How can I pass over an other three long months without seeing you? You spoke some thing about going into the service again. Honey, you don't mean it, for if you do, I shall know you don't love me as well as I do you; for I could not stay from you any longer. I want you to promise not to go in till I will release you from the promise. I know you will say I am simple to try and bind you in this manner, but love dares all things. You write as though you thought it a task for me to write to you, but I can tell you better. It does me good to do any thing that will give you pleasure, but there is allways a sameness about my letters which cannot interest you every time. I have but one theme—that I love to dwell upon, besides our darling baby, and that is how well I love you; and still I can not express the half that my whole heart would tell you. Come home, darling, and then, oh! joy, how can my heart hold so much pleasure? Laura too, Papie, will tell you how she loves her Papi. She is not well yet. Her mouth is broke out with the thark, and every time I wash it, the blood just streams out. It would pain you so much to see the little darling hold her mouth and cry when it hurts so bad.

It seems like bud Gily will never get well. He was so much better last week, he took too much exercise, and yestady he was quite sick. I have not heard from him to day. I am staying with aunt Kit, and we have a very pleasant time together. Laura loves to stay out here: the children all love her so well she just does as she pleases. Aunt Kit has some little ducks, and Laura trots after them all day. She tries hard to catch one too. Saturday morning/ Feb 1. I have nothing new to write, so you cannot be much interested. These dark days always depress any one's spirits, but at night I am happy as long as Morpheus throws her slumberous mantle over me, for I dream sweet dreams of my absent love which make me have pleasant thoughts in my waking hours. Oh! if those dreams could be fulfilled I would be happy indeed, far hapier than I deserve. I think you can get a furlough soon, and I do want you to be shure to try and come, for I know you don't want to see little Laura and I near as bad as we do you.

I can't come down to see you if I must leave Laura, for I would not be satisfied to leave her. She has not been well for some time. I don't know what to give her: some times I think she is wormy, but then I think a baby of her age are not troubled with such things. She sends a great many kisses to her Pappie and says she loves her Papie a heap. I know you are tired of this nonsence, so I will close. Write soon, or something better, come, and I will be so glad,

Your true and devoted Kate.

27

Camp Lee, Feb. 4th, 1862[14]

MY PRECIOUS DARLING KITTIE, I am under tenthousand obligation to you for the sweet & devoted letter I have just received from you. I felt like shouting when I read it. I will never forget this *letter letter*. I was in the City when I got it. Never was I so happy before. I know, my love, you adore me, & so do I you & Laura. Honey, you asked me to promice you that I would not go into the service until you said so. My *dear*, I will not. I never intend to leave you any more when my tearm of service expires. I love you so much that I never want you to get out of my sight again. It seems if I could see you now I would be satisfied. Oh! no joy could exceed that of being with *you*. The letter was characteristic of your devotion. Honey, I want to express my feeling to you but I cannot. I could show you them by actions if I wre with you. I would hold on to you[r] lovly form until you got tired of me. Honey, you will have to excuse me. I feel to proud of you to undertake to write anything to you that has much sense in it. My heart is to full of love for you to express myself. A heart so impressed with you as mine can never love any one but you & Laura. If it were not for you & her, I would wish to die, it seems to me. I lay here in my tent & think of you & Laura all the while. Tell Laura that Pappie will give her a great many more kisses when he comes home than she can send. I set here while writing & hear the beautiful strains of a male voice mingling with the notes of a Gitar singing that go[o]d old tune, Hazle Dell.[15] I can only associate it with you & L. As it is beautiful, it makes me feel sad. I wish you were with me to drive the sadness away to joy that could not be even imagined. Jim Caswell is here. I have to day bought Sweet Laura's shoes. They lay here on the table by me. Oh! how I wish I could see the little thing put them on to see how proud she would look. I am afraid they will be to large for her. I will send your pin & Miss Laura's shoes by him. He starts home thursday next. Honey, I will not try to come home until week after next, as we will not get any more pay until then.

I am going to try to get a furlough then. I donot know wheather I will succeed or not. If Laura is sick, if you will get Dr. Watkins to write a little note to me that my presence is necessary to the wellbeing of my family, I will be certain to get off, as that fills the recuisition for a furlough. If you can get him to write it send it to me in you[r] letter & then their will be no doubt about my getting off. If you cannot do this, I cannot get off. You will have to come to Savannah &

---

[14]Postmarked Feb 6, Savannah, Geo.

[15]"The Hazel Dell," by G.F. Root, included in *Heart Songs dear to the American People*, ed. J.M. Chapple, pp. 212-3.

bring Laura with you. She will be in no danger of any disease there. I will direct you how to come after I find out that I cannot get home. I am obliged to see you & L., & that very so[o]n. I cannot do without it much longer. I will write to Dr. Harlan to night to try to get him to take the place back. He may have it back if he will give me my notes & two hundred dollars. This will a great sacrifice, but am willing to make it under the circumstances. I think we will move down below Savannah in a few days. I begin to think we will have no fight at the city or else they would have made an attack ere this. Their does not seem to be the least fear about the Yankees' taking Savannah. The longer I put off comeing home the better, from the fact that the time of stay will not appear so long for me to stay afterwards. Honey, you need not send me any box yet. I hope I will come to bring it myself. I am getting along finely with all the men in the Regt. I do not think I have an enemy in camps. I believe the longer I am with them the better they like me—at least I hear no complaint nor my friends hears of none. I am sorry to hear of Giles' being sick so long. I do wish he would get well. My darling, write often. I will always answer evry letter imediately that I get from you. It is all I can do to keep from writing to you all the time. May angels watch over you & our little jem until I get to see you & all the time from now until the end of eternity if their is any end. My love to all. Go[o]d by, Honey.

Go W Peddy

28

Franklin, February the 4, 1862

MY OWN DARLING,

Your sweet letter came Wendsday as they always come, ladened as messengers of joy and happiness. How eagerly do I read each word of love, acting as the elixir of my soul reviveing and nourish[in]g again those flowers of affection which spring spontaneous in my heart for you, causing them to exhale such delicious odor as would turn the head of almost any being. Never was mortal man so entirely loved as you; how every throb of life beats for you, yet with all my devotion, I can but sigh sometimes when I think of how many noble hearted inteligent women are doomed to live out their lives with a man not capable of appreciating their good qualities. It is woman's highest ambition to be loved with a whole individed heart, but I never dreamed it could be my lot to inspire the devotion and love of one of nature's noblemen as you are; and well do I know that with all my faults and deficiencys of attraction I an not worthy such love. You have set up an ideal as every one has and imagine that I come up to it, but as love hides a multitude of faults, so I can account for your loveing my unworthy self. Earth teems with a thousand beautiful things, yet none are more lovely than two hearts united with the Geordian knot of true love. In all the ills of life there is the sympathy of a true heart, making the burtheon lighter, and causing our hearts to bless the Giver of good gifts for such blessings. Honey, I hardly know what to write to you. I write to you so often, and all my letters are merly the same every time. You will get weary of this sameness. You said in yours you wished I would write every mail. I have done so every mail since you left. You should have received two letters at once when you got your last. The water has been so high that the mail could not be carried three or four times lately, so that accounts for the delay in your letters.

I have just returned from aunt Kit's. You should have seen her and me, pearched up in a two horse waggon on the meal bags behind Bob with a perfect crowed of children. It was our only chance to ride home. It was just fun for me, but often coming down a rocky hill it was rather rough than pleasant. Pa's buggy is broke and we are just a foot. He has been looking at a buggy down below here, but has not traded for it yet. Pa received a letter from bud Nick last Wendsday. He was at Orange Court House, but thought he would fall back to Gordanville. They had marched from sixty to seventy miles and slep on two rails with a piece of a rail for a pillow, and just one blanket, yet he was in excellent health and the rest of the company was in better health than they ever was. He met up with uncle Winfield. He did not know bud Nick at first, but on learning his name he was so glad to see him. Uncle told him he would give him any office in his staff, bud Nick thinks he will accept the place you spoke of. He will come home on a furlough and stay some time. I have not heard what brother John is going to do, he has not written to me in some time.

Dr. Watkins has got into the service at last. Tomasson's company are to pay him a dollar a head monthly. He thinks he will get other companys two. William has returned and is in very bad health, he thinks he has consumption. I have not seen him yet. Joe Shack[le]ford is very sick with fever, I don't think he will ever be much of a soldier if a few days lays him up. There is at least four or five of Tomaston's company at home sick now. In reference to the corn, you can get any quantity here at a dollar a bushel, but Pa says he don't think it will pay to ship it down there. He says he would not speculate on the necessaries of life. He would on horses for men who want them, are able to buy them, and should give a good price for them. I don't want you to be a speculator no how: it is treating the government to badly, though I know you would not do such things.

My little sow has six pigs, and they are fine ones too. I am very proud of them, I can tell you. We have had some very cloudy weather and warm. Every thing is putting out so fast, which brings to mind that you will soon be here too. I asked Laura over at aunt Kit's if she wanted to go and see Annie. She said yes, Papie too. Every thing she finds she says is her Papie. Uncle Joe wrote that Irish linen was the same price there that it used to be. If you can find any you had best to buy three or four yards for shirt bosoms as there is none here at any price.

Horses are still in great demand here. Pa says he don't see any chance to buy you the horse you spoke of at any thing like a reasonable price. He don't think Grimes would part from him at any price. I am very sorry you will be so disappointed in not getting him, but I am in hopes you will find one just as nice as him. I must close, for I have nothing more to write that will interest you. Aunt Kit sends you her love. All her family are well. Laura sends Papie a sweet kiss and a good hug. Write soon, my darling. I wish I could be in this letter when it gets to you. Then I would be happy a long time. Good by, honey. Your devoted Kitie.

29

Franklin, Feb the 4, 1862.

MY EVER DEAR HUSBAND,

I have written to you since I received any letter from you, but I have concluded to write to you every mail, for no doubt you like to hear what is going on in this country. Aunt Kit received a letter from uncle Joe last mail, and he said you all did not get your box we sent by John Winchester. I never was so sorry about any thing. I sent you a great many nice things, and also I wrote you a long letter and sent it in the box, for I thought it would go as safe as any way. I intend to send you something as soon as I can by express. It distresses me more than any thing to think you can't have every thing that is good to eat. When will these dark days ever end, and this cruel seperation be at a close, for sometimes I think I can't spend an other day without sewing [*sic*] you. Truely this would be miserable world if the sunlight of your presence was not around me. All is joy and gladness when you are here. None of life's troubles press as heavily on me as now. I often think of the difference in us, for you are self-relient and independant, able and competent to battle with all the whims of fortune, while I am but a weight that retards and keeps you back from the position which nature designed to occupy. I am simple, as you will say, but nevertheless it is true. I never think of it but a wish rises in my heart that I could have something besides a heart entirely devoted to you to compensate for all the pleasures you have bestowed on me. I love my little darling baby more every day because she is the very image of her father; and Papie, she talks about you every day in her little baby talk. She is the sweetest child living, which you allready know. I do wish you could see her. She is getting well of the thrash. I sent by Mr. Jeans to La Grange to get her some shoes, and he could not find a single pair there that would fit her. I would be glad if you could send her a pair by some one as soon as you can. Mrs. Jeans sent you some sausage in the box that was lost. She would not sell them, but said you had done her throat good when all the other Drs. had failed, and she wanted to return the favor if she could. I am going to commence gardening as soon as I can, for we have very pleasant weather now. I don't know who I will get to fix up the pailings. All the carpenters are buisy at something else. I want to have a nice garden, but I know I can't without you wer[e] here. If Dr. Harlan would only take the house back I would be so glad. Then we could get us a nice little place and fix it up to suit us. Dave Grimes says he thinks I ought to pay him some of the money I have on the aco[u]nt he has for goods we received for cost—those he sold last year. I have not paid him yet nor will not till I hear from you. I paid an account at Milton Woods of 20 dollars. He said you promised him to send him some money the first you got. I don't think I would have a dollar if I paid out all that want to be paid. I will pay as you direct. Houston's note was only 19 and 35 cents. I have paid that sum to him. I have nearly a hundred dollars now, and you must say who else to pay it too. I don't think I will buy the first thing I can possibley do without, and then I will pay cash. I am sometimes sorry I asked you to buy that pin for me but I wanted to have your ambrotype so bad. I thought I had rather have it so I could always have it near me, so I could look on those dear features as often as I wished. Billy Mozeley started after Ben Gillespie yestady morning. He is very low. The old man has a hard time of it. I am going to see Ben's wife tomorrow. Bud Gily is still very sick. He says you must come home: he would be glader to see you than any body in the world, but I know who would be glad if you should come home. I don't see what could keep you now. The Burnsides expedition has failed and they can't have any excuse now so I will look anxiously for you every day. All send their love to you. Laura is in for her share of Pappie's love. Don't forget to come if you can. I have no news now to write, so will close.

Yours as ever true and devoted Kate

30

Camp Lee, Feb. 6th, 1862

MY DARLING, I write you again to night to let you know I have expressed a box to Newnan marked to me. I hope you will send up by the first passing & get it home. It contains my saddle books & case of splints. Well, my ever dear wife, the Yankees have demanded a surrender of Skidiway Island or they will take or storm the batteries in six days. We will move down in six miles of their tomorrow. I expect we will get into a fight. If we do, my sweet darling, & I get killed, I want you & *Little* sweet Laura to know that I have died in defence of your rights & fathermore that I did loving you two far above all things on this earth. My hole heart, love, affections are consentrated upon you. I cannot think I will be killed if we get into a fight. It would seem hard for me to have to leave my two dear ones to drift about in this cold & charitable world. If any misfortune befalls me, I want you to try to raise our little dear as nigh right as you can. Suffer her to keep no bad company. Keep her with you & I know she will always be in the best of company. Take good care of yourself, my darling one, until I see you again. If you will send the note from Dr. Watkins that I spoke of, I will see you ere long if I live, & I do hope I will have the pleasure of being with you once more at least. Know joy on earth could be greater. Never would one love be so happy as mine. My whole happyness in this lif is in the hand of you two dear ones. My love, I will write to you in a few day after we get to the new camp. I hope you will be cheerful & lively until you hear from me again. We will not be in less than six miles from the fight if it comes off. We are ready & willing to meet them on equal tearms. We have a great many gallant troops here to fight for us: we will be entrenched in our new camp & I think it is very doubtful wheather they take the Island or not. We will be located one & a half miles from the City below two miles from the river in no danger of shell. Their will be a dense thicket of large timber between us & the river, & they are not going to make any attck from that direction. They cannot come up the stream because of Batteries on the Bank & obstruction in the channel. Let me hear from you often, my darling. I will close at it is getting late in the night. I will write you more at length in my next. My love to all relatives & friends.

Yours forevermore G. W. Peddy.

31

Camp Defiance, Feb. 10th, 1862

MY DARLING KITTIE, I read you sweet & interesting letter. I was glad to learn that you were well, my dear. The thing that I most regret about the loss of the box is the long letter that was in it for me. You cannot tell how well I like to read them. They do me good for many hours afterwards. The lines you write look like they are written with gold & the words seem to mean volumes to me. Honey, I wish I knew what to write that would interest you. I am shure I would gladen your heart more—that is my greatest design to make you joyful & happy. I can sit here & imagin how those sweet little eyes of yours look. I would almost give my existence to see them, they are so lovely, gentle, sweet, & kind. They would be far brighter to me than sunlight or any other luminary on this earth. We are now located 2 miles below Savannah, a very beautiful place to camp. I am now fixed up nicely in my tent. You said in yours, my darling, you had always been in my way & retarded my progress. Why, my love, do you say this? Nothing short of your *grand & lovly self* has put me whare I am. I feel proud of you evry time I think of you & want evry body to see you so that they can remark what a beautiful, lovely, & glorious darling I have. It seems to me that no one is so blessed as myself in that particular. The mo[o]n shows brightly to night. Oh! that I were with you & our darling Laura. I do love the little sweet thing so well because she is part of her noble ma.

My darling, I have this day sent you two hundred dollars per express. It may [be] stol in the express office in Newnan if you do not get it by next Saturday. I expect you had better send to Newnan after it. I will send you more in a few days. I expect to get pay for my horse tomorrow. If I do, I will send the money imediately. You may pay to Dave Grimes the amt. of the cash account if it is not over fifty dollars. If it is, just pay him that amt. & no more. If he has got mad about it, donot pay him one cent until I get home. I want your Pa to buy me Dr. Watkins' case of Trephineing instruments if he can get them for ten or twelve dollars. They are rusty, but if the case is compleet, tell him to get thim for me. Your Pa need not tell him but what I lost mine. I am offered $90.00 dollars just for my case of amputating & trephineing instruments. They only cost me at first $35.00 dollars. I think I will sell them if I can get Watkins' little trephineing case. My assist. has an amputating case that we can both use. Let me know, my dear, if I must sell them. I donot expect I can get any more if I let them go after I get home. Your Pa may get them very low or for a great deal less than ten or twelve dollars if he will try & not let Watkins into the secret. I can sell them if they were mine for twenty five dollars. My dear, I donot know wheather we will get into a fight or not. We may, & that very soon. The Gens. begin to think we will in a few days. As for my part, I canot tell wheather we will or not. I am perfectly easy about it. I have been looking with a glass for the Yankee fleet but cannot see it. They say their are 36 vessels in Warsaw Sound but it may not be so or it may: you can hear anything in the world you want to hear here.

You said in your last you would write to me evry mail. Well do so, my darling, for I do cincerely love you above all things that can be thought off. You are the pride of my existence & the solace of my stay on earth, & in dying thy gentle hand & sweet vioce alone can comfort me. I sent you per J. M. Coswell Laura's shoes & your pin. I hope it will suit you; if not, send it back & I will get you one that does if their is one in Savannah. Anything else you want, my darling, let me know what it is. Yours true & devoted forever G. W Peddy.

32

Camp Brown, Feb. 14th/62

DEAR GEN.[16] With much pleasure I write you a few lines to let you know what is going on in this section. Evry thing is quiet in the vacinity of Savannah. The Yankees are pretty thick below us. I went down to fort Jackson yesterday. I saw six Yankee vessels. They fired at one of our Gun Boats to day that was on its way to Fort Pulaska. No one was hurt. I don't think that they will ever pass the fort that I was at & the othe[r] Batteries that are about it. We have plenty of canon here for all practical purposes. We have fine earth works two miles below the city, with canon mounted on them. I think they will take Skidiway when they attempt it. Dr. Arington is Surgeon of a Regt. in Right's Legion on Skidiway. He was up to see us yesterday. He says that the Yankees will take the Island. He is for the war & seems to be in fine health & spirits. The big men seem to think that we will have a fight in a few days, but I cannot think we will. I think they know that we are to well fixed for them. In my feeble judgement I do not think they will make an attck by land. I think they will from the river, & if they do, I think we will get them just whare we want them. Their's eleven Guns on fort Jackson & nine on some earth batteries bellow & nine large ones on the opposite side of the river & five more just above on the same side. If they will give us ten days longer they never can take the City, & I doubt very much their ability to take it even now. Arington says they will all be taken prisner if they are not removed from the Island. I hope he is wrong or mistaken in his

[16]Judge L.H. Featherston, Dr. Peddy's father-in-law.

judgement. I would like to come home, but I donot think I will try to come as long as the prospect for a fight is so eminent, & rearly I donnot think I could get off under the peresent circumstances. It requires a certificate from a Dr. that the condition of one's family is such that his presence is necessary. I wish I could come home. Nothing could please me better. I rec'ed a letter from John to day. He is well; so is Nick. Evry time I begin to talk about comeing home, Neely begins to put on a long face. I will make an effort, I think, ere long if I can get the excuse that I wrote to Kittie for. If I cannot get to come, Kittie must come to see me. I would like to be at home now to see how the fellows take Brown's proclimation. The boys that know Boyd are all anxious to see him just after reading the unwelcomed message. I think he will go into spasms before the fourth of March. I want you to advise me what to do about my future course. I think I had better get me a position in the Confederate Service. I expect their will be a draft about that time. I have got two hundred dollars of the money on my horse. Their is yet due fifty dollars. I will get it the next pay day. I will send it to Kittie the first chance, or by express if the other goes safe. I donot care what they say about my promices to them.

Kittie had better buy us about two hundred lbs. Bacon. I suppose that will be enough to do us. I am afraid it will get higher than it is now. Thom Battie has bought a horse & has let me have him to ride. I sent my saddl by Jim Coswell. I wish I had it back, but donot sent it until I write for it. I think I will let my instruments go: I can get four times what they cost me. If I had Dr. Grimes' horse down here I could get four hundred dollars for him. He is just the horse for the market, but you must not let him know it or else he will send him here to sell. You never saw horses as high in your life. I do wish I could see you to let you know how I want things done about home. I see a great many chances to make money now if I was just out of the war. Tell Kittie I will send her all the money I get, only liave enough to buy me something to eat. Kittie must write to me every mail as I am very anxious always to hear from her. I will reply imediately to hers, I have just learned how to write to her so the mails will take it directly through. I would send you a box of shad if I though[t] they would not spoil before you got them. We get as many as we can eat.

Let me hear from you soon & oblige. Yours evr G.W. Peddy

My love to Kittie, Laura, & the balance of family.

33

Camp Brown, Feb 16th/62

MY DARLING PRECIOUS KITTIE, I have been looking evryday for several days for a letter from you & I expect you have been looking for me to come, but that, the greatest of pleasures, has not been granted me. I have not yet applied for leave of absence. We have been expecting a fight evry since we got to this camp, but it has not yet come off, nor I donnot know wheather it will or not. All seem to think it will soon. It may, I cannot tell. Oh! how I wish I could be with you to night. No joy in this life would be so great. I donnot know that I can get off if you donnot send me the showing from Dr. W[atkins] that I sent for. I have just rec'ed a letter from Dr. Harlan stating that he would take the place back, if I would take the two notes he holds against me for it. That would be intrust & all about nine hundred dollars. I am a great mind to take him up at his offer. I will loose about four hundred dollars & the intrust on it two years. I want to know what you think of the trade & tell you[r] Pa about it & get his advice. If I was to take the offer I would get out of debt by the time I get through here, if I live to get home. I will not say any anthing to him about taking his offer until I hear from you. I was so in hopes when I rec'ed the letter that it was from you I liked to shouted. I often set down & study about how I could bear to be with you & Laura. I am afraid the joy would be more than I could bear. I wish I did know exactly how you two look. I know you are the most beautiful object in the world, but I am not satisfied with this truth. I want to be with you so that I can enjoy that beauty. We are having some rainy weather here at this time. We have been greatly blessed with favorable weather since we have been here. I would like to be at home to see how uneasy the men are about Brown's proclimation. I am sorry for the poor wives & children of those who have them to leave to go to the war. I hope no one will ever be so bad off to see any one as I am you & L. b[l]ess her little soul, her pa want to see her & her Ma so badly. I sent you two hundred dollars per express. I hope you received it ere this. I have the same amt. to send you when I get a chance & hear that the other went safe. I wrote your Pa a letter last night. I expect you will get this about the same time. I donot want you to stop writing to me with the expectation of my coming home. I may come & I may not. I think I will try after I hear from you again. I hope you will send the scrip I wrote for, then I will be shure to come. I would not be absent in a fight for nothing. You must not think that I donot love you & Laura by my not coming home to see you. If ever one did love, I do you & Laura. I wish I knew what you & L. likes best, I would get it for you. I know you had rather I would come home than anything on earthe, & I would do so if I were not afraid of injuring my command. My heart will leap with joy when my time to go home expires. How I will enjoy muself with my dear lovely little family! You[r] happyness is my pleasure. I wish we could be satisfied apart until my time is out, but it does seem to me that I cannot do without seeing you & our dear little Laur[a] longer. It seems to me that I have been gone from home always. It will appear to me the time will like it did just a few days after we married, & when I think of those days I always e[n]vy my enjoyment of that time. Let me hear from you soon, my own true love.

G W Peddy

34

Franklin, Feb. the 17, 1862.

MY DARLING,

No doubt you are wondering what can be the reason why I don't write if you are like me, allways thinking some evil has happened to you, but I will soon explain the reasons why I am so long replying to your dear letter. Nothing would have prevented me from performing the most delightful task that mortal can have, but sickness. Laura has been very sick. She was taken with colra-morbus, and for two days I was very uneasy about her. She hardly recovered untill I was taken with diarea, and I never was so sick in my life for three days. Ma gave me laudnum and blue pill untill I was relieved. I don't want you ever to leave us again, for I never get frightened when you are here. My darling, I commenced to write to you a good letter, one that my heart always dictates, not to trouble you with a history of a few days' sickness, but Pa wrote to you by the last mail that I was not well, and I was affraid you would be uneasy, for you must know that no ordinary circumstances prevents me from writing to you. Pa had just returned from Newnan, where he learned you were expecting a fight every hour, and I did not want you to be distressed on my account for we all thought you could not get off under any consideration. Every day and hour I live makes me love you more, if such as thing can be possible, and long more anxiously for you to come so I can tell you so, for I cannot write it. It is my greatest happiness to give you a moment's joy. It looks indeed like I can't wait till old time rolls his slow wheels around to the time when we will meet. Oh! then what joy! Honey, do you ever think of that hour? It certainly will never come. Earth would be rob[b]ed of all its joys, if you were not here. I never could understand why so many married people seem so cold toward each other, because they were never loved like we do, for I allways judge you by myself in that instance. Matha Woods and Newt Reed married last Thursday night. What a crowed of happy memories comes up now as I look down the vista of two short years ago. I stood by your side on an other Thursday night a happy, loving bride, with high resolves in my heart, that I would make the noble being I had promised to love, honor, and obey, happy if humane devotions could accomplish it. It is a bright, lovely picture which warms my very existance and makes me forget for a while the sad reality of the present. Do you ever think of those days, love, when all was happiness and joy? The future seemed radiant with gladness for us. Then when our lovely babe was given us, how proud we wer[e] of her beauty, how beautiful she looked, how like a little angel on earth she was, when her little soft heair was curled around her snowy brow, and her blue eyes dancing with baby mirth, we thought there was no treasure like ours. Oh! those days—the memory of them stirs my heart with deep emotion. I love to linger over them. We have the same little being now to live for, and we will try to raise her wright so she will be our joy in after years. I must stop for to night as I am not very strong yet and can't sit up longer. Tuesday night. It has been raning almost incesantly for two days and nights. The whole earth is well saturated, and the river is fuller than it has been for years and still rising. I am uneasy about the mail, for I don't think it can be brought tomorrow. I almost dread to hear from Savanah now, for fear you are hurt or some of our brave men. Darling, remember us when danger is nigh and avoid all you can. I don't want to live longer than you, for then there would be nothing worth living for. All my happiness and pleasure lie bond up in you love. Would I were with you this night! I could but faintly express how much love dwells ever in my heart for you, and I know of no being that I could bestow it on, so much my ideal of manly perfection as you noble self. All that is noble, grand, and good are united in making up the caracter of the ideal of my love. You should have seen Laura when I put her little shoes on you sent. She danced and laughed and talked of Pappie for a long time. They were a little too large, but will be just the thing for her in Summer. Papie, we both thank you so much and send you a thousand kisses for our presents. Mine was what I always desired, and I would not take any amount for that dear face in it; the eyes seem to be smiling that same sweet, sunny smile of love for me that used to thrill my heart so in by gone days, and I always feel like you were thinkilng of me when you had it taken. Pa got the two hundred dollars you sent by express to me when in Newnan. It came safte, and your box will also be here soon. The roads are almost impassable now. I will pay out the money as you directed. Dr. Watkins went over to his plantation last week and can't get back in consecuence of high water. Pa has not seen him since I received you[r] letter. Pa says you can't get such instruments as yours again if you sell them. He thinks it not a good plan to sell, but you know best what to do.

There is a new company just commence voluntaring here. Nalls has given up his school and is going; Sam Boggus, Bill Tommasson and a good many others have volunteered. You know there will be a draft out soon if they don't raise a company. Pa says Pace and several others are frightened about the draft. Dr. Northen has his own fun, making out he is spitting blood, and a great many other complaints when the draft is spoken of in a crowed, just to see how men will make excuses to get off. I would not care much if some of these specalators had to go; they must as well do some of the work as a few to do all: it is nothing but justice.

Tobe Oowens came very near killing Charles Mathews last week by stabbing him in the back. Owens, they said, jumpt into a battaux and went down the river. He has not been heard from since, though he is not much loss to the country, I don't expect. Mr. Spencer Gems lost his oldest son too last week. He was killed in the mill some way. He was nearly grown, and was crushed to death. Bud Gily is improving rapidly. His trouble now is to get enough to eat: I never saw such an appetite as he has. I saw a letter to day from brother John. He was well, but the health of the company was very bad. Billy Favor is about to die; his father has sent for him. Columbus McSwain died a few weeks ago, and several were very sick. One of the Furlow boys went after his brother's corps and was taken sick and died in too days after he got there. They brought both of their boddies back together. I must close, for you will get tired, I know, of this humdrum letter; but first let me tell you that Mrs. Oliver has a fine daughter. She went up to see her sister and caught. Mr. Oliver is overjoyful at his good fortune. I am nearly well now and Laura is in the best of health. Eddy says don't forget him down there. All send their love to you.

Ever thine, Kate Z. Peddy

This is my last sheet of paper. You must send me some by the first passing. Tell me when you are comeing.

35

Camp Brown, Feb. 19th/62

MY DEAR DARLING KITTIE, With much pleasure I write you again to day. I have written you several letters recently without getting any answer. My darling, you promised in your last to write to me evry mail. I do wish you would, for nothing gratifies me so much as a letter from your lovely hand. This world look near enough like a baron waste to me, & it seems worse when I fail to get letters from you. I recived a letter from you[r] Pa dabefore yesterday. I was glad to hear from him. I have sent to you to day per express a package containing $375.00. It is not all for you: $200.00 dollars of it is yours. You must take good care of it & donot let any one have any more of the money I send you. I have sold my case of instruments to day that cost me $35.00 for $125.00. I think that is a pretty good proffet. I will send the money to you in a short time. I have bought a better case of instruments f[or] $90.00 from Dr. Smith in Grantvil[le]. I am offered $130.00 dollars. I believe I will let them go for that price as I have as many as I want to use here with me. If you[r] Pa has bought them from Watkins I wrote for, I will make a good proffet on them. I expect you will have to send to Newnan for the money I sent by express to you. When you get it, donot let any one know that you have it & they will not be after it them[selves]. I am as well, my sweet, as you ever saw me, & I am getting to think we will have no fight here. I believe that they are just keeping us here to keep us from going to the upper part of the State, or just beond whare the[y] are whipping our army. I can find out no preperation they are making to attact us, though we may have a fight. We are well fixed for them now & I think they had better not come unless they bring about fifty thousand troops. Then I think we will drive them back under cover of their Guns. My darling, I thought by this time I would have been enjoying the greatest of pleasures, i.e. in being in your presence, but alas it is not so, & I shall not come, I recon, my darling, unless you send the note to me from Dr. W[atkins]. In fact, I donot think they would let me off unless they had a showing of that sort. Say to your Pa I would like he would get me the surgeon's place in some of the new Regts. that ar[e] forming in the State; & Dr. Wily, who is now in the Q.M. department, wants Gen.'s assistants to try to get him as Quarter Master in the same Regt. that I am in. I expect, my dear, I had better go in again as Surgeon or I might have to go as a private. I do wish I could spend the ballance of my life with you & Laura, but it seems that the fates are determined to seperate us. I am coming home to see you before I go in again & stay as long with you as I can, & I will not go in the army anymore unless I am compelled to do so. My only pleasure in this life is with you & our sweet little child, but circumstance are such that I may be compelled to forego the pleasure of your society until peace is made. If you do not [*sic*] send me the scrip I wrot for, I will come home; if not, I donot think you kneed look for me until my tearm of service expires. If you want to come down here, come on. Mrs. Lihew Watkins is here. If you come, when you get to Savannah go to the Gibbon house & write me a note & I will come to see you & stay with you. Let me hear from your evry mail. I will write you again soon. I believe I will by you a fine Bureau & Arm rocking Chair & Laura a nice little rocking Chair. Let me know if you want these things bought. Your evermore G. W Peddy

36

[22 February 1862][17]

MY BELOVED,

It was as I expected: the mail did not get here and I concluded to send an other letter in the same invelop. I am now nearly well except a very sore throat, which is unpleasant. It has been sore nearly a week. It would not surprise me much if it turned to the putrid sore throat, but I do hope it will not. I do not write this to make you uneasy, for it is nothing serious. Laura has entirely recovered from her spell and looks as well and rosy as any child. She gets more and more like you every day she lives. The other day I roached her hair and turned it under all round like you do yours, and I nearly killed her with kisses, she was so much like you. Papie, I know you would give any thing to see your little sweet baby. She is the greatest comfort to me of any thing else since she can say a few words right plain. February is nearly out, my dear, and you are not here yet. I have looked till I am weary, but in vain, for your dear familiar face and voice. I don't want to be put off much longer. I never did want to see any thing in the world as bad as you and I don't think I will ever let you go back when you do come home. Every one is excited very much about the result of a battle in Kentucky, which lasted four days. At the end of the first, our troups had repusled them killing 500, and only 25 killed on our side, but they were renenforced with 8000 and our force only amounted to 1500 at fort Donalson. They then surrounded our men and obliged them to either surrender or be cut to peices, but they fought their way out. Reenforcements were sent from Bow[ling] Green, and they are still fighting, but perhaps you have heard all about, and in a more explanatory manner.[18] Watkins has come home at last and Pa went and looked at his instruments. There was eight peices that belonged to the case. They were only second handed when he bought them and he gave $10 dollars. He says you can have them at the same price. He has also a few other instruments for amputating. Pa says you can't get such as yours are soon and as cheap. Nalls has bought Grims' fine hor[s]e. I don't know what he gave for him: Nalls has joined a horse company some where on the coste, and of cose wanted a good hor[s]e to show of to advantatge. He will start off in a few days. Pa says he will go down near you; he is in Phillips' Brig. I don't know any thing else about it. You can get as good a hor[s]e as that was, I know, any where; he had fell off and did not look well any how. The Garden at the hotel is

---

[17]Date from the postmark

[18]Fort Donelson fell on 16 February 1862.

all down, and the hogs have broke into ours several times from there. I am almost affraid to plant any thilng down there, for Mrs. Pace's chickens just live in the garden. I have had a portion broke up, but the weather is so bad I can'lt get the time to do much. I hope you have not been had as much rain where you are, for I don't think you could live through it. I am writing a very uninteresting letter to you, I know, but some how I can't help it. I know if I just could have the sweet privilege of seeing your dear self I would be content for a while; it looks like a year since I saw you. I long for the days to pass away soon, but yet I dreat lest some accident may mar our joy. I must close, love, but let me tell you that I love you with all the heart devotion that any one can have, and only aske to be remembered by my darling. Good night. May angels keep their guardian watch around my beloved and bring him safte to me *soon*. Laura's little lips comes in in for a kiss. *Kate* Peddy

---

37

Franklin, Feb. the 25, 1862.

MY HEARTS DELIGHT,

Tis night, and I sit by a comfortable fire with my table drawn up close to enjoy its genial warmth while I hold sweet converse with my darling. But Oh!, how much pleasanter it would be to have you here where I could tell you how dear your are to me and receive an answering of affection such as used to be mine in the happy days of our love. Honey, I know you are tired of this sameness in my letters, and will begin to think I had better copy all the rest from the same letter; but when I begin to write, the thoughts of our happy love comes naturally first. My heart is allways overflowing with an ever during love for you, my darling, and it is a wonder that I naturally commence in that manner and end the same way, for the holy Bible says "out of the abundance of the heart the mouth speaketh."[19] Little Laura is asleep now, bless her little bright eyes, which are just like her Papie's. She gets more interesting every day. She often trys to sing. I do wish you could see your sweet little darling. I am so uneasy about you I don't know what to do. I am so uneasy about Skitaway iland. Pa says if you are not sent there he won't be so uneasy about you, but it looks like every thing goes wrong now any how. The Yankees have taken Nashville,[20] and

[19]Matt. 12:34.

[20]Nashville was abandoned by the Confederates after the surrender of Fort Donelson; by 25 February 1862 Nashville was under firm Union control.

it seems that they will overrun Tennessee, and then Georgia comes next. You will say I am only borrowing trouble, but I get very low spirited sometimes and can't think of anything that can throw a gleam of sunshine across the darkest future that we ever saw. To night I do feel so sad some how and I ought to be rejoicing, for Mac Glover has just come back with Tom's remains, and he said he staid nine days in bud Nick's company, and just before he started back, bud Nick had received permishion to come home on a furlough to get men to reenlist for the war. 18 of his company had reenlisted and would come home with him to stay sixty days. Mac could not remember but few of those that had reenlisted. Brother John had not, but would have done so if bud Nick had not persuaded him different. I expect his health would not permit it, for Mac says he is allways complaining, and I am affraid he will yet have a long spell. Mid Hood, they thought, would be shure to die that day he left. The Physician said he could not possible live through that day. I don't know how glad I will be when bud Nick comes home; and if you would come too, I don't think I could stand it. If joy ever did kill any one, I would be uneasy if such a thing would occur. Honey, you must come home. I do want to see you better than any thing in the world. I have so much to talk to you about that I can't write. I don't think you will ever get away from me in a month. Pa wrote to you about the house and lot. I don't know what is best. I am like you: I want us to get out of debt some how.

Pa was so well pleased at your long letter you wrote him, but I was cast down, for you spoke in it about entering the service again when you time is out. I don't know what is for the best. Certainly but I dont want [you] to leave me any more if you can possibly avoid it. I know that I ought not to be selfish, for so many women have to bid adiew to those they love as well as I, and Oh! how I pity them from my heart. Sometimes I think if you did come home, you would not be satisfied to stay with me any more. You would still want to be in the service. I saw Dr. Northern this evening at mr. Watts. He enquired very particular about your health and when you would come home. Almegro is quite sick today. I would not be surprised if he did not have a spell that will finish him. He breaths somewhat labored. Tom Hale came in there while I was there. He is also sent back to get up recruits. He said he had rather fight for 5 dollars here in Ga. than for 20 in Va. He says they have very hard times there. The mud is so deep they can hardly get provisions hauled to them. He said he could hardly keep from crying every time he looked at an old cow to think how soon they would be eat up if they were in Va. Tom looks a good deal stouter and healther than he did when he left here. He says they can't get any licker of any kind. Every trunk and box is broke into and every drop taken out. Alec Lane lost two quart botles taken out of his trunk by the officer. It is a good thing for some of the boys that love the *creter* too well. I have written all that will interest you and had better quit for fear I tire you out. I wrote to you in my last that Nalls had joined a horse company, but he has changed his notion and is going in this company. I recon he thought there would be a good chance to get Capt. place, but Bill Tamasson thinks he is entitled to it, and several others, so it will be split up as the first company was. Nolan has broke up his school and is going. Sam Boggus has moved back to the old mans and lets Dr. Grimes have his house for nothing if he will take care of his place well. My fire has burned down and I must close.

Come soon, darling. Yours forever Kate Z Peddy

P.S. I am in the same condition I was when you left home[21]

38

Franklin, March the 14./62.

MY OWN BELOVED,

Again it is my delightful task to tell you how dear to my heart is the thought that amid all the allurements and pomp of life, when all seem darke and drear elsewhere, one heart is mine, all mine where the halo of true undying love for unworthy me ever plays. My darling, I have often told you how like my own life is the love ever dwelling in my whole heart for you, but how little deoes words seem, how cold and pashionless, to the warm soul thrilling love that is yours from me. I often sit and think for a long time how I can render myself worthy of you love, but poor me, it will never be so. It seems like months scince you went away. I did want you to stay awhile longer. I have been so lonesome too. Sometimes I think I will start anyhow and go to see you, but then I know that will never do. Laura, too, talks so much of Papie. Every thing she has, Papie gave it to her. I know she will not forget you any more. She is standing now by the table quareling about her chair. Papie, you have a sweet little baby at home, you know. She has not taken the mumps yet. I hope it will not hurt her if she does. I have had the toothache ever [since] you left. I went down to get Dr. Northern to plug it. He said there was but one remedy for that tooth, and that was pulling. I could not let him pull it no how. I told him you would have more patience with me than any one else. He said I had a splendid set of teeth with

[21]Dr. Peddy was at home on furlough some time during the first two weeks in March 1862.

that exception, and he did want to get that one out. Bud Gily has succeeded in getting a school at Friendship and will commence Monday. Nalls intends to run for Major and so does Tobe Wood. Tobe says he would not give up to any man when it comes to drilling, but I should judge differe[n]t myself. The company has left. They will be in the field soon; no time to drill or to return home again. I am so sorry for the poor faimilies that are left. They don't know how much joy there is when the one most loved is at home. I don't think I can let you go again. It is almost as bad as to be shut up in prison for that length of time. I saw Wyat Wood yestady. His time is out and he has returned home. He looks very robust and healthy. Two of bud Nick's company is sick. They have left Centreville, as perhaps you already know, perhaps. Mr. Sims has just returned from Va. He spent three or four days with bud Nick and said all the boys seemed to think a great deal of their captain. He heard not a word against him, as he did when he was there before. Mr. Sims hired a substitute for Bob and brought him home to send him to school. Almegro Watts has been very low for several days. Three or four times they thought him dying. He will hardly live much longer. Mrs. Averzena Wilson has a fine daughter—so you see we have some little Yankees here too. If it had happened a little sooner, you would have been called in. Fannie will be married next Sunday two weeks to mr. Ab Keith. That is the fact this time. Every body has been making enquiries and guessing so long it is a matter of fact now.

I was so lonesome after you left. I went over to see Mrs. Sugart and stoped and got mrs. Foster to accompany me. I enjoyed the day so well. They are such clever, agreeable people, and above all, thinks so much of you. They wanted to see you very much. Abe Foster will go in the next company from here. As I came back, I say Nancy Copelan. She said to tell you she wanted to see you as bad as I did, but I told her not to think of that for a moment; there was no comparison. She is a good girl and looks better than I ever saw her. Mike DeLacy is here yet. I think he spends most of his time at Dave Grimes', and the next news, Sallie and him will be engaged. Tell Ambrose he had better watch close or his sweetheart will give him the mitten. I paid Dr. Grimes the money you directed should be paid. He seemed satisfied.

I can scarcely write, for Laura thinks she must write to Papie and won't let the paper be still, but has her a pen with no ink to help mother write to you. You forgot to return Pa the office key, and he has to go through your shop, which is some trouble. If you have any convenient way to send it, do so.

Honey, I wish I could interest you some way. I would gladly do it. Time rolls so slow to me now, without your presence to render the hours joyful and happy. When again will kind Providence unite us to make us truly happy, for all is void and dreary where you are not. To me, it is not half so bad as it might be. I often console myself in thus thinking, but it don't do so well.

John Favor has returned from Va. and is now lying at the point of death. He caught the measels when in Richmond and now has typhoid disentery. He is a good clever fellow, and it would be a pity to lose such [as] he is. Old man Kite is still very sick. He has not heard from Samy, and that makes him worse. I can't find any thing more that will interest you and had better close. I am afflicted with the blues just now; and when I get in one of those spells, I can't think or write much. I will do better next time and tell you the cause of my felling so bad. Laura says Papie must come back again. She sends so many kisses I can't count them, and talks a great deal about you. I could not get her to say one word about you before you came home, but now she never tires. I too will think of those blissful hours as the one green oasis in the dreary lonesome time that I have passed through in four months. I hope it will soon come round again for us to taste again those delightful meetings. But I must close. Write soon. Yours ever. Kate Z. Peddy

39

Camp Brown, March 18th/62

MY EVER DARLING KITTIE, I am proud to state to you that I have got entirely well & am once more permited to enjoy the pleasure of writing to your lovely self again. I have suffered more since I left you that I ever experienced in all my life togueather. Oh! I did want to see you so badly while I was suffering so much. I wish I had have taken your advice about leaving home. I would not have been so bad off. I have this day bought you a fine Beaureau at $28. & an arm chair at $10.00. I intend that you shall have some easy setting. You ought to be sot up for the world to admire anyhow, with Laura by your side. I would have bought the rice for your Pa, but could not buy it for life. It cos[t] four cents nor no less number of lbs. than six hundred & thirty. Tell him to let me know if I must buy. I will do so if he wants it. It may rise in price again before I can hear from him. I sent you in the Beaureau drawer, twelve yds. bleached homespun, & twelve yds. linsy. I paid fifty cts. a yard for each piece. It was very high for both. I believe that is all you told me to buy. If you want anything more, all your have to do is to write. I have written to Charley McDaniel for the Surgeon's place in his Regt. I expect that I will get it. If I do, I donot know wheather I will come home or not. I wish Gen. would go or write to him to try to secure me the situation. If I get the position I must have Grimes' Horse at any price. I have written to Dr. Harlan to go & take the place back. If he gives you up the notes, you will find the deed in my Diploma Box with the Diploma. Ambrose sot the cand[l]e down on my fine Vest & burned it up. I had to buy me a new one to day. If I donot get into McDaniel Regt. my time here will soon be out. Then I will get to see my own dear again perhaps for some time. What a happy time we will have! Honey, I got to camps safe with the eggs. None broke but about ½ Doz. They came in the best time in the world. I eat them while I was sick. You have never seen me so reduced after I got up from my bed. I am fatning up now again. I had your Furniture marked to Gen., Newnan, Ga., O.W. When I come home, if I stay any length of time, we will go to Ala. to see Pa & Ma. They would be so glad to see us & our little darling child Laura. You must learn her to rock in her chair like Ma does in hers when she gets it. I recon it will be in Newnan by next week. Who halls the Furniture have to be very careful or else they will get soiled or broke. You and Laura will set the Furniture off so nice. You must try to get one of the rooms from Dr. Harlan to put the ballance of our things in down at home. If you have to buy any corn, you had better buy it at once or else it will get higher. Lou stayed with me very close while I was sick. After I got up, I got after him about drinking. I have not seen him in three or four days. I expect he is mad with me about saying any thing to him about it. If he is, I will not get freted with him. You all must not let him know anithing about my saying a word about it. If you do, he will be shure to get mad with me. My darling, write to me often for, dear, you donot know how much I like to hear from my love. You are my only solace in this life. Kiss Laura for me. My love to all. Yours ever loving

G.W Peddy.

At top: Take good care of my dog, Jef.

40

Camp Brown, March 20th/62

DEAR GEN., I wrote you a few days. ago, but did not write all I wished to write. I have got entirely well but weigh less than I have in several years. I have been trying to get into McDaniel's Regt. as Surgeon, but donot know how I will come out. I expect to hear from him tomorrow. I may yet get in, but I hardly think I will. If I could have got to see him, their would have been no trouble, but as it is, I think it doubtful. You may say to Capt. Spearman that he can get his company in to Col. Way's Regt. that he is getting up. He told me he would send him marching orders at any moment he would get in the notion to go, so you may say to him to get ready at once if he wants to get in the service. Gen., I want you to buy Dr. Grimes' horse for me at once if you can get him for $250.00. Ambrose & D. Williams are going to buy him to go into a cavalry company. I will make money on him at that price. I will then have left, after my tearm of service expires, about $500 or $600. in cash. If you buy him, put him in the stable & cover him with a blanket & give him six years of corn three times per day & have him rubed daily; & when I get home I will sell him for $350. to some one going in a cavalry company. I have written to Dr. Harlan to take his place back. I have not heard from him since. I recon he will be glad of the chance to do so. If I donot get a position in the army before I leave here I will go into the practice again when I get back home. I do not think Harlan will do anything if he comes back. I having been off for some time in the Army will give me a new start into the practice. If I go into the service again I will need the horse spoken of before in this. If I don't, I can make money on him. I would like to stay in the service about 8 or 9 months longer if I could. I could then be able to buy me a snug little place to farm on as well as practice. My great desire is to make my little family comfertable & get them a nice home. I am willing to forego any pleasure of home & their society for their benefit. I hope if you see any chance to do better than to stay at home, you will get me in. I wish I had got you to go to see McDaniel. Then I would have had a position for the war. I hope Nick will get into your Brother's Staff, as I want him to. He will then have one of the prettest positions in the army. If you cannot get a letter to him very soon, you had best telegraph to him. I am quite anxious for him to get the place. It has been raining all day. No chance for a fight here as I know of. The Confederates have evacuated Skidiway & falen back to the Isle of Hope, four miles nearer the city. Tell Kittie I want to see her & Laura as bad as ever. I hope she will be pleased with her Furniture when she gets it. If I get a favorable hearing from McDaniel, I will go to his Regt. imedeately (resign here). Let me hear from you as soon as convenient. Tell Kittie to write to me often. I have had no letter from her since I got back to camps.

Your ever true G.W Peddy.

At top of letter: The Furniture is marked to you Newnan Ga. O.W.

41

Wendsday, March 20th/62

MY OWN DARLING,

I have been quite uneasy about you, for we have had no mail in a week now and I could not hear anything from you, whether you had got well or not. I knew if you had anything, like a spell, you would send for me, for you promised me that. Honey, I do want to see you so bad, it is just like it was before you came home. I thought then I could get along firsttrate the balence of the time, but now I feel worse if possible than before about your being gone. I want to be always telling you how much I love you, but I never can express it in words, for they seem cold and meaningless compared to the love itself. Shurely no woman was ever so blest as I am, or one so suprimely happy, when I think of my loved ones. They are both all that heart could wish: noble, hansome, and good: I am ever thinking of the years of quiet happiness which is in store for us if kind Providence will only spare our lives. When, though, will we ever gather round the hearth stone of home sweet home, a happy little family blest in each other?

We have had some little excitement in our quiet village. Fannie Watts was to be married last Sunday morning, but Almegro was so low they had nearly put it off two weeks longer. Sunday morning Fannie was too sick to sit up. Keith was going to start home, but the old lady and Fannie told him to stay as long as he had come so far, and came near being drowned. She would not disappoint him, so Sunday night they were made one. They started the next morning to his mother's and returned yestady just as Almegro was having the hardest spasms he could possibly have to live. He took them again last night. They sent for Ma to go and wait on Mrs. Watts. She nearly dies every time he takes one. I am very sorry for the family, they do grieve so much. He takes spells with his head and goes into spasms. I can't see what can produce them unless his spine is affected. I have not heard this morning whether he is dead. Mrs. Rollins is here packing up to move to her mother's. She has been sick a long time. I went out to see Su Hale yestady evening. She looked fat and well; said she would have come to see you if she was not affraid of the mumps. Tom is here yet: he has been sick for several days, but thinks of starting back next Sunday. It is reported here that the regment he is in is taken prisner. There is a good deal of excitement in consequence of it. It is court week, but very little business done. Some of the extortioners are catching the indictments, and it is no matter for them. I have just heard that your brother William and Dr. Becum was in the service. Becum had moved his family up in your Pa's yard, and that Frank was staying in camps with Godfrey. Your mother had worn out her cards and could not get any more. She is in a bad fix with so many little children to clothe and factory thread so high. We have not heard from bud Nick since they moved their camps only from passer [*sic*] down the train. I am affraid it will make them sick. Bud Gily has commenced his school. I have not heard with what success. He is boarding, I think, at Ise David's. I have no news to write, therefore this will be an un[in]teresting letter. Laura sends a great many kisses and askes for some of Papie's candy. She thinks it never gives out. I must close and go and look her up, for I am affraid she is out in the rain, as it has commenced.

Yours ever, Kate Z Peddy

42

Franklin, March the 21/62.

MY OWN DARLING,

I am again seated to perform an ever delightful task to me. Perhaps you will get weary of my too frequent letters when they are nearly the same in interest. I am sitting by a glowing fire with curtains drawn down and the warm rosy light shedding comfort on all within. How I wish you were sitting here by my side, and Laura over in the corner in her rocking chair. We could talk of so much that would make us happy, and I know I could enjoy talking with my tongue much more than my pen. But your letters always breathe so much of affection, it nearly takes my breath in reading. Although I feel the magic power of love's spell, yet I am not gifted in telling it so well as you. I have been very low down lately with the blues in consequence of thinking something was [w]rong with me. I have been very regular in my monthly times untill this last time, which is about six weeks. I tell you I was uneasy: I knew you would hate it so bad, I could not stand to think of it, but I am all right now. I have not been well since you were here, but I think I will be better after this. Laura is shaking me, so it is impossible to write any. I asked her what I must tell Papie. She said, candy. The other day I asked her who loved her. She said Papie, and I had not ta[l]ked about you before that day. Her little cheeks are rosy and her eyes bright to night. Papie, she is a pretty baby. You know it, don't you Papie?

We have had two deaths in 24 hours of each other this week. Almegro died at a little past six on Wendsday night, and Thursday night nearly the same hour, Mr. Hicks died. Almegro had hard spasms for some time before he did die. He suffered so much. The Drs. dissected him to see if the effects of the wounds he received last year killed him. They said his left lung was entirely destroyed, and his kidneys were diseased. They will have to sware whether he did die of the wounds. He complained of his head all the time. Dr. Grimes said the matter or pus that was formed in his lung was absorbed by the vains and arteries through his whole sistem producing Putrid fever, but I don't think either one of them knows much about it. The family take it very hard. Mr. Hicks has been gradually sinking for some time. He will be buried tomorrow evening. Pa says you must write back word how much medicine Bill Barker bought for you of Dr. Howel. He was going to credit it on the old man's account and did not know how to settle it. He has some money now, but won't keep it long, for they tell me he likes to take his dram too well to keep money.

We have had so much rain lately, I have been affraid we will have no mail again tomorrow. I was so disappointed Wendsday, for I expected to get two letters from you, but how my hopes were blasted. I could not believe I did not get one. Any how, I could [not] help bursting out in tears, for your letters are next thing to your dear self, and I always feel so happy for a long time after I read them. I know you love me, Honey, but I am so childish as to love for you to be continually telling me so. Men get tired of such things. They have something of more interest to think and studdy about, but woman, poor weak being, her whole world consist in the love she bears the beings that are tied to her heart by the cords of love. Yet it is proper, and I am glad it is her privilege, for how could I live if those that make life sweet did not claim all my devotion. It is perfect extacy to love, and where the being who inspires it is of a lofty nature it is sweeter still; but, Honey, you are tired of this nonsence, I know. We have not heard from the boys in Va. since they moved. I am so uneasy about them. They will be exposed so much building winter quarters again, it will be bad on them, but we have come to the point where we must endure any thing. I see in the papers where some man has anilized Rye and said it was very injurious to the humane sistem. What do you think about it? I must close as Pa is about to start to the office and I must send this letter. Do write to me soon. Laura is up this morning looking very well. She puts up her little sweet lips to send Papie a heap of kisses.

Yours ever more, Kate Peddy.

43

Camp Brown, March 22nd/862

MY OWN LOVE KITTIE, I have just finished reading your dear letters to me, which always fills my heart with emotions of pleasure. I do wish I was with you again, but we must learn the unplesent lesson of being away from each other. Thank god, if we live & have good luck we'll will be with each other in one more month & I will have for you a nice lot of money for you to spend. I am so anxious for you to get your furniture to see how you are pleased with it. I hope it will just suit you, but I had much rather you could have picked it out yourself. Then you would have been better suited. My time will be in about one month. Then, oh then, I will have the exquisite pleasure of seeing my two darlings again. Never was any one so much blessed with a lovely little family as I, and both of you are all that could be embodied in such noble perfection of nature. Your letters do do me so much good. They are the next thing to being with you, & for that reason I want you to write often & long letters. Your Pa wrote to [me] for me to enquire the price of shugar & salt & the faceletees for shipping. I will do so by Monday. I would tomorrow, but it is Sunday. I will give him all the points about the matter & he will get the letter by Saturday's mail. I wrote to you[r] Pa to buy Grimes' horse. I still want to do so. I will have money enough left then to do us a long time. I have not yet heard from McDaniel. I donot know wheather I will get into his Regt. or not. I wish I could, notwithstanding I do hate to leave you & Laura. If I donot get in with him I will stay at home sometime when I come. I have written to Dr. H. to take the place back. I suppose he will do so. I want you to write to Mrs. Glover if you know her Postoffice, which you can learn from B. Oliver, & try to rent her place for us the ballance of the year. If you would like to live their; if not, name the place you want to live at & we'll have it. If I can buy it for four or five hundred dollars, I believe I will do so after consulting your Pa about it. I am quite sorry to hear that Almegro is so ill. I know Mrs. Watts is distressed to death about him, because she is so devoted to her children. I wish Fannie all the pleasure that the earth can bestow. She is one of my best friends. Tell Averzenia to name he[r] little Girl Laura & I will give it a nice dress. I am glad to know that you went to see Mrs. Shugaret. She is a good friend of mine.

I have one glorious consolation now: that is, if we get shet of the place, we can get out of debt when we want to & be free with what we have got. I intend to work night & day before any of your property shall be taken for my debts. With the sta[r]t we have, we can make something for ourselves & our little sweet child. Kittie, I feel so happy when I get to thinking abo[u]t the genuineness of my two dear ones. My heart leaps with joy to contemplate the hour when we will meet again. Their is so many in my Tent talking that I can think of nothing to write that would interest you. I am anxious to know what give you the blews. I hope nothing serious. You need not be affraid of anything. I expect that's the cause of your blews. Let me know if that's what you are lamenting over. Let me hear from you soon. Your forever

G.W Peddy

44

Camp Brown, March 24th/62

DEAR GEN., I wrote you a letter yesterday in reference to the horse. I write you to day to let you know the price of the articles you wrote to Dr. Lane about. Letter A shugar is worth 17 cts. Salt is worth $20. per barrel. I suppose a barrel will hold about a sack. Coffee is worth 65 cts per pound. Rice is still four cents. Write to me what Quantities of each you want & I will buy them for you. Evrything in the provision line is riseing evry day. I would advise you to buy at once. I thought when I wrote you about the rice that I could not get less than a tierce, but now think I can. Lou & Dr. Lane is quite will & getting on finely. I hope Giles has a good school. Evrything is quiet in the vacinity of Savannah. I see no chance for a fight. If provisions should rise before I get an answer from you, I will use my own judgement about buying. I would like to be at home with you all very much, but think I can stand it one month longer. I will get my pay by the time I hear from you & will buy any thing you want. You may do as well to buy the articles in Atlanta. You had better try there first, but donot delay for fear of a rise in evrything. Tell Kittie I am well & getting on finely. I hope she is also. I hope she has her furniture by this time & I hope it is not broken or injured in any way. Buy the horse at $250. Yours ever, G.W. Peddy

At top of page: Shipping facilities are very good.

45

Tuesday, March the 25/62

MY DARLING,

I received your precious letter last Saturday, which gave great relief as well as joy to know of your recovery, for I had heard from aunt Kit's letter that you was sick. I was shure that something of that kind was the matter or you would have written sooner. You can hardly imagine how anxious I was to hear from you, and now that I know you were sick, how I wish I could have nursed you while you was suffering. Not that I am a very good nurse, yet it gives me great pleasure to wait on you when you are well, but sick, it is doubly dear to nurse you then. My darling, I love you more than any thing else, and yet it is not my privilege to be near you. Fate is a severe master this time, yet I hope we will yet taste of the joys of domestic bliss where we will forget this cruel seperation. March will soon be gone, then one more month and you will then come home. But I am affraid to indulge in joyful anticipations for fear like nearly every other joy will not be realized. If you do go in the service again, I am going with you. We will have some trouble here about the negroes. They are grown insolent. Seven negro men ran away down in Troupe last week. Pa let Lin go down to Corrinth the other Saturday night, and he is getting above himself. He told the overseer the other day he was not affraid of no white man. Pa says he will sell him as soon as he can. Dr. Harland came last Saturday. He stoped on his way down to Friendship the next day to see us. He seemed very glad to get back. He shook hands with Laura. I told him that was my little one. He said he knew that from her striking resemlance to her father. He came to town yestady and gave up you noates, and Pa got the deed, but you will have to sign it. Pa will send it down to you soon the trade is complete, all but that, and I will move my things tomorrow. He told Pa he could still occupy the same room he has for an office, but Pa says he will get an other place and move your medicines with his books; but I am affraid they will be injured unless you was here to attend to it. Dr. Harlan gave directions to have the garden and yard pailed in directly, as he would move as soon as the weather would permit. Pa is very glad he took the place back. He thinks we could do better in some other town. Meat and Corn are both going up rapidly. I don't know whether to buy any meet or not. If you stay at home any time, we will need it; if not, we won't. Pa has bought 500 pounds of bacon from your uncle Levi and he charged 25 cents. We heard it was one dollar a pound in Augusta. It is so distressing to have to buy now at such prices. I was truly sorry to hear of bud Lu's disipation but you must not get angry with him, for he is young and don't know how much danger lies in the intoxicating bowl. Pa says he thanks you for it and wants you to use your influence to prevent him from associating with those who do drink. I saw Grand Ma the other day. She insisted on my going out and spending several days with her, said she had been looking for me ever since you went away, but I know a few persons. I wonder if you get lonesome as I do when night comes, for then I miss you most around the fireside. It seems so lonsome. No matter who or how many are here, there is a vacancy none but your dear self can fill. Why is it so that no one can be perfectly happy without the object on which they lavish their affections are not present with them? I never dreamed before we were married that I could love any one as well as I do you. It seemed a matter of imposibility to love as well as I do now, and if I continue to love on more and more every day I will become simple and foolish about you, as I often fear you think of me now. I don't care what others may say, but as long as you love me it is all right with me; but darling, I write so often and such long letters, you may get weary reading. I hope ere this you are entirely recovered and will soon come home. Laura is well and fat as a pig. She sends Pa two kisses. Jef is doing finely. He gets after Laurence every time he can. He evidently thinks Laurence is a great black rat with his shirt tail always out. Tell bud Lu I wrote to him some time ago and he has not replied to it. Give him my love. I am, as ever, your true wife. May angels guard you from temptation is my wish. Katie

---

46

Franklin, March the 28/62.

MY LOVE, I received you ever welcome letter by the last mail and now hasten to respond. I am rejoiced to hear you are regaining your health very fast and I do hope you will not be sick any more away from home. Today is a beautiful one: the bursting buds and singing birds denotes the aproach of spring. Every one is buisy in feild and garden, which forcibly reminds me of our gardening, how we watched with delight our success in our first year's planting. Every evening we wandered up and down the walks with Laura perched up in Papie arms as though she could understand and take on over the growing plants. Poor little thing, Pa don't have that pleasure now. She loved Papie so well then. He can recolect all about her baby antics. She is not very well today; having a severe cold makes her feverish and fretful. I don't think she will have the mumps, for it will soon be three weeks since you left, and she has no symptoms yet. She tries every morning to get me to sit in her chair, and sometimes just to please her I make out I am setting in it. She thin capers around telling Sis to look at Ma. I have no doubt but what I will be pleased with my furniture for you can select any thing a great deal better than I can and have a great deal more taste in all things of beauty than I ever did. How my heart leaps with joy every time I think how blest I am thus to be loved and cared for by one worthy the admiration of an Empress. How little do I do to reward or be in any way worthy of such ennobling love as yours. I felt a little bad the other day on hearing that some malicious person talked as though she was surprised that we should have married, but that every body that did marry did not always marry for love, and a good deal of just such nonsence. I told the one who tole me if that girl could get a chance to marry it would be no consequence to her if there was not a thimble full of love on both sides so she married. I know that what she said is not so, but it will cause unpleasant feelings for several moments. I always judge your love by mine, and that is lasting as time. I do not nor cannot measure it. I only know that it is my life's life and without it Earth's joys would be void to me.

I don't believe every one has such intense devotion as mine; not that I am that much better than others, but they let other joys come in and mar their feelings till the fountain is almost froze.

Honey, I don't hardly know what to do with all our things. Ma has not room enough to move all up here, and if you still stay in the service, Mrs. Harlan may not want to give up her room for such a long time. I don't like to put them in the Hall House. It is so badly torn up and they might get abused. If Pa would only let me get a room of the hotel I could better tend to them, but he don't want any thing to do with it. He says you had best rent Tom Glover's place for next year, and he thinks she will then be willing to take a low price for it, say three or four hundred dollars. He says he would not give more than five hundred for no place now. He thinks you can get a sergeon's place in the regments that will be formed out of the troups down on the coste who will reenlist again. Dr. Ashford of La Grange has been appointed by McDannel. The company from Troup would not vote for any one for Col. unless he would appoint Ashford as surgeon. I don't know whether it is your friend or his brother. Bill Tomaston told Pa he saw Beasly just from your camps and he said that all of uncle Joe's company had reenlisted except uncle Joe. Pa don't want bud Lu to go in any more, or at least in a long time. He thinks you have so much influence there and is known better there, that you had best hold on and try to get a situation in some of the regments there as he sees no chance now of doing better. Pa thinks bud Nick would not like to be confined to Va. all the time, as his health won't admit of his staying in such a severe climate, and uncle Windfield will be permanently settled there. You could perhaps get him in a good office in the regment you get into as it would be best for both of you to go together. Pa has written to uncle Winfield about bud Nick before, and he says he wonn't do it again, for if he don't see proper to give him the office any how after his writing to him once, he can just let it alone. Dr. Grimes has raised the price to three hundred and don't think he will take that. Three men from Alabama came over this week and are buying up every horse that is fit for any thing and giving big prices for them too. Mr. Housan Jackson got two hundred and 75 dollars for his sorrel, Dave Grimes 1 hundred and 75 for his horse, and a great many others that I can't recolect. You can't hardly buy a horse when you get home for any price. He says he wont buy the horse you spoke of untill he hears from you again on the subject, as Grimes has taken a notion that you want him and he can get any price for the horse from other horses selling as high as they do. Ma has gone over to aunt Kit's and I am housekeeper, which you know by experience is a very sorry one, but I will learn maybe to do a little better. Laura has waked up from a long nap and of corse Ma must take, so I will have to throw down the pen for a while.

I owe Billy Mozely a bushel of Salt and now it has got up to 25 dollars a sack.

If you can get any cheaper than that, you had best buy a sack and bring it with you when you come home. He does not need it now, but will before many months. Capt. Spearman's company will join Stil's Regment so they think, but I don't think they will go untill the next call.

Mat Brichell is going to move here soon. I saw him some time ago and he told me to say to you he still had those tops of boots you sent him and if you wanted them fixt to let him know it. I must close as I have run out of something to write. Laura sends Papie the sweetest little kiss in the world and her mother sends you as many as you want. Don't be too anxious to stay away from us: I want you satisfied, but I don't care if you do not get in any other Regment. You can then stay with us. Good by, darling, with fond hopes we will meet soon to enjoy each other's society. Yours forever Kate Peddy

---

47

Camp Brown, March 29th/62

MY PRECIOUS SWEET KITTIE, I have just Rec'ed yours & you can't imagine how highly I apprecated it. You spoke in yours of how much pleasure it gave you to write to me. It is my happiest moments when I sit down to write to you. Nothing could afford me more joy unless it is to see you. You need not think that I will ever tire of reading your letters. They are the very life of me when I am away from your lovely self. Your nicely written letters always sends a thrill of pleasure through my whole system. Honey, we have such a nice little Girl we ought to be so proud of her. She is the next thing to you in my affections. My whole heart is yours & hers. I have nothing but friendship for any one else. I wish I was able to make you more happy. I wish I could be with you always. My greatest pleasure in this life is when I am with you, but the thought of having you at home is a glorious reflection to me. I am so happy to think that you are all right. I would have been so sorry if it had been so on your account. I donot want your beauty soiled by bearing children. I never want you to suffer any more in that way. If I could take the suffering off of you I would not care so much. I have been so anxious to hear from you on the subject. I have hardly been comfortable since you gave me the first hint of it.[22] I am sorry to hear of the death of Watts & Hicks. I donot know what Mrs. H. will do, but it is the way

---

[22]Despite these sentiments, Dr. and Mrs. Peddy had five more children, a boy and four girls. All but the boy were born in post-war years.

we all have to go. They are only a few days in advance of some of the rest of us. If I thought I had to be absent from you & Laura all the wile, I had as soon go on that way in a short time as not. I am having a better time in camps now than I have ever had—nothing scarcely to do but think of you & L.—, bless her little heart. Pappie wishes he was with you & her tonight. We could enjoy ourselves so much. Your letter that I have read today was eight days comeing to me. I wish you would write to me evry mail. It does seem to be so much company for me when I am sad & lonely. Their is so many in my tent bothering me I can scarcely write you anything that has any sense in it. I hope when I hear from your Pa he will have bought the horse for me. I will make money on him if I can get him. I hope you have rec'ed your furniture by this time. When you get your chair, you & Laura can have a fine time rocking. I expect she will want your chair as it looks so much better than hers. You must let her put her clothes in one drawer of the Beaureau. Let me know in your next what corn is worth in Heard now. I can buy from Ambrose for one dollars per bushel. I will buy a large quantity of it from him if your Pa thinks I can make any money on it. It is worth $1.75 per bushel in Savannah. If your Pa has not enough to do him he had better buy it now, for I think it will be a great deal higher after awhile. I hope you wrote to me on Fryday last, so that I will be joyed again soon. Let me know how my dog comes on. I hope he will be good for squirles by the time I come home. My love, you must take good care of yourself & Laura until I come home. If you Pa has bought the horse, you must take good care of him until I come. Have him rubed so that he will look fine. Let me hear from you often, my own sweet Wife. Kiss Laura for me & tell Laura to kiss Ma for Pappie

G W Peddy

48

Camp Brown, April 1st/862

MY PRECIOUS KITTIE, I have just Rec'ed you[r] much esteemed letter of the 28 ultima. I was truly glad to hear that you was all well & getting along in the same way. I rec'ed also a letter from your Pa of the 29th, asking me to buy him a tierce of rice. I will have to pay five or six cts. but will buy it any how, & the salt also if I have to pay more than I wrote him it is worth. I will buy us a barrel also, I believe. I am sorry that I did not buy Grimes' horse when I was at home. I told you all their was money in the trade. You need not buy him at that price. As soon as I get home I will go to Ala. & try to buy me one. Any purchase that your

Pa might make now in the provision line he can make a proffet on. I am not uneasy about getting me a position after I leave here. I can go before the medical board of the Confederate States & get a position in a hospital at any time, ranking as I do now. So far as the reenlistment of Dr. Lane's company is concerned, their is not a word of it, so you cannot get even one in the Regt. to do so until they go home. Their will be no more State organizations I donot suppose, & unless their is a new call made by the President on the State, their will be no use of reenlistment. Not the first man of Lane's company has done so; nether will they do so until they come. McDaniel said the reason I did not get the position in his Regt. was that he did not know that I wanted it or would accept it. He never got my letter nor dispatch until the appointment was made. Honey, I would like to know who is busying theirselves about our affairs. I should think they ought to be satisfied if we are. I am perfectly so & bleive you are. If I did not think so, I would be miserable all my life. But their is one that ought to be dissatisfied & that is your Pa. I have no doubt that he would be better & more confortably situated if I had you in a house of my own & not trouble him so much with my business. I am sorry that I am compelled to do so. He shall not, nor any one else, be looser by it. I am willing to pay for all the trouble & expence you & Laura are to any one, & thank heven, I am now able to do it. Honey, I donot know what to say you must do with our things. You must get them out of Harlan's way, if he will not spair you a room, if you have to put them out of doors & co[v]er them with bords. I know their is not room at your Pa's for them & I donot want you to trouble him much about them, for I fear we will weary his kind patience out. We can never repay him for his kindness & that of your Ma's, but we must try to do so somehow. I want you to be shure to write to Mrs. Glover about the renting of the house, or I will do so, if you will write me the name of her Post Office. Maybee Olive has the management of it. If so you may rent it from him or get him to write to her about it. I am not going to leave Franklin yet awhile. I expect to make some money there before I leave the place.

I recon I will go into the service in a month or two after I come home, but if my life if spaired, I expect to enjoy myself with you & Laura for a short time at least, for with you two is all the real happyness that I have, notwithstanding the decleration of our friend, who ever that be. She is only sorry that she is not married. She will have my kindest regards by attending to her own business if she has any. You & Laura, of course, has the right to claim my wole affection, & you do have them, if I have any honor in me. Let me know what the one who talked about us bassed her remark upon. Neather of us as I know have been recreant to our promice to each other befor[e] we married & at the time of our marrage. Their is no news of importance to write you, only the 13th Ga. Regt. captured 15 Yankee. They shot at them six hundred yards in a boat & killed one

& wounded two more & kept shooting at [t]hem un[t]il they held up a white handkercheif & s[t]arted to whare our men was on shore. It is only twenty four days now until we will be mustard out of service. Then I will be with my two darlings again to enjoy the bliss of their presence and more. Let me know what to bring you & Laura when I come home. If you want a set of Kushion bottom Chairs like your rocking Chair I will get them for you. I can get them for twenty dollars. Let me hear from you soon, my own sweet Kittie. Your forever.

G W Peddy

At top of p. 5: I will go to town in the morning & buy the things your Pa wrote for.

49

Franklin, April the 8, 1862.[23]

MY DARLING,

Once again I am engaged in the pleasant task of talking through my pen to my own dear husband, nor can I be better pleased in your absence than to write and receive your letters, for I know if I do commit errors with my pen, your loving heart will always excuse me, and I am shure to find sympathy in every thing that hapens. Oh! what a delicious thought, and one that is a little selfish too, to think between me and the cold world there is a manly form to sheild and protect me from the rude blast of unfeelingness that is always to be met with along the rugged path of life. But the future is gloomy any way now: we can not tell what this war may lead to; one cannot have any shure foundation to build their hopes of happiness on. Yet " 'tis woman's lot, to be friend when others fail, to look on death and fear it not, to smile when others' cheeks grow pale", and we must not now when the dark clouds of adversity lowers, to give up all and not throw in our mite towards helping the brave gallant men who are driving the craven hearted foe from our suny South. I received a letter from your Father last Saturday. The family were all well. He says he has not recived but one letter from you since you went into the service and none from brother John since the 26 of December. He thinks you two have forgotten him. He is so anxious to have you go out there when you come home. He thanked me so

---

[23]Laura's pencil scribblings are at the top of the letter.

earnestly for writing to him, I could hardly keep the tears back. Tom Rechum had gone to the war, was in the fight at fort Donnelson, was taken prisner, and was then at St. Louis. His family was still in Cosa. Your mother had gone down there. Your brother William was color bearer in a regment of light horse. He did not say where he had been sent. His family was at your father's. You must write to your father, Honey, it will do him so much good, and he is way off he can't hear none of the Georgia news.

I have been staying with Mrs. Oliver while Mr. Oliver went to Carrol court. She sends her compliments to you and says she has got the prettiest baby in town, yours not excepted. She thinks Laura is the very image of yourself and gets prettier every day. Now ain't that a nice way to pay you a compliment? Mr. Oliver says he is going to name his baby Laura, for she is the prettiest child he ever saw. You ought to have seen Laura when she saw the baby. She was amazed as its having a head and eyes, insisted on holding it in her lap. Fannie Keth sends her kind regards also. She moved home yestady. Keth does look so young and boyish. The same kind friend that doubted our loving each other said she heard that Fannie told Keth she would marry him, but he must not expect her to love him as well as Bill Martin, for she never could love any man as well as she had loved him. I don't believe she did say any such thing. John Hopson is flying around one of the misses Dukes. I see them together continually. Mack Peddy went to curry his horse a week or too a go and got strangled with dust, which caused him to cough so violenly that it produced bleeding at the lungs. He is in very bad health now and won't get well soon, so bud Gily thinks. He was up Saturday, and has a very good school. Every one is well pleased with him as a teacher. Some are sending two and three who did not want to send any. I must trouble you again, honey, to buy me a hoop if they can be got cheap. Get a stif good one and bring it when you come. Don't buy the chairs you spoke of. We don't need them, and you know we must not spend one dime we can do without. Pa says practice economy. Laura calls herself Papie's little lady, and sends you a dozen kisses and mother also sends them with her love. Yours ever more, Kate Peddy.

50

Camp Brown, April 8th/62

MY PRECIOUS DARLING,

With great pleasure I respond to your sweet letter. It is the best letter I have read in my life. I'll declare, Honey, you ought to write a work on some subject.

Your tallent shouldn't be waisted at home silently. The world is in need of just such a work as you could write. I am proud to think that I have one that I can call my own that is so sweet & has such an intilect & such an education. I am sorry that all men are not so nobly blessed as myself in this respect. I have awlways been unfortunate until I could press you to my bosom & call you mine alone, but since that, I have been as happy as any one on earth. Honey, I wish I could tell or write to you how well I love you. When I undertake to do so I am at a loss for words & language strong enough to express it. In fact, my letters fall so far short of your[s] that I am ashamed to try to write anything. You wrote in yours that you wished you could be in your letter when I opened it. Oh! my, I do wish so to[o]. I would have been overjoyed to that extent that I would have caressed you until you would have lost your breath. We have now just 16 days to stay in camps. Oh! how proud I will be to meet you once more! If I donot get to stay with you more than one week we will spend the time we are together so sweetly. My heart will be so full all the while I am with you that I will not know how to conduct myself. We will go fishing & evry whare else you & Laura wants to go. I hope I will not be sick again when I get home, as I was the two last times I was there. Gov. Brown has been down here for several day[s]. We had a grand review of the State forces. Their is a great many of them. They have been solicited by the Gov. very strong to reenlist in the State service on the same terms that the Confederate States offers. His propposition was as fair as could be offered, but I donot thing that scarcely any of them will do so. They will have served out their time in a few day[s] & are all now a[n]xious to go home to see their friends. I thought of you often on the day of review. I wish you could have [seen] the grand display. Their was a large concourse of Ladies & also Gentlemen out to see us. It come of in the city of Savannah. Lou nor Dr. Lane will not reenlist. I am going to apply to the Gov. for another position. I expect I will get it. If I do succeed, I will be in for two years & a half. That's a long time, but I cannot make anything at home & might have to go into the service as a private. I am almost affraid to make the adventure to get a place for fear I get it & not get the chance to go home. Honey, I am so sorry I did not get Grimes' horse. He would just suit me in the service, but I must not pay all my earnings for a horse. If I do, I will have none left for my two darlings. I will start out & find me one when I get home. If I cannot find one in Heard I can in Ala.

Honey, Dr. Watkins is a fool: he cannot make a contract with a company unless the Surgeon of the Regt. agrees to it & he cannot do consestlently with the responsibility resting upon him. I will make the prediction that he will not stay in the service three weeks. Honey, I am so glad that Nick got the position suggested to his pa. That will make his bitterest enemies respect him. It is the prettyest position in the whole service. I am as proud as if Brother John had it, for I feel as deep an interest in any member of your Pa's family as [I] do for him,

& feel as near to him as any one on earth except you & Laura. I wish Giles had the position of aid de Camp to some Gen., but I would not ask of his uncle to[o] many favors. I forgot to mention that Gov. Brown is going to keep up a State army & he says he will give the troops now in service the preference. It I get the position, I am going to keep you close to me, if it cost me all I make. I donot expect to ever stay from you as long as I have so long as we both live unless I am compelled, for my whole existence depends upon the pride I take in my little but noble & sweet family. Oh! how bad I want the sixteen days to go off! Time never did go off so slow to me. One day seems the length of two because I want to see you much. One of our companies go out on the 18th inst.—only ten more days to stay in service. Some of my friends are trying to get me the position of medical director of the State of Ga. I had much rather have that than the one I now have. I would not be in the field then. I hope I will get anothe[r] letter from you tomorrow. The[y] do me so much good to read them. I have heard to day that Capt. Mabry is dead. I recon it is not so: I hope not anyhow. If I donot get a position before I leave here you may get W. L. Mozeley to meet me in Newnan with a horse & Buggy on the morning of the 26th inst. I will get the Linnen. Let me hear from you soon. Your forever

G W P.

51

Franklin, April the 11, 1862

MY OWN DARLING, This is the only piece of paper I have at the house and therefore you must excuse this rough letter. Paper is scarce here at any price and we have to put up with any sort we can get. I have just finished writing to your father, but I did not write a good letter, for I have been nearly sick for two days with a cold. I went down to take up my big unions to plant out in Ma's garden, and while there, it began to rain hard, and I got very wet, but I had not had a cold in so long I did not think I could take one. I finished moving yestady all of my things, scoured and cleaned up, and delivered the keys and deed to mr. Watts last night. I felt very sad in one respect and glad in an other while down there, for I could not help from thinkover the past, for in that house I had lived two short happy years with one who is dearer to me than life, and there, too, our little darling first opened her sweet blue eyes to bless us with her presence; but then again, I considered it would relieve you of so much anxiety on account of paying for it. You would not have to work so hard, and that is the greatest item with me. While I was sitting down there looking the negroes scour, Julia Grimes came in and took a seat. She said there was but one thing wanting to make every thing look natural and that was yourself. She sent her best wishes to you. It is the first time she did not say any thing of Tom Boddie. I think she rather give up the chase, as Mike De Lacy has been home and she is on a different chase now. I heard something bad the other day about a certain young lady in this town, but I will not tell you now, for I know it [will] be a big fuss and we had better not say a word about it any way. Charlie Grimes has returned home. He looks more manly, and has grown a great deal. They were over joid to see him. Dr. Grimes has been sick and we did not have any body to give medicine then for Dr. W. started last Sunday. Imagene Watts has been [and] is now very sick. I am affraid she will be a good deal like Almegro, for her spine has been affected a long time. Old Man Boggus has one of his spells of palsie again. He sent for Redwine. He come and shocked him but could do him but little good. He never can get well as long as a jug of licker is close by. He said none of the Drs. here had done him good, and was going to send for Roberson, but Roberson said he would not take a case which every Dr. had practiced on, and nearly killed them, which made the old man mad, and he then sent to St. Cloud for a Dr. They found your battery, but it did not opperate well, as some part of it was loose. I here Laura quarreling with some body. She says she is going to tell Ma too. Her[e] she come[s]. Papie, I tell you she is a dirty face little kitten, but I don't care: she is worth all the babys yet. Mrs. McArthur came up to see us this morning and invited me down to see her—don't you think there will be a storm after this. I am shure I don't know what will happen. Pa says you must buy some salt if you find any cheap as you come home, for he has borrowed some for three or four months, but don't know where he can get any to pay back with. It can't be had at all here. The wheat has the rust now very badly. Some places the crop is very much injured. Pa is not hurt yet though. Milt Wood got his foot hurt and had to come home to day. His company was sent [to] Corrinth. They had some of their men poisoned with whiskey. I must close, for I don't feell like writing any more. Ho[n]ey, excuse me this time for writing such a dry letter. Yours evermore

Kate.

52

Camp Brown, April 12th/62[24]

MY DEAR SWEET KITTIE,

I have received no letter from you, my darling, since yours of the 4th inst. I do hope I will get one tomorrow (Sunday). I feel so bad because I got no letter from you to day. All the forenoon I was reflecting about how pleasantly I would spend the eve in reading a letter from your dear hand, but alas! I was disappointed. Our misfortune in the fall of Fort Pulaska makes it bear more heavily upon me. Yesterday the fort with all the Garrison was surrendered. What a sad thing in this dark hour of our infant Republic! We are expecting an attack daily on the City. I presume we will have a fight now in a very short time, perhaps tomorrow. I do hope if we do that I will live to see you & my dear child again. Our time likes now only twelve days of being out. So much I want to see you, my darling, & sweet Laura worse than I ever did in my life. It seems to me that I have been gone from home more than a year. Oh! how happy we will be when we meet again. It will be the most joyful thing to me that has every happened. Rest assured, my own love, that when you think of me, always think that [you &] Laura has the genuine affection of my whole heart. With pleasure in old age if we should all live we will dote on our little child as the idol of our hearts & be proud that we first loved. I reflect of you with the greatest pride. My whole mind soul & body is enamored with the profoundest feeling of love & adoration for you. You are the grand pillow in the edifice of my affection & life. The though[t] of you though absent alwas cheers me in my darkest hours of sadness, & even when in the hight of glee, I am more so. When my thoughts revert to you, evry incedent, wheather melancholy of gleeful, turns my thought with admiration to you. The low muttering of the enemies cannon that caused the fall of our fort, spoke to me of you as did also the glorious victory in the West of our gallant Beauregard.[25] I am quite well, my dear. I hope you are not sick that prevents you from writing. I judge the recent rains has prevented the mail comeing to & from Franklin. I expect a great deal of news in your next. You will not have time to write me many more letters befor I am at home with you if I am so fortunate as to live. I wrote you in my last at what time I would [be] at home. I suppose I will be there at that time. If the enemy put off their attack until the morning that I am to leave, I of course will not come until it is

[24]This letter is stained and torn in places.

[25]This probably refers to the Confederate victory under A.S. Johnston and Beauregard on the first day of the battle of Shiloh (6 April 1862).

over. I think they will make the attack before that time if they make it at all. I am glad to hear of our prospects for hogs. You must [borrow] corn from you Pa to feed the until I get home. We must keep all of them fat until the[y] get large enough to eat. Let me know if you[r] Pa has got the rice & your furniture. Let me hear from you soon, My own dear. Yours always.

G.W Peddy

53

Camp Brown April 14th/62[26]

MY SWEET WIFE, With much pleasure I reply to your very much esteemed letter of the 11th inst. You need not expect much of a letter from me to night for I have the headache for the first time since I left your happy presence. I wish I was with you so bad I know you would cure me. We have considerable excitement in Camps about the passage of the Conscrip [tion bill]. Our soldiers are very much opposed to it & I am also. It is one that never was intended for a republican governmen[t up] to now. It is the same law that France has & she is nothing but a military despot. The people of the Confederate States will revolt against it. I was sorry to hear of Imogeans Watts' health. She's a good Girl. I regret it much. You must treat Mrs. Mcarthy civilly when she come to see you. Let us forget the past. It is best for us to court the favor of evry one. I have this day bought one barrel of salt for you Pa & one for myself. I paid $28.00 each for them. I think your Pa will be pleased with it. I think you are mistaken when you say we owe Billie Mozeley a bushel. We owe him one half bushel & two flat pan fulls, at least that's all I recollect off. Honey, I wrote to you that I would be home on the 26 inst. You need not be disappointed if I am not there for I may get a new Commission before I leave from the Gov. If I do, I donot know when I will come home. It almost greaves me to death to think that I have to be away from you & Laura so much, but honey, it is perhaps best for us in the long runn. The future is dark & gloomy, but let us not forget to love. The happy thought of you, my dear, breaths life into my soul. Honey, in your last you did not tell me you loved me [a wee] bit. I will co[n]so[le] myself with the idea that you do to the utmost of your effection. You know, my love, that my admiration of you cannot be any greater. Tell Mrs. Oliver she will have to use different tools

---

[26]This letter is stained and torn in places.

before she can have a baby as pretty as Laura. Laura is the prettyest child that ever was born, & she has enough of he[r] Mother to make her one of the sweetest & one of the most lovely children. Emenation from such as intilectual Mother, she is obliged to be one among the most tallanted after awhile. Honey, if I get another position I will keep you & L. near me all the while. I can never stay away from you longer unless I am obliged to, than I have stayed. You must take care of our sa[lt] for it's near [*four words lacking*] money. I will ship it in the morning. I have sent my trunk to Newnan. Tell your Pa to carry it home when he gets his other things. I will get you a hoop if their is one to be had. You shall have any thing that I am able to buy you. Honey, good night: think of your Babie who thinks of you evry moment of his life. Let me know the one the tale is on & what it is. Your yours, yours ever devoted G W Peddy

At top of first page: Honey, do not talk to the best friend you have at home about the story or tale on the one you hinted at, for it might get you into a scrape that would cause me to injure some one. You shall not be ronged or abused by none on this earth unless they be held stricly accountable to me for it. Your pure purson & character must not be assailed by any one unless their is just cause for it, & I hope you will give none.

54

Tuesday, April the 15./62

MY OWN DARLING,

I received your ever dear letter, and always wishing to give you pleasure, no matter if only for a moment, I will again write to you, as this may be the last time I can write for you to get it before you return home; and I am truely glad it is so, for as dear as your letters are, you are a milion times dearer. I have nothing of interest to write about, consequently you will find a dry letter. Somehow to day I wish to see you worse if possible than I ever did. We heard the Yankees had taken Fort Pulakia, and if that is so, they may attempt Savannah. Oh! how I do wish something would prevent them from attacking the place, for I am fearful some of our brave men will get hurt. You promised me not to run any risk, and I rely on that, but you know I must feel very uneasy any how. Don't let bud Lu be placed in a dangerous position if you can prevent it. He is very rash, never dreaming of danger like all boys of his age. Honey, I don't expect you ever get the chance to have the blues, surrounded by so much excitement all the time. If I did not know your heart so well, I should be almost affraid you would hardly ever think of me and Laura, but brigh[t] eyed Laura would be hard to forget, woulden't she Papie? Papie knows we love him so much, and want to stay with him all the time, no matter where he s going to stay. Honey, I recon you think paper is scarce, and you think right. I sent down to Pa to get me some and he sent me this saying there was none in town, so you must excuse half sheets untill we get some paper, which I am affraid will be some time yet; but I am so glad we don't have many more letters to write before we are permitted to see each other, but all the joy will be lessened by thinking you will have to go back again, but I will not pain you by complaining, when you think it for the best. So many thousand are deprived of that pleasure, for their hearts idol lays stif and cold in a soldier grave with no hope that on Earth they will meet again; or they may be a prisner like Dr. Bechum in a strange land surrounded by foes who care not for his life or feelings. I saw a man the other day from uncle Joe's company. He said all was well, and I think from the way he talks bud Lu must be a great fellow down there.

Dr. Strichlan of Grantville was here the other day and offered Grimes his price for his horse. He would not part from him at no price, says he has declined the idea of selling him for he can't get another that suits him so well. Dr. Strichlan is Capt. of a horse company in Coweta. You said something about getting Billy Mozely to meet you in Newnan. He has no horse now, nor is there a horse in town now that we could get. Pa will have the buggy mended so you can come in that. He has just come back from Carrolton. He thinks you could get a good horse up there. He saw a good many fine ones there. They raise a great many also. It has been raining for three days, and every thing looks so fresh and green. The crops are doing finely. If we don't have frost, we will have plenty after this. I must close as I fear I have already wearried you by this dul letter. I hope I will get a letter from you tomorrow.

Laura says Papie's coming every day just to fool her ma. Katie Peddy.

55

Camp Brown, April, 16th/862
[and 18 April 1862]

MY SWEETEST DARLING, with much pleasure I write you again to night to let you know that all is well with me as yet. I wrot to you in my last of the 14th instant that you need not be uneasy if I was not at home on the 26th inst. I judge I will be home by that time if the officer in command will let me go. We will be from now until our time is out in the Confederate service. We are all turned over to the Confederate army & will be under the command of an officer in that service until our tearm of service expires, & perhaps longer, if they are amind to keep us here. They may conscribe all of us & get me in as a private. That will be pretty tight on me, will it not, my dear? It seems to me that I am obliged to see you & Laura for a little while after I get loose here. I intend to stay as long as I can with you & Laura, for when I leave you again I cannot tell in what capacity it will be in. Oh! what a good time we will have if I live to get home! I will have the delightful pleasure of hugging you to my bosom & kissing those lovely sweet lips of yours. Honey, you must not kiss any one but Laura until I get home. You must save all the sweet kisses for us, for we love you better than any other two on earth. We will do more fore you. The chances are very good for a fight before we leave here. Their has been some picket fighting below here three or four miles this eve. We heard the guns plainly. I have not heard the result of the engagement as yet. I will learn early in the morning. I expect their is several killed from the way the guns cracked. None of our Regt. was in it. It was part of the 13th that done the fighting. The enemy were trying to land & a great many did do so, I suppose. I judge they run back to their boats from the length of time they fought as they did yesterday. If we are conscribed & I cannot get to go home, you must come to see me, but I think after the excitement wears off we will be honerably descharged. My chances for getting a position now similar to the one I now hold is quite doubtful. If Gov. Brown had the management of things I could get it quite easy, for I have learned that he is favorably impressed with me. I learned this from the Surgeon Gen. of the State. If they turn me loose here & press me into a position as a private, I will get permission to go before the medical bord & then I will get into a Hospital with the same rank I have now. I have bough[t] me some nice Linnen to make me some shirts. I will send it to Newnan by a man I discharged to day. I shiped the salt to day. I cannot tell when it will get to Newnan. If I am not at home by the 30th inst. you must write to me. Yours, yours forevermore, G.W.P.

Honey, knowing that you would not get the letter I have written you on the 16th inst. I concluded to keep it & write you more to day the 18th inst. We all went over on Whitmarsh Island yesterday with the 13th Regt. to attack the Yankees they had fought the day before. After getting their & skirmishing the Island all over, to our utter supprise we found all of them gone. If they had been their we would have had a bloody time. Our Regt. has nearly all gone back to day to scout the Island. I did not go with them. While we were their yesterday we found two of our men dead & two seriously wounded who had lane out their all night. They I say were our men, but they belonged to the 13th Regt. Their was only one hundred & fifty of that Regt. fighting eight hundred of the enemy.

Our men had to retreat & leave the dead & wounded. The wounded wer literally eaten up by the sand flies. Honey, I cannot tell as yet wheather I will come home when my time is out. I have not got the late Conscription act of Congress. I donot know wheather it will affect our organization, & if it does, how it will. No one can tell anything about it, all is confusion & perplexing about it. Honey, you ought to have seen us when we got back to our camp last night. We ware the muddyest set you ever saw. We were in mud up to our nees & sometimes up to our waest. I was so tired when I got back to camps I could hardly stand up. I could have slept on a rock soundly. How much I did think of you & Laura no one could imagine. The thought came to me often what a condition you & Laura would be in if I got killed. The thought of leaving you & her was all I had to oppress me & what an indigent condition you would be in. I do hope I may live at least until I can make enough for you & Laura to live comfortably on. Honey, you cannot imagine how often I think of you & our dear child. Their is no joy for me when I am away from you, all's gloom. My dear, if I do have to stay here I donot know what I will do about seeing you. One of our companies time went out to day & the authorities refused to muster them out. They are the madest set you ever saw, & I donot blame them. Lou is not 18 years old, as I know of. If he is not, I will make him come home when his time is out. Dr. Lane is coming & is not going in any more, he says. Oour Regt. on the Island has no fight as yet. I suppose their is no Yankees over their today. If so, they would have seen them ere this & it is now 4 o'clock. I will go over whare they are tomorrow as they have to stay 24 hours.

Tell your Pa to write to one of the member in Congress & get permission through them for me to go before the medical bord, to be examined for a position in the army. If our organization stands, I will still hold my place, I expect; if not, I come under the Conscription law & am subject to be called out at any moment.

May heaven bless your pure heart & genuine soul is the sincere wish of your true & devoted lover for ever,

G.W. Peddy

Kiss our sweet Laura for Pappie evry morning, & tell her to kiss ma for me. P.S. Honey, you must buy me a nice hat by the time I come home—N 7 or 7 1/8. Get one with a wide brim. Their is not one to be bougt in Savannah. Be shure to get it. I will think so much of one you would pick out & give to me.

Part II.

FORAY INTO KENTUCKY

19 MAY 1862 - 31 DECEMBER 1862
56-93

By mid-summer 1862 the Confederacy was about to launch counter-offensives in the west as well as in Virginia. The former, it was hoped, would liberate the border state of Kentucky, while both together might lead, if successful, to European recognition of the Confederacy. The two Confederate generals involved in the foray into Kentucky were Braxton Bragg and Edmund Kirby Smith. Unfortunately, neither could give orders to the other, and more unfortunately still, Bragg, who devised the two-pronged strategy, was, to say the least, inept. The course of Kirby Smith's rapid advance can be traced through Dr. Peddy's letters: from south of Chattanooga through northeastern Alabama and Tennessee (Knoxville and Clinton) into Kentucky (Cumberland Ford, Lexington, Mt. Sterling). He won promotion to the rank of Lieutenant General and the thanks of the Confederate Congress, but the numbers of both forces were insufficient to consolidate the gains, and the reaction of the people of Kentucky was lukewarm. After the inconclusive battle of Perryville on 8 October, the armies of Bragg and Smith were finally brought together, but Bragg had lost his nerve and could not be dissuaded from abandoning Kentucky. Thus Dr. Peddy found himself in Selma, Ala. en route to Vicksburg.

56

Monday, May the 19./62

MY LOVE, Again is it my sweet privilege to write to you for although you have been gone but a few days. Yet I know that it will cause a throb of joy in your heart to read a few lines from those you love at home. Oh! how my very heart aches with pain when I think perhaps a great many days and weeks may pass before we are permitted to enjoy those halcyon days that have passed like a golden dream of joy untarnished and without alloy. My darling, you know that you are my heart's treasure and that noth[ing] on Earth is as deare to me. Therefore do not expose yourself so that your life will be endangered. When I opened the letter Col. Watkins wrote you, the room seemed to grow dark around me, for I well knew you went off with such bright anticipations and for them to be so suddenly destroyed by one fell blow. I was affraid you would get into some trouble with Watkins. Yet I knew you would act as you ever have done, the very soul of honor; yet it would have been very hard to let him pass if he had not given you the position. I have been very uneasy and low down with the blues since you left. One thing I well knew, you carried all my sunshine of your love, in which I basked and lived, away, and it threw a shadow over me I could not shake off. Laura is standing at my side saying, ma give me titty, please mam. Now you know I can't write much of interest. Lu has a fine girl. She got through very well. Uncle Joe attended her. I have not been out to see her yet, but will soon. I must close, for Pa wants to seal the letter to send off. Yours ever more

Kate Z Peddy

I am looking so anxiously for Wendsday to come, for it will bring me a letter I think from my darling.

57

Camp McDonald, May 19th/62

MY OWN DEAR,

I have spent the most miserable time since my arrival here I ever spent in my life. For the first two days I was here without Col. Watkins saying a word to me about my position & went off to Atlanta without saying a word to me, only treating me corteously. I went down to Atlanta to see him last Saturday. I asked him about the matter. He said that it was all right & for me to come back & go to work right & do the thing up brown. He has sent on for my commission, although I still have some misgivings about it. The Liut. Col. is opposed to me, I suppose. I have heard so at least. I hope he cannot affect anything. I will be uneasy until I get my commission. If I donot get the position, I intend to come home to see you once more. I do wish I could see you, I love you so much. If you were hear, you could share my troubles & console me so much. I will not suffer myself troubled about it any longer. I will conclude that it is all right & go ahead. I will not have to go before the Medical bord now. I will after awhile. Honey, I will have to have a negro to cook for me. Tell your Pa Peter is no use to him & if he will send him to me by some one comeing up here I will not let him do any thing for any one but myself, & on a forced march I will let him ride my horse. I will keep him in the tent with me & see that he is well taken care off. If he cannot let me have him I will have to get one from someone else. He shall fair as well in camps as I do. If he is killed or lost, I will pay your Pa a fair price for him. Let Puss work in his place, if you have not hired her out to any one & your Pa wants to keep her. I cannot get in any mess here & if I donot get him I will have to cook for myself. We will stay here six weeks I have understood to day. If we do, you must come to see me. I will write to you when to come. Their is a hotel at this place that you can stay at while here. You can bring Laura with you & perhaps Lou will want to come also. I would have written to you ere this, if I had my appointment certain. I am not exactly certain yet but think it will be all right. Col. Watkins will be up here again to day. If their is any thing rong, I will find it out. I have some good friends in the Regt. that will stick to me all the while & will let me know if anything is going wrong about me. I donot want you to send the Books I wrote for but want you to send the following by Peter if he comes. If he does not, send them by some one else: Woods, *Practice of Medicine* in two volumes; *N. S. Dispensatary*; & Dunglingson's *Dictionary*. Send them in a small trunk if you can get one or that box I gave you. My horse is getting on finely. Let me hear from you, my own love darling. I have been sad hearted since I had to part with you. Be cheerful, my dear, we will meet again some day. I feel a little sick to day, but think I will be well in a short time. Let no one see this letter but you Ma & Pa. Yours ever

G.W Peddy

Direct you letters to me: Big Shanty, Col. Watkins' Regt.

58

Atlanta, June 6th/1862

MY OWN DEAR KITTIE,

With much pleasure I write you from this place whare we are camped. I don't know how long we will stay here, perhaps for some time, & perhaps we will leave in a short time. Their is no telling. My dear, I must see you before we leave here; if not, I do not know when I will have that pleasure again. I have got a house for you to bord at & I want you to come back with Mr. Boyd as he comes. He will come back about next Wenesday. So as soon as you get this letter begin to prepare to come as he returns. It seems like a lifetime since I saw you last. I cannot do without your presence longer than the time for Charlie to return. Honey, you have no idea of the estimate I place upon you. Language is insufficient to give you least notion of how much I love you. I never expect to have any more pleasure only in your society. The more I see of you & know, the more I want you with me. If you donot come Wenesday, come Thursday & I will meet you at the car shedd. I will go their Wenesday evening expecting you. Honey, I know it will be a great deal of trouble to you to come & you will not like to do so, but you must forego a little pleasure for me once. I expect you will think it simple for me to be writing for you to come so soon but I cannot avoid it easily. If we move from here, I donot know when I will get to see you again. If Nick comes on before that time you can come along with him & put up at the Atlanta Hotel, & Nick can let me know it so that I can carry you to the place I have picked out for you to bord at. You must bring you[r] money with you. I guess I will have plenty, but you had better bring you[rs]. Tell Nick he had better get off pretty soon as he will be conscribed & put in the ranks. I expect I will kiss you untill you are tired of me when you come. Oh! I do want to see you so much. I know you are so lonesome when I am not with you. I do hope the day will come ere long when I & your sweet self will enjoy the presence of each other in quetude. Life would be such a pleasure to me under such happy circumstances. We have a nice place to camp here about three hundred yds. from the Depot, but a very hot one. We have splended water, which adds greatly to our comfort here. Boyd is perfectly delighted with camps. He gets the dinnus [*sic*] pretty fast, which pleased him above evry thing else. Honey, be shure to come up, & I will be so happy & give you a nice present to take home with you, if you will have one. I sent your Ma a pair of Cotton Cards. I expect she will be quite proud of them. Bring all the news with you when you come. I have subscribed for a paper for you for four months. It cost two dollars for that length of time. Mr. Boyd will hand you this letter, after which you must prepare & come along up here to see me. Foster is getting on finely & is well pleased.

Yours ever more, G. W. Peddy.

59

Franklin, June the 9/1862

MY DARLING.

I wrote to you that I could not come to see you, which I then thought was true, but since I come home and studdied about it I thought I would go any how. So you may meet me and Laura at the car shed either Wendsday or Thursday, as Mr Boid does not know what day he will go yet. I must close as I am very busy at this time. Yours in haste.

Kate Z Peddy.

60

Chattanooga, Ten., June 16th, 1862

MY OWN DEAR KITTIE,

With many feelings of deep regret I left you alone with no one to cheer you but our lovely little sweet Laura. I never regreted leaveing you so much in life as I did in Atlanta. I hope you got home safe. If I had know[n] what I do now, I would have stayed with you that night. Oh! what a joy that would have been for me & you also. We arrived here safe the next morning after I left you in the eve. I never slept any all night for thinking about you. I heard from Lt. Stephens that you would not ride after the horses you started with. I am sorry, for I know how miserable you are when you are frightend o[f] horses. I wish you would forget fear of gentle stock. We are getting on finely here drinking lime water. The Yankees are about 20 miles below us on the other side of the river about six thousand strong. We have about the same number of men or more here. We intend to try to hold this desolate place. The Lime water here does not effect me in any way. I am still quite well. I expect we will have a fight here in some two or three days or week. Regt's are arriving here evry day. Kittie, you need not think about us getting into a fight, for I know just about as much when the enemy will some as you do. Kittie, I do not know when I will see you again. I hope I will ere long. I have plenty to do here. I have scarcely time to write. We have a great many cases of measles & mumps but no one is seriously ill. I often think of the many happy hours we have spent togueather. Oh! how I wish we could have a similar time. No pleasure on earth is so great as that of being with you & realizing that solid fact of our devotion to each other; & Little Laura, the most beautiful & lovely of all beauties, purtakes of the same nature of that angelic mother from which she sprung. No one can be so blessed as myself in respect to family. It is only Laura that portray[s] the outlines of her mother's beauty & lovely disposition. Darling, their is no fiction about the above lines. They are the sentiments of one unworty heart that beets alone for you & our little lovely Laura. I can see her & you in my imagination all the time: those little blue ribbon looked so nice on her little sweet shoulders. They looked as yours did the memorable night we married, the most pleasant one I ever spent before. I am alway when I am at leasure thinking about those Halcyon days of our life, which we have spent in one glourious feeling of love & admiration for each other. Oh! I do hope that their is other glorious days awaiting us like them we hav just passed through when I was permited by the state of the country to stay a home & enjoy the bliss of my existence. Let me hear from you soon, my dear. I have not time to write you more. Let me have from you & long & lovely letter as yours always are. G. W. Peddy

Yours forever.

P.S. My love to the family.

61

Chattanooga, Ten., June 28th/62

MY OWN DEAR KITTIE,

I have just had the glorious pleasure of reading your two letters, one of the 17th & the other of the 27th Inst.[1] With pride & pleasure I heartily respond to them. I feel proud that I am well & have the noble privalidge of writing to one who holds a higher place in my affections than all the wide world with its jems & buties. I have been quite well since I left you in Atlanta. The water here is very bad to drink cool, but full of lime. To my utter supprise, when I opened the nice pants made your own dear hands, I found a sweet letter from you. Honey, no one has such jewel to love & worship as I have. I wish evry one was so bless as I am, but cannot see how it could be so unless every man had you, the noblest of

[1]These letters are missing.

all on earth. Honey, you cannot imagine how much I esteem you. Ideas, thoughts, words, & even evry act of the human mind sinks & falls to far short for me to try [to] undertake to tell you any thing about what my feelings are towards you. Indeed, I fear you will never find it out from the fact their is no mode by which I can exemplify it to you. Honey, the pants are so nice. I have not tried them on. I suppose they will fit. I am going to wear them because you made them wheather they fit or not. Our Regt. was ordered to Knoxville. We went up there, but after staying there a few days, we were ordered back to our old camp, where we are now. I like this place very much notwithstanding its a desloate looking place: Evry body has left it but soldiers. Plenty of them here to defend it. If the Enemy had it, I donot know as we would be injured by it materially. I saw some of the prettiest country between here & Knoxville I have ever seen in my life. I have almost got in the notion to move to Ten. after the war is over if we live. I am in hopes the war will close in a short time, if we have whiped the enemy [before] Richmond. The news is quite favorable so far from that section. I hope its true.[2] Darling, if the war would just close, what a happy time we could have with our sweet little Laura around our own fireside. Let us not dispair of ever having a plesent life togueather. I do hope we will be spaired by kind providence to enjoy each other's society sweetly at our unkown home that is awaiting us. Honey, I would have written you ere this, but have not had time. I have been travling from pillow to post ever since I left you in Atlanta. I have been buisy making out my monthly report, but have it all right at last. I have been having a very buisy time indeed since we got back from Knoxville. My Assist. has been absent all the while & has not returned yet. I do wish he would: I am so wearied. A great many of the Regt. is sick with the measles. It has been my misfortune to get into a Regt. of fresh troops evry time I have started out, but we will get thtough now, I hope, ere long. I sold my horse at the price offored me for him in Atlanta. I have bough[t] another at $225. He is the prettiest little horse you ever saw. He is just like Dr. Grimes' horses. If I & he lives, I am going to bring him home with me when the war closes & give him to you. He will just suit you; & get me another.

Foster is getting along finely. He is now examining my pants you sent me. He likes them admirably, he says. You did not write to me what Mrs. Featherston says of Laura. I know she thinks she is pretty. Honey, I wish you could wean her. I want you never to look so thin as you did when I was at home. I want you to improve in flesh if their is any chance. When you get so reduced I am uneasy. Evry time I look at you, I am led to imagine without any foundation that my darling is leaving me in this unhappy world by littles or latently. I know if you would quit nursing Laura you would get healthy & fleashy. If you & Laura was

[2]The Seven Days' Battles about Richmond began on 26 June 1862.

gone *Lord Lord,* I would say let me go with you through death as well as through life. All joy, happiness, all evrything would be a nuisance to me & me to evry one else. Foster says let Lina know he's well, & he wants you to write if any thing happens to her & his children. He wants to know how they get on. Honey, I will have to close as it is growing late. Let me hear from you often. I will write to you as often as I have time. Give my love to all at home. I am anxious to see them & would like exceedingly well to see Mrs. F. Your ever true lover

G.W Peddy

62

Chattanooga, July 5th/62

MY EVER LOVED DEAR, As Mr. Boyd is going to start home this eve I thought I would drop you a few lines. I am sick to day with Diarrhoea: eat some fish last night. I suppose that's the cause of it. I think I will get well soon. It does seem so hard for me to be sick & be away from ; you, my only solace in life. I would give all I have to be with you. It does look so hard for me to be kepted away from you, one that I love so dearly as I do you. Honey, the idea of not having the pleasure of being with you in some time is almost more that I can bear. I would freely give up evrything if I could be permited to stay with you all the time. One moment with you & Laura is worth more to me than all the money that I could make away from you in three or four years. Oh how happy, how surpemely glorified I will be when I am permited to stay with you & our little sweet Child. She did look so beautiful when we were in Atlanta about the time she pointed at the fly in the butter. Honey, if you can devise a plan or advance an idea that will console me away from you, I would be glad you would do so. I am miserable all the time that I am away from you. I have no news of importance to write you, only what you have heard, that is, our glorious victory at Richmond. We have rec'ed news of a perfect triumph of our arms. Honey, I fear this is an unhealthy country we have got into, but will not conclude that I must get sick because this is a sickley country. Honey, you must save me all you sweet kisses. Oh, I wish I had some of them now. I think they would cure me. Woodruff Dollys is in our Regt. a private. He is a good fellow, but a man of sense you ever saw. I donot think him worthy of her, for she is a talanted Lady. Our Regt. are nearly all sick & what is well are about to get sick. I see no prospect for a fight here soon although we may have one. I am so sorry that Laura got sick. I hope she is well now & will remain so until she gets grown. I wish she could stay little & sweet like she is now. Honey, let me hear from you as often as you have time to write. Make me a Haversack out off that Oil Cloth of ours & send it to me per Boyd. Make a large one.

Yours, Yours, ever ever
G W Peddy

63

Camp Ledbetter, Twelve Miles below Chattanooga, July 10th/62

MY DEAREST ON EARTH KITTIE, I sit in my tent this rainey eve while the rain is patting gently on my tent to drop you a few lines, which is always so much pleasure to me. I have just read your sweet letter of the 7th inst.[3] Your letters, like your advice & placid words, always come, it seem to me, in the best [t]ime they could. I have been sick for a week. Last night I never put over such a night. I was deathly sick for about five hours with Diarrhoea, but am a good deal better to day, but have done no duty, nor do I expect to until I get perfectly well. I hope I will be so in a few days, if I can keep from eating. After reading your letter per Mr. Miller I felt so much better. That is why it came in such a good time. You spoke in yours of our happy hours spent at the rocks. Oh! Honey, how I do wish we could spend some of them there now. It seems that I have been the most fortunate Creature on earth in marrying such a noble, grand, sweet, & beautiful Lady as you are, but the most unfortunate in having to leave you, and whose beauty excelence & loveliness excells all on earth to me. In evry hour of sadness or glee my heart turns with pleasure & pride to you & our sweet little one at home. Home, sweet home: the place where the dearest object of my heart is & whare the inclinations of my heart are. Honey, sweet one, you spoke in yours of the ocean of love their was in your heart for me. If my whole system was converted in to a heart it could not contain the love I have for your dear self. The poet may be inspired to speak of love & the youthful heart m[a]y pulsate it at evry throb, yet never could eather speak, think, or feel it with that enrapturous spirit as that which animates my bosom of it for you; & that which gratifies me most is that you are so worthy of that bestowed on you by me, & so much more worthy that I disdain to speak of one that would be worthy of you.

[3]This letter is missing.

Dear, you spoke of wanting to see me. Oh, nothing would gratify me so much as to see you if it were not but for five minutes. But Darling, loved one, I see no chance for me to come home. You know I would come if I could. You must not think I donot love you by my not coming home, for I am always as a[n]xious to see you as I can possibly be & will let no opportunity escape to see you that may present itself. Evry time I open your tru[n]k I think of you & think of the many times you have toumble your things over in it while at school long before you knew me or took me to yourself to trouble you. How oft those little lovely lilly hands have been busy about the trunk now by my side. Honey, I will forego these plesent reflections as they tend only to mystify how I was so fortunate in getting one dearer & better than all others. The unholy war may continue & I may be kept away from you in the most crewel manner & treated in evry way that's unplesent. Yet never will I seace to love & admire your & my little darling girl. Honey, I wish I could write something half expressive to you of my love & admirati[on], but I fall so far short that I become freted at myself.

Honey, tell your Pa not to let Lou go into the service at all. I think after the present Conscription is over their will be no more. The Act says all those between the ages of eighteen & thirty five will be subjects of conscription on the fifteenth of June. It does not say what disposition will be made of those that will be eighteen after awhile, but provides that all those in the survice not 18 & over thirty five will be discharged after the expiration of ninty days after the passage of the act. So from those considerations I donot think that Lou will have to come. Honey, you must not give yourself no more uneasiness about me than you can possibly help. I will take care of myself the best I can, awlways having in view your future happyness. Honey, I would make any sacrifice on earth to gratify you. Honey, when you think of me, always bear in mind that evry thing I do is with an eye single to your future pleasure. Give my love to all. Let me hear from you often. Your ever lovingly

To my Dear Wife, Kittie Peddy G.W Peddy

64

Twelve Miles Below Chattanooga, July 12th, 1862.

MY DEAR DARLING KITTIE, I write you a few lines this morning per Mrs. Able to let you know that I have gotten well at last. The object of this letter is to get you to buy me in Franklin a pair of thin shoes of some kind. My feet are nearly ruined by those boots you saw me buy in Atlanta. You can send them to me by some one passing from home to camps. Honey, I donot know when I will see you again unless you come to see me. Their has been an order issued that no resignation shall be tendered, no furlough sent up to head quarters, unless upon Surgeon's Certificate. So you see, their is no chance for me to come home unless I get quite sick. But my own Darling Angel, if I donot see you in twelve months my love to you will grow no dimer but *brighter* all the while. To love you is my happyest thought. The reason of my loving you so dearly you can give by reflecting about the jenuineness of you own lovely self. Honey, I can write nothing that is half good enough for your eye to see. Oh how I do wish I could look at them this moment. I wish I had got your & Laura's Ambrotype while in Atlanta. Darling, if you have the chance, have them takened & send them to me. My love to all. Kiss Laura for Pappie. Your forever.

G.W Peddy

P.S. I donot know how long we will stay here. We may leave in a few days, but continue to direct you letter to me at Chattanooga & I will get them. Give me all the news when you write about the town. My love to Dr. Lane & your Ant Kit. I do think so much of them.

G.W.P.

65

Camp Ledbetter, July 13th, 1862

TO THE DEAREST ON EARTH, MY DARLING ONE KITTIE,

I wrote to you on yesterday but owing to the fact that I have this day sent to you ninty dollars per Express, you may look out for it. You may have to send to Newnan for it. Honey, I want you to awlways keep on hand about three or four hundred dollars for fear that you or I need it. I will send to you three hundred & twenty four or five dollars as so[o]n as I draw, & perhaps I will send my horse home to you also. I cannot get anything to feed him on but Clove Hay. We have been out of corn for three days. I am quite well to day; I do hope I will keep so on your account. We have a great deal of sickness in the Regt., mostly Remittent Fever. We have pretty well got through with the Measles now. Honey, you need not be affraid of us going any farther north than we are. I think we will do all our fighting on this side of the Ten. River. The Enemy, as you will see in your paper, are crossing the River below us, intending, I suppose, to march to Rome, Ga. I think if the Yankees get into Ga. that Gov. Brown will call out the ballance of the men that's not over forty five to defend their homes with pikes such as he has made ready for use. Mr. Boyd reached here to day well & brought me a sweet letter from your genuine self.[4] Oh! my, it seem[s] a hundred years since I saw the beautiful & lovely [one] that kisses me so sweetly & treats me so lovely & kindly when I am with her. Honey, you write to me to come home, & how I long to do so, but Lord only knows when I will come. I try to be merry & lively here, but at the same time my heart is almost broken by absence from you. I never hear any on[e] talking about the nobleness of their wives but myself. I expect I bore many by speeking in tearms of adoration of you, but I cannot help it, for wheare the heart is there is the thought also. How often I do imagine how you & little sweet Laura looks & enjoy yourselves togueather. Oh how I wish I could share a part of that joy. Honey, in reference to your cloth, you can do as your good judgement directs, but I would keep it. I will weare it out for you after the war is over with Laura to help me. I want you not to work while I am gone. I want you to take good care of yourself, for if you were gone, I donot know what I should do. Capt, Spearman says you look better than he ever saw you. If so, I donot know how I would content myself if I were to see you could improve in beauty & Loveliness. He says I ought to stay away from home all the while if it is that to improve you[r] looks. Honey, I do long to see the day come when peace will be made & we will be permitted to enjoy ourselves togueather the remainder of our short stay on earth. What little joy I have on this earth is when I am with you. Your presence alone with our little one is more happyness to me than all the wealth of this world. Write s[o]on. Your evermore G.W.P.

66

Camp Near Bridgeport, July 17th, 1862

MY OWN PRECIOUS SWEET DARLING KITTIE,

With mingle feelings of pleasure & pride I write you a few lines to night, though very much wearied, & its growing quite late. My Assist. has been taken sick & gone home & left me as usual all the work to do. I have had a much harder time here than I did in the State Survice. We have so many more to see

[4]This letter is missing.

here, but with all my trials, hardships, & perplexities I have the prowd & happy reflection that it is for the benefit of one more noble & lovely than all else on earth & also for one that I love & cherish with the most exalted of all feelings. Honey, oh! that I could fold my arms around your lovely form this night. It would be more pleasent that the reception of all the goods of this earth. Honey, [do] you think of me with as much joy & pleasure as I do of you? If so, what a happy mortal I ought to be. Oh! that I could have the pleasure of consulting your wise and lovely head about all my business. When I am home & get perplexed, the gentle words of consolation that drop from your sweet lips mellows my irritableness into perfect pleasure. I never [k]new my darling what a monument of wisdom I possessed in a wife until I left home. Alwease advise & console me when in trouble & made me happyier when in good humor. Oh! that I now had the benefit of that councel now. Honey, my headaches so much to night you must look over the manner in which this is written. How happy I would be if I were at home now, but Darling, I see no chance to get their in I cannot tell. The Yankees are just across the Ten. River from us shooting shells at our picketts occasionally. I am in no danger myself or our Regt., only when on picket duty. I never go out with them, only when the whole Regt. goes. I am the best pleased with Col. Watkins of any I nearly ever saw. He is a perfect gentleman in evry sence of the word so far. I doubt not that he will continue so. I am proud that I am under such a man. I have got well now & can do as much buisiness as any one in the Regt. I am as well pleased here as I want to be—if I only could have my own dear wife & Little Laura with me or whare I could see you once in a short while. Honey, let me hear from you soon. I am so sleepy & tired I will have to go to bed thinking of my treasure at home. My love to all at home.

Yours ever with a heart that's all love for you & yours. G.W. Peddy

Direct your letters to me at Chattanooga & I will be apt to get them.

67

Jackson Co., Ala., July 20th, 1862

MY DARLING KITTIE, It is my happy lot to reply to your very welcomed letter bearing date of the 15th Inst.[5] Honey, how sorry I was to hear of the accident that hapened to our dear friend Mrs. Turner. I hope she has gotten well by this

[5]This letter is missing.

time. She is one of our best friends. You must attend to her good. I am also greaved to hear of the death of my t[w]o friends C. Shugaret & Phelpot. Poor Charlie, a braver, nobler boy never lived than he. I cincerely condole with the bereaved family. I hope they will take it as lightly as they can. One should not murmer at the dispensation of kind providence, but it almost seems to me that it was wrong for noble Charlie to die, but such is alloted to evry man. I know the sad accident will nearly take the life of the oldman & old Lady Shugaret. Honey, I am not a foot again. I sold the little horse I bought for you at $225. for $300.00. I made $75.00 dollars in the trade, but am sorry I let him go. He would have just suited you to ride. I donot know wheather I will buy another or not. I believe I will not unless I see a chance to make something. All the staff want to turn over their horses to me to trade off for them. I will not accept, but will do my own trading & divide proffett with no one. I have made since I left home in two horse trades $125.00 cash. Ask your pa if he thinks it a fair speculation. If so, I will buy another tomorrow. Brewer Lane has arrived safe at Camps with his Wagon & Team. Honey, I wish you would write to Brother John often. I donot have the time. Honey, the Dearest idol of my heart, I want you to go down to see Jane Lane & go with her in the store & buy you one of those silk patterons to make you a dress. I want to give you a nice present, & if you donot get one of those silk dresses, I donot know when you ever will get one. Brewer & I have been talking about them to day. He says the triming is all their for ether of the patterons you may take. You cannot buy one in Atlanta for a hundred dollars. Brewer lets me have ether of them at the old price. You can take the green or Black one just as you choose. The reason I want you to take one is that I am going to get me a nice suit ere long, as I am needing one badly. I will pay Brewer for it up here. You need not pay Jane for it. Let me know which piece you take so we will know how to settle. The money I have made on the horses is enough to pay for both of our Suits. Tell Kitten Pappie will buy her something nice after she gets large enough to wear fine dresses. She is sweet and pretty enough now but to[o] little. Honey, how badly I want to see you. If their was any other chance I could not do without seeing you longe[r], but their is no chance for us to meet soon unless you come to see me. But darling, [k]no[w] this truth that never has any one loved one so dearly as I do you. I would be perfectly happy with your presence under any circumstance of life, but oh! to contemplate the day when wee shall be seated by our own fireside with our darling child to prattle around us is an extatic thought. Oh that it were sow now, how happy how happy would we be. I cannot imagine the glory of such a thought. Honey, I have not drawn any money from the Goverment as yet. We will get our pay before long. Then I will send you some more money. Honey, let me hear from you often. It does me so much good to hear from you. It does not cost me scarcely anithing to live. We get sugar at th[r]ee cents per pound. Good night, my darling Babey. I must go to sleep. [Would] that I could sleep with you by my side.

Yours forever G.W. Peddy

68

Camp Near Grahams, Ala., July 27th, 1862

MY DEAREST KITTIE,S

With feelings of the deepest joy I have just received & read your sweet & nice letter.[6] It is one of the best I ever read. Few as good are rarely written. Its length & tenor was just as I wanted it. It fills my heart with the deepest emotions of love & happyness to think I have a dear one at home who loves me with so much pleasure. Honey, when you are loving me your utmost, reflect that their is one distant from you who loves you in the same way all the while. I cannot do justice to the subject of how I love you with my pen. If I were with you, I would act in such a manner that would convince you tha[t] my affection for you was real. Honey, donot write about your inferiority, for you are to none on earth, but far to[o] sweet lovely & modest for the one who regards you a perfect *angel* in evry respect. Darling, I know well that if I were at home & their was peace in the country we would be an example of pure happiness on earth if such a thing could be. Honey, I am so glad you have weaned Laura, but it griaves Pappie to think the little sweet child has to do without her jugs, but Ma you must let her have them no more. You will get corpulent now. Oh, how I want to see you so much since your Ma accused you of looking so well. You look well all the while & their is but little room for improvement if any. If you look any better than you always have I donot know how I will conduct myself when I see you. When I am at home I never can kiss you enough I love you so well. I am always thinking about the pleasure we spend in plessing each other warmly in love. Oh! my, would that that time should come again. Happy, oh happy, would I bee. Honey, you wrote to me in reference to some close. I want you to make me a nice suit of light colored Gray Jeans & Vest & all. Have it as *light gray color* as you can conveniently make it. I want it cut like a Military Coat & the Collar & risbands Black Cloth. I do not know how you will get it cut out. If it is real nice suit I will not buy me one out of the Store. It cost so much I hate to buy it, but

---

[6]This letter is missing.

you must be shure to buy you[r] silk dress & make it by the time I get home, if I should live to get their again. Honey, I will write you a better letter than this in a few day. Sig Owens is here & is about to leave for home & I am in great haste. I wish I was at home to eat beans with little pig. Kiss her for me. My love to all. Your always. G W Peddy

---

69

Knoxville, Ten., Aug. 3rd/1862

MY DEAR KITTIE,

We have been so busy moveing about since I reced you[r] last that I have had no time to write until now. My darling, when I read your last letter,[7] unmanly like I had to take a little Cry. The chastizement you give me for writing to you as I did in the letter I sent per Mr. Boyd, honey, I like to have died with the blews after reading it, but darling, do not think because I wrote to you in that way that I dislike you in the least. I love you with my hole heart knotwithstanding the unchaced letter I wrote you. Honey, if I should ever write to you in that way again, please donot scold me about it, for it is the love I bear constantly in my bosom for you that promps me so to write. You are the only woman on earth that I have ever hinted such a thing to & I think for that reason you should forgive me. Honey, you'l find out if we should live that I love you with all my heart, mind, a[nd] soul. The language of our country is not elastice enough for me to give you any definite idea of how well I love & worship you. Although I am far from you, & perhaps long absence may cause that love that I imagine you cheerish for me to wither, yet rest assured, my heart's delight, that so long as this eye can see, this tongue can speak, & this brain can think , I'll ever love & cheerish you as the only idol of my heart in this life. I do adore & worship you I fear to a dangerous extent, but thank God, I am proud that I do do it. My deepest regret is that you cannot be taught to realize that firm & everlasting fact. You & your dear little child is all I desire in this life. Once restored to your presence, happyness will overcome me. Tonight, my dear, I will sleep pleasantly on my cot & in my nice tent for the last time. I will have to abandon them & evrything else but my shawl & blanket. Tomorrow is fast approaching which will set us out for Clinton, Ten., from thence to London, Kantuckey, all

---

[7]This letter is missing.

the way to march through the country. I know not, me dear, when I will see or hear from you again, perhaps never. I hope we will be succesful in our tour. If not, we will do all in our power to take care of ourselves in the best way we can. As for you, darling, you must do evry thing you can to preserve your health. Do [not] think off me so much that you cannot see any peace, but reconcile your self that if I get killed you have lost one who love[s] you more than anyone is capable of doing. Y'r hea[l]th, prosperity, & happyness is all I desire. If I could have a guarantee that these three things would be your lot, I would be reconciled to almost any fate. Honey, if you have not gone to Ala., I recon you best not go. I am afraid for you to leave home. I had rather you remain at home until I can get an opportunity to go with you to see my good parents, whose heads are whightning for the grave. They no doubt think I am unkind in not writing to them. If so, I donot intend it so for I love them as well as I ever have. You & our little sweet child occupies my whole mind to an extent that I have hardly got time to think of any one else. Honey, you must not listen to the tails you hear of my miss treating the men. It's all falts, & so far as being killed in battle by them is concerned, I donot fear them in the least. If the Yankees were to attack us I would be more uneasy for fear they would run over me in retreating if I were behind them than to think they would shoot me, & so far as my partiality extends if any difference I have shown it from the company from our county, the whole staff think the world of me. Col. Watkins & Slaughter tell evry body that they have got the best Surgeon in the world. They say I suit them to a fraction. If you will notice over the signature of M.J.C. in your paper of the 31st ultimo, you will see how I stand in the regt. with men who have some sense. Fools like some here from Heard I care nothing for, & so far as Copelold is concer[n]ed, he's the worst liar I know off. He pertends to be the best friend I have, but I care nothing for his friendship or malice. He's a nuisance any whare you put him. No doubt their are many in the Regt. that dislike me because I will not give them furloughs & discharges, & also frequently mark them for duty when they are trying to play off all these things with other conected with my deportment, them not only dissatisfied with me but evry body else. Honey, you may adress me at Knoxvile, Ten. until you hear from me again. I recon the letter will be sent on to the Regt. I have my commission. Our Regt is the 56 Ga. in Gen. Leadbetter's Brigade. Honey, do nothing to injure your & little Laura's health. I do hope you will keep well while I am gone. Darling sweet one, I am getting quite sleepy. It is growing late, & a long day travel before me tomorrow. Excuse this. I'll try to do better in the future.

Very Respectfully
Y'r ob't Lover always

To Mrs. Z. C Peddy
Franklin Ga

G. W Peddy

70

Clinton, Ten., Aug. 10th/1862.

MY DARLING KITTIE. With the most unalloyed pleasure I write you a few lines to let you know my whareabouts. I am at this place, but do not know how long we will remain here—but a few days, I suppose. I think the intention of our people is to drive the invader from the soil of Ten. & Kentuckey ere our campaign ceases. We have the upper hand of the Yankees at this time, if we can only keep it. I have marched forty miles, evry step on foot. My horse was left behind, but has caught up at last. You donot know how glad I was to see him. The march wearied me very much, but I stood it as well as any one in the Regt. We waded Clinch river twice. The rock in the bottom liked to ruined my feet. Honey, when I was so wearied I did want to see you my *Dearest* so badly. My heart almost melted into tears when I thought of the comforts & enjoments of home & my *dear* little family, the leaver of my existence, & the pride of my very soul & heart. Honey, no one can imagine how badly I want to see you & Laura. I would freely give all I have made since I have been in the army to get to see you one hour even. It appears to me that I cannot forego the greatest of all pleasures, viz. seeing you much longer, but darling, their is no chance under the heavens for me to get off to see you under six months, if then. Honey, we will have to foregow seeing each other to an extent that is fearful in length. I do wish I could be at home for a week or two, or a much longer as I could get leave of absence, to enjoy the privaledge of your socity & to see Laura eat Watermelons, Beans & c. I know she loves them so well. I have not eat but one piece of melon since I have been in the survice. Honey, you spoke of wanting a buggy. You had better not get it until I send you more money. You must & shall have any thing you want, if it is in my power to obtain if for you. As soon as I send you more money, get your good Pa to go to Altanta & buy you a nice fine boggy & fine harness. Tell your Pa not to get one to[o] light or to[o] heavy, but meadun, such an one a[s] Paces' or finer one with side springs & *Box Body*. Ma, you must let little Pig ride in it as much as she wants to. I intend, if the war ever coloses, to bring home with me a horse that will just suit you to ride & drive. Honey, if you need the Buggy before I can send you, send your Pa after it at once. Let me know if you have got your silk dress—if you have made it. We have at this time about thirty women that have come to camps to see their husbands. Mr. Watkins is here to day & he is going to present a flag to the Regt. at nine this morn.

I wrote old Gallespie a tight letter for talking about me in my absence. I have heard of some of Beckie Packston's writing about me since I have been in camps. Notwithstanding the talk about how the Regt. despises me, I get all that's written from home about me. It does not affect me in the least, what anyone says of me , if they let you & Laura alone. So you & she loves me that's all I care for. The happy thought of having you affections sinks evry sentance of slang into insignificance. Honey, do write to me often. I have not heard from you in some time. It matters not how long or how far I am away from you, I will always love you with whole soul mind & heart.

Your ever more
G. W Peddy

Direct your letter to me at Knoxville Ten.

P. S. I forgot to tell you that I am Brigade Surgeon.

71

Boston, Ky., Aug 19th, 1862

MY DEAREST ON EARTH KITTIE,

We arrived at this place last eavning, had a skirmish with the bushwhackers just as we got in town. No one hurt on our side. We killed six of them. I was detailed on last Monday to go with the 43rd Ala. Regt. to Huntsville, Ten. to whip out the Yanks their. We did it very nicely. We fought about two hours. Three of our men were wounded. We killed ten of the Hessians & wounded several. We captured a great quantity of Coffee, Sugar, Clothing, Shoes, Horses & mules, Guns &c. The trip like to worried me to death, but got well repaid for it in fun of various sorts. Honey, you can't imagine how the bulletts whistled around me, but fortunely no one struck me. I thought of my darling often while in the engagement. Honey, fighting is nothing but fun to our troops. This place is in the rear of Cumberland Gap. We have the gap surrounded at this time. I think if we donot whip the Yankees out of their soon, we will perish them out. I am quite well at this time. Foster is also. When I get [to] see you I will give a full account of my travels & scares since I last beheld those dear pritty eyes & lovely form of yours. Honey, I will send this letter to you by John Lipham, who is going home. You can get some wool from him. If you will get it soon to make my clothes out of, I believe I will not get me any other uniform but the one you make. Honey, pad the brest & make me a nice suit. I wrot to you to make me a round jacket, but can make it to suit yourself. I want to wear that only which you thinks looks best. Honey, your last was the best letter I ever read.[8] Oh that I could encircle you, as you said, in my arms! I would not let you go for a month. I do love you so well I cannot content myself. Honey, donot think I donot love you because I donot come home. I would come home evry week if it was in my power, but it is not. I would give the whole world to see you & Laura. She is such a lovely little thing, only the image of her angelic mother, the most lovely of all ladies that live. Honey, I cannot express myself to you. You can imagine how I worship & love you. Think of the past & always think that I love you more & more evry day, if possible. If I were not to see you in twelve months or twelve years, I would love & worship you as much as ever. Honey, you must continue to love me as heretofore. You must not look out for some one else until I get back home. Donot think I am lost for good. I will get to see you again some day, I hope before many months or many days are weeks. Honey, we took a store to day, confiscated it. I got you a nice hoop & a nice pair of shoes. I will try to get Mr. Lipham to bring them to you as he brings the letter. I wish I could see you when you get my suit done. You will be so proud of it & so will I. I want you to be shure to buy you the Buggy. You need it & must have it. I have not drawn any money as yet. The government owes me over four hundred dollars. I will send it to you as soon as I get an opportunity. Give my love to y'r Ma & Pa & all their little children. Write to me as soon as you can. Direct you letter to Knoxville as heretifore. I am coming home the first opportunity. Foster wants Lina to write to him. He says tell all at home howdo for him.

Honey, I hate to have to quit writing to you. I could keep on with pleasure writing all night, but some of the boys are waiting for medecine & I will have to stop until I wait on them. Good by, my dear. I will write you again soon.

Yours forever, with a heart that beats alone for your & Little Laura, our bright eyed beauty,

G.W. Peddy

Aug. 21st, 1862, My darling, We will leave here tomorrow, I suppose for Comberland ford in the rear of Comberland Gap. I received you dear sweet letter to day.[9] Honey, you have no idea how happy I was to receive it. The pleasure that I experienced in reading it is indescribable. I love you more & more evry day, if such a thing could be possible. I am so sorry Lou has to come to war. You have no idea what hardships we have to undergo. We frequently have to march all day & night. I will let him ride my horse when he get tired, & he can mess me. Foster can cook for us both. I hope, my dear love, I will see you

---

[8]This letter is missing.

[9]This letter is missing.

before many more days or weeks. Rest assured that I will come as soon as I get off, & rest assured that if I donot see you again, that I love you more than any one on earth can possibly be loved.

Your forever & forever

G.W. Peddy

Written across the letter: I send you this letter in a Yankee envelope.

72

Cu[m]berland Ford, Ky., Aug. 26th, 1862

MY OWN DARLING SWEET WIFE KITTIE,

Once more, after passing throught the land of Bushwhackers over the Cumberland mountain to the rear of Cumberland gap, I am permited through the intervention of kind providence to perform the delightful task of writing to you again. Nothing could gratify me more here surrounded on all sides than to sit down quietly & write to you, the greatest & most lovely of all beings on earth to me. It seems hard, Honey, for me to be kept away from you so long, but it cannot be hope at this time. I do wish I could see you, my dearest, I know you would be so gratifying to us both. If I am not killed by one of those Bushwhackers, I think I will see you between this & Christmas. We have the Yankees between our force in front & rear. We captured their supply train consisting of about three hundred wagons & teams, the best you ever saw, loaded with Sugar, Coffee, Flour, Bacon, & evry thing that is eaten by the Yankee army. We will starve the enemy out at the gap in a few days. I think they will be compelled to surrender, if a very heavy force does not come to their rescue in a few days. We got around here by comeing through Big Creak gap across the Cumberland & Pine Mountains in Ky., from thence to Boston, & from their to Barbersville, then to Cumberland Ford, the place we are now at. Your Pa can tell from this outline how we got here. We have a large force gone up towards London, Ky. They are to check the reinforcements to the Gap. We have taken on our rout about one hundred Prisners. Our Regt. is quite healthy at this time. I suppose when we leave here we will go on towards Lexington, Ky., i.e. if we donot meet with to[o] strong a force. Darling, donnot be uneasy about me if you can help it. I will be at home as soon as I can to see you & our little sweet Laura. Honey, I want you to buy me a pair of sadlebags. & send them to me by Lou. You can get them out of Mozely & Lane's store. If you cannot get them their, tell you Pa to get them some whare. I am obliged to have them. Their was a nice pair in the store when I left. I expect they are their yet. I wish your Pa would go as far as Atlanta with Lou & get me a nice Gray army cloak. I donot care what it cost. I have spent no money, & I can afford to buy me a cloak, hence I want a nice one. I have drawn no money yet no[r] will I until I get back to Knoxville. I will send it all home to you as soon as I get it. Honey, be shure to send me the saddlebags & Army cloak for a surgeon. I am not going to wear anything, only the jeanes suit that you are to make me. I will get the badge of my rank & put on it. If Lou could stay at home until you got my close done, I would like it very much. Honey, I must close. It's growing late at night & I have been marching all day. I will try to give you some idea in my next of how I love you if I can find language to express it. Darling, if I stay away from you tine years I will love & worship you as I always have done. Give my love to all your Pa's Family, you[r] Ant K[it] & Uncle Joe. Tell Dr. Lane & your Pa to write to me. I would be proud to hear from them at any time they want to write. Yours forevere, my own dear angel Kittie,

G.W.P.

P.S. Direct your Letters as before. I will write again soon.

73

Cumberland Ford, Aug 27th, 1862

MY DEAREST SWEET KITTIE,

I drop you a few more lines this morning. I have nothing new to write. I am quite well this morn. I have had as fine health for the last month as I have ever had in my life. I expect we will have to fight here in a short time. I cannot tell, though, about that—perhaps we may not. The object in writing this scrip is for you to tell Lou if he starts with my things, not to let them get out of his hands. If he does, some one will steal them. He had better come as far as Knoxville & their find out when a wagon train is comeing to supply us. He will be apt to see their some of the men that belongs to this Regt. comeing from the Hospital to camps. If the enemy evacuates the Gap before he comes to Knoxville, he can get along quite easy. My darling, I awoke this morning think[ing] of how I loved you so much. It seems to me that I would give my life for a few moments with you & my dear little Laura. You must not let her forget Papie. Tell her I love her more than she will be able to retaliate. Yours true & with the strongest devotion of heart, G.W Peddy

---

74

Lexington, Ky., Sept. 5th, 1862

MY OWN EVER DEAR LOVE KITTIE, With no little pleasure I write to you to night. I have had no opportunity of gitting a letter carried back to you until now & donot know wheather this will reach you, though I hope it will, for I know you want to know my whare abouts as bad as you ever wanted anything. Honey, you need not be uneasy about me: I feel as safe here as I do in any part of Tennessee. Darling, this is the prettyest country I ever have seen in all my life & do wish you could bee here. I never saw people so enthusiastic in my life. Our presence fills them with so much joy they are nearly crazy. The road sides are throunged with Ladies waiveing their handkerchiefs & Confederate flaggs. We can hardly get about our camps for them. They bring loads of provisions to our camp evry day. They have been oppressed by the Federals so long that in a great many instances they burst into tears at our approach. Nothing they have is to[o] good for us. They would not let us stay in camps at all if we were to go home with them evry time they invite us. We had a fight at Richmond, Ky. & give them the worst beating that ever a people got. We taken any amount of arms, army stores, amunition, & better still, we taken four thousand five hundred prisners. Parolle them & they are gone to their homes. We captured at this place evry thing the enemy had, the worth of which I will not attempt to mention. At both places I would guess we captured twenty or thirty millions dollars' worth. I am happy to say to you, my dear, that I am as well as I ever was in my life. Oh how I want to see you, my darling, but it is out of the question now. I will come as soon as I can get an opportunity. Amid all the enthusiasm & excitement I think of you & wish you was here to enjoy it with me. I do love you so well, my dear, that you cannot imagine how it affects me to stay away from you. Honey, I would have written ere this but it is the first opportunity I have had in several weeks. It is such a pleasure for me to know that I have once more the opportunity of holding sweet converse with you through the meduim of a pen. Our Regt. is generally well & seem to be in good spirits, notwithstanding the amount of marching they have done. I donot know whare we will go to from here. We may not stop in Ky. I cannot say. Honey, I cannot portray the intensity of the excitement in this country. The K[entuck]yans have made up for the Confederacy in this country to day two Regts. of infantry & one company of Cavalry. We will get at least fifty or sixty thousand troops for the Confederacy out of this state. I will tell you when I see you how things exist in reference to the people of Ky. Such a state of affairs never was known, it seems to me, in any Government. We have a large army here sufficient for all the Yankees that can come. The people of this state have just found out, that the object of the Fedral government is to abolish slavery. My sweet darling, do take care of yourself & our little bright eyed Laura. She bears the impress of her noble Mama. Without you the world would be a perfect blank to me. You can never appreciate how dearly I love you. Your presence & councel is worth more to me than all the treasure in the world. Oh if I could this night behold your lovely form, I would give, it seems to me, my whole existence, but the fates may keep us from enjoying each other's presence; but their is one thing that cannot be crushed, & that is the genuine love I bear for you. I worship you as a perfect, lovely & angelic being no pureer, no lovlier on earth. I will write to you as often as I can get a chance to send letters back. Direct your letters as before. I have had no letters from you in several weeks. Give my love to your *good* Ma & Pa, you uncle Jeo & Kit, & all enquireing friends. Give me in your next all the news about Franklin.

Yours forever,
G.W. Peddy.

75

September the 24, [*1862*]

MY HEART'S DELIGHT,

Although I am somewhat tired, having been very busy all day preparing your suit, yet I can not lay me down to sleep without penning a few thoughts to my darling, who is far far away from all that loves him. I am almost blinded by fast falling tears when I sit down to write you. My heart grows faint when I think how long you will be gone from us and how much evil may happen to you or me when you are away. Oh! I am almost ready to give up, my heart is almost broken some how. I fear that comming events cast their shadows before, for I never felt so sad and desolate as I do now. It has been nearly three weeks since I heard from you, save by some one passing who said you had gone on to Cincinatta and there was no possibility of getting a letter from you in two or three months. I don't know how I can stand that, for you letters was my only enjoyment, and to be deprived of them is a great misfortune. I have been quite well untill last night. I was threatened with an other spell of cramp colic, but I am relieved of it now. I do hope I won't be sick while you are gone. Every body is getting frightened about the Smallpox. Tom Vaughn came home last week, and traveled two day with some soldiers who had it. Two or three men of St. Cloud come with him. They are going to stay off to themselves untill they find out whether they take it or not. Dr. Harlan is vaxinated, but I cant stop makeing your suit now to be sick with vaxination.

Honey, I am so distressed to night, it is impossible for me to write any thing sensible. I have just heard a rumor that your regment was taken prisner. Although I put no confidence in the report, yet it makes me reched to think of such a thing being possible. You can't imagine what joy I would experience to even know where you are this night. In a few moments I will lay my head down on a nice soft pillow and sleep pleasantly on a good bed; but where is my darling, does he even have the oppertunity of sleeping at all? Honey, we never knew how well we loved each other untill this cruel war. I think of you more and more each day, and oh!, how ardently I long for your return; but to think I can't even get a letter from you, it is too bad. I do hope to morrow will bring me some word from my darling. William Watkins has got him a substitute, as his health is very bad at this time. His wife is very sick at this time with the fever. Mr. Turner has had a great deal of sickness in his family of late. Mrs. Turner said she did not know how much she would miss you untill all of family was sick. They had six negroes down at once. She will be so lonely if Mr. Turner does go off, for she has neither father, brother, nor any one to go too in her troubles. Brewer and Billy are hear yet. Billy is not well. He can't walk without his crutch. He spent the day here last week with several others. I showed him the saddle bags I bought for you. He was completely taken with them, said I could not have bought them at 20 dollars in Newnan or Atlanta. I give 5. I hope they will please you at any rate, and if they do, I shall be more than pleased, for every act of my life I intend shall be for your pleasure and comfort, if I am capable of making you happy. Good night, darling.

76

Mount Sterling, Ky., Sept. 26th, 1862

MY SWEET & EVER LOVED KITTIE, Once more I have the opportunity of enjoying sweet converse with you through the medium of my pen. I have had no chance to get a letter to you in more than a month. I have been quite well since I wrote to you last & am now in as good health as you every saw me. You cannot imagine what pangs of grief I have suffered on your account. I know you imagine you will never see me again, but darling, keep in good heart. I think I will, if I donnot die from disease. This is the finest country you ever saw, & the best people inhabit it in the world. The ladies are kind & generous. Nothing they have is to[o] good for us. I have seen many beautiful & accomplished ladies since I left you, but none so lovely, so sweet, so angelically great as yourself. Doubtless you think, my dear, that I have forgot to love you, but you need not. So long as this heart beets it will beet tones of love for you. Honey, if I get a milion of miles from you & am gone twenty years, I will only love you the more. Without you the universe would be blank. I do hope you & little Kitten have been well since I left you. If I could but know that much even, how happy I would be. My only desire as I cannot see you is for you & Laura to keep well. Our march has been as brilliant an affair as ever was undertaken. Our force has been in four miles of Cincinati. I judge we will take that place before we stop. We could have takened it once, but we would have had to evacuate it again.

Darling, rest as easy as you can about me. Always rest assured that I will ever love you as dearly as ever under all & any circumstances. It's my pride & my heart's delight to do so. So long as this heart beets it will beet alone for you & little Laura, two of the greatest & most lovely of all human beings. I do love you beond what I can express. Honey, take good care of yourself & Laura. I do want you to keep well so bad. Pappie will see you again some day. Honey, do try to raise Laura right. I know you will do that without my asking you to do so. She is such a pleasure to us, I wish I could get to keep her company as you do. Oh how pleasant it would be! I look forward with bright antisipation to the time where we will meet again. How happy we will be! I often imagine how happy we would be to see each other. Tell Lou if he has not started yet to be shure to bring me a fine military cloak from Atlanta. Let him buy a Surgeon's cloak. He can come to us now if he wants to. I want him with me. ours forever more, G.W.P.

Give my love to you Ma & Pa, Dr. Lane & Kit, & all the rest of the family. Let me hear all the news. I have the best horse for you in the world. If I had to come home I will bring him to you.

At top of letter: Direct your letters to me Lexington, Ky.

77

Mount Sterling, Ky., Sept. 28th, 1862

MY DARLING PRECIOUS KITTIE,

I wrote you a letter yesterday. For fear you donot get it, I will start another to you to day, Sunday as it is. Honey, I have ere long found out that their is no happyness one earth for me only in your presence. Oh how proud I would be to spend this day with you & Little Sweet Laura! If ever any was truly worshiped in this life, it is you & Laura by me. I think their is none on earth so pure, so lovely, so evry thing that is great as you & her. I often think about what happy moments we have spent togueather with our little girl. I used to have some pleasure in reading your dear letters, but I am now cut off from that enjoyment. How glad I would be to get a letter from you! I will keep writing to you. I donot expect that you will get them all. I wish you could. I imagine they will be some consolation to you. Honey, you must not greave for me. I will come home some day, I know not when. I am in a fine country, get plenty to eat—no danger of starving here. I enjoy myself as well as anyone could under the circumstance, but no one can have much pleasure who loves you & Laura as I do. I see nothing beautiful but what it reminds me of you, the lovliest of all on earth. I have often thought what a mystery it is for a man to be so perfectly carried away as I am with my little family. Honey, I donot know how long we will stay at this place. We never stay more than a day at one place. We have marched since we left Knoxvill about three hundred miles. Our boys seem to stand it very wwell. Capt. Spearman's company is generally well. Say to Hiram McDaniel that Bud is getting on finely. Lt. Stephens we left at Richmond, Ky. quite sick. I hear he is getting well. I supposes he will get up in a few days. Lt. Cato is in bad health, though he keeps up all the time with the Regt. Nute Read is a little sick at present; I suppose will be well in a short time. I know nothing of our destination next. We may march into Ohio ere we stop, though any idea that I would advance in reference to our movements would be intirely speculation, for no one knows but our May. Generals. We will have Ky. clear of the enemy in a short time—I think we will hold it against the world. Kayntuckians are rellying to our standard by the thousands. I never have seen people so proud to see one people as they were to see our army. They welcome us with joy, outstreached arms, & open doors. Their is not end to their hospitality. Honey, if I just had you & Laura with me how I could enjoy their benevolence. Evry child & Lady I see is only beautiful as it has some resemblance of you & sweet Laura. Darling, if ever I get home I can interest you for awhile with a history of my travels through Ky.

Honey, I have two horses now. One of them I will send home to you by the first one with whom I can trust her. She is the prettyest animal & the easiest riding I have ever seen. If you had her at home you would not take seven hundred dollars for her. Foster is getting on finely. I have not seen a Southern paper in two months. Cumberland Gap is now open. I suppose we will have regular mail rout established to Lexington. You must direct your letters to me at Lexington via Knoxville, Tenn. Honey, you must let me know all the news from the boys who are in the army & also about Franklin. I am anxious to hear all the news in the section of country about home.

Give my love to all the family, Dr. Lane's, & Honey, do think of me as often as it is plesent for you, & always remember that their [is] one far away who love[s] you with his whole heart. Kiss Little Kitten for me. Donot let her forget Pappie, for he loves her dearly.

I hope Lou will come on a short time. Yours even more with a heart full of love for you,

G.W. Peddy

78

September the 28/62

MY DARLING,

I cannot abandon my self to the pleasurs of dreamland untill I hold sweet converse with my darling, although I often try to express the entire devotion of a heart entirely yours. The queen of night in all her radience and splendor looks down and sheds a holy light on many thousands various scenes, and listens to thousands of expressions of devotion from humane beings, yet on none does she unvaile her loveliness to, that loves with an undying devotion as I do. I have been thinking of you more to day than ever before. Shurely you are in no danger. That makes me feel so sad about you. If I could see you once more, you don't know how glad I would be to see my dear. Honey, I am quite well to night, and Piggie is just as fat as any little thing you ever did see. I tell her of you often, yet I fear she wount know you, for it seems to me you have been gone for a year. Mrs. Turner has heard that her brother, John P. Rains, was killed in the fight at Richmond, Kentucky; but she is not satisfied about it and wishes you to enquire of the people or who ever knows about the battles there; and write to me soon all you hear.

I went down to see Mrs. Oliver this evening. She has been quite sick for several days. I think so much of her: she is a good friend [of] ours, and is so anxious for us to live down close to her. Mr. Oliver says Laura was a very pretty baby but no prettier than his.

Honey, I have just been to hear a man from Kentucky preach. He is a refugee driven from home and loved ones. He is a great preacher. He carried us back in our imagination to the time of our innocent youth when a loved mother fondly pressed our brows with loving lips, and bade us live in accordance with God's holy word, which we thought then we would do, but afterwards, association with the world drove off those feeling, and the heart had wandered off in sin far from a good kind benefactor. My darling I thought of you more then than I ever did, for I knew that you have a good mother whose heart has been often wrung with agony when she remembered her dear son exposed to death so often and yet unprepared to meet your God. Oh! how our poor hearts are torn with grief when we bid those we love dearer than life adieu, when perhaps we may see each other once more, but in the vast eternity we must part forever and forever. My darling, I know this is an unpleasant subject to you, yet I can't help but tell you how happy, how very happy I should be to know that you had given your heart to God, and that when life, which is but a troubled dream, is over, we may live to gather in that better land where no bitter parting are known. I have just heard of the death of Dr. Redwine of St. Cloud. He is very much missed by the people, for Drs. are scarce now. I don't know what disease killed him. Pa was sent for this evening to go out to assist in burrying him in Masonic honors. Honey, do be careful of your health, for I am uneasy about you. I do want to see you so much. It nearly grieves me to death to think what a long time must pass away till you can [come] home. Honey, I always commence with love and end with that delightful subject. I know you don't have the time to think of me as often as I do you. *Good by.*

79

Oct. the 9, 1862

MY LOVED ONE,

How can I stand it much longer, not to hear from you? My darling, where are you oh! where can you be this stormy nigh[t] while the wind moans and howls arou[n]d the house and through the trees? I do feel desolate and broken hearted—nothing to live for. Honey, have you forgot your poor babie or have you ceased to love her? Shurely this Earth never had so much Sorrow in its beautis. I read over all your letters, and oh! it give me such intense joy to read those words of love. It flows through my heart like a perfect torrent of delight. Honey, you will doubtless think very strange that I write to you so much at once, but I can't send the letters, so I will keep them untill your cloths are sent. Then you will have a long letter to read if you like them. Grand Ma sent for [me] last Thursday. I spent several days with her very pleasantly. She speaks very kindly of you; said you must never come back unless you come to see her. She excused you the other time because you did not have any conveyance. She is now engaged studying her plands for moving to Newnan. Your Mother and William came Monday last. They left all well but Ann. William could not stay long enough for her to get through brother John's cloths. I will go home with her and stay a short time. As your father is so anxious for me to go, I don't see how to get out of it, but I can't stay long, for I can't hear from my darling. I know you will not be displeased with me, honey, for you know I love you better than all else in this world. I can get shoes out there for something like a reasonable price. Here I can't get them for no price at all, for all the shoe factories are working for the government.

Oct. the 14, 1862

I have just written to you and sent it by mail, but perhaps you will not get it, and I will send a long one to tire you out by bud Lu. I have been so distressed to[o] about your coat. I thought it would not fit and was almost miserable for several hours. Pa tried it on and said he knew it would fit just as nice as any thing could; but I do hate to work as hard, as I have thinking all the while it was going to be extra nice and just as I finish it, be disappointed, but I do hope it will be just as you like it. I have wove and spun all of it and therefore must be pardoned for being some what proud of it. We have just heard that Hugh Vickers was dead. I can hardly believe it, for shurely it can't be so; but many brave and gallant heart lies cold and stif to nigh[t] wrapped in his soldier blanket in solitude and gloom. No friendly eye above them weep, no flowers around them bloom, but there is one noble brave heart which I earnestly trust will be spared, and is you, my darling. Oh! how long will it be ere I am clasped near its strong beatings and feel that the cold blast of the world unfeelingness can not be felt by me, for I am she[l]tered securely in my darling's love.

Honey, we are far apart, but one in heart and what ever may come let life's cares be chased away by the blessed light of true love. I know it beguiles a many weary hour to me. But, my love, it is getting late in the night and I must close, for I am somewhat tired sewing so steady. So Good by, love. Laura['s] little bright eyes are closed in sleep. Honey, I am just going to start to see you father in the morning, but can't stay but a short time. Kate

---

80

Tazewell, Ten., Oct. 23rd, 1862

WELL, MY DARLING, ONE OF THE SWEETEST OF ALL ON EARTH TO ME, After marching over the state of Ky., the most fertile & beautiful country on earth & inhabited by the most hospitable people, the land of Clay & the home of the lamented Daniel Boon, we have returned to the Land of Dixie, the dearest land to me because it is the land of my hearth, my native home, the place whare my dearest idols are, whare resides you & Laura, the fairest of the fair & the most lovely of all to me. Honey, you cannot imagine how proud I feel in getting back to the South whare I can hold sweet converse with you through the pen. I feel like their was a mountain moved off of me since I got south of Comberland Gap. The Comberland between Ten. & Ky. is in the way greatly to the acquisition to our Confederacy [of] the State of Ky. I am afraid now that we will never get Ky. It is gone, I think, with the north; if so, the South has lost the finest country in the world. You may say to Esq Oliver that we went to Lexington, Frankford, & almost evry town in the State. We have marched since we left Knoxville about seven hundred miles. Our troops are well nigh worne down. We lost a great many men that had to be left in consequence of sickness. We have been into no fight since we left, but come very near several times. Honey, you must not conclude that I think of you less often by receiving so few letters from me. I have had no chance to convey letters to you until now. The last I received from you was at Georgetown, Ky., bearing date of Aug. 29th.[10] I have just received a letter from Mrs. Glover, making enquiries about her son, Mc Glover. I will answer it in short time. Mack is quite well. He has been sick twice since he left home, but is now as well as he ever was in his life. He is tired of marching. Isac Gorden is quite sick. I am keeping him along with me. James Paschal has been, but is now getting well. He has been as low as men ever get to live. Bud McDonald is sick at this time, threatened with Pneumonia. I keep him along by walking & letting him ride my fine mar or yours. Honey, I hapened to get with the best man in the world for a Col. Col. Watkins is one of the best man that lives except your Pa. Darling, the news is that we will be

---

[10]This letter is missing.

stationed at Blains & Roads, seventeen miles above Knoxville, Ten. If Lou wants to join our Regt. he had better come to us now. Honey, I am as near naked as I have been in my life. I want you to send my close on just as soon as you can. I wish a roundabout, coat, vest, & pants, & some wolen shirts of some kind. If you do not send them by Lou, send them in a box with my name plainly written on the box per express & take the express receipt for them to Knoxville. I will need some socks also, but Darling, donot work to[o] hard to make them. I had rather buy them if I could find them to buy than for you to tire yourself making them. You & Laura are my only jewels & you must take care of yourselves, for if I should loose you I should not want to live longer. Honey, please send them to me imeditely, for I will be out of a coat to wear by the time they get here. Darling, I have not drawn any money yet. I will draw in a short time. The Confederacy owes me now over eight hundred dollars, & I will send it to you as soon as I get it. Darling, I would try to come to see you, but think it would be us[e]less, for I have no idea that I could get a furlough. Nothing could make me more happy than to see you now. It seems to me that I have been gone from you two or three years. I am so glad that you were proud of the things I sent you from Boston. I will send your Ma some if I can find them. Honey, I would give any price if you had my fine Mair at home. She will just suit you to ride. She is the prettyest thing you ever saw. I have been offored in Ky., whare horses are cheep, three hundred & fifty dollars by several. I ask six hundred for her. I think I will get it if I can get her to Georgia. I gave three for her. I wish your Pa could see her. I think he would want to give me a thousand for her. Honey, I have the prettyest dressing box for Laura you ever saw. It was a present to me. I will send it to Laura the first opportunity. You must Kiss Laura for Pappie & tell her he loves her evry day & evry moment. Honey, let me have in your next all the news, how things are & how the people talk & get on. I will write you again in a few days. Let me hear from you as soon as you can write & send the clothes as early as possible. Lou had better come on to the Regt. as soon as possible if his Pa cannot get him a position any whare. Give my love to all the relatives. I close, my dear, with the fond hope of seeing a letter from you soon & also, if an opportunity presents, of once more beholding that lovely form of your[s] & kissing those sweet ruby lips.

Your truely until death,
G. W Peddy

To Mrs. Z. C Peddy
Franklin Ga

P.S. Direct your letter to me Knoxville, Surgeon, Gen. D. Ledbetter's Brig.[11]

[11]Dr. Peddy was at home on furlough during the last week in October 1862.

81

Atlanta, Ga., Nov. 1st, 1862

MY DARLING, I cannot get me an overcoat no way here. I want you to buy the jeans at Mozeley's & make me one by the time Capt. Spearman comes to camps. He has a furlough for thirty days. I have drawn my money here up to date. I will send you the greater part of it per John Daniel or Nathan Fomely, [?] who is at camps. From your true lover, G. W. Peddy

I am getting better, I think. Honey, when you think of me, alway think I love you better than all earth combined. If you want any sugar, send up here & get it. You can buy good sugar a[t] sixty cents per pound. G W Peddy

---

82

Lenoir's Station, Ten. Nov. 9th, 1862

MY OWN SWEET DARLING, it is my good pleasure this morn to drop you a few lines per Mr. John Daniel, who leaves for home to day & will bring you five hundred & fifty dollars for me. Honey, always keep on hand about two hundred dollars. I have recovered my health compleetly. I am as well & as corpulent as I was before I was taken sick. When we take up winter quarters I want you to come to see me. I expect we will leave here in a short time. Evry body says I have the prettyest suit they ever saw & I tell them it was all made by your dear lovely hands. I admire it the more for that reason. My heart leeps with joy at the thought of having for my companion the perfect embodiment of all that's lovely, inteligent, & wise, one of nature's noblest ones. Honey, I am so lonsome since I left you. I do wish I could stay with you this winter, but oh, their is no chance unless you come to me. You must keep little Kitten warm this winter. Honey, I often think of how corpulent & sweet you were when I was with you last. It seem I cannot get the chance to send Liz to you. I do wish you had her: she would suit so well. I suppose we will go from here to Myrphyburrough. Can't tell, though, as yet. We all have tents now. We are getting on finely; great many sick. Honey, tell Lou to spurr up Brickell about my boots & be shure to bring them & my Cloak you are making wtih him. You must have the cape in front to come toguether before the edges of the coat meet. May your life ever be one continual stream of happyness. Your forever

G. W. Peddy.

83

Lenoir's Station, Nov. 15th, 1862

MY DARLING, THE SWEETEST & MOST PRECIOUS ON EARTH, It is my good pleasure to reply to your sweet letter per Mr. Boyd. I read it with great pleasure & joy as I always do. They always bear the sentiments of love to my unworthy self. I am proud & almost overjoyed at times at the happy thought of your accomplishments, your greatness, & your high feelings of love for me. Honey, I am so tired of this war. I do wish I could pass the remainder of my life in your dear presence. It would be one of continual happyness.

Notwithstanding it has been but a few days since I left you[r] lovely presence, I want to see you worse than ever. It seems almost like a life time. I do wish I could be with you to day. How happy I would be, but oh. I cannot nor know not when I will meet your lovely form again uneless you come to see me. That would be so much trouble to you & such an expence that I forbear to ask it of your noble self. Honey, I have sent you my fine mair per Foster. I expect if he has had good luck he will reach you ere this letter does. I hope you will ride her down town to the Office to get this letter. She looks very rough in consequence of having to take the weather. She will look all right by the time she stays in the stable a short time. You had better buy about ten barrels of corn before it rises. Let me know how you & your Pa is pleased with her. You must not sell her for less than six hundred dollars, if that. If you like her & she suits you I will not sell her at any price. I will keep her to carry your dear sweet self. I would give no little am't to see you dressed up & on her. I would go into extices. My evry effort is to render you happy & plesent. If I can accomplish that, I will ever feel relieved to no little extent. Honey, I hate to trouble you to make me an army cloak, but to save money I will have to ask it of you. I intended that you should buy the gray jeans that Moseley & Land had to make it, but they have brought it away since you looked at it. You must get it done if you can & send it per Capt. Spearman. If you donot, I will have no chance to get it. Evry body brags on my suit you made me. I would not take nothing in the world for it because you made it with your own dear hands. We will leave here on Monday next for Murphisburrough, Ten. I donot know as yet whare to tell you to direct your letter to. Mr. John Harris wife got here last nighgt. She came to see her son Abe, who I had sent to the Atlanta Hospital the day before. I was glad to see her indeed. We sat up and talked a great deal last night. She taken supper & breckfast with me. Honey, let me hear from you evry opportunity. Tell Brit Ware his nephew Strong is in the Hospital in Atlanta. I tried to furlough him, but could not. My love to all. Yours ever G W Peddy

84

Bridgeport, Ala. Nov. 18th, 1862

THE SWEETEST OF ALL, MY DARLING WIFE KITTIE, We arrived at this place today. We are on our raid to Murphysburrough. I was in hopes we woud stay here three or four weeks so that you might come to see me, for it looks like I cannot do without seeing you longer. I often think of our unalloyed pleasure when at home, which constrains me to want to see you worse than anything else. You were so fat & pretty, I nearly go beside myself thinking about you. Honey, I do wish you could realize how well I love you. I think no one on earth can love as I love you. The more I am with you, the more I desire to continue with you. If I could get out of the service any way honorable, I would do so, so that I could enjoy the greatest of pleasures, which is being with your dear self. Darling, if I knew whare we would stop at & wheather I could get a house for you to stay at, I would ask you to come to see me with Lou when he comes, but not knowing this fact, I am obliged to forego the pleasure of shaking that lovely little hand & kissing those ruby lips of yours, which speak words of love to me when I am with you that vibrate in my ears for days after I leave you. Your lovly self is often in my imagination. It appears I can trace evry feature as though you were with me, but oh!, drawing you up in my imagination is only a foretaste of the pleasure of being the reality itself. Honey, I cannot tell or describe how happy it makes me to see you. Language is inadequate to the task.

You can tell Lou & Capt. Spearman whare we are, and we may stop before we get to the above mentioned place. I donot think we will leave the rail road again at least until spring. I am in hopes we will go into winter Quarters about Chattanooga o[r] some whare near. If we do, darling, I will send for you, & what a happy time we will have. The winter is to[o] cold for you to sleep without me. I want Foster to come back with Lou. *Darling*, send me something to eat per Lou—some potatoes anyhow. I eat a splended breckfast in Chatanooga this morning. It made me think of being at your Pa's. Honey, you must send me a good letter per Lou. I must close: the train is about to start.

Give my love to all.

Yours forever more

G. W Peddy.

To Mrs. Dr G.W Peddy
Franklin/Ga.

85

Franklin, Nov. the 19, 1862.[12]

MY OWN DARLING,

With a heart full of love for you, my darling, I will commence a letter to you. I would send it by mail before bud Lu goes, but don't know where you are. I heard two days ago your regment had been sent on towards Nashville. Honey, while I write, the rain is pattering softly on the top of the house produceing a pleasing kind of langor and enticeing one to try the pleasures of dreamland. I always enjoyed such nights before you left me. Now as I lay me down on my soft good bed I wonder and wish that my darling was enjoying such comforts. It robs all such pleasures of their keenest enjoyment. I am not very well to night, hony, therefore cannot interest you very much. Foster got through day before yestady. I am delighted with my horse. She is a beauty. Every one thinks that of her. Pa says she is too nice for me, I don't deserve such splendid looking animals. Ambrose Williams will take her tomorrow. He wants to brake her to harness as you wished. I have not rode her, bud Lu says she is very scarry and thinks her too much so for me to ride her, but I think I will try her any how soon. Honey, I do want to see you worse than any thing on Earth, for no pleasure is like that which your love and presence gives: it is an elixir that thrills heart and being with a joy as intense as it is lasting and pleasant. I get your good sweet letters sometimes and read them. While I do, it seems to me I must see you soon, for all is dark, drear, and lonesome without you. My love, you write me such nice letters. Oh! how they bring back the features that joy used to wear, causeing the heart to throb with renewed happiness. Yet there is an echo of sadness breathing over all the joy, a spell which tell too unmistakeable that all is not weil within, and that unhappiness is caused by your being absent and surrounded as you are by temptations which try all the strength of manhood nobler instincts to resist. The inebriating bowl comes before a worn weary soldier in a more tempting and excuseible form in camps than else where, for he thinks that it can do no harm when he is so tired, so he indulges for a while, thinking it will do good, untill he cannot resist, and it fastenes him as one of the many victims of an untimely and ignominious grave. But, my love, I need not thus talk to you, for I know your nobleness too well to think you could ever do any thing to make yourself or our blue eyed darling to blush, for you have too much sence and then love your two babies too well to cause our hearts to ache with grief. Honey, I do wish I could always be with you. Then it matters not

[12]Envelope addressed: Dr. G.W. Peddy, 56 Ga. Reg., Col. Watkin[s] Command; Care of L.H. Featherston.

what any one can say about me. It does not hurt me one bit. I have worn your cloak twice, and I heard Mrs. Grimes had considerable to say about it, but I try not to think of it. I intend to have the cloak altered to fit me, but won't untill I get ready. Honey, don't less us settle here, for I don't want to raise Laura in such society. She will be surrounded all the time by people who don't have any of the characteristics that make a noble creature. My love, I cannot write any thing interesting to night. I am nearly done your over-coat and I think it very nice, but it cost high. Next winter I will weave you a fine one that will look nicer than this one. I don't think you will get cold this winter, for you will have such warm clothes, and it gives me infinite satisfaction to think that I have done all that I could to render you comfortable while endureing so many hardships. We have just received a letter from bud Nick last mail day. He was standing camp life very well. His position is a good one to protect his health. He don't think brother Johni in any danger of taking the smallpox, if it realy is that, for he is in advance of the regment. Little Kitten, papie, is the sweetest child in the world. You ought to have heard her singing "Lottie Love" today. Ma says if you should never come back, Laura would never forget you, for she never saw a child love a parent as well as she love you. It is all she thinks about, all she loves. I asked her to day who loved me; she said, papie. I then asked he[r] how she knew. She replied: he kiss you. Every day she begs to ride Lizzie Welch. Bud Gily says my horse is the best riding horse he ever saw. Ambrose Williams got on her yestady to see how she rode and he was delighted. He wants her to ride untill the ground gets dry so he can break her. I am sorry for bud Gily. He can't get suited in a boarding house and he was in hopes you would conse[n]t for me to go down to keep house. Chippie has been down too and does hate it so bad. I think they will have a good school next year, that is, if the war don't have a use for bud Gily and he can't get off. My love, I had a perfect feast of the heart and mind to day, for I had two sweet letters from you. It is impossible for me to tell you how much pleasure it gives me to read you loving letters. Honey, I can't see how you can love an unworthy being as I am so dearly. If I could by any act of mine do any thing which would justyfy you in being proud of me, as I am of you, it would give me joy indeed. If we should spend the remainder of our lives in each other's society, we could then know the extent of our love for each other. You spoke of doing all you could to make me happy. Honey, I cannot look back on our past lives but what I see all a long the past every act of your life was kindness and love to me, and it seems to me I can never repay you, but Darling, I do love you more than I ever thought a humane being capable; and it is my very life to love you so well. I hardly ever pass over a day but what I am surprised to think that I am so much more blest than most of women. What is life worth living for but to love, if the object is worthy? Honey, I can't tell you how proud I am of my darling, and I talk so much of you that no doubt I tire some people out, for I think all who knew you should love and esteem you. Pa thinks my horse the finest saddle horse he ever saw. He rode her to La Grange yestady and it did not complain of being tired at all. He says he must have her any how, but she is very wild. She came very near throwing Pa twice. He says she is more dangerous than Nell. Hony, I am afraid you disfurnished you[r]self to send me your horse, for you have to ride so much you should have a easy rideing horse. I am so proud of her I don't know how to thank you for your kindness. If she will only work kindly to the buggy, I will be so delighted. If you could only get off from this cruel war, we could be so well fixt to enjoy life. I have paid Mr. Pace. You owe him, Dr. Grimes, and Jim Hales. You did not say any thing about yours and Mr. Mabr's settlements. If you owe any one else, write me word and I will pay them. I don't want to think of our being in debt again. Hony, I do want to spend this Winter with you, but I think it will cost so much. You can't afford to spend so much just to be with me, though it would give me more joy than any thing in the world. Pa says if you take up winter quarters any where near Myrphysbourh, he will go to see you, for all his relatives live in and near that place. I do want to stay with you any where. I don't care: it would be bliss to me, but a great trouble to you, my love.

86

Tallahoma, Ten. Nov. 23rd, 1862

MY DEAR DARLING WIFE KITTIE, It is my sweet pleasure to write you a few lines. I am not well at this time, but think I will be in a short time. I have got well of my diarrhoea & am looking as well as you have seen me. I suppose it is cold that achs me when I lay down at night. I cannot sleep for headache & soreness all through my back. I am so sore that I can scarcely turn over when I am laying down, but after I get up, I feel very well, the pain & soreness all leaves me. Honey, let me hear from you by Lou. It gives me no little pleasure to hear from you. Dear, I would be so happy to see you, but it is impossible. I wish the war would close so that I could be in your dear presence. I will never be happy until I am in a condition to be with you all the time. It does look so crewel to spend the bloom of our lives absent from each other. I have got Lou a nice position as Brig. Q[u]arter Master Sergent, which puts him on a horse & takes him out of all danger. You must not say anything about it for fear something might happen that he would not get it. I told the Maj. Q.M. that I would write to Lou's Pa about it to day & he said he might depend upon his giving it to Lou. He will rank as orderly Sergent.

Honey, I have the headache a little, which puts me in such a woold gathering condition that I cannot write. I have heard that we go from hear to Manchester, Ten. I donot think we will stay in this portion of Ten. long. I think we will winter on the South side of the Ten. River. If we do, honey, you must come to see me. Direct you letter to me at Tullahoma, Ten. Honey, if this reaches you before Lou leaves, give him $25.00 to bring me. I heard to day that Foster stayed in Carrolton to day (Sunday) was a week ago. I am glad to hear he got on safe that far with Miss Lizza. I have heard bad tales about the women in Carroll. That society is going to nought. Your cousins, Marry & Chippie, have been to see you. Perhaps they told you about them. They say in Carrolton on mail days the women from the country come to get letters from their friends in the war, & such things as are carried on is to sad to tell off. I hope the women of our county will let no such reports get out on them.

My love to all.

Kiss Laura for Pappie. Yours, yours, yours,

G W Peddy

87

Nov. the 23, 1862.

MY DEAREST ONE,

It is God's holy sabbath day, one in which he has set apart to do his holy will more perfectly in regard to prepareing to live in a better hous when life's troubled dream is over. Honey, you must forgive me for talking to you of such things, and I know I am very imperfect myself, yet I do earnestly wish you all the happiness in this life and perfect happiness in the next; and I know to secure that, we must try to do the will of him who sitteth on the great white throne and in whose presence alone is joy forever more. Ah! how it wrings our hearts with the bitters agony that mortal beings know to say that dreaded word farewell to our heart's treasures, but it is only for a short time, and if we should be so unfortunate to bid each other adieu in that final day, how terible, and then it is for eternity. My love, never does a night pass over my head before I close my eyes but I aske a kind father, who never slumbers and who is able to keep you from all harm, to guard and surround you with his care and to bring you safely back again to me. I know you have not time, and surrounded as you are by circumstances so opposite to any thing which renders man better, yet I do wish you would do that which will secure you eternal happiness. Honey, don't be offended by my writing to you about this subject. I know you have never loved to hear of it.

Nov. the 24. My love, I am again seated at an ever delightful task of writing to you, though I fear by the disconnected uninteresting way in which I have written this letter you wil get weary before you are half through reading. I had rather talk to you now than to write, for you know I am an untireing talker when with you. Bud Lou does hate to go so bad [I feel sorry for][13] him. You must be kind to him, but I know you will. He is often rash and hasty in speaking, yet he is one of the most generous hearted boys I ever saw. I don't know, hony, whether you will like your coat or not. I never noticed a military cape and don't know how to make one fit. Yet I have done the best I could. Hony, get some one of your lady friends to sew on your buttons for you. I did not put as many buttons on it as should be, but you can have more on. Don't buy any buttons from Brewer Lane if you can get them any where else. Mr. Oliver and Pace have had a quarrel about some hogs. Mr. O[liver] wanted to fight, but could not get the chance. It [is] bad for two men living so close to fall out that way. Hony, please send me that bolt of cloth you have by the first one you can trust it with, and if you can get any worsted cheap up there, get me and L[aura] some dresses. There is no dress goods here at no price. Brother Giles wants to buy your cloak you had on the coast last year. He can't buy one nowhere. He will give 15 dollars or more if you want to sell it, so be shure to write me word as soon as you get this what to do. I don't think I can alter it to make it look well for me. Honey, I am affraid we will have trouble this winter with the negroes. I do wish you could get off and come home Chrismast and then I would not feel uneasy at all. I should think you would get off. This morning Laura was sitting talking and I writing. She looked up all at once and said, Mama, write me one yetter. I asked her what for. She said to send to her papie, so I wrote her one just to please her. I had just got up and was walking to the fireplace with her when I hurt my foot severely. I sat down in the first chair I [came] too. She looked like she was distressed to death for fear I would cry. All at once she looked up with a brightened face and said, Mama, hush, Pappie will tote you. She is like her mother, believes you can make all things right. Ah, if I could only be [n]ear[14] you to night! How happy! It seems to me that I get more anxious every day to see you than ever. Instead of getting use to staying away from you, I get worse, It seems so many months instead of weeks that you have been gone. Honey, you know how well I love you almost, for I know that I do love you a great deal more than you do me. I often dream such sweet dreams of you. The other night I dreamed of having my arms around you. When I awoke, I was almost certain I had you, but it was little Kitten. She had laid on my arm

---

[13]The top os the page is torn.

[14]There is a hole in the page.

till it was almost dead. Ambrose Williams is going to sconscript all to forty now soon. Uncle Joe is bothered nearly to death, for he will have to go as a private. I expect he wishes he had still mad[e] up his old company, for there is a good deal of difference in a private and captain. Bettie, his little girl, has dipthra. It is proving very fatal here now. It keeps me in continual dread about Laura, for you know she once had the throat affection, and it might prove fatal if she takes it. Annie is very sick now. I am affraid she will never get well. Dr. Harlan came up this morning and said she had the intermittent fever. There is considerable sickness about here now. Honey, please send me some writing paper by the first one passing. I write so much it takes a good deal to do me. You must write as soon as you get this so I will know where to direct my lett[er]s. Foster has just come in to tell us all good by, and it made me think of the time when he came in for that purpose, the first time you left, how it touched you even to see a negro telling his home folks goodby. It is the thought that gives me the most happiness of all others to think how much you grieve to have me, for I know you do love me then or you would not dislike leaving so much. Honey, I am nearly sick with a cold to night. My head achs severely, therefore you need not be surprised to read a very uninteresting letter. All sent their love to you, but I send as much as you want and will keep a supply till you come back, which I do hope will not be many days before it is my happy lot to wellcome you home again. Pa is going to Atlanta Thursday with bud Gily to have him examined so that the conscript won't take him.

Yours ever more. Honey, I do hate to quit. It nearly kills me to say good by. If this war continues two more years, I fear it will run me crazy or kill me one.

Kate Peddy

88

Manchester, Tenn. Dec. 3rd, 1862

MY DEAR WIFE KITTIE, It is my happy pleasure to write you a few lines this eve. Kittie, I am quite unwell at this time, but hope I will get right in a few days. I feel much better this eve than for several days previous. I will come home if I donot get well before long. Honey, I feel sad. I have lost about $225 in my pearse, which was stolen from the Wagon train in Chattanooga on the way to this place. I will never get him I have no idea. I will have to buy me another. I am so glad I sent the Mair home. She might have been stolen to if I had not. I ought not to grumble: I have always had good luck before; but that is a back set that I am very poorly prepaired to receive at this time, for you & Laura stands in need of evrything I can make. I will not dispair at that but live closer to try to make it back in some way. If I were to loose all by you & Laura, I would feel immensly rich then, for you, the perfect imbodiment of evrything that is beautiful, lovely, & grand, is enough to cheer any one to the highest pinicale of faim & honor. Honey, all who knows you must join in praise of your greatness unless it's some one who envies your position in life. Honey, I am encamped close to a good band. When it begins to play, it always reminds me of you & makes me think more about you. I do love to live to admire & worship you & our dear little Laura. Lou & Capt. Spearman has not come yet. They will be here this eve or tomorrow. How proud I will then be. I will get to read a sweet letter from my loved one. I hope they will bring an Army Cloak & Boots. I am in great need of them, for we have very rough weather here. It seems to be moderating for the present. Honey, we have some of the finest Apples here I ever saw, but I can get no chance to send you any. If I do, I will send you enough to do you some time. There is no express up here by which I could send them or I would do so. Honey, send to Atlanta & get you some & you can their buy cakes of all descriptions for you & Laura. You had better buy you some flour & shugar. You can then do your own eating at home. I hope you & Lizza are getting on finely. I will buy me a cheap horse so if I loose him I will not loose much. Honey, you must direct your letters to me Manchester, Tenn., Gen. Taylor's Brig., 56th Regt., & I will get them. It seems like to months since I got a letter from you. Honey, you must write to me often, for I do love to read your dear letters. I think if the enemy will make a demonstration in front we will fall back to Bridgeport. Then you can come to see me. Then how delighted I will be: my heart would be overwhelmed with joy at the sight of your dear lovely self. Give me all the news about Franklin & what the conscript is doing & who it's taking. I fear it will take off many whose families will suffer.

Give my love to Dr. Lane & wife, you Pa & Ma, the Children &c. Kiss Laura for Papie. Tell her to kiss Ma, sweet Ma, for me.

Yours forever more truely,

G.W. Peddy

89

Franklin, Dec. the 5, 1862.

MY OWN DEAR DARLING HUSBAND,

Words cannot express how much I long to see you again. Every day and hour seems longer ten fold than it did when you were here. I love to live to love you and Laura. You sometimes sayed I did not seem to think as much of you as you did of me, but ah! you little know what an ocean of affection that is only stired by your love. Perhaps you will think me foolish and void of any delacacy to be thus all ways writing, but to save me, I can't think of any thing else. I wish I did know what would interest you most. Laura, the little darling, gets more interesting every day. She tries to say every word she hears any one else say. The other day Amanda came up to dress Laura and brought a very red apple that her brother gave her the night before, and just as soon as Laura saw it, she would not be satisfied till Manda gave it to her. I tried to get it away, but no, she would scream every time we would go towards her. I then bought it from Mandy, though I hated to let Laura take it all away. She went to the farthest end of the room and set down and munched it all up. This is a long story about nothing, you will say, no doubt. Brother Gily has gone up to St. Cloud to get him a school. He has been once before, and thinks he will succeed in getting a very good one. He says he would be the best pleased in the world to go down to see you but thinks it would cost so much.

We heard the other day that bud Nick and his company was on the way home, but don't know how true it is. Brother John or bud Nick either has enlisted again. Brother John says he will go over to his father's and make him up a company and go, but don't want to go in that company he is in. The petition signers did not affect much by their smartness. Pa went to see Gartrell not long ago. He was very friendly and sayed a great many complimentary things about bud Nick as an officer and a gentleman; and that he knew nothing about he pe[ti]tion whatever. He thought the company generally was well pleased with their captain, and when he went back, he would do his best to stop it. Gartrell and the commissary, Wilson, had a difficulty and several others, so that the noted Col. has but few friends excep amongst the low rowdies.

Jessy Winchester was brought home a corps yestady and burried to day with marshal honors. He died with typhoid pneumonia. I was very sorry to hear it, for he was truly a clever boy. Henry Free also died a short time ago, with measels. He was the grandson of a very old lady by the name of Parker, who lived up at Tom Johnson's old place. He was all the support she had, and now he is dead, she is truely in a distressing condition. Six of Lee Williams' company have died. Tobe Wood is back now on a furlough for sixty days. He has rumatism. I have not seen him. Mabry is here yet. He got ready, and the very morning he was to leave, he took a hard chill and has been laid up ever since. Mrs. Mabry was up here this morning and insisted I should come to see her soon. I did not say what I would do. Mrs. Grimes has open a select school. She has three sholars. I think the girls are quite cresfalen because John Boddie did not call to see them when he was at La Grange the last time. They said they knew he would be shure to come, and would be so glad to see him. They intended to fix him up a box and send it by uncle Joe, but he was coming home and that was so much better. Lizzie Filpot married Chrismast eve to Dr. Britton. They had a good large crowed.

You must try and rent the Garden and patches that belong to the hotel where Houston lived when you come through Newnan from Wilkerson. I am going to plant our garden and have it all ready when you come back to have plenty of vegetables. Lance Boggus says he will let you have some corn, but I don't know how much. I would be glad to get any. I have not received a letter from you in over a week. I am like you. I want to hear from [you] every week and oftener, if not interfering with your duties, I am so eager for every mail and every letter. I think may be it will tell me the glorious news when you are coming. I dreamed you came home the other night, and I was nearly crazy with joy, but you seemed indifferent. I wanted to know if you did not love me. You said, yes, but did not love me as much as you did before you had learned to stay away. I awoke in great distress, and all the next day it would come into my thoughts oftener than I wished.

I must close, for it is late and very cold. Don't say this is such a short letter. I will do better in future. Goodnight, darling, may angels keep their gentle watch over you while you slumber and from all harm when you awake. Laura sends a kiss from sweet little lips and a hug with her little chubby round arms. All the children send their love to you and bud Lu. Tell him I will write to him soon. Ambrose Williams is getting well and will start back soon. Henry Turner is here yet. He is not well, but is improving fast. You had better get you some cloth as you come through Savanah[15] for a shirt and let me make it while you are here.

Once more, good by. Kate Peddy

P S Alen Pri died last week.

I thought last night I would not write any more, but this morning being refreshed by a good night's sleep, I concluded to finish this page, though I have no interesting news to write. Laura got up soon this morning and is now laughing and playing with Eddy. I asked her whose baby she was. She said, Pappie's. She can say some words right plain. I know you would nearly eat up

[15]A mistake for Atlanta.

the little sweet if you could see her. She sometimes call[s] me big sis. I have the toothake this morning. I think rather it is produced from cold. Have been weaving very steady for over a week and I think some how I took cold. I am going out to see Lu Hale soon. I have not see her since you went away. Eddy is calling me now to give him the letter to carry to the office. Kate.

90

Readyville, Tenn., Dec. 10th, 1862[16]

MY OWN DARLING SWEET KITTIE,

I read with pleasurable emotions y'r sweet & joyfully interesting letter brought to me by Lou. Honey, y'r admonition was very good. Any advice you give me is worth miriads more than all that could be given by the rest of mankind. Honey, I cannot tell you how proud I was to get that letter & the one from little sweet Laura. I do wish she was able to write to me, but if I can get letters frequent enough from you, I will be satisfied. Honey, you cannot imagine how much I love you. Hea[r]t only knows to tongue can speaketh it not. If I were with you. looks, words, & actions would speak to you, tones of love more real than I can write it. Honey, I cannot tell when I can get to see you again. I suppose it will be some time unless you come to see me. We are now twelve miles north east of Murfreysburro. If y'r Pa wants to come to see his relations, he [can] do so. I expect we will stay here for some time, but cannot tell. We may be ordered of in a few days, or we may remain here for weeks. We are in a fine country here for getting something to eat in the way of meet & bread. Honey, I am so proud of my cloak. I am under everlasting obligation to you for your trouble of making it. I would not take a hundred dollars for it. Their is no chance for me to get cold now; & Brickell sent me the greatest pair of Boots you have ever seen. I wish you could see them. You must repay him for them. Darling, you must not let Ambrose keep up you Mair more than three weeks. I want him to work her in a buggy all the time. I donot want him to ride her, & Darling, you must not let her be rode only with a stiff Bar bit. If she is rode much with the common smooth bit, her gaits will be ruined. You must attend to this, darling. Take the bits of y'r Pa's Buggy Bridle. Honey, I want you to ride the mair. I got her for you to ride. Their is no danger in her if you will put on the bit spoken of before with

---

[16]Envelope: From G.W Peddy, Surgeon 26th Regt Mrs. Dr. G.W Peddy, Franklin, Georgia Per the politeness of Rufus Fergerson

Mortingals. Lou is here & seems to be very well satisfied. I will make him as comfortable as I can so long as he remains in the regt. with me. If the QM gets well, he will take Lou with him. He will then have to leave the regt. Honey, you must direct your letter to Murfreysburro. I will get them—Gen. Taylor's Brig. Honey, oh how I do wish I was with you this lovely eve. How sweetly we could talk & enjoy ourselves togueather. But oh, I must longer with pain forego that pleasure. Let me hear from you soon, my own sweet Wife, the pride of my heart. Their is at this moment a Brass Band going by playing Home Sweet Home. Oh that I were their to enjoy its pleasures & luxuries! Kiss Little sweet Kitten for Pappie.

Yours yours evermore

G W Peddy

My love to all relatives & friends. Consider how you would feel if I were to feel if I were to step in & kiss you after you get the last word of this letter written.

Yours ever
G.W. Peddy
Act. Brig. Surgeon.

91

Franklin, Dec. the 22/62

MY DEAREST ONE,

I know you are like myself, delight[ed] to read letters from loved ones if they are ever so often on hand. My darling, I have been quite sick ever since I wrote to you last untill now. I had three hard chills and high fevers afterwards, which left me very much debilitated. I thought for several days I should have a hard spell of sickness, but I have missed my chill for three nights and now begin to feel better. Honey, you can't tell how much I miss you when I feel sick. Then I remember with tears of sorrow the many thousand tender words and acts which you so fondly bestowed on me and which by their soothing kindness almost banished my pain. My love, I know that I miss you a hundred times more than you do me. I have been thinking all day of the joy I should feel if you should come. It would be two much joy, I fear. Honey, I had the blues last week. Sometimes I thought if I had a severe spell I should never feel the preshure of strong arms around me nor see the fond look of tenderness which you always gave me nor hear the love tones of your dear voice fall with such rapturous melody on my ear as of old. My dear, I am perhaps simple, but when the grim monster comes, I should like to have my head pillowed on your bosome near the heart whose every throb of pure undying love I covet and prize dearer than all else besides. But I will not indulge in any more such fancies, as I know you dislike to hear them. Pappie, you have one of the sweetest little darlings here in the world. She was sitting up late one night. When she happened to look out of doors, it was quite dark. She says, mama, it is so dark. I told her yes, and poor Papie had to sleep out on the ground. She looked, distressed nearly to death for some time. Suddenly she looked up and says, mama, oppen the door so papie can come up tairs and sleep wid us. She then turned round and tried to make sis get out of our bed so her papie would sleep with us. She loves her papie more than she does her mother. Pa has been appointed judge. He received congratulations from all parts of the circut. We have not heard a word from bud Nick or brother John since the battle.[17] I fear they have been hurt.

Tuesday 23.

My love, I am somewhat perplexted to know what to do. Ambrose Williams came up to day and says if he keeps my horse much longer, he will have to sell one of his, as corn is so high and he is charging nothing for keeping her. He has worked her in duble harness some. She works very well there. He wants to keep her this coming year or untill you want her. If he only works a little and then sends her home, Pa won't work her any, and she will only be to breake over. Corn is hard to get at 1 dollar and a half a bushell. I can't find any it seems to me at no price. Honey, I want you to write me word what to do with my horse just as soon as you get this. I don't have any one here to curry and feed a horse. The negroes are always buisy, so if you like it, I will let Ambrose keep her untill he brakes her well. He says he will give me 350 dollars for her any time. He is well pleased with her. I told Pa I could do nothing untill I heard from you. Pa says you must look out for him a fine horse as he will have to have one. Jessy Jackson marries to night. Bud Gily has gone to wait on him. I only wish they may be as happy and well contented in their marriage as I am in mine. I often wish I could live over my life again. What a happy time! At least I would be with my darling, and that is bliss. Honey, I can't get any shoes any where here, it seems. I have tried for some time. I am affraid it was for the want of thicker shoes that I had those chills. I have Amanda and Laura some shoes, so that much is good. Honey, do come home. I will love[18] you nearly to death. I never

---

[17]The battle of Fredericksburg, Va. was fought on 13 December, resulting in the repulse of Union forces under General Ambrose E. Burnside.

[18]The remainder of the letter is written upside down across the tops of the pages.

did want to see you so much as I do now. Honey, I received a letter from you a few days ago telling of the loss of your horse. I should have got it two weeks sooner. I am sorry for you, for you work so hard. I dislike so much for your work to be distroyed without reaping any benefits from it. Mrs. Harris said he was a fine horse two. Pa was so sorry. He talks of it continually. Honey, I don't want any shugar or any of the luxuries of life as long as you are denied even the comforts of life. I hardly ever think of them unless I am sick, as I was last week. Then I give a good deal for just enough shugar to sweeten my coffee. I must close. Kate Peddy. Pappie, Kitten says send her a nice Chrismast present, pese sir. Write as soon as you get this. I want to know what to do with my horse

---

92

On Board Boat, Dec. 30th/62[19]

MY DARLING WIFE KITTIE, I write you a few lines to let you know I am getting on finely. I do wish you were with me. How happy we would be! Lou is well & highly pleased. I did not get his Boots. They were not done. You must be shure to see Lt. Stephens, get him to bring them & a bridle Copeland at Corinth is making for me. I will write you more at length when we get stationed. Let me hear from you, my dear angel, when you can find out whare we are. My Saddlewallets were not found that anyone in the regt. knows off. Kiss Pig for Pa, & let her kiss you for me also. Yours, you know, devotedly,

G.W Peddy

93

Celma, Ala., Dec. 31st, 1862

MY DEAR WIFE, I write you a few lines to night to let you know how I am getting along. I am quite well as to my physical system, but feel miserable sad because I had to leave you so soon as I did. Oh how divinely sweet it is to be in your presence! No mortal on earth was so loved as I do you, my darling one.

---

[19]Dr. Peddy was at home on furlough during the last week of December.

Evry thought, word, & action of your[s] is enough to move the heardest heart of tones of the most genuine love. Honey, it is vain for me to admire & love you as I do. I expect I often weary my friends in talking to them of your loveliness. I cannot help it. My evry pure & genuine thoughts are of you & our sweet little child, Laura, great because she has the inteligence of her noble mother. She will learn from birth the greatness & lovelyness of her mother when I get time to stay with her long enough to tell her. Honey, I believe I will not get my suit. I think I am to extravigant for mine & your future good. I bought you several pieces of music today & mailed them to you. Hope you will get them. I want you to learn them by the time I come to see you again, if I should be so fortunate as to have that good pleasure. Honey, one word you spoke to me while at home has made me very unhappy oftentimes since I left you, that was that you & your Pa did not know I was in debt so much. Darling, I was dissatisfied to make you mine at the time I did because of your better condition in life than mine, but my love for you was of that genuine purity that I could not withhold the propesition that you was so unfortunate to acceed to. I am proud you did so & am proud that I have such a noble one, & if I deceived you, I cannot but ask when it's to late your pardon, with the unhappy thought lingering ever in future about me that I deceived one so noble so pure & lovely as yourself. If you did not know my pecuniary condition in life, I thought you did. I often told you, as I thought, that I had nothing & was in debt. I do hope I will live long enough to make you & Laura happy after I am gone. If I do not, I will die wishing that I could have let you alone, so that you might have married some one that could have taken better care of you. I have done my utmost to do so so far & I will continue until the last nerve is paralized. If undegoing privations & hardships in this life will make you happy, I intend to undergo them. Great God, what shall I do to heal this breach commited on an honest innocent family, & get read of the unhappy thought?

Honey, those tears of yours which dampened my cheaks as I kissed you last I hope may some day be repaid with feelings of joy more lasting than a few short days or months but in years of unalloyed pleasure.

I wish, Honey, you would buy Williamsons Woods' saddlebags for me at ten dollars. That's what he said I could have them at. I will never see mine again I recon. If you can send them by Lt. Stepens, get them; if you cannot, let them alone & I will save you ten dollars by so doing. They will be very convenient for him to bring Lou's Boots & my bridle in. I will leave here tomorrow for Jackson, Miss. You must direct your letters to me at that plase. Be shure to have 56th Ga. Regt., Gen. Taylor's Brig. on them. Honey, you must quit working for me. I donot intind my deception shall ever again weary your dear lovely self in working & working for me as you have done for the past few months. Honey, do get some one to make those shirts of mine. I did not get you to do such things. I got you to love, adore, & worship as one of nature's noblest works, & shall continue to do so until death. Let me hear from you soon, my dear sweet Kittie.

Yours with an undying affection & a happy thought that I have a wife more lovely than any other.

G.W Peddy

Part III.

VICKSBURG, CHICKAMAUGA, CHATTANOOGA

6 JANUARY 1863 - 18 APRIL 1864
94-166

The strategic assault on the Confederacy down the Mississippi River began with Gen. U.S. Grant's capture of Forts Henry and Donelson in February 1862 and continued through the Shiloh campaign in April of the same year. In the same month Admiral David G. Farragut captured New Orleans and extended his hold on the River as far north as Baton Rouge. It was the task of Gen. John C. Pemberton, a native of Pennsylvania, to prevent the two Union forces from joining and to hold Vicksburg. After five unsuccessful operations against the city, Grant's campaign began in earnest on 29 April 1863. In a brilliant manoeuvre reminiscent of Napoleon, Grant defeated Pemberton's possible rescuers and laid seige. Vicksburg capitulated on 4 July. The South had been cut in two, and Grant's forces were free to turn elsewhere. For logistical reasons Grant paroled Pemberton's forces, so that Dr. Peddy returned home. He rejoined the army in Tennessee immediately after the carnage at Chickamauga on 19-20 September. Grant arrived in Chattanooga on 23 October to take personal charge of the situation. The battle of Missionary Ridge, at which Dr. Peddy was present, was fought on 25 November. Gen. Braxton Bragg, who was nearly captured, withdrew the Confederate forces to Dalton, Ga. The stage was now set for the most famous operation of the war.

94

Camp Near Jackson, Miss. Jan. 6th/63

MY DEAR PRECIOUS KITTIE,

After arriving safely & well at this place last night, my first duty of this morning is to write to you, the most pleasant of all duties is to write you a few lines. No difference whare I am or what I am doing, my happyest moments are those which are spent in reflecting about my dear, happy, little famely at home. Never did I spend two days so plesent as those I spent with you last. They appear like a plesent dream, or the realization of some unexpected boon. They are only a foretaste of that continual scene of happyness which I am to enjoy when this protracted & unholy war shall find a terminus. Their is no way that I can cyper it up for the war to last more than six months longer. Then, oh then, what a happy time I will have with you & Laura, two of the most beautifull & lovely of all on earth! Ma, you must teach Laura to love papie for something more than the little presents that I bring her when I come home. They are not even the foreshadowing of my unbounded love for you & her. We had quite a plesent trip comeing out here. Only two of our men got sick. I had such a nice time I wished you along with me. We have a beautiful camp here. I was in the City of Jackson yesterday. Their are a great many good there. I will send you somethings if I can find out that the express is safe to send them by from this place. I met up with one of the professors of my college in N[ew] O[rleans]. He was proud to see me, & I him. I will get up to the City to see him as soon as our horses get here. We are looking for them daily. The Yankees have all left this part of the country. They have all gone to help out those who have been so badly whiped by Bragg at Murfreesburo. I donot know whare we will go from here. It's said we will go either to Grenado, Miss. or Murfreesburo, Tenn., whare we came from. We left there in a good time to keep out of the fight. I whish we had been there to help our men out. Not that I am dissatisfied with this country, the home of the President and your Uncle['s] Country. Each part of the Confederacy is equally important with me to defend with the exception of the spot whare my darling is.

You can hire y'r Negro out about Atlanta for $125 dollars per year, & her clothing & shoes will be furnished, but I had rather you would hire her for less about home. She would not be so liable to take the prevalent diseases. Do as you think best, my love. I leave all my business at home with you & you have so far managed it excelently. Let me hear from you, my dear, devoted one. Give my love to all my relations & especially to y'r Ant Kit.

Your evermore devotedly
G.W.P.

P.S. Inclosed you will find a bill of articles that I bought from Wm. Z. Barker, belonging to Dr. Howel.

95

Jackson Miss. Jan. 9th/63[1]

MY DARLING WIFE KITTIE,

With a thrill of joy I write a responce to your sweet welcomed letter.[2] I am that proud when I get a letter from you I no not hardly [know] how to content myself. They always bring with them such sweet sentiments of love that it will fill my heart with pride & the joyous reflection that I have a darling one that can by her inteligence depict such vivid strains of love as they exist. You are, my darling, the most beautiful of all beuties, the most lovely of the loveliest, & your inteligence, I am proud to say, towers far above the common order of your sex. I went to the City to day & bought you one calico dress, at one & 75/100 dollars, also and pair of shoes at fourteen dollar, & kitten one little dress at three dollars, & forwarded them the Newnan per express. The above articles are enormously high, but you & Laura must have something as well as myself. They were the cheepest I could get. Lt. Stephens arrived safely in camp with my four shirts. They are the nicest I ever had. I am so proud of them they just fit. Honey, I don't know how I am to pay you for your kindness towards me. Honey, I love you with all my heart, but that is poor pay; you ought to have something more than that. Honey, when you want any thing, write to me & I will get it for you if its to be had in the market which I am at. You will have to pay the express or freight. When you get your goods, you must have some one to bring them to you from Newnan. I did not direct them to Franklin. Honey, you need not be uneasy about y'r Lizzie putting out her fore foot. She has been at that ever since I got her & before, it's just her pride. Tell y'r pa she is not like common horses. If they stick out their feet, something is the matter with them. Not so with her, she does so to be different from the lower order of horses. Do not let any one ride her hard. You must get her fat.Honey, she is not half so. Honey, I am glad you hired Puss out. If you had sent her to Atlanta, you could have got one hundred & twenty five dollars for her, but I had rather have her

---

[1]Letter misdated /62.

[2]This letter is missing.

where she is. You must make Mathews pay you the note you have against him. You hired her for more than I would have done if I had been at home. You are the best trader me & Laur has in the family, better than I am. Honey, I am so glad that Mabry fell in my debt. Send down the note with the account for Mrs. M. to settle, as she was so anxious to dun me when I was at home. Keep sending to her until she pays it off, & charge interest from the time the account came due. Lou is getting along finely. I have got him to quit cursing. I tell him I will do that part for the family myself. I received the two potatoes you sent. Lou did his boots & socks. He is very proud of them. He can sell them for fifty dollars if he could get another pair. Honey, let me hear from you often. You can imagine how much good it does me to hear from you.

Kiss Laura for me. Give my love to all at home. Let me know if y'r Uncle Joe has his company.

Yours with all my heart
G.W Peddy.

96

Jackson, Jan. 18th, 1863

MY DARLING WIFE, THE IDOL OF MY HEART,

With the most pleasurable feelings of love I respond to your letter of the 7th Inst.[3] Never did my eyes before behold such a one; its inviting pages is music for my eyes. Such heart felt sentances of love, such intiligence as is manifest on its pages, is nearly found in the writing of the most able, in fact, it was just a letter that would melt the rudest heart to love & make my heart bust with joy to think that I was so fortunate in woing one so noble, so beautiful, & so evrything that's grand & sublime. Honey, I am so proud of you. I wish you could realize how much I appreciate you. Language is not supple enough for me to give you the faintest idea of my deep & fathomless affections. Evry word that I have heard from your ruby lips sounds yet like the pleasant tones of the Eolian harp, evry motion is angelic, & lastly but not leastly, that voice when mingled with the notes of the Pianno sounds more pleasant than that of the nymphs. Oh, that I were with you to tell you these things rather than write them! Honey, you say that you intend to come back with me. I hope you will continue in that mood until I come home. I have no idea when I will every get back home. I see no possible chance for me to come. I do wish you had come with me when I was at

[3]This letter is missing.

home last. What oceans of pleasure we would have had, but as it is, you are their & I am here with no chance for us to see each other unless you come to see me. Never, no never do I expect to have any pleasure that real out side of your lovly presence. You know it's with a sigh I make this declaration. Honey, I was so sorry to hear our little angel Laura was sick. Ma, don't you love her? You must love her some for me because I am not capable of loving her as she would be loved on account of her noble Mama. Pappie will bring her a heep nice presence when he comes home, if he should ever come again. Honey, to think of the many happy hours we have spent togueather, & then realize our present monotinous condition nearly overwhelms me notwithstanding my indisposition to be sad. It is said that it's best to be away from the idol of one's heart at times to make it the more admirable, but the promptings of my nature says to me that I need no such evidence to cause me to realize the significant fact that I dearly love you. I hope ere this that even you a[l]so have been forced to acknowledge the cincerety of my true affections. Have you not? I think you will say yes.

Honey *you* & *Laura* must be *vaccinated* at once. We have the Small Pox in our Regt. I would be affraid to come home if I had the chance, but have no idea I will get that chance. Be shure that it takes on you & Laura both for I would not have you or her to have it for a world. Honey, do not put it off one moment after you get this letter. My horse has come through safe. I hope yours is doing well. Lou & Foster are getting on finely. This is the hardest country I ever saw. We have had nothing but beef for three or four days. I hope we will get some in a short time. Let me heare from you often. I am so happy when I get a letter from you. Honey, you must not become heartless about the war. I hope we'll have peace before long. The Yankees have not taken Vicksburg.

Give my love to the family, to y'r Uncle Jo & Ant Kit. I will cal y'r ma my ma after this.

Yours ever more
G.W Peddy

If you want any thing that I can get out here let me know, but I believe you can do better in Atlanta.

97

Camp Near Vicksburg, Jan. 28th/63

MY DARLING WIFE,

With great pleasure I read you sweet letter of the 10th Inst.[4] Honey, I had the blews when I received it, but as soon as I read it I was all right. Honey, no letters I get draws my attention in the least but yours. They always fill my heart with emotions of pleasure & joy unspeakable. I wish I could portray with my pen the feelings of love which cours through my heart for you when I read one of your sweet letters. It would startle you to think any one could have so exalted an opinion of one as I have of you.Honey, it does seem so hard for us to be seperated so long. Sometimes I donot know what to do & how to do about it. I recon I will have to become reconciled about it in some way. Honey, you spoke of your feet, sweet little feet (I wish I was with you to wash them for you). Oh, if I could be with you I could hold them in my lap all night if necessary to keep them warm. Honey, I do not think it immodest for you to write to me about such things. I like for you to let me know all about your dear little self, for their is my intrust & my all embodied in you. I am sorry, my loye, that you ar so near out of money. I have some for you if I had any way to send it. I will wait until I get more, then I will send it by express. Honey, I hope to hear in your next that you have received your goods I sent you per express. I could not get any shoes for our little sweet Laur[a]. None will fit her little sweet foot that I can see.

Honey, I expect we will have a fight here before long. The enemy are in large forse beond the river from us, not near enough to shell us. They have a great many transports, & only three Gun Boats as yet. It is thought they will land below here & attacke our fortifications. It's said the enemy are sixty thousand strong. Honey, I donot know what I will do about seeing you. You will have to come to see me after awhile. I see no chance under the heavens for me to get off from here; if I could, I would come any time. Kiss our little Laura for me. Tell her papie wants to see her worse than he ever did. Honey, if you want that silk dress at Mozeley's & can get it for thirty three dollars, I believe I would get it. The Calico dress I sent you cost $19; the silk dress is worth two of it. Honey, if you want it get it, it is worth three or four Calico dresses. It would cost as musch to buy another Calico dress here as it would to buy the silk one.

Lou is well & fatter than you ever saw him. Give my love to all, Dr. Lane & your Ant Kit. Kiss Laura for me & tell her to Kiss you for Papie. Your forever

G.W.Peddy

P.S. Let me hear from you often.

---

[4]This letter is missing.

98

Camp Near Vicksburg, Jan. 31st/63

MY DARLING WIFE KITTIE, I was again made happy at the reception of your sweet letter per N.J. Read.[5] I received it the 29th inst. & would have answered it immediately but had to go on picket ten miles below this place. Parden me, my darling sweet, for not replying sooner. You have no idea how I think of you & how pleasent it is after reading your letters. Happy thoughts of you ever linger about me, but more so at the reception of your unparallelled letters. Honey, oh! how much I want to see you. It greaves me nearly to distraction to have to be kepted away from you so long. I write the above often, but oh, it does not bring any relief. I often have pleasant & sweet dreams of you, but how sad I am when I awake & find that they are not real.

You wrote in yours about a dream you had of me. I would like to know what it was. I know it would gratify me no little if it was a good one. Honey, when danger & hardships afflict me most I love you if anything more. You and Laura are my only hope for happyness in the world. How hard it seems to me to think that we have to spend the flower of our lives away from each other. I am willing to make any sacrifice on earth to get out of this war that does not reflecting any discredit on you, Little Sweet Laura, & my self, so that I can get to stay with you & her. It will ever be my highest ambition to act in such a maner that the purity & sanctity of my lovely little family be not in jepardy. Honey, this is not from the lips, but from the heart. Honey, I will answer evry letter I get from you if I get one evry hour in the day. You cannot write to me to often. Lou is not very well to day. Had a bad Boil on his neck I presume is the reason. Darling, I wish I had some news for you but I have not. I haven'[t] seen a paper in several days. The Enemy seem to be making arrangements to attack this place, but I do not think they will ever take in. Nearly evry family in the City have them a cave dug to go into when the enemy begin to bombard. Let me hear from you often. Honey, I wish I had been at home when you was so wearied. How proud it make me when I can sooth you in your weary hours. I always think I have accomplished wonders when I can do you good in any way. I feel proud of it afterwards. Honey, donot forget to be *vacinated.* I *would not have you & Laura to be exposed to vareola for no price.* Honey, write to me in your next wheathe[r] you have been or not, so that I will be satisfied about it. Several of our Brig. have died with it, one out of our Regt. Darling, you had better hire you weaving done. I am afraid for you to do it. Women frequently become diseased just from that cause alone. Honey, I did not get you to work; I got you to worship & love & am proud to say that my idol is more than worthy [of] my admiration. *So, darling, quit the weaving.* Honey, write me all the news about Franklin: what is said & done. Enclosed you will find a letter that contradicts the statement that my old friend over the rive[r] made about me.

---

[5]This letter is missing.

Darling, I will buy you a cloak if I can find one & away to sent it to you. Give my love to all. Yours ever more truly

G.W Peddy.

99

Vicksburg, Miss. Feb. 13th, 1863[6]

MY DARLING, THE OBJECT OF MY HARTE ADMIRATION,

With pleasure unspeakable I read your sweet letter of the 31st ultimo.[7] It had been so long since I heard from you that I began to get impatient. Honey, donot let it be so long before you write again. You[r] letters are the only consolation I have, therefore I like, you know, honey, to read them. Honey, I am here in tent to night by myself. Lou has gone on picket. Nick has just left me after returning from Jackson, whare he went before the ordinance board. He stood a splendid examination & I think, if justice is done him, he will ere long be ordinance Capt. How proud I will then be. I feel as much intrust for any member of the family as I do for myself. They have alway been so kind to us I feel it would be a breach o gross injustice to be otherwise. My whole ambition is to do all in my power to make any sacrefice for any of them. I am so proud that I am so perfectly wraped up in you all. Because they have been so kind to us in only the fainteste cause. I love them on account of their raising their purety, their evrything that [is] grand, noble, & good. Nick, whose highttoned character as a gentleman & whose pure heart like yours knows nothing of evil, has my warm admiration, but the secret is not yet told. You, oh you, honey, whos[e] lovely form & body bearing must necessarily gain possession, it seems to me of all virtuous hearts is the cause of my admiration.

Would to God, Kittie, that I could tell you this sad night or impart to you through the medium of my pen my profound love for you & our little sweet Laur[a]. Knotwhithstanding our indebtedness, our absence from each other, & the reflections of the many troubles which particularly have had in all my life, we should feel proud that we have arrived to the point we have. We have a great many things to make us proud: 1st & most important, our dear little Laur[a], whose beauty & intelect is rarely surpassed in children of her age; 2ndly, our deep & heart felt at the joyious reflection that your are mine, that I was so extremely fortunate in marrying you; & not speaking ironically, I did you an

---

[6]Written along the side of the page: "Direct your letters to Vicksburg G.W.P."

[7]This letter is missing.

injury in not letting you alone for some one who could have treated you beeter than I could, both as regards personal comfort & genuine unalloyed pleasure. My wants in youth were many, my extravigance was great; now, alas, I see to late my folly. Instead of my reaping the bitter rewards of my indescretion, it has fellen with a crash on those who are dearer to me than my own life. Honey, while I speak the above, the silent tear, though unmanly as it is, steals slowly down my cheek, whare you have often pressed your warm kisses. Darling, I wish you knew my feelings to nigh[t]. I experience a lashing of concience that's nearly felt by others. You have acknowledged at last that I love you. I am proud to know you think so. I do with all my heart. It will ever be my greatest ambition to act in such a manner as to keep up that truthful thought. Honey, I do wish I could come to see you, but their is no chance nor will their be, I suppose, befor the war closes. I may have to do without seeing you for some time yet, but I donot know how I am to do so. The trancient hours I have spent so happily with you for the past fourteen months appears like a dream or something that's not rearal. I want to be with you always in order that I may alwas be happy & in the heghth of enjoeyment. I am glad your Ma thinks I love you. What I can write to you can not even give her a faint idea of my affection for you. Whatever I go to do, it is my happyest thought that is to redound to the good of you & Laura. Your are alwas first & last in my mind. No thought is pleasant only as it associates you with it. Your advice is worth more to me than all else. I do wish I was whare I could get the benefit of that graceous boon. Honey, at every effort I fall so far short of giving you one idea of how well I esteem you, I become almost deshartened. Spring with all its lovliness is approaching here on the banks of the broad Miss. Its waters are beautiful, the froggs croak, & the turtle dove mourns sweetly only when they remind me of my dear ones at home. The place whare my loved ones are the place whare my idols are & my hearts warmest affections lye. Honey, I bought Nick a fine horse for three hundred dollars while he was gone to Jackson. He is well pleased with him. He is encamped about four miles from me. I have not had the pleasure of getting aquainted with your Uncle[8] yet. I think I will go over in a few days. I am so glad Nick is so close to us. I never was prouder to see a man than him. I do hope we will stay close togueather until the War closes. If I cannot see you, I have the gratifycation to know that some one very near & dear to me because they are to your noble self. Lou has been sick with the jaundice, not so much as to go to bed. He is now well. I was so sorry for him. Honey, you did not let me know wheather you had been vaccinated or not. I do feel so uneasy about you & Laura. You must have Laura vaccinated any how—it will not hurt her—on account of her having the Whooping cough. Poor little thing, Pappie wishes he could have it in her place. I am willing to take all of your & her suffering on myself, if it will relieve you any both mentally & physically. Kiss her for me & speak of pappie often whare she is. Quit weaving, honey, & let me hear from you often. Good nigh[t], my own love, G W Peddy

[8]Gen. W.S. Featherston

100

Camp Near Vicksburg, Miss. Feb 26th/63

MY PRECIOUS WIFE KITTIE, After returning from a two days' picket duty, my heart was made glad by your sweet letter being handed me.[9] I was so tired, but assure you I had a pleasent & joyfull rest while reading it. Such a sorce of gratification as it was to me no one rearly knows. Your letters get sweeter & sweeter to me evry one I read. They are emblematic of the pure & lovely one who writes them. I am satisfied from several years' observation with a good field before me than no one loves as I, dout fewer have such a worthy object or jewel as I. I am so sorry to learn that you have the headache. I wish I was with you to rub your sweet head—perhaps it would get some easier. So long as you and Laura keep well I am tolerably well satisfied, but when you get sick, my all is then involved & I become restless. Honey, I hope you are well ere this time. I will always do your suffering for you if it was possible for me to do so. Honey, your letters are few but are very sweet when I get them, so write oftener if it is not to much trouble for you to do so. If you could imagine how happy they make me, I know you would send them evry day. Honey, if it wearies you in the least to write often, donot do it, for it is not my intention to ever make you the least unhappy or unpleasent, but my greatest desire is to do any thing in my power to make you happy. If I at any time make a request of you that wearies you in the least, donot comply with it. I am willing to forego any pleasure to render you happy. Honey, I have Dysentery to day. I cannot write you anithing that will interest you. I hope I will get better soon. You need not be uneasy about me. If I get bad sick, I will telegraph to you. Honey, I long to see the month of May come, when I will have the pleasure of a visit from you. You must be shure to come with your Pa when he comes to see us. I will nearly eat you up when you come. I would be so overjoyed that I would hardly be able to govern my self. Honey, I have to go before the Medical Board to be examined in a few days. I cannot tell how I will come out. I may be rejected, but I hope not. I know if I do that the ballance of the Surgeons in our Brig. will go up the spout. Dr. Whitaker, my Assit. Surgeon, is not going before the board. He's afraid they will throw him . You must not say anything about this for fear he gets hold of it. I expect by this time Nick is installed in his office. I am so proud about his success. Honey, I have just received your letter of the 16th instnt.[10] Stoped writing this to read yours. Honey, Honey, I am sorry to hear of you being sick in bed by a[m] made glader when you write you are nearly well. Honey, I am frightened about you. I fear you [are] taking the Small Pox. They come exactly like a bad cold. Honey, if you have them not, do for my happyness & the sake of y'r sweet little child do be vaccinated. You know not what hour

[9]This letter is missing.

[10]This letter is missing.

you may be exposed to that lothsome disease. I hope your Pa has a fine horse. If he has, it is the first one he has had since I knew him. I have one that I am offerd $350 for. I think I could get four hundred if I would let it be know[n] that I would sell him. Honey, you wrote to me about coming home. You know, darling, that I would do so any moment if I could, but I see no chance for me to get off from atall in many months. All the way I can get to see you is for you to come to see me. You must quit teasing y'r Pa to much about this outfit. Honey, I donot think we will have any fight here soon if at all. I am afraid we will all be sick here. We have miserable water: the best we get is rain water that drops from our tents. Darling, I will write you a better letter in a few days.

Kiss Kitten for Pappie. Your evermore G W Peddy

101

Vicksburg, March 1st, 1863

MY PRECIOUS & DEVOTED WIFE KITTIE,

With many joyous reccolections of this beautiful Sabbath day when we used to strol happly in our Garden to see our sown seeds germinate; many, many pleasing coincidence have I this day pondered in my mind. Oh! that we could realize such blessings we were enjoying, whareas now we a[re] seperated from each other having no idea when we will meet again. It seems crewel, yet our cinditions could be worse. We may yet have to look back even to this day as a bright one in our history. I hope not. I hope, Honey, you have get entirely will ere this reaches you. I do hate to hear of your being sick, & darling, I cannot bear the idea of you getting poor. It is my great desire to see you moderately corpulent. Honey, perhaps if you would travel about you would get in better health. You must not distress yourself about me. Perhaps that has something to do with your waisting away. I hope also that your ear has got well & did not rise. Honey, if I were with you I would try to act kindly enough to you that you would forget your suffering, if such a thing is possible. You speak in your of our former joys. Oh! it is my greatest desire to enjoy them again. I love you, if possible, more than ever. It seems that the joys of former days would fall far short of the jenuine pleasure we could have if we could again be togueather at home. Honey, do not ever think again that you letters are tiresome to me. I rearly get wearied in doing an act that is my greatest pleasure. Honey, your letters are emblematic of your pure, lovely, & jenuine self. They not only combine inteligence, learning, & wit but modesty, virtue, & chastity. Honey, it [is] my happy reflection that I have the best, purest, & most lovely wife in the world. You may have defects, but they are all lost in my imagination by virtues. It appears to me impossible for you to do something rong.

Darling, I make effort after efort to give you some idea of how I love but find I fall far short of it. Honey, I fear you are to anxious about my wellfair. I fear you donot enjoy yourself on that account. You say I s[h]ould not want a wife that is neather usefull nor ornamental. Your are more usefull than I desire you to be. I fear it renders you unhappy; and as an ornament of beautify, virtue, & intelect I chalenge Marnerva hurself to excell you. You have not the idea of beautity that I have. If you did you, like Narcissus of old, would go frantic the first sight you got of yourself. Oh! that I were at home to day to stroll in the beautiful sunshine with your new dress. The beauty of any dress that you wear is alway absorbed in the superior beauty of the wearer. Lou is getting along finely. I have the diarrhaea now. I will be well, I guess, in a few days. I hope Little Sweet Laur[a] will get well in a short time. Pappie does want to see you and her so much. Tell her pap love her & she need not think I donot becuuse I donot come to see her, for I would come any time in the world I could get of. Sometimes I think I will write for you to come & stay close to me all the time. If the war does not stop before long, I think I will. I want us to enjoy ourselves while will do live. I don't think we should much longer forego the pleasure of togueather on accont of looseing a little money.

Honey, let me hear from you often. I will write more next time. Kiss Laur[a] for me. I am sorry Dr. Lane did not get his company. Give my love to all.

Yours yours now & forever
with all my heart

P.S I [s]end you another peace of music with this letter.

102

Vicksburg, March 5th/63

MY PRECIOUS KITTIE, THE PURE IDOL OF MY HEART, With great pleasure I write you again today while the Regt. is on picket. No one is in camps but myself & the sick. Evry thing is quiet, hence a good time to write. It appears to me that we will have no fight here in some time, if we ever do. I believe the attempt to take this place would be futile. The enemy may undertake it sometime, but not soon, I think. We have more sickness in our Regt. now than we'v had in some time: evry one seems to have Diarrhoea. I have not been will of it in a month. I am taking medicine for it now. Lou has gone out with the regt. He is getting on finely, has a slight attack of the prevailing diarrhoea. Honey, I sent you to day per A. J. Lowe of Newnan, Ga. four hundred dollars, which you can make any disposition of you wish. Pay some of it to Mozeley.

You must keep a good am't on hand in case of an accident. Honey, when you or Laura kneed anything, buy it. Two more months will pay us out of debt, then I will be free so far as indebtedness is concerned. The ballance I make after that, we will keep for our future purposes, to buy us a place to live happyly situated at home, out of debt. If we have not money, we can make the greatest bounty to live upon as none of it will then will have to go for debts. What a happy though[t] it would be to me if I was to die, that I would have a plenty for you & Laura to live the banlance of you life bountifully upon! I have no anxiety for myself in this life. I am anxious only for your & Laura's happyness. I never have no desire to do an[y]thing unless their is a prospect of its redounding to the benefit of my two angels at home. I do wish I was at home so that I could verify to you in unmistakeable tearms & actions that you are the only two that has all my affections. I love you, my dear, as never did mankind love before. I regard you my love purer that it's possible for humane to be. Oh! that we could always live in each other's presence. Ne'er would their be a waive on the calm oc[e]an of our love. The lookers on would be bound to acknowledge that their is an example, true love unalloyed by policy. Never could one be made so happy as myself if I could be in your angelic presence, their to feel the realities of your love. It is a woman's grand prerogative & her worthy mition to give comfort to man. I know I realize when I am with you the truth of this saying more than any one because of your true devotion. But, oh, is this presumption on my part that causes these utterances? I hope not, believing myself to be so constant is what give me such unbounded confidence in you. Honey, I am affraid you will eventually get tired of the same old song, the details of my love to you. I write them because these ideas linger with me always.

Honey, you spoke of making me some pants. You can make such as you like. I donot want you to put yourself to any trouble about them, though. Honey, I wish you would send me & Lou a box of meet & butter. We have had nothing but the poorest beeff you ever saw to eat in a week. I cannot tell when we will get any. But I have just heard that our Quarter Master is ordered to have his mules shod & the wagons fixed up preparatory to a move. We may go away from here. I cannot tell. If you can find out anyone coming, send us one an[y]how, & if we donot, send it per express. Wait until you hear from me again. We may go back to Tenn. I hope we will. Their is going to be the place whare the most fighting is going to be done. I hope we will not go any father west. I am sick of this country already. I want to get nearer to you, if possible. I wish I was post surgeon at some place, then you could come & stay with me. You will have to send to Newnan after the money I have sent you. Let me hear from you often, dear. My love to all. Your evermore G.W Peddy

103

Camp Near Vicksburg, March 7th/63[11]

MY OWN DEAR LOVE KITTIE,I wrote you day before yesterday. I write you again today in responce to your sweet & interesting letter of the 27th Ultimo.[12] I received it yesterday. I have been reading it ever since, I like it so well. I am so glad to learn that you have got well. I do hope you & Laura will remain so until I get home to stay. Honey, you say you alway find a hearty echo to your deep felt love. Yeas, my dear, & you ever will with feelings of the deepest pride, I am fearfull John's flame in Va. will turn out like his one in Heard. If she does, it's time enough for him to marry unless he can get such a noble *angel* as I did. You ask me in your last did I not wish I had not married so that I could have got the most gifted in the land. Honey, I got the noblest one of that sort & am perfectly satisfied with her. Honey, you ask me to express myself candidly about what time I thought I would come home. My dear, I hate to think about the length of time that will be. I donot think their is any possible chance for me to come before next Christmas. Their is no chance for me to get off from here unless I get sick so that I will not be able for duty in a good long time. I would freely come home evry month if I could get off, but their is no chance to get a leave of absence. Honey, you say you wish it would not be nine weeks longer before I would come home. Darling, I do whish I could think I would be home in that length of time again. I would almost uxult with joy. The only way for us to get to see each other is for you to come to see me. That, you are at liberty to do an[y]time you see propper. I would be rejoyed no little if I could see you out here. Honey, when the war is over, we'll, if both are alive, bask in the scene of pure enjoyment. Honey, I wrote to you that perhaps we would leave here in a short time, but now I think we will not. I want you to send me a box of meat, sausage, & butter. If you cannot get any one to bring it, send it per express. A box weighing one hundred lbs will cost seven dollars. You had better pay the express on it at Newnan, & take the express receipt for it & send it in a letter to me. I would rather you would get some one to bring it if you could. I had as soon have side meat as any other sort—anithing to get meat. I have had none in some time. It sells here for one dollar per pound. Honey, I wrote to Fannie Copeland about how Asbury was & stated that Bud McDonald was detailed to go on board of a Gun Boat, but I was mistaken about that. I want you to rectify that as soon as you get this, for they will be uneasy about him. Tell Kitten, Ma, she must not forget her Pa. He wants to see her so much. Tell her also Pappie would take that troublesome cough away from her on himself if he could. Honey, I do love you & Laura so much it does seem so crewel for me to be kept

---

[11]*At top of page:* You must not be very particular about sending me side meet, for that will do negroes better than me.

[12]This letter is missing.

away from those I worship so devotedly, but such is life. Honey, I have had a worse spell of Diarrhoea for the last week than I had at home when I got back from Ky. I am better now. I think I will be well in a few days. I expect Lou will regret much Tressie's marrying. I think he has a very strong Puppie love for her. He will be back from picket directly & I will let you know in my next how he takes it. Honey, the swelling buds, the sweet warbling of the Birds of Spring does make my heart & soul full of dear & loved thoughts of you. Let me hear from you often. Give my love to all. May heaven's choicest blessing rest with you, my dear love, Kittie.

Your G W Peddy

Lou has just got back. He is quit[e] well. He does not believe Tressie will marry.

104

Vicksburg, Miss., March 18th/63

MY DEAR WIFE KITTIE, My heart has again been made glad at the reception of two sweet letters from y'r dear, lovely hand.[13] Honey, you have no idea how much pleasure I experience in reading y'r letters, sweeter far than evrything else in this land. Honey, you do write such sweet & beautiful letters it's an honor for any one to get them. I feel proud that I have such a lovely one to write me. You have no idea how happy it makes me to reflect that we have the most perfect little girl in evry particula of any other two. She has the noble & lovely disposition of her angelic mother. Honey, I do wish you could see the interior of my heart so that you might realize the debths of my unbounded love to you. Honey, I forgot to write to you about sending you the *Soldier's Friend.* We get it hear evry week. It's a good paper for any one to read. I often read it but donot, I am sorry to state, obey its teachings. Honey, I read the letter your Ma wrote to Lou. It was such a good one. I told him he could never do bad concientiously again after reading that letter. Y'r Pa also wrote to him a good one. He is very proud when he gets a letter. Boyd Lane & Lin have arrived safely to camps. Honey, you wrote to me you wanted to sell Lzzie Welch for six hundred dollars. I donot think I can take less than seven hundred for her. Six hundred looks like a big price but I could get a thousand for her if she was here. If you will have her rubed well she will bring seven hundred in a short time. If any one comes to buy her again, get Ambrose Williams to show her to them. Any one that knows

---

[13]Both letters are missing.

nothing of her gaits can make her go then. She goes all the gaits perfectly if any body knew how to make her. No one does but Ambrose. Honey, if the mair is sold for the above am't, ask y'r Pa if he had not better buy for us Hiram McDonald's place at two thousand. I can pay for it quite easy by next Christmas if I live. I expect their is money in it at two thousand dollars. If y'r Pa thinks so, let him buy it. Honey, how would you like to make that kind of a traid? I will be governed by your say so in any trade of that kind. I donot want you to think that I want to get in debt again. I will go in debt under no consideration unless it is for the purpose of making more money for your & Laura's enjoyment. And I would not make any trade of that magnitude without y'r consent. Y'r judgement is worth a fortune to any man. I hope ere this you have received your money, which I sent you, which will nearly pay us out of debt, that happy day I have long look for on y'r & Laur[a]'s account.

Honey, you ought to see me tonight with my fine uniform on. I am the finest dressed man you have seen. The Ladies would turn round on the streets to look a[t] me.

Honey, I wish I could tell you what a dream I had of you last night. I will tell you about it when I get to see you. Oh that I could realize such facts as the dream perpetrated! Honey, I am sorry to relate the fact of the death of Roberson Brigman. He died in hospital on the 17th inst. when I was on picket. I cincerely condole with his bereaved wife & relations. I tried to send him home, but the Rail Road would not carry him.

Hony, I will take as good care of myself as I can. Honey, you have no idea how proud I was on the reception of the sausage you sent me & Lou. We enjoy it finely. Hope to get some more from your dear ha[n]d when D. Lane comes. Let me hear from you often, my darling. Your Pa & Ma knows I cannot stay away from you longer if I could help myself, but oh, I cannot help myself.

Give my love to y'r Ma & Pa & all the rest.

Yours ever true

G.W Peddy

105

Vicksburg, Miss. March 24th/63

MY PRECIOUS DARLING WIFE KITTIE, I wrote to you in Lou's letter that we were on the verge of leaving here for Yazoo City, but instead of that, we are now quartered in the best & finest houses in Vicksburg. I am now seated by a pleasant fire in my neatly carpeted room, furnished with evry thing necessary for comfort, without its costing me a sent. I hope we will remain here all summer, & from what I can hear, the prospect is very good for us to remain as we are for a good length of time. Honey, the position I am in now is enviable, to good for a sold[i]er. If I had past the Board now I would feel much better. I expect to pass, but you know I cannot help to be uneasy about it. I feel anxious about it, you know, which is a natural consequence. I will go before them in a few days. Honey, if you were just here now, how happy I would be. You are all that's liking to make me as pleasant as I could be made. I do want to see you & Laura worse than ever before, if possible. The more I stay away from you, the worse I desire to see you. Oh! would that I had you here to enjoy the pleasure of my fire & nice room with me. This is the first time I have had the enjoyment of sitting by a fire in a house since I sat with you at home. Honey, I have no news of importance to write you, only Gen. Featherston has won himself quite a reputation in whipping the Enemy above here a few days ago. Nick is about sixteen miles from me now. I have wrote to him to come & get Lin, but has not come yet. He's not had an opportunity to come. It is an impossibility for me to get off. Now, my dear, if y'r Pa come out to see us, please come with him. I am so anxious to see you I donot see how I can do without seeing you much longer. Honey, Boyd tell me he thinks y'r Shoes are nearly worn out. Let me know if it is the case & I will send you some more. My great desire is that you must have evry thing you need or want that I can furnish. Honey, if you were here how with me I could stay with you all the time. Their is a good Boarding house next door to me.

Honey, I have had a bad headache tonight. I hope you will excuse the length & stile of this letter. I have not had a letter from you in several days. I hope I will get one tomorrow. Give my love to all

Yours ever more happyly

G.W.Peddy

106

Vicksburg, April 1st/63

MY DEAR KITTIE, I write you in a great hurry. Nick stayed with us last night. He said he had no use for Lin & requested me to send him back home. He has to travel about so much that Lin would do him no good. Honey, I have rec'ed two sweet letters from you recently[14] & one to day from brother John. He speaks in

[14]Both letters are missing.

high tearms of my beautiful & devoted little family. I know without anyone telling me that I have the most lovely one in the world. Honey, this is not a reply to your two last. We are ordered a few miles above Vicksburg, hence I have not time to write & I have been waiting to go before the Medical Board so I would know what my fate would be in reference to being a Surgeon in the army longer. You said Chippie read my letter & thought you had the most affectionate one in the world. Honey, she could scarcely get an idea of my unbounded love for you & Laura from that letter. Honey, shugar is worth fifty cents per pound here. It is about as cheap in Ga., hence I will not send any. If I could get it cheap I would send hom by Lin. I give Lin $25.00 dollars to take him home. Honey, I will answer your letters in full as soon as I know wheather I pass the Board. Honey, I do want to see you so bad. It looks like a thousand years since I saw you. Honey, their is but one way for us to see each other—that is for you to come to see me. I will come the first opportunity, you know, but I cannot tell when that time will come. I wish I could come now, but oh, I cannot.

Honey, excuse me for not answering your two last for when I write I want to inform you of my triumph before the Army Medical Board & thus showing to the world that I am in evry way worthy the position I hold here, by thus succeeding I will reflect credit on you & Laura. My great desire, as I have often wrote, is to always act so a[s] to reflect honor on you & Laura & not myself.

Honey, I wish I had time to write you more. Let me hear from you often. Give Chippie my love, kiss Laura, for me & let her return the sweetness. Nick & Lou ar quite well. Foster wants Lin to stay & let him go home awhile. Yours ever truely & devotedly

G.W Peddy. Surgeon

107

Hed Quarters 56th Ga. Regt.
Camp on Deer Creek, April 13th/63

MY DARLING PRECIOUS KITTIE, This is the first opportunity I have had since Lin left of writing to you, that is, since I went before the Army Med Board. Honey, I felt very uneasy about passing it as they had rejected several surgeons before me, but fortunately I passed them, & after the examination was over they paid me a compliment, which of course I felt gratified for. Honey, you have ho idea how happy I was when they give me a certificate of my qualifications to discharge the duties as regtal. surgeon. As I rode back to camps I felt so proud to think I had again at the hour of trial reflected no discredit on you & Laura. I did want you with me to rejoice over my success. Of course on my arrival in camps my friends complimented & exulted with me, but their is not one that can share my joys & woes as you. Whare the heart is their is no one with whom pleasures can be joyously mingled. I have by passing the Board gave my enemies no clew at me in the future. I am now a defacto Army Surgeon with no chance to be thrown out, only for some misdemeanor, which I have no idea of being guilty off. My greatest ambition is to get higher & to add to the prosperity of my now as heretofore noble little family. If I cannot be with you, my love, it is a happy thought to realize the significant fact that I have the most enviable little family at home of any one else. Honey, I cannot discribe to you in what great admiration I hol[d] you. You are the most lovely, the most jenuine of all others on earth. Honey, the more I stay away from you the greater is my desire to be with you & the oftener I think of you. A great many of the officers have their wives now with them in camps. I never see them but what I want you with me not in camps by near by me in some nice house. We are now about one hundred miles above Vicksburg. We came Yazoo river to this place to run off a party of the enemy who were out here stealing negroes. They have all gone back to the Miss. River to their boats. We will go back to Vicksburg in a day or two; we only came here to run off the above mentioned party. You must continue to direct you letters to Vicksburg. I think we will stay their all summer. I rec'ed a letter from Brother John the other day. I was glad to hear from him. I have not replied to him yet for I have had no time. Lou is quite well; so is Foster. I expect Lin gave me a bad name when he gets home. I made him stand around when he was with me. He is the sorryest negro in the world. I think the most impudent. S.W. Faver wishes to know how much I paid him. It was fifteen dollars. I paid it to him in front of J. Swinney's grocery. Say to Chippie she can only get a faint idea of my love for you by reading the letter she did. If I could only write it as I feel it for you, she would be astounded. If she will let me find her a sweetheart after I come home I will find one that will love her as I do you if their is one capable of so doing, but I doubt any one doing so. The am't of money sent you by J. Lowe was four hundred dollars, that by the man in Carrol, one hundred, making five hundred. I am glad y'r Pa is being complimented in the discharge of his duties as judge. I wish to know, though, at the same time if he cannot outrank Ebin Duglas. I see him complimented as high as y'r Pa in the same peace. Tell y'r Pa he must post up his strikers better or get them to leave off Ebin. Honey, I want you to write to me about y'r sickness. I always want to know all about you. I will not receive y'r apologe for writing to me about y'r being sick. I want you to let me know all about you at all times. I wish I was at home to help you feed y'r horse and hogs. Ma, you must not hurt little Kitten by sticking a needle in her, for she is papie's little sweet girl. Tell her she ought to love Ma the best, for Ma is the best woman in the world & stays with her all the time. She ought not to love pappie because he stays away from her so long, but would not do so if I could do any better. Honey, I would almost give my life to see you. It looks like I have been away from you all my life but a few days of it.

Honey, you & y'r Pa must come to see us. Their is no chance for us to come to see you. If the Army would leave Vicksburg we might be ordered back to Tenn. I am gitting plenty to eat up in this country, but when we get back to Vicksburg, then we will be in a tight again. It [is] eather a feast or a famine with us. We will try to take a good many chickens back with [us]. Let me hear from you often, & you may tell my friends of my success before the Board. I am anxious to know what Dr. Lane is going to do about his Lieutenency. Capt. Thomasson will resign if Dr. Lane come in a short time & leave him Capt., so he said to me. Donot say anithing about that. This will be mailed in Atlanta, as their is a man here that will leave for that place in the morning. Kiss Laura for me. Tell her pappie loves her if he cannot get to see her.

Yours forever more truely

G.W.Peddy.

108

Head Quarters 56th Ga. Regt.
Camp on Deer Creek, April 16th/63

MY OWN PRECIOUS DARLING KITTIE, With no little pleasure I write you a few lines this morn to let you know how we are getting on. We are quite well & doing as well as could be expected. I heard heavy cannonading down about Vicksburg last night. I expect they have had a fight their.[15] We are here more for picket duty than any thing else. The citizens are all leaving this delightful portion of country. Citizens are all very wealthy & the finest plantations you ever saw. The country abounds evry thing that's good to eat. The enemy have taken of as many as three hundred negroes from some of the plantations. Nearly evry one has lost more or less of their negro property. The enemy destroy evrything that they can as they go. We are constantly looking for orders to go back to Vicksburg. We are catching a plenty of fish of the finest kind here. One of the soldiers has just brought in a fine Buffaloo fish weighing 14 lbs. I wish I could send it to you & let you enjoy the pleasure of eating in company with your little sweet Laura. Honey, I am afraid you will let Laura forget me. I recollect one time when I came home from the cost she did not know me. I never felt so bad about anything in my life as I did that. You must tell her often how

---

[15]Admiral David D. Porter got seven gunboats, a ram, and two transports past Vicksburg to the south on 16 April, and this was the first step towards General U.S. Grant's later assault on the city.

well I love her & how anxious I am at all times to see her, & you, but alas I am kept away from the dearest idols of my heart, those whom I love better & cheerish more fondly than I do my own life. Honey, I will have to forego the pleasure of writing you more as the courier is now about leaving. Let me hear from you often. You must come to see me when y'r Pa comes. I think the fight is still going on at Vicksburg as I hear cannon in that direction, but I am satisfied that we will be triumphant & victorious at that place. Yours ever more.

G.W Peddy

How happy I feel about passing the Board!

109

Camp on Deer Creak, Miss., April 21st/63

MY EVER PRECIOUS DEAR KITTIE, With a heart overflowing with pleasure & love for you I paroosed your two sweet letters one of the 1st inst., the other of the 10th.[16] The last date is my bearth day. I never want any better celebration of it than for you to write me a letter. I do not expect you thought of that when you was writing to me on that date. I was twenty nine years old at that inst. I am getting old very fast in years; in feelings, I am as young as ever. I must make it if I live by the time I am forty twenty thousand dollars or more, for Laura will need a great deal by that time. She must have a classical education if it takes all we can make.[17] Honey, I am proud and I hope you are too in having such a beautifull & sweet object to live for, as she is the perfect embodiment of her lovly & angelic mother, bless her little heart. I would fail if I wore to attempt to tell how much I love you & her, but suffice it to say that I love you with all my heart & as I do myself. Honey, I cannot express what consolation it gives me to read your letters. I was perfectly fretfull at the time I got your letter. You have no idea how pleasant it made me feel after I read them. Darling, I am often carried away at the thought of having a dear possessed of such a briliant mind, so liced are your ideas, so perfect & so sweet the tenor of your letters. I am perfectly astounded to think that I was so fortunate in marrying you, the dearest of all on earth to me. Would to God I could be with you now. It seems I cannot do without your presence longer, but I do not know how I am to help

---

[16]These letters are missing.

[17]Laura received her M.A. degree from College Temple in Newnan, Ga. on 26 May 1879. College Temple was the first American educational institution to grant the master's degree to a woman.

myself. Honey, I could sit down & talk & love you now for forty eight hours without sleeping a wink. Honey, I wish you knew how much I though[t] of you. I will let you know by my actions when I see you again if I should ever have the happy time to come. I yet see no chance in the world to get home with you. You will have to come to see me when we get back to Vicksburg, if we get to see each other soon. Honey, it seems so crewel for two that love as we do to be seperated so long. The beauty of the different seasons have lost all their charms for me in consequence of not having your sweet, silvery voice mingled with the aerial warberlers. Your eyes, your lips, which look & speak the sweet tones of love to me, & your hole charming face & form I have not drawn on the tablet of my imagination as durable & as lasting as the pillows of Herculese. I am sorry to learn from your letter that your Pa had declined comeing to see us. I was in hopes he would come & bring you with him. Honey, they cannot press your Lizza Welch. They could do so if I was not in the army, but being a soldier in the service, the regulations does not allow my horses to be interupted. If these facts are made know[n] to the Quarter Master who impresses, then he will not do so; & again she could be run off in a few minutes if one was to attempt it, so you need not be uneasy on that score. Honey, in reference to McDaniel's place or any other place, I would not under any consideration buy a place unless you ware perfectly satisfied with it. Always have this idea that I am desireous of pleasing you in evry thing I do. I was sorry to learn that Laura had been sick. Bless her little heart, when Pappie does come home he will get her anything to eat she wants. I donot blame her for not letting you leave her while sick. I would not myself if I ware at home sick. I am sorry to hear of the misfortune of Mr. Ben's. He has a good wife. Tell you Pa I read every line you write over & over again & donot have half enough to read then of your production. Honey, you tell me not to think to much of the Ladies here or you will get jelous. Your knowledge of my affection for you would not suffer you to get so, I hope. I get to see Stubbs here occasionally, your second intended husband. I think I would have a right to be jelous if he was not in the war as I am. You are also jelious of my ability to pull teeth, for I tried repeatedly to get you to let me pull your tooth while I was at home, but you would not consent, but had some one else to do so in my absence. I wish it could have been saved, for I had rather loose one than to see you do so anytime. I want you to mantain as long as possible your pristine beauty. I will save my close until I get to see you in them. It [is] the prettyest suit I have seen since I have been in the survice. Honey, you say you hate to hear of my being home sick & you are afraid I do not enjoy myself & that if I had not married you that you & Laura would not trouble me. I admit I want to come home, but I, as to enjoying myself, I get along in that particular as any one in the survice, & as for being troubled about you & Laura, it is the most pleasant really enviable. If all my troubles ware such as you & Laura give me, I could be perfectly happy. Honey, you must not shed tears about my long absence. I would come home in a moment if I could. Tell Laura to feed Pointer as much as she wants to for he is her pappe's dog that he has had much sport with. Honey, if Factory cotton is going to get up to $20 per bunch, you had better buy some to sell. Buy it & hold it a while & you will make money on it. You may buy any article & keep a short time & you will double your money on it. Honey, you spoke of being an intruder. If you ware to walk in my room, it would be pleasent intrusion, I assure—such as I would like well at any time. Honey, you say you get tired of living without Sugar. Darling, send to La Grange & get you some. If not, I will send you some by the first one I see coming home. [Ho]ney, I am glad to say that you will never again see me dejected in consequence of being in debt. I have finally worked out of debt, knotwithstanding I have had a hard row to wead thus far through life. But the happyest part of my life has been spent in your dear presence, & I hope to spend the ballance of my life their. Honey, I can get beef here at twelve cents per pound & bacon now at turty three. If I had know[n] it was so high at home I would told you not to have sent it. We are living finely on fish at this time—get as much as we can eat.

I was sick at the time I wrote you the letter about something to eat. I could not eat any thing, I thought, bu[t] something from home. Honey, keep Lizza fat. If you do have to pay $3.00 per bushel for corn, we'll make it pay on her yet. It is quite common for horses to sell here for $1000 or $1100. Honey, I would not buy any cotton. I donot think it a safe purchase. The Goverment might take it from you. Honey, I am sorry to learn that you are not well. I wish I could come home: I think I could benefit you. Honey, you put one of my letters in Lou's letter. He read it nearly through before he found out the mistake. He said he thought you was getting pretty heavy to begin to call him honey. Giles writes him some good letters. I hope y'r Ma is still getting on well.

Tell y'r Pa that my asst., Dr. A. S. Whitiker, did not pass the board. He was rejected & will soon be relieved from survice. I am very sorry of it: he is a good fellow, & it will mortify his Brother, Jerod I. Whitiker, of Atlanta. You nor y'r Pa must not say anything about it. No one in the regt. will know it. He will resign as though nothing had gone rong. If I was him I would not tell my wife of it. She will think him a poor doctor. Fortunate for me, I passed all right. Let me hear from you often. Donot let seven days pass between the time of one letter & another. I guess you will be tired of this letter before you get through reading it. Your every true

G.W.P

Kiss Laura often for me.
Give my love to all.
Foster & Lou is well. Honey, donot forget to have my watch cord made as soon as you hair gets long enough.

110

Vicksburg, May 7th, 1863

MY DARLING PRECIOUS ONE KITTIE, With great delight I have read your five last letters.[18] Nothing affords me more gratification than to think that you are well enough to write to me. I have spent some miserable moments about you & Laura having that disease which baffle the skill of the medical world to prevent the uncomely scars it leaves. My great grief is that you were not vaccinated. The first time I wrote to you to be, but oh, it [is] to late to talk about that now. You write to me about being vaccinated again. Of course, be vaccinated evry three day until it takes. You do not say wheather you have had Laura vaccinated. Honey, do for God sake & for the sake of one who is willing to die for you *continue the application of the virus until it has thoroughly taken on you & Laura both.* I have been maserable ever since I heard Lin had it. I would not have such a time again for a world. Honey, donot let any of those who have had it come near you unless you are thoroughly vaccinated. You will be in danger of it for months. Tell your Pa to burn up evry [cloth] those negro have. Do not suffer a rag of cloth or anything in the world [to] be handled that will be likely to convey the contagion. Honey, you had better leave home for fear of taking the disease by accident. You can go with impunity anywhare that all have been vaccinated.

Honey, I am so distressed about you I canot write anything that would interest you. I think we will have battle here ere long, though I cannot tell. We are prepareing for it with all our might. Our Regt. is about ten miles below here. I am only here for a few hour for seing some sick we left in camps. I will return in a short time. I donot have time to write you as often as I would like. I will write you often as soon as we get temporially stationed. I saw Nick in Vicksburg to day. He is in fine health. Lou & Foster are also well. Tell you Pa Lin came in contact with some one whose in the R.R. It is in all the towns & cityes. Honey, I can not let Pa have your Lizzie. Tell him that she is ow[n]ed by me & another man, & on that account I could not let her go. Honey, have Puss, Manda, & evry one of y'r Pa's family vaccinated. I send you another scab that is pure matter. Let me here from you often at least evry mail until their is no danger of getting the prevalent disease. Honey, have it put in at least six places in one of your arms at each vaccination. Eight day from the time the matter is first put in is the time for other to be vaccinated from it, if it takes. If vacinated from anyone's arm at that time it will always take. Donot vacinate from one to another after that time for fear of making a bad sore.

Yours ever more G.W Peddy

---

[18]These letters are missing.

111

Franklin, May the 12, 1863.

MY OWN DARLING ONE,

With a heart filled with fond proud devotion I have read your dear long interesting letter from Deer Creak.[19] Shurely no one can excel you in writing words that make all the heart to throb with a deeper thrill of love untill life becomes as a beatiful dream with so many pleasures to link the chain of love to. I did not think of you birth day at the time I was writing, for I thought it came on the 11. I would have tried to write you a good letter if I could be capable of doing such things. I do sincerely hope an other birth day will not pass and find you far away from those who love you better than life. Honey, you spoke of being fretful. I don't think it could be possible for you to get very fretful, for you have borne so patiently all my faults. How I do wish I could tell you how much I love you. Language cannot tell half how much of devotion dwells in my heart for you. Every letter I read of yours tells too unmistakably how strong the cords of love bind us together. You think me jealous, do you? I know too well that every throb of pure love is mine that fills you heart & I hope to retain the noble fondness of devotion that any woman, no matter how gifted, might be proud of, but I see you never forget a *joke* spoken in thoughtlessness. I think you are some what mistaken about the tooth I had pulled. It is not the one you wanted pluged, but a wisdom tooth & a very small one at that. I suffered so much it seemed like I could get no relief any way untill it was taken out in your absence. Honey, we have such nice pease and the finest lettuce you ever saw. If you but get to enjoy eating it, I woud be so glad. I did hope that you would come home soon, but I fear such a happy thing cannot come to pass. We have heard you was fighting down around Vick and I can't hear wheather you have got back from Deer Creak. It is terible to be in suspense & anxity so long about those we love. You tell me not to grieve about your absence. How can I help feeling sad in your absence when all my happiness is centered on you, & then, my love, you are exposed to every danger and temptation? Honey, I am so glad you passed the boad so well. It fills my heart with pride and pleasure. You say you would not have told me of it. Honey, I am the one to share all you sorrows as well as your successes. Honey, I am so thankful that I have escaped thus far that horrid disease, small pox, and know that you are glad too. Nearly every night I dream of you being in trouble, and it must be the case. I have been so uneasy for fear you would come off by yourself, and so many Yankee scouts prowleling around. I do wish it could have been so I could have telegraphed to you every day how we was getting on. The little children who had been incoulated are getting well. I don't think any more cases will break out from it.

---

[19]*Supra*, No. 109.

We have just heard of the death of Stonewall Jackson.[20] I am so sorry, for he was worth ten thousand men to our cause. I fear it will protract the war longer. It looks like we will soon be ruined any way.

William Martin was mortally wounded and has since died, and two more of Mabry's company are killed. He himself was judge advocate in a courtmartial and was not in the fight. We have not heard the full account of the casualties yet.

Your father sent me word by Andrew a few days ago to let him have Liz untill I heard from you, and if you objected to it, he would send her back. I did not let him have her, for I knew you would not like for her to go so far from home. I never was so troubled about any thing. I am affraid he will get mad with me about it, but I did what I thought for the best. You must write to him not to blame me for doing as I did. I dont like to do anything contrary to her [*sic*] wishes if I know it. He sold his horse and don't want to buy one till fall. Liz is getting fat now as she can be. I do wish she was gentle. How much pleasure I miss by not riding her. Your sister Fannie wrote to me, and says you have forgotten she is your sister, sends you her best love. She sent Laura a little ring mad[e] out of ivy. It pleased Laura so well. She says, papie, her mama is weaving her a nice dress and will soon have you some clothes done too. She kisses me every day for papie. Honey, I write to you nearly every mail & you don't write near that often. I would be glad to get a letter every mail. Honey, do for my sake take care of yourself. Good by my love. Katie Peddy

112

Vicksburg, May 3rd at night/863[21]

MY DARLING PRECIOUS ONE KITTIE,

I write you a few lines to let you know that we have got back safe to this place an occurrance of which I am very glad, as we were surrounded on all sides by water when on Deer Creak & liable to be cut off by the enemy. We will leave here in the morning to be gone three days. We'll go below here some fifteen miles. I suppose we will have an engagement dow[n] whare we are going. We have been fighting the enemy for three days a[t] Port Gibson. They beat us back at that point, so I hear to night, by outnumbering us. We have heavy reinforcements that will arrive there to night, enough, I hope, to beat them back again & rout

[20]Jackson was mortally wounded at Chancellorsville on 2 May.

[21]Misdated 862. Envelope addressed: Mrs. Z.C. Peddy. Franklin, Ga.

them. Honey, donot be uneasy about me. I will take care of myself the best I can on y'r & Laura's account, for I know you would not live happy if you knew Pappie would not come again. Honey, I love you more dearly, if possible, ev'ry day. It is not man['s] province nor his good fortune to love so purely as do ladies, but if any one lo[v]es better on earth than I do you, I cannot imagine how it [is] done. Honey, I have not time to write you only a short letter. I rec'ed a letter from Nick to day. He is quite well & doing finely in his office. Lou & Foster are well. Lou seems to be gay & lively all the while. The only objection I have to him is he keeps me thinking of you every time I look at him. Nick is in command of the Or[dnance] Department at Jackson in consequence of the officer over him being arrested. Capt. Maring will be here on Monday next. I suppose he will bring my box, as you have sent it. I hope he will. If I had know provision was so high at home I would have not asked you to send them. Honey, I have the finest buggy horse you ever have seen. I got him for $250. I will sell him in a few days of $500. I have sold my pistol of $75 this eve. I expect I had better kept it, but I must get out of debt. Honey, if you want to make money, buy a lot of good tobacco as cheap as you can & hold it awhile & you will double your money on it. It will be worth ten dollars a pound before next Christmas. Honey, pay good attention to Laura's teeth. Also do not let her get gross in her habits or maners. It's no use, though, to tell you of these things, for I know y'r good judgement can tell you how to act better than I could write. Honey, let me hear from you often. I am so proud when I get a letter from you. Honey, my pants are nearly worn out you made me last winter. I cannot buy any wool in this country. I need not troubl yourself about making me a great many garments. My overcoat will last me, if I should live, two more winters. The coat you made me last winter will also last me a great while yet. Give my love to all. Tell Giles I will get his muset & send him in a short time. As for my watch I was offered to day $75 dollars for it. Yours evermore,

G W Peddy

To his dear Wife
Z. C. Peddy

113

Franklin, May the 15, 1863.[22]

MY OWN DARLING,

I sit down this lovely sunset hour to write you again. It is always a great pleasure to me to look at nature's beauties. It fills the soul with wonder and admiration and causes the heart to gush with thanksgiving to nature's God for such lovliness. My love, how I would be delighted to sit by your side now. Such pleasure is rarely mine. I think of it in the day and dream often of it at night, but alas! it seems we will be seperated a long time now. I can't help looking for you, although I know it is impossible for you to get off. I was so disappointed when Mr. Miller came home & brought me no letter for me from you. Bud Lu wrote to bud Gily. I heard from it that you was expecting an attact every hour. It gives me a great deal of uneasiness, for I am not shure you are safte, and bud Lu is too ventursome. You must try and get him to listen to reason and not go on any more dangerous work as he has been on. Pa was very much amused at bud Lu's description of his trip up the country. Honey, you don't write half often enough. Pa & Ma say it is perfect folly for me to write twice a week, says it is spending money too freely for postage, but if it adds any thing to your pleasure for me to write often, I am going to do it, for I consider money well invested when spent to secure no such pleasure as letters give. I feel so sad if a mail comes and brings me no letter. You always write such good, inteligent, loving letters, it would be very strange if I did not welcome them with a glad heart. Honey, my words seam cold and pashionless, but could you see the fountain of love in my heart that gushes forth, filling every portal and avenue with devotion for your noble self, you would wonder why I could not express it in language more forcible than I do. Laura is well. She gets resless every night and screams out in her sleep. I am going to give her some Vermefuge. I think she needs it. I had our little cow brought up to give her some fodder, for she is very poor. Laura calls her Peggy. Every day she comes to me and puts her sweet face close up to mine & asks if she may have little Peggy. She is perfectly carried away at the idea. I believe she is the smartis child I ever saw, but she could not be otherwise & be like her father. I do hope we will raise her right, to walk the the straight and narrow path which leads to that place where the good & pure in heart meet to part no more. I want you to read a great deal in the Soldier's Friend just for my sake. Do so: you will find there a good many things which will tend to make you

[22]Postmarked Franklin Geo May 16. Addressed: Dr. G.W. Peddy, Vicksburg, Miss., Gen Taylor's Brig. 56. Ga. Regment. (Maj. Gen. Richard Taylor, C.S.A., the son of President Zachary Taylor, commanded the District of Western Louisiana.)

think of religion with respect, and I do sincerly hope it will lead you to seek the "pearl of great price" that is all you like to make you all that heart could wish on Earth. Honey, don't begin to be uneasy for fear of a sermond, but I think of your situation a great deal and can't help writing of it. I have no news to write that you would care to hear, no new cases of smallpox. Lew has not been brought home yet, nor will not soon. His feet & legs are swelling so he can not walk well. I think I will get off from here when he does come back for fear of an accident. You must be shure to send me some vaccine matter by some one. I am frightened yet, and will be untill all danger is over. The excitement about it has somewhat subsided.

Ambrose Williams & Hence Baggus are going to be sent to camps in ten days. The duty of enroling is assigned to men who are not able for military duties. It will be quite a severe trial to them to have to go off into hardships. I do wish you could stay with me and not go to the army any more, but it is the decree, and we must brave it out even if it does wring out hearts with agony. Honey, write me word wheather you will have to have an entire suit this fall of jeans. Wool is selling now at four dollars off of the sheep's back. It will cost a good deal, but if you need it, why just write to me so I can get the wool in time to get it made before it gets cold weather. Yours & bud Lew's summer suits will soon be ready, if we could only find any way to send them to you. I know you must need them Uncle Ben was here a few days ago. He asked me what I would take for Liz. He bought one for three hundred. I will close by asking you to write as often as possible. Yours ever more.

Kate Peddy

114

Franklin, May the 18/63

MY LOVE,

I am so sad & low spirited tonight it would be useless to attempt an interesting letter. We heard today the enemy had taken Jackson, Miss.[23] If such is the case, we cannot even hear from each other. I am so uneasy about you I

[23]Jackson fell to Grant on 14 May. Joseph E. Johnston, now in overall command in the West, withdrew to the northeast with the intention of joining forces with Pemberton, who was defending Vicksburg.

can't have any peace. Honey, I have not had a letter from you in a long time. It seems every one else gets letters every mail but me. I write every mail too, but can't hear one word from you. I have not heard from you since we had the small pox here. I know you are nearly as wretched as I am, for it seems impossible to get a letter through in a long time. I would so much like to hear what you think of the campains in the west or at lest where you are. I don't know where I could wish you would be sent to now, for at every post there is a prospect of a fight, but darling, let fate do her worst, we will have the joyful knowledge that our hearts are one joined by the holiest ties that nature ever bound two hearts with, and through storm & sunshine we will love on to the last. I get so anxious to see you sometimes. It does seem hard to wait longer for the sweet privilege of being with you, my love, but we will comfort ourselves with the comforting reflection that we are still spared to each other, while so many are denied such a blessing; and our little baby darling is a perfect little cherrub; says she loves her papie *60* pounds and a *half*. Hony, you stey away so much and so long she will not feel as dear to you now as she used to, I fear, but we love you, papie, if we could, a thousand fold more. I wish you could hear some of her little baby talk. It would amuse you; & now she is sitting in my lap waiting patiently for me to finish this letter to rock her to sleep. Now, papie, ain't she a spoilt baby? I don't think you will get an oppertunity of leaving me, for I will be near you as long as I live. We never have appreciated the pleasures & blessings of life untill they have been snatched from us. I wish I knew where you are to night. It might add to my suspense, but I don't think it would now.

May the 19. I have been very buisy all day. The only way I can get any relief when troubled about any thing. We heard today the Yankees did take Jackson, but was compelled to evacuate it. I fear they intercepted the mail, and now I shall get no letters. If I don't get a letter tomorrow, it will be too bad to think of. Honey, my health is better than it has been since you was at home. I am fleshy too. I do hope I will keep well for a long time. Laura is also as fat as a pig. Dr. Watkins passed here a few days ago and told Ma Jane was in a bad condition. She coughed so much, she could not sleep any at all, and he could do her no good yet. Don't tell Brewer, for I know he will be frighened, but it is thought she has consuption. I saw Mrs. Ben Spearman the other day. She was very uneasy too, not having received a letter in three weeks. You will think women are very simple to get so uneasy about such things, but I can't help it. Pa will go to Newnan the last of this week and get some vacine matter from Dr. Calhon. I had rather wait for you to send me some, but it may be too late in the Summer. The small pox in Boudon, Carrol Co. and at a great many other places. I fear it will spread all over the country. It is a fearful time shurly. Lee run away from the overseer to stay. He would not take a whipping, so he left. Pa has determined to sell Lin as soon as he can. I would have let him go a good while ago, but he disliked to seperate him from his wife. Hony, you don't say much about the war closing now. I think even the most hopeful give up the thought of peace soon. If it would close now, we would be too happy, I fear. You are tired to death of marching from place to place, I know, by this time. Honey, all the medecine is about to give out in town. You must send me some blue mass if it can be found where you are, and some fhis to draw blisters. I will get Dr. Harland to make me some paragoric, as I have the ingredients necessary. I don't know what people will do if there is much sickness this year. I am very tired to night and sleepy, so please excuse me if I must say good night and leave you. What would I give if you was only here to say that word to! Come soon, darling, and you will find a heart war[m]ing welcome.

Yours ever more. Katie Peddy.

115

Stone Mountain, Sept. 23rd, 63[24]

MY DEAREST KITTIE, With a heavy heart I left you & will be to, so long as I remain from you. I am always happy in your presence, so much so that I want you to come to me. I cannot come home again soon. Honey, I can get a good place for you to stay at. If you come, you must not bring a servant with you, & I expect you had better leave Laura at home. It will be much cheaper to do so, although you can bring her if you wish. I can stay with you nearly all the while. It's generally thought that we will remain here a month or two, at least a month. Honey, you can start next Tuesday morning & get from home & get here a[t] 8 o'clock. Lane can bring you to the R.R. Tuesday & get you a seat & you can keep it until you get here. I sold the Grimes horse for $1800.00. My part of the proffit was after the table expenses was paid was $141.00, or a right nice proffit to make in ten days. Now you see, if I had taken your advice I would have been minus that am't. I have bought a ten dollar gold piece for fifty dollars. I will make a hundred dollars on that.

Honey, be shure to come Tuesday, for I want to see you badly. I will let you stay until we leave here. I donot know what to do without Andy. I expect I will have to take him away from you. If you want to keep him, though, you shall do so, & I will get another that I can trade on. I have not heard any thing about the

---

[24]There are no letters between 19 May and 23 September. Vicksburg capitulated 4 July, and the garrison was paroled. Some time afterwards, Dr. Peddy apparently was home on furlough.

Lt. Place in the company as yet. Bob Tharp is here. I am staying with the company now. My camp chest has not come yet. I am looking for it on evry train. I have no place to write, only on my knee. Honey, I bought as much corn as you want from Jep Daniel. I expect you had better borrow the money & get twenty barrels. I have plenty of money, but no way to send it to you. You must come & git it. I will close, honey. Come on to see me.

Your as true as life

G.W Peddy

P.S. I am to get the corn at two dollars. If you can get it from Uncle Joseph Lane, I had rather have it, but get it soon for fear it rise.

G W Peddy

116

Stone Mountain, Sept. 24th, 1863

MY DARLIN SWEET KITTIE,

I wrote you a letter ysterday to come to see me next Tuesday. You need not come, as we are ordered to join Gen. Brag. How sorry I am. I was in hopes that I would have a happy time togueather again, but oh, I fear our enjoyment is at an end for the present; but we must not despair. I hope we will meet again before long. Honey, prepair my clothes as quick as you can. I will need them soon. Also make me a shusrap. I donot know whare to tell you to direct your letters. I will know ere long. Your ever more
Kiss Laura for pappie.

G.W Peddy

117

Chicamauga Station, Tenn. Oct 3rd/863

MY DARLING SWEET KITTIE, It is my sweet pleasure to write you a few lines this eve. We left Decatur in the evening after you left in the morning. Honey, I did regret to see you leave so much. I was very well satisfied in camps so long as you were near, but now you are fair away & I am miserable. I hear no war news to write you. If I could be with you all the time, I would be perfectly happy. Without your presence in war or peace I am not satisfied. Let pleasure with all its allurements cluster around me, let my heart be light & my air be gay, let news of victory to our army be rife & cheering, let evry thing which serves to cheer up the mind of man in this life come like an avalanch: none affords such jenuine as your dear presence. Honey, you said to me when with you last, I would not love you now, but if it is possible for my asteem to be increased, I think it's now. I thought that nothing could increase my love for you, but to my great supprise, after many though[t]s & diligent research into the deep recesses of my affections, I find that I love you better than before I saw you last. Honey, when you think of me, you may be assured that I will ever love you & be as constant to you as death is certain. Honey, donot get sad while I am away. Keep your sweet heart buoyed up with the reflection that I *love* you *fondly* & will *cherish* and *reverence* you as the good christian does his maker. Honey, think when you are sad also that it shall be my greatest pleasure to keep you cheered up. Honey, this crewel war cannot last always. Then if I live through it, what rapturous series of pleasure we will have! Honey, what a happy though[t] when I think about the beauty & perfection of our little darling Laura. I have not got my Chest as yet. Poole is at home & will bring it to me as soon as it comes to Atlanta. I wrote for it today again. Honey, get my close done as soon as it possible. If [we] move from here, I think I will send my trunk home. I brought Andy on the train with me. He is d[o]ing well. Honey, I have to pay 85 ct per pound for meet. I must try to get my meat from home after you kill hogs. Honey, I am going to save all the money I can for you & Laura. I cannot get anything to eat in this country but meat & breat, but I am willing to live almost any way until we have peace. Honey, how proud I feel when I think of the perfection & loveliness of my little family. To night while groups of soldiers are singing praise to god with one perfect cord of music, I sit here writing to you & can imagine that my heart at every pulsation beets a stronger affection for you than any hea[r]t beats can. Honey, I know not what to say about Lou's case. I know it's better for him to be here if he expects to get the position he has been speaking of, but your Ma is so opposed to his coming, that I could not advise him against her wishes. If Lou comes, he mus[t] inquire at the express office in Atlanta to see if my Chest is there.

Direct your letters to me Atlanta, Ga. & they will be forwarded to me. G. W Peddy

Side: With an ever rushing sentiment of love, I close this.

Top: Write often, honey. Let me know all the particulars about home affairs. I expect we will have a big fight here soon.

118

Chickamauga, Tenn. Oct. 6th/863

MY PRECIOUS DEAR SWEET KITTIE,

It is my sweet pleasure to write you again a few lines this pleasant eve. I have not heard from you since I left you. How much pleasure I would have in reading a letter from your dear sweet hand. Honey, it seems that it's been years since I left you last. Oh how I wish I was with you now! What sweet converse we could have. The lovely look of those lovely little eyes will ever be fresh with me. My heart leeps with joy when I think what a perfect little being I have as my lifetime campanion. How pleasant I could spend the remainder of my life with you if I had the gracious opportunity. There is no news from the front today. I visited the battle field yesterday. Thousands of the enemy are yet lying there in a state of putrefaction unburied. They smell awfully. Our dead are all buried.[25] Honey, I sent you Pa's saddle & bridle to Hogan[s]ville per express. You must pay the express on it. I got a letter from Dr. Houston yesterday about the fifty dollars he owed me. I wrote him to express it to you at Hoganville. You will have to send their for it in about two weeks. I have not yet drawn any money to send you. Lou has some colored shirts here that Poole brought out of Vicksburg. Honey, I donot want you to do any work while I am gone. Let me hear from you often, how you are getting along in evry particular. I will write you more at length when I hear from you. Kiss little Kitten for pappie.

Yours forevermore

G. W Peddy

---

[25]The battle of Chickamauga was fought on 19-20 September. Union dead numbered 1,657; Confederate, 2,312.

119

Chicamauga, Tenn. Oct. 7th, 1863

MY OWN DEAR SWEET KITTIE, Lou arrived her safe last eve with many acceptable favors from you. They came in quite as favorable time as they could have. Many good wishes to Mrs. Hales for her kind faver. I hope I will be able to return the compliment in future. Among the many good things sent was a little billadew from your lovely hand, the contents of which I propose to notice closely.[26] I am glad to hear you had a pleasant trip home, also that you found friends evrywhare. I should have been happy to have accompanied you on your pleasant tour. I am under lasting obligation for Mr. Purgeson['s] kindness to you. You say you can never get accostomed to live without my presence. Honey, I donot wish you to. As for myself, I know it's impossible for me ever to be happy only in your presence. Honey, there is one expression in your letter more marked & expressive than any that has been in any heretifore, which is this, when I told you that I had an idea of doing better in the future, you write that it makes your heart ache with joy evry time you think of it. Honey, after the many stiring & pathetic appeals of love I have made to you heretifore with my fun, after all my efforts both in actions & words to make you realize the genuine purity of my love, after doing evry thing that I thought was in the province of man to do to teach & impress upon you the debth of my affection, I find I have fallen far sho[r]t of my desires! The fact of you leavening me & going to church when I first came home from Vicksburg, the fact that nothing can elicit such soft expressions & such pleasant ones from you as the one on the second page of this letter, teaches me that your affections are concentrated upon divine things & the nearer one through faith approaches deity, the more you love them. Hence I am forced to the conclusion, as anyone is compelled to be, that I am an unworthy & unfortunate creature & share only a finite portion of your pure affection. If this be so, alas for me: better far that I never had been born. My appeals to you have been of the most pathetic kind. It has ever been my highest ambition to do evrything I could to make you think I loved you dearly. Evry affecting sentance I was master of I have wrote it to you. You have been writing to me now for over two years & you never made use of as good a one as the one aforesaid.

Honey, I love you & Laura solely; you, me partially.

I wish I could have seen Laura petting. You I know it was affecting. Perhaps pappie will be home again some of these days. Then I hope I will enjoy the luxury of he[r] little sweet caresses. Honey, let me hear from you often. Honey,

[26]This letter is missing.

alway remember when I am in sadness or in pleasure that I love you with a devotion rarely experienced by anyone else.

Yours ever more

G. W Peddy

120

Chicamauga Station, Tenn. Oct. 16th, 1863

MY DEAREST IDOL KITTIE, I have reced no letter from you yet. Their is so much derangement in the postal department I presume is the cause of it. I begin to want to hear from you so much. A letter from you would be a rare treat now. I have written you three since I have been here. I have no war news of interest to write. It is rumored that we will fall back south of Dalton from here. I know not wheather their is confidence in the report or not. Honey, I have got Lou a furlough for 40 days. I feel almost as proud of it as if I had it myself. Honey, do you not think you had better keep Puss at home next year to wait on you & Laura? Your comfort, pleasure, & happyness in this life is all I desire. I know you cannot get along well by yourself, & for that reason I want you to take her at home to wait on you. Bless your little heart, if I was their with you I would wait on you better than any one else. Oh! that I could be! Honey, do not work anymore after you get my clothes done. *You must not suffer yourself to become fretfull at Laura & the negroes*, for it all amounts to nothing & can only redound to your injury. Honey, remember this when you get ruffled in your feelings. Use yourself as heretifore & I will be perfectly satisfied, because you have always acted in a manner so becomeing a lady that I idolize you, love you more than the suppleness of language can speak. Honey, a fine Brass band has just struck up the tune of Lorena. Oh! how I wish you could stand bi me to hear it. I cannot enjoy it because of your absence. The 7th & 8th Ga. Regts. are camped in a hundred yds. of us. I have seen & see evry day Brother John & all the boys of Brown's old company. Indeed I was glad to see them. I have an Asst. Surgeon, a nice fellow from Va. I have but little to do. The band is now playing *Home Sweet Home*. Oh! you cannot imagine what strange feelings run through & over me. I cannot tell them. Home Sweet Home, wheare linger those that I love & whare my earthly a[n]gel sleeps & wakes, I hope to think of me, unworthy as I am. Great God, can I live through this crewel war to enjoy your presence, which is more desired by me than all else? Honey, do not let Sweet

Laura forget me. I think of you oftener than ever before & if possible love you more. It seems to me that I can not possibly stay away from you longer. I could always stay away from you better than now. Now it seems that I cannot. Poor Kittie, I often think, I began the hours evry night thinking of your pure precioss self. I am so proud that I have a pure lovely one to worship. It seems to me if I were with you I could not suffer you to even raise your hand without my assisting you. I could treat you more kindly & tenderly now than ever in my life before. But darling, as I can't be with you, pleese try & be as merry as you can. Nothing will help you along so much as that. Take good care of yourself. If you take Puss home, keep enough meat & bread for her. Honey, it seems that I could write to you always. Good by, my sweet angel. Let me hear from you often, honey, the pride of my heart.

G.W Peddy

121

Tiner's Station, Tenn. Oct. 19th, 1863

MY DARLING SWEET KITTIE, I drop you a few lines with my pencil. I have rec'ed no letter from you yet. You must direct your letters to me at Cleveland, Tenn., as we are going to that point this eve, & from their on towards Knoxville. You may say to Lt. Cald & Stephens not to bring any trunks or boxes for they will not be allowed to have them halled. I will ship my trunk home per express with my uniform in it. I will not need them this winter after I get my suit from home. You must hang them up in your wardrobe & keep them for me nicely. Honey, I donot want to be dressed up finely unless my da[r]ling could see me. Honey, direct your letters to Chickamauga, Tenn. instead of *Cleveland.* I will ship my trunk to you at Hoganville, Ga. Dearest, you must please send my clothes by the first one that you can safely trust them with. Honey, I am so anxious to hear from you. I fear that my love is not well. I hope you are. Honey, do take good care of your dear precious self, for you know without you I could not exist. You are my life in every interprise in every thing in this world. I think I would have rec'ed several letters from you, as I had told you to send your letters to Chickamauga. Oh! how I want to see you! It hurts me worse to be away from you than ever before. Honey, Lou must get an extension of his furlough. I cannot get him another soon. Send a certificate. I will write to [you] often. Yours ever true. A kiss for you & Laura

G.W Peddy

122

Franklin, Oct. 20 th/63

MY PRECIOUS DARLING,

With feelings of love such as is seldom dreamed of by mortals do I attempt, though as I always do, without fullfiling my wishes, to tell you how dear you are to me. Honey darling, you could but see the deep love which sweeps like a wild torrent through my heart, you would never dream of such love dweling in any being's heart no matter how noble the object of the heart's admaration. It is not surprising to me that I do love you so well, for you are all that humane beings can be to cause the spontaneous gushing of undying love in any one heart. I never see or hear any thing lovely, grand, and magnificent but my first wish is that you too could be with me to enjoy it. Pleasures lose all their zest while you are far away; sorrows are more unbearable without your dear voice to soothe the pain away. Honey, I have never read or seen any kind of devotion that is half as strong as mine for you. All seems cold and pashionless compared to the love I cherish as my happiness in this life. Honey, you said in your letter that you did not think I loved you. Darling, I know you can't doubt it, for it seems to me every word I have ever written and every line ended in telling you how like my own life, a life was the blessed love making glad every nook & corner of my heart. Bud Lu came home Sunday night. He brought me the best letter I ever read in my life. I have read it with the tears chaseing each other down my cheeks for days. Honey, don't be uneasy about me. It grieves me so much to think how much you are troubled about me. I know you think now your share of trouble is great. Of course I can't expect to be entirely as well now as usual, but I am doing finely. If you was only here, how supremly happy I should be, but honey, I will try to do as you tell me, & if you will write to me such sweet good letters as you did the last one, I will only be so happy that nothing but your presence could surpass it. Honey, I dream of you nearly every night. Sometimes I am nearly distressed to death about you; then again, I am so happy with you that it wakes me. Darling, you *must* take good care of yourself, for you can't tell what bitter agony I would be plunged in wer I to lose you, the source of all my joy. Honey, if I could only feel those dear arms around me again it would give me joy too great for language to express. I do miss you so much. I think sometimes I must see you, it has been so long since I last saw that face dearer to me than all else besides. Hony, I have been sobing tonight while writing this letter till it seems like my heart will break thinking of your being far away in every danger while I am not with you to share it. Honey, don't think I am childish: it is the love I have for you that makes me wish to be near you every hour.

Oct. 21. I did not finish my letter last night, for my light gave out. Laura was restless all night. She is not well, though she never complains. Puss came over Sunday & tells me she is in the same condition I am in. Mr. Mathews had made her & two other negroe women raise a crib, and she was not well. She had the logs to haul too to make the crib out of. I wrote him a note telling him to send her home if he could not give her such work as a woman ought to do. She looks very poor & bad, says she is not well no day. I will try to hire her here in town next year. Honey, it would be spoiling me too much to keep her here to wait on me. Don't you think I had best go out and see about her now? Mrs. David has refused to let me have any more corn. I only got 5 barrels from her. I don't know where to get more now. Every body is waiting untill it gets up to five dollars a bushel. I think maybe I can get some from Mr. Mathews. Write to me often, and I will do finely. I must stop now. I am so glad you & brother John are together. I am as ever yours forever. Katie Peddy.

123

Near Loudin, Tenn. Oct. 22nd, 1863

MY DARLING SWEET KITTIE,

I have a chance to write you a line or two. I am quite well & hope you are sweet one also. I expressed my trunk to you at Hoganville. Hope it will come up safe. Honey, I have recd no letter from you yet. I am so anxious about you. Acy Smith his shot his hand, & I will send this letter to you as near home as he can get. We have marched here. We cannot get but 12 miles farther before we encounter the enemy. My darling, with many kind & sweet wishes for your welfare & happyness I remain yours forever G.W. Peddy

P.S. I have no coat to wear, but my overcoat & my pants are worne through. I sent my uniform home in my trunk. GWP.

124

Sweet Water, Tenn. Oct 27th/863

MY DARLING KITTIE,

It is my sweet pleasure to write you a few lines this evening. I have no news, only we are here in a bountiful country. I am living on pork at this time, but my diet has been awfull for the past few days. I have rec'ed no letter from you yet. I want to hear from my precious little family very much indeed. I will wait as patiently as I possibly can. Honey, I want my clothes so much. You must keep a sharp lookout for my trunk at Hoganville. I will send you the key by the first one I see passing, & if no one goes soon, I will send it to you in a letter. I have not heard from my Mess Chest as yet. No one has inquired in Atlanta for it in a long time. Honey, you cannot imagine how much I want to hear from you & our little sweet darling Laura. Tell her pappie loves her if possible more than ever. You & her are my idoles, my happyness, my evrything that's noble & good. Oh! would that I could be at home to see you & talk to you. You have no one to tell your secrets to; neither have I to tell mine to. Honey, it's going to rain. I will have to stop writing. I have no tent nor any place to write to you on. Honey, I think of you at all times & feel proud that I have such a noble one to worship as you are. Honey, I wish I could write the true sentiments of heart's love to you. You would be astonished to think that anyone one was capable of loving so dearly. Tell Lou he must have my boots made & bring them to me when he comes. I am doing all I can for him. I hope he will succeed in his expectations. He had better send a certificate back before his furlough runs out, as the commanders are getting very particular. Honey, let me hear from you often & write me all the news. Kiss little pig for me & tell her to kiss you for me also often.

Yours ever truely

G.W. Peddy

P.S. Direct your letters to me at Chickamauga, Tenn.

125

Franklin, Oct. the 27. 1863

MY OWN LOVE,

Again I am seated by a comfortable fire at the ever delightful task of writing to my precious love. Nothing gives me so much pleasure when you are far away as to read such words of affection as your love dictates, words that will live in the holiest place in my memory as long as my heart throbs with life. My darling, you often think me cold and void of those warmer feelings of love which you often give expression to, but you can't even imagine the debth of pure unalloyed love that you dear self have inspired. I sit here sometimes thinking over the many pleasing incidents of our lives since we have coned the same sweet pages of love together. I was thinking a while ago of your coming up stairs in search of me, as you always do when you come from town, & I hid behind the window curtain. You looked all over the room but did not find my hideing place, and turned away with so much disappointment depicted in your dear face I could not stay away from you longer. Such an incident served only to amuse me then, but now it tells me in unmistakable language the strength of the chain of love which binds our hearts together. Ah! how I do pity those unfortunate beings who never felt love throbing in their hearts making it a rich garden filled with every flower of affection which sheds a rich perfume along the otherwise dreary path of life. Honey, I am tolerably well to night, but am tormented with the most frightful dreams you ever knew and wake up scared almost to death. I will soon have your suit done. It will not be pretty, but will be a very good warm one. I have grived so much over its being carded so bad. Honey, I know you will not sencure me for it. That is something you don't find in you noble heart to do, but I did wnat it to be so nice, for I had rather your apparel should be nice than to have the finest dress you can find. Your matrass has been done some time, but I could get no one to carry it. Brewer went yestady, but said he was too heavyly loaded to take it for me. Two or three will start in the course of a few weeks and I think I can send them to you. Bud Lu has gone to Bowden to get your leather. He engaged Brickell to make them for 20 dollars and you furnish every thing. It is very high, but no one else can fit you as well as himself, though I don't think I can afford to let him make mine. I am troubled about corn now. No one wants to sell untill it gets higher. I think Jef Danniel acted badly about his corn. He also promised Mr. Oliver to let him have some at 2 dollars, and had the money offered to him at the same time. He now refuses to let him have it at all. Mr. Oliver says he will sue him for damages, and if he does, maybe I can get mine too, for I sent the money to pay for all but they declined it. Honey, you never [saw] such nice hogs as ours is. It would do you so much good to look at them. I am affraid they will get so fat. I can't let them run till January. Don't engage our meat to any one in camps, for I think I can sell it for more money here at home. Pork is selling at 1½ dollars now, and every one thinks it will go to 2 and maybe more. There is a pressing officer from Bragg's army now down below here taking all the cattle from the people but milk cows. Pa thinks they will get our little cow, but I will not hear to it. Every body is frightened about their stock and have killed nearly all they have. I don't know what is to become of us no how. I do get so low down thinking on every thing, and the greatest of all troubles, your being absent. Honey, I am affraid you will be sent over on the mountain where those mean bushwhackers live. If you do so, I shan't rest easy a moment till your return. Honey, I must stop tonight, for it is late and I am sleepy. One good night kiss for your sweet lips from one who loves you dearer than life. Laura is well says send a *bag* of *apples*. Katie Peddy.

126

Hed Qr. 56th Ga. Regt., Louden, Tenn., Nov. 2nd, 1863

MY DEAREST ANGELIC KITTIE, With feelings of overwhelming joy have I received & read your two sweet letters of the 17th & 20th ult.[27] No one has such a cause to be proud as I have, for no one has such a loving & intelligent lady as I have. Your condition demands, it seems to me, that I should be with you. No one can possibly be so kind & tender with you as I could. Oh! that it was in my power to be. I am shure, & I hope you are, that it would be my greatest pleasure, but alas for this unjust war, I am forced to stay away longer still. Honey, you can imagine how fondly I could caress & express my feelings of love to you in many other ways were I in your presence. It seems to me if I were with you I could not suffer you to do anything in the world, not even walk. I should want to carry you tenderly with my own hands. While I pen these lines my heart is deeply affected & the pure feelings of love which hover in my bosom for you swells the sympathies of the heart to that extent that it speaks its own language by sending the silent tear down my cheak. Honey, you say I will think you childish for writing me such letters as your last. My sweet darling, they are just such as I like to get from you. Anything that appertains to the distribution of your affections I am always proud to hear, especially when I am blessed

[27]The first letter is missing; the second is 122.

partisipant. Honey, you spoke in yours as if you would like to be at a home of your own. Then you could prepare some thing that you could eat. Honey, if you want to, you can rent Mrs. Boon's house & take Puss home & you & her live their togueather. You can either do that or let Ma know your condition. No doubt she would be better satisfied & tell you better how to get along than you know; but Honey, all confidence in anything you do or your ideas of what to do, I am always satisfied with anything I can do to make you happy. I am willing to do if it is in my power. It is my greatest desire that you have evry comfort & pleasure that you wish. You & Laura are the pride of my heart, my life's life, my solace when far away, & my joy when at home. Would to God that I were able to write you evry feeling of love which throungs around my heart for you. You would be astounded to think that frail man was capable of loving so deeply. Honey, I want you to take *particular care* of *yourself*, for if you were gone, the pail of sadness would drop before my eye forever. No form, no revalry, no joy, no happyness or pure bliss would be mine again. A gloom of dispondency would ever hang around my brow, if such a dreadfull catastrophee were to befall me. I have my Mess chest in Atlanta. I can get it anytime I wish to. I am so glad of it. As soon as I get my wagon, I will be fixed up very nicely. I want Lou to bring my matrass. He may not be able to get it father than Charleston, Tenn. If he can get it no father, he had better get some Citizen to take charge of it until we can send after it. I expect he had better bring the Mess Box also that far & get some one to take charge of it too. I will send you my trunk key in this letter. Honey, donot work yourself, but send my clothes with two pair of yarn socks as soon as you can—I mean the suit you are to make for me. I am so sorry it was spoilt in carding. We are this eve ten miles south east of Louden. I expect we will beat about here for some time, then fall back to Chickamauga. Send my gloves you were to nit for me if you can. The seat of my pants are all out. I cannot get or borrow a pair or get them patched. Let me hear from you often, my own dear. Kiss Laura for pappie. Your love ever more G W Peddy

127

Franklin, Nov. the 3, 1863.[28]

MY DARLING ONE,

I have received two short letters from you in the past week, and am so sorry that you have read no letter from me yet. I know you are uneasy about me, which grieves me so much. Honey, you have enough hardships to endure without being troubled about me. Yet it is very sweet to me to know you sympathise with me in everything that pains me the least. I thought this morning the first thing, if you could only be here now, I could endure almost any thing, for your presence gives me so much exquisite joy it seems to act as a cure for all evils. What a magic charm love has, and it has woven a spell of enchantment around my heart which is more lasting than time. Nothing can ever brake it lose. I love to live just to love you, but always unbidden comes the thought [that] I am not worthy to were the [ring] which you gave me and which [would] enrich the noblest woman that [ever li]ved, though no being, no matter how refined or elegant she may be, ever loved man as I do you my love. How I do wish you could always stay with me! Then I could express to you in actions more striking & convincing than cold feeble language can express. Honey, I am well as you could expect. At night I am tormented with the most frightful dreams I ever had & nearly always something about your being wounded or sick. I wake screaming, then I am nearly tired to death. I can't sleep well no time. I think I will sit up till ten or eleven o'clock and see if that won't do some good. I can't say I am sick, though not well. Laura swallowed a pin a few days ago, which scared me nearly to death. I never suffer her to have such things, but she got one from some one else. She is well now though. I went up to aunt Dump's and got your coat stiched nicely. You will have such a good warm one too, but honey, if it had not been naped, it would have been so pretty and fine. It is a pr[etty] color too. I don't know who I can [send] them by. Bud Lu has gone to [ ] and he will see if any one w[ill be going] from there soon so I can send by them. I am so sorry to hear how scarce of clothes you are, but if I could get them to you, it would not be so. Jeans is selling at 20 dollars a yard and hard to get at that. I have enough left of your suit to make Laura a nice cloak. It will be a pretty one too for her. I don't know whether I can get your boots done in time to send them by the one who carries your suit or not, but will try to get them to you as soon as possible. Mr. Jackson made me such a nice bit. I had it sewed on to my bridle, and now I have as nice outfit as I could wish, if I only had

[28]The letter is torn in the bottom left corner.

Andy to ride. You must take good care of him, honey. I have promised myself a good many easy rides if I live and he comes back. I never saw a horse I like half as well. I am so glad you have him with you to ride. Honey, if you want my bridle-bit, I will send it to you [by Bu]d Lu. Perhaps you can sell it [for a] good price, as I won't need it [until yo]u come home. Then I [will need it] far less. Uncle Ben is down here now come to the sale of Grand Pa's mills. They brought 17 thousand dollars. Grand Ma was the purchaser. She paid a good deal over their value. What would you do with Puss next year? She is going to trouble me to get some one to hire her. I don't need her, and corn is so high it will take too much to keep her at home. I am sorry for you with so much worthless propperty as you have on hand. I can get corn from Honsand Jackson at 3 dollars and will buy four or five barrells. I think you ought to see our little pigs. They eat all the time under the pen of the other hogs, and they are just as fat as they can be. One in particklar Ma nearly has fits over it as a perfect guinea. Honey, I am so uneasy about you. I don't like for you to be so near the enemy. You must not expose yourself. Remember your two babies in time of danger. My dear, it looks like you might off and come home now you have a good assistant. Pa wants to know if there is any [place to] get a young horse that the gover[ment] has condemned. He is obliged [ ] I cannot hope now. I [ ] gone. Write often [ ]. Laura kisses Ma every day for Pappie, is distressed every night it rains about you sleeping on the ground.

128

Camp Above Louden, Tenn., Nov. 4th, 1863

MY OWN DEAR ONE KITTIE, I wrote you yesterday.[29] I write you again today. No news of importance, only I am quite well, hope that you are also. No one is so much interested in your health & wellfare as I. I am always planning out for some way to try to render you happy & comfortable. My great regret is that I fall far short of my desire in that respect. I am messing with three men. Foster is making for your Pa twenty dollars per month. If I were disposed to be troubled with a large mess, I could make him make forty dollars per month. Gabe Spearman is coming to camp in a few days. You can send my clothes by him. The car runs now in two miles of us. They made the first trip yesterday. You can send me anything you wish and I will be apt to get it. Lou need not bring when

[29]Probably No. 126.

he come anything in the line of bedding but our matrass, as I have got some blankets sufficient for us. He had better send a certificate back, for I could not get him a furlough again soon. I want the oil cloth very much to keep my bedding dry. I sent my toothbrush home in my uniform pocket. I would like you would send it back to me. Honey, I do want to see you so badly. I imagine you would look sweeter now than at any other time. If so, I would go into extacees over you. Honey, be of good humor all the time I am away from you. It will be better for you. Donot get mad with little Kitten, for I know she loves you dearly. Let me hear from you often. May guardian angels watch over you in my absence. Yours ever G W Peddy

---

129

Lenoir's Station, Nov. 11th, 1863

MY OWNE SWEET DARLING KITTIE, I send you my Mair per Foster. I can get to send her no other way. When he gets home with her, let him stay a few days, then send him back with Benj Spearman; if not by him, as soon after as possible. You will have to give him money to come back on. He had better come through with Lou & Spearman. Tell Lou to spurr Brickell up & make him have my boots done so that he may bring them. I told B- to call on you for the money for the Boots. You must pay him. I donot know how long we will stay here—not long, I think. I expect we will go to Nashville. Honey, I can hardly live away from you. Since I left you I can scarcely sleep or eat for thinking of you. You may rest assured that I think of you enough, but that it does me least little good. I do wish I could realize the stubonne foot [*sic*] of your presence all the time. I am quite well now. I hope I will remain so. We may go into winter quarters ere long. If we do, I will send for you to come & see me, for it seems I cannot live without your presence. I will write you again in a few days when I am in a less hurry than I am now. Direct your letter to me at this place, or send me a good one per Lou. Kiss Kitten for me. You must take good care of your Mair. I make you a present of her. You must not take less than six hundred dollars for her. Ask more than six.

Yours ever

G W Peddy
Surgeon 56th
Ga. Regt.

130

Chickamauga, Tenn. Nov. 11th, 1863

MY DARLING ONE KITTIE, I write you a few lines to let you know where I am. We have moved back to this place and will take over positions on the line in front of Chattanooga. I bought in east Tenn. a pair of nice mules for six hundred dollars. I gave my note for them. I sold them for one thousand dollars. I had them only three days. Pretty good trading, wasn't it? If a man had have not deceived me, I would have made a thousand dollars in another trade. If I could have sent the mules home, I could have sold them for fifteen hundred dollars. I thought four hundred dollars to be made in three days was doing well enough. I rec'ed a letter from you a few days ago. How glad I was to hear from you! Honey, you had better kill our beef and let your Pa have a part of it before it is impressed. Dry some of it. I will not sell any one our meet, for we will need it ourselves. I have been here two days without a mouthful of anything to eat except flour without any grease in it. I will start Foster home in a few days, I think, after some. I have plenty of money for you if I could see some one to carry it. If the note is presented to you for payment I gave for the mules, you must pay it off. Honey, send my clothes to me as soon as you can, for I need them very much. If anyone starts to the Regt., tell them to come to this place. We will be stationed near here all the winter. Honey, if I cannot get more corn to feed my horse on than I am getting, I will have to send him home. I let some one keep him for his feed. Take good care of yourself, my sweet one, for it is you that I love above all others. Kiss Laura for me. Tell he[r] Pappie loves her as well as ever. I do want to see you and her so much. Let me know all about how you are getting along.

Yours forever
G.W. Peddy

131

Camp Near Chickamaug. Nov. 12th, 1863

I have sent you per Foster $340.00.

MY DEAREST KITTIE, I wrote you a letter with a pencil yesterday.[30] I write

[30] No. 130.

you again to day & send it by Foster. I need my clothes so badly & something to eat that I cannot wait for any one to bring them. He will bring my Mess chest from Atlanta. You must send me something to eat from home in a small box as you can. I expect that Lou had better come with him as far as Atlanta. Then he can go back home. I want him to come back by Wednesday night. It no doubt looks very extravagant for me to send him home, but it will only cost ten dollars to carry him home and back & I will make my Mess pay their part of the expence of the trip. They are all sending for boxes by him. I will be pleased to get a good letter from you on his return. Morrow Wood will be home soon on furlough. I have just rec'ed a sweet letter from your dear sweet hand. You cannot imagine how much good it done me to read it. Evry line breathed that proud spirit of love which I am proud to know ever exist in your noble bosom for me. It seems like presumption in me to say the above, but I am judging you by myself. Honey, I am sorry you have those horrid dreams that you speak of in your letter. I do wish I were with you. Maybe you would not have them. If you did, I could console you after you awoke from your troubled sleep. Honey, I would give anything to see you in your present condition. I can imagine how sweet and lovely you look. Honey, write to me if your folks or any body has found it out; if so, what they say to you. Honey, you must write to me about your condition often, for I am so afraid about you all the time. Honey, I will send you some money by Foster. I have not drawn any from the Government as yet. They will owe me a good chance of it. Honey, send me as much butter as you can get onto. You had better get 10 barrels of corn from Parkson[?]. I do not think it will get any cheaper. Perhaps you had better buy more than ten barrels. If we do not need it, we can sell it again. I will write to you again soon. Honey, remind Foster not to loose any thing that he starts to me with. Yours ever

G W Peddy

132

Franklin, Nov. 22.[31]

MY LOVE, With much pleasure do I write to you to day, although it has not

[31]Envelope addressed: "Dr G W Peddy, Chicamauga, Tenn., 56 Ga. Regiment, Gen. Cummin's Brigade" (Brig. Gen. Alfred Cumming, C.S.A. commanded the 3rd Brigade. He was exchanged after the fall of Vicksburg and reorganized his brigade in October 1863. He was severely wounded in the battle of Jonesboro, Ga. (31 Aug. - 1 Sept. 1864) and was invalided home.)

been but a few days since I wrote to you by Foster.[32] I hope he has got safte back to camps. although your suit could not pleasure you, ruined as it was, but I think it will keep the cold off. Bud Lu came very near being taken up by the guard on the train. He was very uneasy about it. He is going tomorrow to get it extended. His expenses was 7 dollars and a half. Mrs. Spearman is to pay half. When I kill my hogs, if a box can be found, you shall have as many spear ribs, back bones, & sausage as I can send. Honey, I do wish you could come home and see our hogs. They are just as fat as hogs ever was. Every one tells me that I am wasting corn to feed them longer. Pa's in the other pen are not as fat as ours was when you left and he can't get them much fatter. He sees now what good feeding does. I have paid out since you send me the money by Foster 2 hundred and 50 dollars for 15 barrels of corn. I got ten barrels from Mrs. Dansly for 3 dollars a bushel and 5 barrels at a sale for four. I did not know what price corn would be next year, especially if wheat crops is not good, so I thought the saftest plan would be to get enough now. It is higher now than it was when I bought. So you see I have paid out 3 hundred dollars this year since I have had my hogs up, including the 5 barrels I got from Jep Danniel. Your Grand Ma & Mack Peddy both died the morning Foster left. There was not 20 minutes difference in their death. Uncle Jack Lane will start in the morning out after your Father & Mother to come out and be at the sale, which will take place as soon as they get every thing arranged. Aunt Katy and Uncle Jube came the Sunday before Grand Ma died & are here now. If you wish to buy any thing at the sale, you must write to me by just as soon as you can so I will get an answer. Every thing, including land & negroes, will be sold. I wish you could be here. I was sick last night all night. I don't know what was the matter unless it was jumping a little ways off of the fence day before yestady when I went to feed my hogs. I thought it was a spell of cramp colic, but it did not wear off as that usually does; but I am well this morning as usual. Honey, I don't let any one know when I feel bad or sick, only you. If you could see me you would not know there was any thing wrong. I don't show it by my appearance or my health because I never complain only of being tired. Now, darling, for my sake don't let any one see my letters. It would mortify me nearly to death to think that any but your eyes should see this. I cannot tell you all my troubles, it seems, for I don't want any one else to know them, and if I thought you would be the least unhappy by my telling you these things, I would not do so. I am going to making cloth, hony, to sell. I think I can make Puss's expenses that way. It troubles me to have to keep her here on expenses, so we will both go to work and try to make it back. I must stop now. Write often, hony, and tell me what to do in all things. Yours ever more. Kate Peddy

---

[32]This letter is missing.

133

Dalton, Ga., Nov. 29th, 1863

MY DEAREST DEVOTED KITTIE, MY TERESTRIAL ANGEL, With the most pleasing emotion do I embrace this, the first opportunity I have had to write you since I received your generous donation from that most pleasant locality, home. I am quite sorry to inform you that I have lost most all of them. I saved my butter & ham my mate at Mess had. My beautiful pillow that you so nicely fixed up for me is now in the hand of the basedali enemy. My cooking things, too, are all lost for the want of a wagon to transport them, which I had not loaned Foster, & my horse, my blankets are also. I am proud to say myself are safe at this place. My clothes fit me most beautifully. They are universally admired by any one who sees them. All regret that they have not a suit like them. Honey, I do feel so proud of you and your unparallelled generosity toward me. I wish I could pay you for them in some way. I love you, my darling, of which you are aware, more than the emotions of any other heart are able to feel. Would that I could express to you what pleasure I have in knowing that I love & adore you more than is capable of being taken. Your sweet letter, which I rec'd by Foster, was no little consolation to me. It breathed that spirit of burning love for me which always receives hearty response of love, which chimes in perfect cord with yours at all times. Honey, so far as killing your hogs are concerned, you can do that when you get ready. If you need salt, I can buy it [in] Dalton at any price. I would have bought salt for you if I had not thought that you had plenty. You can make such disposition of Puss as you think best. If her health requires, you had better keep her at home. Honey, I am afraid you will need her. I hate for you to have to attend to so much business. You had better get your Pa to take charge of your business. I fear it will trouble you to much. Honey, our army have all retreated to the aforesaid place. Our Brig. fought, tho, very galantly in the battle of Missionary Ri[d]ge, and none exerted extreame might, but two of our company were much hurt. Will Spradlin, I suppose, is dead. No one else in the camp were injured. We lost five killed out of our Regt. & fifty four wound[ed]. The loss of the enemy was great in front of our division. The loss in our army will not amount to five hundred killed & wounded.[33] I donot suppose the Brig. of Ala. that gave way and caused us to

[33]Dr. Peddy's estimates are conservative, to say the least. During the fighting at Chattanooga, 23-25 November 1863, the Confederate losses were 6,667 (361 killed, 2,160 wounded, 4,146 missing), 14% of the 64,165 effectives. Union losses were 5,824 (753 killed, 4,722 wounded, 349 missing), 10% of the 56,359 effectives. In later years Dr. Pedy said that he performed so many amputations at Missionary Ridge that the piles of arms and legs were high enough to shield him from the bullets.

loose the day only had two killed & fourteen wounded. It was disgraceful thing for that Brig. to have acted so badly. We had been victorious all day until this aforesaid Brig. gave way. If [it] had held out fifteen minutes longer, it would have been dark & the enemy would have retired. Honey, I expect you are all disheartened at home about the result of recents. I wish they could have been happier. I am yet hopefull about the success of the South. Honey, I do wish I could be with you. I hope the war will soon end so that I can be with you all the time. Honey, I never will be happy only in your presence. I am glad you told your ant Kit what you did. I am glad to know that you are not ashamed of your condition. I am shure I am proud of it if is your desire to be so. Lou must bring us something to eat when he comes, as times are very hard here about eating. If I had a wagon, I would ask you to send an other matrass. I would like you would let Lou bring me a pillow. Honey, I enjoyed the cake you sent me so much. Let me hear from you often.

G W Peddy

Honey, I will send you some red flannel the first one I see going home, & if I can get some apples, I will express you a box of them. Yours ever more G W Peddy[34]

134

Dalton, Ga., Jan. 7th, 1864[35]

MY OWN DARLING SWEET KITTIE,

With no little pleasure I appropriate a few moments to write you a few lines to night. Many are the sweet recollections of the few happy moments we spent togueather last year. I hope the new may be hallowed to us by having the pleasure of passing far more than we had last year. This being leape year and being one in which the fates have dedicated to the Ladies to act in the supremacy, I expect a good deal of them. I hope their wisdom and prayers may have some influence in bringing this unricheous war to a finale. I am having a

[34]The postscript is written across the tops of the first and last pages. This letter is so faded that it could only be deciphered by ultra-violet light.

[35]There are no letters for December 1863, when Dr. Peddy was home on leave.

fine time reading in camp. You have no idea how much I enjoy my stove and candles. Without them, I would be very unpleasantly situated. I am reading now as much and more that I would were I at home, for were I there, I would be happily fondling with you, whom I adore & love with an unparlelled on this extensive continent.Hony, I had an awful time getting back to Camp, of which no doubt you have heard in detail ere this. But knotwithstanding my perplexities and my short stay at home, I felt amply repaid for my Trip. It appeared that I could not do without seeing my angelic one longer than I had. Honey, you cannot imagine how much I enjoy the box I brought with me and the one you sent me before I came home. My mess did not break it open until I got back. I am looking for Foster up now every day. You must not let him bring so large a box, he might fail to get it in the train. One as large as you sent by Mr. Williams he can take in the car with him. Uncle Mort will be coming up here next week. Foster can come with him. I and he are going to buy some horses and mules & he is going to carry them home. I have them engaged so we can make money on them. I wish he was here now so he could start with them tomorrow. Honey, he gave me a nice guinae pig. You must ask him about it the first time you see him. I also engaged our wool from him. You can get it as soon as he shears in the spring. I want Foster to bring me a soothing iron when he comes back. I am a little uneasy for fear he had not got his health good. After he gets here, he will be as well of as if he was at home, as I have a good sharety [?] for him. As soon as Uncle Mort comes up here I will try to get a sow from him that has guinae pigs every time. I donot know that I will succeed. Let me know how ours comes on, especially our little shoat. Honey, you had better get some meal & feed your hogs on that when they get tired of corn. I wan[t] you to feed them all the time like you was fattening them to kill. If we get those from Uncle, we will have the finest stock in the country. I have bought a nice pair of mules at a thousand dollars & a fine mair that's heavy in fold for twelve hundred dollars. Each will bring fifteen hundred at home. I and uncle are going in halves in them. He is to do all the feeding & selling & carrying them home from here. I will telegraph him to come at once after them. Andy, poor fellow, cannot get anything to eat but corn. He does not fatten fast. Honey do not let any of your [hogs die] for want of feed. You can get someone to let you have shuck for them. My darling, I fear I ask to much of you. If so, hope I will be able to repay you for you[r] trouble some day. Hoping to hear from you soon, I will wind up for the night. Honey, be of good cheer while I am away, for you know how bad I would feel did I know that you were sad & unhappy. I assure you, my dear, that no heart throbs more fondly for anyone than mine does for your angelic self. Good night, sweet one. Yours ever G W Peddy

135

Franklin, Jan. 15/64[36]

MY DARLING,

I received the first you have wrote since you left. I was so uneasy about you, for I have never know such severe weather as the day was in which you went to Newnan. I concluded you must be sick by not writing sooner, but am so glad to hear you are well; but I can't say that I am well or have been any day since you went away. I had long spells of cramp colic last week & a very bad cold, which made me wish for your presence more than ever. I thought several times while those spells was on me, I could never get over them, but I am still up yet, although my throat is very sore. You say this is "Leap-Year" and ladies have more privileges. I hope they will not waste them in sentimental foolry, but employ their time in doing acts of love & kindness for those they love and relieving as far as they can the intolerable suffering of our noble soldiers. Hony, I do want you to come home and stay always with me. I study over the bad state of affairs untill I can't think of any thing that could give me any pleasure but for you to come home. Then I might feel the sweet caressing attention which I don't deserve, but it makes me so happy. You can't imagine how impatient I get thinking that you are forced to be away now. I try to do as you tell me, be cheerful, but darling, I have not the sunny buoyant disposition you have. Little kitten says, papie, she knows 5 letters in the book, and you must send her a book with pictures, and got Earth a crack in it and one big round O with another eye in it—that the way she can tell her letters. She gets her book every day, then after she learns awhile, she must sew, and always tries to make her papie some breechis. Seems to be very fussy all the while. I do believe she has more sence than any child in the world. I am very proud of her. I sent for our cattle today to see what they needed, and you never saw such poor stock. The cow nearly fell down while tring to eat. I am affraid we can't save the cow, she is so poor, but I am going to feed them well at any cost. I can swap off the old cow to uncle Jack for a young one he bought at Grand Ma's sale, which is of the best kind of cow, and think we will trade. Our hogs does not look so well this cold weather although I have them feed well. Little Dumpi is not so fat as it was, which is for the best. Tell bud Lu I ricon Laura & I will not get any shoes unless he comes home, for no one will trouble themselves about any wants as he did. If he did run away with the buggy and turn horse, buggy, girls and all over in a pile, he treated me kinder than brothers seldom treat their sisters and I will

---

[36]Letter misdated /68.

always feel grateful to him for it. My shoes are so bad I get my feet wet every time I go on the ground, which keeps me with a cold. I never had the blues much worse than I did a day or two ago. I commenced carding and spinning. The lint got into my nostrils & lungs until I coughed nearly all night. Pa says I must quit carding, as I could not live. I could not bear to think that you would have to be burdened with such an expense as to buy all the cloth we needed. The thought was intolerable, for I know I am trouble enough to help you all I can, but not to work any, I would be a perfect nuisance to you. Perhaps you have heard of the marage of John Harp[?] son & Sallie Dansby. Another one of bud Lou's old flames left him. If they are only half as happy as we have been since we took the marriage vows, it will be a source of great pleasure to number that day of all others the most sacred to them which united them together; but alas, how few think of the great obligations they are under to each other to render as far as possible life's pathway, a delighful path strewn with fragrant flowers. I did not know when uncle Mort left for camps. I think Pa does not like it about your buying stock with uncle Joe & Mort and not let him in. He says he told you he wanted to buy some on speculation, but he was affraid you would be busy and not time to tend to it. I know uncle Joe is the last man you would help to make a dime. Pa received a letter from a Mr. Greg of Atlanta saying he had two notes, one on you, and the other on Col. Slaughter, and you two said you would make arrangements with him or Mr. Oliver to pay it. Write me word if you want me to pay off the note; or will you do it? It is for the mules, and we would be better off to pay off and be entirely free. Pa will get some one to pay the note off if you want me to attend to it.

I must stop now. Remember your promise to write often. Laura send[s] you a kiss, and her mother, a thousand, if you will accept this. Yours ever more Kate Peddy.

136

Franklin, Jan. the 19, 1864

My darling love,

I was so disappointed last mail in not receiving a letter from you, but Pa got one as directed in your hand writing, and he being gone to Rome to court, I took the liberty to open it. I wish you had thought of renting a farm sooner. Now every body has rented the vacant places untill there is none to get. Mr. Mabry has bought the Favor place. I sent down to try and rent it from Mrs.

Mabry, but she is going to tend it all this year. I had much rather have rented Bob Liffoot's place down by uncle Mort's;, if you had thought of it in time, for that is good land and very close to uncle Mort, who is a good farmer and would have assisted me a great deal. You know I am perfectly willing to do as you think best in all things, for I have the most implicit confidence in your judgment in every thing you undertake. Of course Ma & Pa could object to my leaving at any time and more so *now*. If you don't get a place this year, we must try an other, for I don't take care of our stock and it off at the plantation. I had the cows brought up and kept them here two days, but Ma can't get nough shucks to feed her milk cows with and I can't keep them here. If I buy shucks, Pa is so busy commencing his crops I hate to ask him to haul so much. I do believe the old cow will die any how. Foster has not entirely got well. He looks poor yet. Pa is affraid he could not stand the cold yet. I made him hang up our meat to day, and I wish you could see how nice & fat it looks. If I had a house of my own, how much I would fret. Laura says she is affraid papie is hungry and she wants to send him some meat. When Foster comes we *will* send you some of our nice meat. Puss don't eat any hardly, says she can't eat it now, for it makes her sick to eat much.

Tell bud Lu not to be distressed thinking his *lubly* Dinah will go into agony amounting to distraction on the acount of his absence, for she has tried the experiment before and can easily transfer her smiles to some other. John Pendergrass is the recipient of her love tokens, so I am told. Honey, I have not felt like writing in some time, and I know I can't interest you at all. If I could only find language expression enough to convey you an idea of the love that fills my heart for you, such burning words of affection would be penned as never a mortal being saw before, but I have so often tried to tell you and then made a most miserable failure, it is almost useless to try. But then, I love to talk of such things and to think over in your absence how much we think of each other. Sometimes I am affraid you are not entirely satisfied. When you tell me of having made the acquaintance of some beautiful & accomplished woman in your travels, I think perhaps you often draw a comparison between such a lady and homely sensless me, but then I try to banish such thoughts as quick as possible. You must send me your other shirt to put a new bosom in. I heard of several compliment[s] passed on the beauty of your shirt bosom by the ladies out at the party, and I hope that will repay you for disliking to wear marsails bosoms. I don't expect you can read this letter now: all the ink froze that very cold weather. I must stop now. Do write often, honey. Laura sends a kiss.

Yours as ever Kate Peddy.

137

Dalton, Ga. Jan. 20th, 1864

MY OWN DARLING SWEET KITTIE,

With much pleasure I read your sweet letter yesterday. You have no idea my dear how much joy I experience in tracing the lines which your own sweet hands write. I would have responded at once had I not had the worst boil on the side of my neck you ever saw. It kept me from sleeping for four nights. Honey, you have no idea how much I wanted you with me to doctor it. It is not well yet, but is much improved. I donot want to be sick again when I am away from you. Your presence is enough to drive almost any ordinary pain away from me. I was so sorry to learn that you had two spells of colic. I wish I could have been with you. I hope I would have been able to have releaved you. Honey, you had better get you some Compound Spirits of lavender and take it when you have those spells. Honey, I did not think their was enough money in the stock I bought to get you Pa in with me. Rearally, I do not know that their is any as yet. I will know as soon as uncle Mort disposes of them. I thought your Pa wanted me to buy them at a Government sale. Such an one has not come off since I have been here. I can [make] plenty of trades as good as those that I and uncle M. made. The four we bought cost $2250. Your Pa can look at them and see how he likes such stock. If he likes them very well and will send Johnie up with some money, I will buy as many more. I donot know that I can buy another pair of mules as t[h]ose was at that price. In fact, I do not know of any more to sell, but can buy for five or six hundred dollars a peace pretty fair horses and mairs. I could have made a splendid trade the other day, much better than I made for most, if I had had any one to carry them home for me. I offered Nute Read $75.00 to take them home for me, but he would not do it. I wish you, Honey, to send Foster up just as soon as you can. I know Lou needs him. Besides, if he were here, I could at anytime send him home with any stock that I might buy. If you Pa will go my halves, I will buy evry good bargain I see. Tell your Pa I cannot buy any fine stock at the above named price. They are all on the scrub order. Tell him to look at them that Mort brought home and he can tell what sort I can get. Then he can let me know what to do. As for me assisting Joseph Lane in making money in any way, it [is] a thing that I will not do. Uncle Mort has been a good friend to me. I therefore would render him any assistance that I could, but of course I would do anything in the world to farther you Pa's interest much sooner than any one in the world *except you.*

Honey, my proffits in that trade is two barrels of corn and a nice sow with seven guinae pigs. She always has them sort of pigs. I would not take three hundred dollars for her. I expect that Mort will make eight hundred dollars on the four stock, which would have been four hundred a peace for us, but I was affraid that he would not, because of which I made the proposition to him in reference to the corn and hogs. He will pay you two hundred and fifty dollars and the corn and hogs, if he takes all four of the stock. If not, he will call on you for five hundred dollars, which you must pay him. If you do not have enough to pay for the mules I bought in Tenn. and pay Uncle five hundred that he may call on you for, borrow a little from you Pa and I will send it to him in a short time. Honey, those hogs that we are to get from Uncle are the prettyest one[s] you ever saw & nicer than owers. You must feed all of them when you get the others as much as they will eat twice a day, then we will have a quantity of meat to sell next winter.

Lou has gone to Mobile to take a Rebb prisoner whom a court martial had sentenced to work for six months. He may come by home when he comes on back to stay a day or two. I had not made any arrangements in Atlanta for Josep[h] Lane to come up here, therefore he did not get to come, and I am glad of it. Don't say anything about this. Honey, I do hope I will get another sweet letter from you in a few days. I do love to read them so much. Honey, you must get better ink if you can. Honey, I donot want you to card or spin any, for I can make out without your labor and rather you would do nothing than work in the least of pain. I am stout enough to make a living for you and am willing to do it and am proud that I have such noble and lovely creatures to labor for. It is exquisite pleasure to me. Honey, send me a good box by Foster and send him on at once, if you think him able to come. I hope if you are satisfied to live at the Favor place, that your Pa has rented it for me if it has not been rented out. I will buy you a horse and send it to you if he has. Uncle Mort carried my trace chains home. You can get them from him and let your Pa have them, if we donot need them. Honey, you have no idea how much I want to see you. I would give any sum to get to stay all the time with you and little Laura[37]

---

[37]Signature lacking.

138

Surgeon's Office 56th Regt. Ga. Vol.[38]
Camp Near Dalton, Ga.
Jan. 23rd/64

MY OWN SWEET IDOL KITTIE,

Once more I am greeted with another sweet letter from your dear little hand. Would that I could this knight have the pleasure to press it to my lips. I would kiss and press it until it became unpleasant to you. I am quite sorry that we failed to rent the place, but since you spoke of it, I had rather had the Tipford place, it is better land. You may make arrangements, if I live and the war does not close, to go to farming next year. Then, perhaps, we will be better able to go at it. I do not think that the war can possibly last more than another year, though it may. Honey, I am anxious to hear wat you have to say about my last trade and how you like your sow and pigs. I imagine that you will be perfectly delighted with them. You will say, no doubt, that I ought to have made more than I have on that trade. Perhaps I ought, but think I did extreamly well. I would not take any price for the sow and pigs; and the corn is also an item at this particular time.

I am quite sorry to learn the condition of our cattle. I wish I had made some provision for them ere I left home. I expect you can buy shucks from uncle Mort to finish wintering them. I am sorry to hear that Foster has not yet entirely recovered. I am needing him now. Honey, you must get your wool from Uncle Mort as soon as he shears his sheep and have it carded in the summer while the weather is warm. Then it will not nap so badly. It will then, perhaps, be cheaper. He promised me that you should have it. Honey, I want you to send to market and buy you as much sugar as you need. You will have to pay three dollars per pound for it, but I donot care for the price. You must have it. My boil is getting well farst. I am having a good time in camp. I have but little to do, and little of the poorest that you ever saw to eat. I have not eat a biscuit in two weeks. We have to eat our meal without being siftered. I'll assure you it is coarse. Lou has not got back from Mobile. His time will be out next Tuesday. I expect he will go by home. If so, I hope he will bring me a rich box. You say you heard the Ladies at the party compliment my shirt bosom. Did you not hear them compliment the wearer? Also, you ought to have done so if no one else would. I do hope, my love, that you are well and doing well. So long as you get on well I am pretty well satisfied, but when I learn that you have been sick, you

[38]Envelope addressed: "Mrs. Dr Peddy, Franklin Georgia"

cannot imagine how much I am hurt about it, for it is your dear self that I want to be free from pain and mental anxiety. I wish you to be perfectly happy as long as you live, and I intend to exert my utmost resorces to that end. I love you with an ardor that's rarely felt and known by others of my sex. Honey, you must not let little sweet Laura forget her Pa, for bless it's little heart, it has no idea how well I love her. You and her, I am proud to say, are my worthy idols. I do love to live for you. The though[t] of you is always a happy one. I feel for you Honey, in your present condition. If I could be with you, I would not hate it so much, but alas, that's impossible. Give my love to you Ant Kit and Chippie. I would like to see Chip. I hope she will get on well with her school. I never hear from Giles or Nick. Let me hear from them when you get their letters. Kiss Laur[a] for me every day. My love to all the family. Yours ever More

G.W. Peddy

139

Surgeon's Office, 56th Ga. Vol
Camp Near Dalton,
Jan. 25th/64

MY DEAR DEVOTED KITTIE, I write you a few lines per Jack Miller, as he is going to start home this eve. I will also send my shirt by him. I am quite well, my dear. My boil has gotten entirely well. Honey, I wrote to Billie Mozeley to let you have a piece of Casamere to make me a vest. I want it cut like my uniform vest. Make it, darling, and send it to me by the first one that comes up here from our section. Honey, send me a good lot of meat in the box you send me. I cannot get along without it.

Honey, we have the pretty spell of weather I have seen in a long time. It creates a desire in me to want to be at home to stroll about with you. The weather reminds me of the halcyon days when we used to walk out in our garden doting on our heart little Laura. Would to God we could be thus situated again! Then I was spending my happyest moments, but I knew it not. If the weather continues so for ten days we will begin to hear the clash of arms from the Potomac to the Rio Grand. Linco[l]n and company think they have the South crushed and think all that's to be done is to pick up the fragments. I hope they will have a sweet time in doing that. Our troops are in good spirits and are ready for the conflict to begin. I think they will be more fighting this year than any year of the war. The Linco[l]n Government are going to send their legions which they are now fitting out against us from all quarters and all directions. If evry one will do their duty, you need not fear to hear from the result. Honey, inclosed you will find a peace of poetry that chimes in with my feelings accurately; no doubt it will with yours. Honey, I want you to write me often. Be sure to feed the hogs as much as they will eat. I am anxious that they be kept fat all the time. Donot listen to those who tell you that they will not grow if you keep them to fat. I will risk that. Honey, send down to Uncle's after those others as so[o]n as you can. I am anxious for you to see them to learn how you like them. Honey, I want to see you so much I would give my interest in anything to get to stay with you all the time. If peace was made, we would set an example of nuptial enjoyment that thousands would envy. Honey, teach Laura all you can. Tell her she must always keep out of bad company, for that is what ruins many people. Honey, give me all the news in Heard. Give my love to all the family. Remember, my dear, that you always reign supream in my affections. G W Peddy

---

140

Surgeon's Office, 56th Regt. Ga. Vol.[39]
Camp Near Dalton, Ga.
January 26th/1864

MY DEAREST KITTIE, ONE ON WHOM NATURE BESTOWED MORE BEAUTY MORE LOVELYNESS AND MORE CHARMS THAN IS USUAL TO MANKIND, I am proud that you are mine and will ever look back to the day I obtained you as one of the brightest rais of my life. My memory has always and will ever rushd fondly to that time. My great desire is to ever keep up in your hallowed bosom a reseprosity of feeling. Then that pleasant element that's called bliss will ever be mine. I have no right to ever doubt your constancy, nor will I in my opinion, so long as I am conscious in my belief that I have not proved recreant to the trust that you have reposed in me. But no doubt if I were to rong you, as is often done, I would degenerate into the belief that you was getting cold towards me. Honey, so long as my tongue remains free and my arms are unpalsied, I will strike and speak prais and adoration in your behalf, and it will appear pleasant and noble in me so to do. The elements of this cold world may gather

[39]This letter is water-stained.

themselves into a rapid [?] torrent and sweep like an avalanch against me, but that heart that beats happily and warmly for you will never chill. Lou and Foster arrived safely here today accompanied by a nice box with delicious contents, which you may be assured I enjoyed, and better still was a letter from you, a production that is rearly excelled by those who are the most gifted.[40] You have no idea how much I enjoyed it. It was just such a letter as I like to get. Honey, you need not make me any cotton clothes for summer. You will have to get me up another pair of pants like the ones I have. I will wear them out in the seat before the summer is gone. Lou tells me uncle Mort says the sow that he was to let me have has lost nearly all her pigs. I will write him to let you have her anyhow. I learn from Lou what disposition he has made of the horses and mules. I made one hundred dolars to my part on the mules. I think the horse he has an leased now will bring twelve hundred when made fat. I have almost forgot Andy in my letters to you. We should not never forget anything that you fancy so much. He is fatter than you ever saw him, the prettyest horse in the world. I nurse him like he was a child. You expect our next, you say, to be as contrary as his ma. I hope it will be half as lovely. If so I will rejoice with gladness. I am sorry about H. Pendergrass and sympathise with *Uncle* and *ant*. Honey, I will close reluctantly as I am several letter ahead of you. Your ever more G W Peddy

[41]Buy as much flour as you want to use/ Have some meal ground to feed our hogs and I am sorry thay are looking poorly./ Lou tells me that Laura knows 7 letters. Tell her she must learn them all and say them to Pappie when he comes home. I will buy her a nice book as soon as I get the chance./ I will have to live from home as much as I can. If not it will take all I make to pay for my rations. I am paying 75 cts. per pound for poor beef from the commissary and $2.25 per pound for bacon./ Kiss Laura for me.

141

Franklin, Jan. the 31/64

MY DARLING PRECIOUS ONE,

With a glad heart and a deep gush of affection which I can but faintly express did I read you letter yesterday. I felt tired and worried at the time, but how light

[40]This letter is missing.

[41]This postscript written along the top of the page.

hearted and happy I felt after reading such loving words which comes from one I love so dearly. Never does the thought ever for a moment come to my mind of your ronging me by thought or deed. I know the purest instincts of your noble heart too well to ever think of such things. Never did a wife repose more confidence in a husband than I do in you or think more fondly & proudly of the noble elements which compose the character of my darling; and my only abbitions is to render as happy as I possibly can the heart which I prize far more than all the jewels of Earth. I do wish it was so I could go to see you. I never see any one start from here to go where you are but I wish I could go too, but I don't suppose I ever will again have that pleasure. I heard yestidy that the order had been countermanded allowing furloughs. I am so sorry, for I had been indulging in the sweet hope that you would come again soon, for I need your presence so much now. Every thing annoys me more than usual. When you are here, I feel better every way. It has been such good weather for several weeks I am affraid there will be more fighting. There is considerable excitement here amongst those who have hired substitutes. I feel sorry for those who have to leave wife & children, but then they do not theirs [*sic*] better than others who have been in a long time. I do dread to think what this year may bring around. You seem to be hopeful of the result, but I cannot see upon what you have your ideas on. If you have to pay so high for provisions, it shows that the government has not much on hand. Honey, I may be rong, but I think the cheapest plan would be for you & bud Lu to turn off all from your mess, and then what we send you from home, if you are careful of it, would last a long time. If you had been by yourself all this time, the meat we sent would have been enough for some time. I think you would live cheaper & better if to yourselves. I wish bud Lu had carried an other piece of meat also, for men dislike to be troubled with boxes. I still hope, love, you will come after your other box soon. Your brother William and a man by the name of Durrunn is out here on their way to join Morgan. They want to go in cavalry service. Brother John has not got well yet and will not go back to camp soon. John Pendergrass is anxious since Henry's death to go to your regiment: says he would be better satisfied with you. Uncle Mort says he will let me have the sow but not a part of the profets on the horse trade but you must buy them. He says you misunderstood. He never thought of letting them go as part of the profets. He says the pigs are little over a month old and the sow is weaning them now. Pa thinks the best p[l]an would be to buy a shoat and not pay the high prices for corn & sow. He don't think the sow a good one if she weans her pigs so soon. We will have in a few days a good many hogs and I think we can't buy corn and to feed them on at the price it is at. If you want uncle Mort's stock of hogs, I will get him to pick me out a fine little sow now, and next year when we go to house keeping, she will then do us good; but too many now would only be a heavy expense, and to buy them at such exorbitant prices too. Uncle M. says it will be a heavy expense to keep the horse awhile. He is fat, for it will take some time to get him in a condition [to] sell him. You did not say if you had paid for the mules you bought in Tennessee. Uncle Mort has not called on me for any money yet. Honey, I think this vest will be so nice I wish I could see you with it on, but then in camp you will get it soiled directly. I do not like the idea of Mozeley & Lane giving it to you. If you can, I would rather they were paid for it. Some how, though, Billy Mozely would not let me pay anything yestady. He seems to be very liberal.[42] Honey, I know this will be a very tiresome letter, for I don't feel like writing much today. Laura says she will learn fast for pappie. Don't wait until you get my letters to answer them, but write often, my love. It is such a pleasure to read your sweet letters filled with such dear words. Yours every more Kate Peddy

---

142

Franklin, February the 5/64[43]

MY LOVE,

With much pleasure do I sit down by a comfortable fire around the same hearth stone where we have passed some many happy moments even since this unholy war has cast its mantle of desoltion & sorrow on all things beautiful and happy. Such blisful hours which we have snatched from the present, while the future loomed up before us as a black mountain without one ray of sunshine to cheer the bleak aspect, will live as long as memory holds her place and cheers me with the thought that perhaps we may be permitted again [to] quaft the richest joy that ever floated in the cup of bliss. Honey, I admire the piece of poetry you sent me. It is just my thoughts & feelings exactly. How I do wish I had the language and talent to write such pieces, for in my heart are feelings of true love that no pen can tell. It is needless for me to say how much I would give for you to be with me *now*. It may be annoying to you, and perhaps I grieve too much over it when it might be so much worse. Three men who belong to Wharton's command[44] eat breakfast here this morning. They were raised close

---

[42]The remainder written around the edges.

[43]Envelope stamped PAID 10 FRANKLIN GA and addressed: "Dr. G.W. Peddy/Dalton/Ga. 56 Ga. Regiment/Gen. Cummin's/Brigade"

[44]Brig. Gen. Gabriel C. Wharton in 1863 commanded a brigade engaged in guarding railroads in southwestern Virginia. He joined Longstreet in eastern Tennessee and in April 1864 was sent to Breckinridge.

to Murphysburrow and knew all of Pa's relatives & friends. They did not hear from their wives at all. Some had lost all their property and then did not know what situation their families were in. I will not, I think, murmur again if I am permitted to live and keep my loved ones too. You never saw so much excitement as there is here about the conscript law being extended to 55, for it takes nearly all of the croakers who have been so bitter against secession—and I am glad of it. May be they will now know what privation you have to suffer, though I ought to pitty all who have to leave home ties if they are as strong as ours. There is a Surgeon here now examining men over 50. They received your uncle Loun[?] to day. He did not think of such a thing, I recon, and I don't hardly think he can stand much, but he has to try it any how. I suppose it will make aunt Rebecka worse than ever to quarrel with our government. Ambrose Williams has authority to raise a company and uncle Joe will go in it, I suppose. You brother William is also going. I think he has bought or swaped for uncle Mort's gray horse. Uncle Mort sold uncle Jack Lane the one he bought by himself for 58 dollars' profit. He intends to keep the young horse untill he is grown. Every one says he will make a fine horse, but uncle Joe laughs a good deal and calls it my fine stock because he is so poor. I told him if you said he was fine, I could bear any sort of fun, for I knew your judgment of a horse was better than any body in this country. Uncle Mort sends me word several times to send for the sow, but I will not till I see him and find out what he will do about the way she has to be paid for. Hony, I am uneasy for fear our meat will be pressed. I do want you to enjoy some of those nice hams. Pa received your letter sending bud Gily's certificate. I was disapointed in not getting a letter too, so write often. Darling, come home. I cannot bear thy long protracted stay, so sad and lonely is my heart when thou art far away. Yours ever more. Kitie Peddy

143

Surgeon's Office, 56th Regt. Ga. Vol.
Camp Near Dalton, Ga.
Feb. 7th, 1864

MY DEAREST SWEET KITTIE,

Without having as one of your sweet letters before me as usual to night, I attempt to write you. I fear I will fail to interest if I should do so. I hope you will think it's my intention always so to do and attribute it more to my mental weakness than anything else. It would ammuse you to hear me talking to myself about you evry time I am alone. Here is my common expression, viz. bless her little heart, she is the sweetest mortal in the world, and no one will ever find out how well I love her but myself. I am sorry that I cannot act and speak to you in such a way that you could realize it. I often get sad thinking about the crewel protraction of this war. It is depriving me of more rearal enjoyment with you than it seems to me I can bear. Were to God their was a way for us to be with each other all the time! I want no more nor ask no more than to be in your sweet presence. Life would be to me then a fairry tail. All my wants would be supplied a[nd] my earthly stay perfect joy. Honey, I am happy with you as my idol. I love to worship and admire you and feel at the same time that I am doing no one injustice to do so, but you who are worthy of more love and admiration than one man can bestow upon you. The above and stubborn fact, my love, and the penning of them are promptings of the heart. Would that it was in my intilect to give you all the impulses of a heart that throubs joyfully and unceasingly fo[r] you! It would, if their is in you[r] dear bosom a reciprocation of feeling, send a thrill of joy to your heart that would make it almost melt into tears of gladness.

This crewel war may keep us seperated a long while yet, but their is one thing that nothing can accomplish, that is to sever the cord of true love which binds my heart and affections to you with a firmness that no power can sever.

Honey, while I am here alone in my tent I can imagine how, where, my love is sitting around the social fire at home with the light reflecting your unparallelled beauty on the wall. Would that I could only get a glimps of that reflection, as I cannot see the substance! I would be gratified to some extent. Honey, I owe all my comfort to your industry. I do admire my vest so much. It seems that everything you make me just chimes in with my idea of beauty. Honey, if your condition would permit, I would have you with me in a short time. It seems that I cannot do without seeing you much longer. The Col.'s Wife if here again. I was talking with her in his house when he come in to meet her. All they done was to say how do. I says to them, well, well, such a dry meeting as that was I never saw! I told them if they was to see us meet once they would see an example of true affection and happy heart in love. After I told them this, she ventured to kiss him. I had a good laugh out of them on account of their coldness.

Honey, I do hope that you are getting on well. I as so [*sic*] anxious about your welfare. You no[r] anyone else feels such intrust in yourself as I do. I think I have the best right to, for in you willbeing and pleasur lies all my present and future happyness.

Mrs. Watkins is coming to Franklin to live this year if she can rent a house. She will be down in a few day[s] as she is going to start home in the morning and will come right on to F________. Honey, you must be very kind to her because the Col. thinks so much of me and treats I and Lou so well. Lou and Foster are quite well.

Honey, you had best buy your wool early in the Spring and have it carded in the hotest weather in Summer. Then it will not nap any at all. It will be cheaper in Spring than next winter. If you have not corn to keep your hogs perfectly fat all summer, you had best buy some from Joseph Jones, as he will let you have it at four dollars per bushel.

If you have not bought you any sugar yet, I want you to send to Lagrange and get it. You will need it before long and I am anxious for you to have it. Brewer is messing with me. You can get if you want it, two bushels of wheat from Mozeley that belongs to Brewer. He will write to Billie to let you have it if you wish it. As soon as we go to move I will send my stove home in a box, as the winter will be over in a short time. Honey, write to my by evry mail, for you cannot imagine how proud I am when I get your letters. It keeps me alive until I can get a succeeding one. I do have so many pleasant dreams of you these nights. I do wish I could realize some of them Honey, you must keep you hogs fat. We are drawing bacon at this time. Our ham is not gone yet. Brewer brought a nice box. We are living fine off of it. Honey, you need not look for me before June, as I cannot get a leave of absence before then. Keep our darling Laura for me. My love to all. Your ever more

G. W. Peddy

144

Surgeon's Office, 56gh Reg. Ga. Vol.
Camp Near Dalton, Ga.
Feb. 9th, 1864

MY DEAREST LOVE KITTIE,

I now have the exquisite pleasure of responding to your dear sweet letter of the 5th inst.[45] I always feel so proud when I get your letters I can scarcely content myself. I nearly always reply imediately, but put it off for two days this time because of having wrote you night before last and sent the letter per Mrs. Watkins. Honey, I regret to ask you longer letters to me on account of your condition. I fear by so doing it may weary you to much. If it does, I will forgo the pleasure that I experience in lenghty ones.

Well do I remember the many pleasures around the old hearth stone which

[45]No. 142.

you spoke of in your last. I hope the day is not far distant when we will realize more rearal happyness and more lengthy enjoyments than ever before. I am more encoraged at the prospect of affairs in the South than I have been heretifore. If you will read the papers now you will be cheered in you[r] feelings exceedingly. Heretifore I was almost afraid to read and on account of the defection of feelings they produced, but now the tenor of them is quite different.

Honey, I hope you will take encouragement from the statement the cavaliers made you. We ought to rejoice even to be situated as we are. Our condition could be so much worse. Honey, my heart yearns to see you so that it could pour its emotions of love in you[r] dear presence. It seems to me if I could get a leave of absence for twelve month, I could not be away from you one moment. I would hang so fondly around you that I fear you would get woried with me.

I learn from you letter that the conscrip is waking up the powers that be in Heard. I hope evry croker will be brought into the Service. I am only sorry that true and loyal men have to be classed with them. I sympathise with the latter class, the former I donot. I[f] you should see Brother Wm., tell him to go with Ambrose and Dr. Lane. They are both excelent men. Tell Dr. Lane if he will look back over his former life and think of the poor and sorry stock which he has owned, he would not cast any reflections on your fine blooded colt. If he was no count, I would expect you could sell him to the Doct. in a very short time, for that is the sort he always buys. My compliments to him and Kit.

Honey, I admire your short appendage of poetry so much. It expresses my sentiments exactly. Lou and Foster are quite well. Capt. Spearman's going home to nigh[t]. He will bring you this letter. He will bring I and Lou a box with him, he says, if you will fix one up. Get a box and put me in a nice ham and such other things as you wish. Then send it to Brewer's mother and she will finish filling it. We are messing togueather and he will write to his Ma to turn it over to Capt. S________ to bring. My dear, I have had such a pain in my back for the last two days that I can scarcely move without hollowing. I think I will get over it soon. Honey, send me some butter if it is convenient when you send the box. Honey, if you are afraid of your meat bring impressed, you can sell some of it or swap it for sugar, or sell it for money and buy you some with the money. You must get you some sugar anyhow. I donot care what it cost. I want you to have as much as you can use. Evrything that is nice and sweet that you need buy it. It is for your enjoyment that I live and labor.

Honey, you must get Laura to say a lesson to you evry day. Do not scold her while you are teaching her, for fear that she gets to disliking it. I am so desireous that she should begin to learn.

Honey, you ought to see Andy. Now he is the nicest horse you have seen.

Honey, if Mort agrees to take $200.00 for the sow and corn, I should give it, as I think they are cheap at that price. Excuse this letter, my love. I am writing in a great hurry. I will do better next time. I hope our hogs are getting on well and will do so until you get so that you cannot attend to them. Brewer will write to Mozeley to let you have the wheat. Let me hear from you often. My darling, your letters are my only solace when you are far from me. I have the honor to be your ever more

G.W.P.[46]

Give my love to all.

145

Surgeon's Office, 56th Ga. Vol.
Camp Near Dalton, Ga.
Feb. 14th/64

MY DEAREST KITTIE, I have just received your letter of the 9th inst.[47] I imagine you was in quite an ill humor when you wrote it from the tenor of it and the reference to some Lady in Laws about which I was taking on. I assure you that no Lady but you, as I have often told, engrosses any part of my affections, and it seems to me that I have always been so constant to you (a thing that I have no lashings of concience about) that you ought not to doubt me at this late hour. I am so wraped up in you that I never even think that you have the least regard for any one but me. If I was guilty of such an act, my concience would recoil, and I would be a miserable creature unworthy the respect of any plebion. I am a wicked creature, my love, but still I have a concience that would revol[t] at such an idea; and any one guilty of the above offence is ever contemptible in my sight. You also spoke in your[s] to Lou about my failing to write you. I have written you three letters since I got your[s] before the one I am now replying to. This is the first I have had from you in a week according to my recollection. Honey, I am aggreaved that you have to labor so hard that you cannot write me without being in pain. It is your own fault that you weary yourself so much. It is not my desire that you work so. Hope you will cease it. I am willing to make any sacrifice of pleasure to keep you from labor. Your condition does not warrant a course of fatigue, therefore I think you ought to quit it for the sake of one who

---

[46]*On back:* "I send y'r letters back. Please keep them for me."

[47]This letter is missing.

love[s] you better far than you love yourself. I want you for no other purpose but to love and to write to me in my absence. I donot want you to try to get used to it. My sincere regret is that you did not marry some one more worthy than myself and calculated in evry capcacity to render you perfectly happy, not even ever think of work. I am ever ready to render you joyful eather by letters often arriving or in any other way that [is] in my power. Your sweet letter[s] alway cheer me a[nd] make me feel proud that I have such a lovely being as yourself for a lifetime companion, but I have made these declarations of regard so often, I fear you esteem them as an old song. As for myself, ever tender word or sentence that I can catch from your letter finds a responcive echo in my brest.

I hope, my dear, you will not suffer yourself to become sad about the Small Pox being in your midst, as it cannot be remedyed. I fear by letting Laurance to [come] down their it will be the means of getting it into our family. The next thing I expect to hear is that he has ran away from their and come home, which will necesarially spread the disease.

I donot believe I would buy the jeans. I do not want any, only that which you supervise the making of. I regret that you cannot get the wool to have me some pants made. I do not want you to give yourself any a[n]xiety about them. I had rather do without them. I deeply sympathise with you, my love, for it seems that you have more trouble in equiping me than I ought to entail upon you.

I hope our little Cherub ere this has gotten well. I am so sorry to learn that she is so lean. Tell her Pa wants her to take good care of herself and get well, for I could not get well without seeing her bright smiles occasionally, which reminds me so much of her Ma, one whom I do love above all things I ever saw. I regret that she cannot realize her dream about my comming home. I am sorry to hear of the death of you cousin, E.F. You need not be uneasy about me, my darling, for I have gotten entirely well of the dearrhaer. I donot think I will have it again soon. Lou has just rec'd a note from Louise W. knocking him higher than a kight. I am glad to learn that our stock are so prolific. Hope you will keep them as nice as you did the others. You had better watch out for meat, as Congress has passed an act to impress all the meat, only just leaving half the quantity that it usually takes to do family's. Say to yr Pa I would come home once a week and agree to eat nothing while their if I could get the opportunity.

Honey, according to existing orders it will be impossible for me to come home before June. I regret it no little. I hope the day is not far distant when I will be permited to come home and stay with you all the time. No one could be half so proud as I. If such a thing was announced to me, I would make the welcon ring with my shouts of joy. Honey, let me know how you are getting along. I will regard nothing you write immodest in your present condition. If anything goes rong with you, it is nothing but justice to me and to your dear self that you let me know it. Your letters are always stricly private. I never lay them whare anyone can see them but myself. Honey, please write to me evry mail for one month. I fear that you are keeping up to ma[n]y correspondence. Yours with delight until death

G. W. Peddy

146

Surgeon's Office, 56th Regt. Ga. Vol.
Near Dalton, Ga.
Tuesday night, Feb. 16th, 1864[48]

MY PRECIOUS DARLING KITTIE,

To night while you[r] bright orb sends its gentle rays through the meshes of my tent and while the rude north wind hurls its fury against it[s] walls, I attempt to respond to your unusually sweet communication of the 13th inst.[49] Would that you could realize the pride of my heart on the reception of yours, so full of love and evrything which is calculated to cheer the soul in its sadest moments. I thank allwise providence that he permited me to select from the casket of jewels that *one* which is most precious that and which I most admire, that and which composition of mind and body is better suited to my happyness than all others, unlike the one whose nuptials you spoke of in yours. I will never have the remorse of conciens that I fear some one will have, when he reflects he espoused a private prostitute. Such shamefull strategy as I imagine was to enduce him to such deads are to be abrogated and renounced as one of the most wicked designs which the human mind can purpetrate. No doubt that many nice young ladies whose pride and virtue are untarnished envys her in her position, but hats the evil deeds which was wrought to induce him so to act. He is quite a gentleman and a warm friend of mine and one who is in evry way worthy of a virtuous lady. I imagine that I can almost hear the quiet soliloquy of many ladys, saying I wish it could have been my fortune to have done that well in point of means and inteligence. Often have I seen young ladies whose virutu was undoubted cater to his smiles and regret even to day that they are not the happy recipient of his affections.

---

[48]Envelope addressed: "Mrs. Dr. Peddy/Franklin/Georgia"

[49]This letter is missing.

I am proud to know that I have a precious boon in you, about which their is no menacing of concience. Honey, I am so proud and well pleased with you. My great besetting genius is that I had not sufficient means to render you happy. I have self esteem about me enough to think that I am as well worthy of a nice wife as almost any one who possessed no more than I had, but fear that it may, some day when you see others better situated than us, cause you to regret not having obtained one who is capable of taking care of you and rendering you perfectly comfortable so far as this world's goods are concerned. I hope that is is a hallucination of mine, that such things rearly enter you thoughts. Honey, I am anxious to know who was your gallant on the night of Giles' Party. Hope you had a nice gentleman if any. Do you suppose that their was one thought of me that night only what eminated from your precious intilect? I fear not no[r] care not so long as I have the undivided affection of you pure heart. I can get along noble even if the world of mankind were to discard me. As you say, I donot ask more of this world's goods than to be permited to be in your gentle and loving society all the time. I am so sorry, my love, that I cannot be with you to caress and pet you when you feel so much wearied. I do sincerly hope that you may be free from pain in my absence as well as when I am with you. My dear, donot let any one see this, for it is rather dirty in part. I will not write so again. I fear that your lovely trait, modesty, will revolt at the reflections in this.

Honey, Brewer sets by me now talking sadly about his departed companion. I deeply sympathise with him. I can imagine the heart rending agony at so great a loss. I do hope to God I will never be deprived of my noble love. Such are my affections for you, my only love, that without your smiles and enchantments this life would be a reached one.

Lou is quite hostile about y'r Pa not giving him a party while at home. I told him he ought to have acted like an obedient son, then his good Pa would have rendered him evry comfort and gratified evry desire that he might have had consistent with sound reason. He seamed to regard the significance of the idea. Honey, in your last you did not say anything about our little Cherub. I suppose you forgot it, but you ought not to forget her. She is to little to read or Pa would write to her every week with pleasure. Let me know what Giles is going to do in reference to going into the war. I do wish he could stay at home. Honey, write me another good letter soon. Without frequent letters from your dear hand in camp, I am almost miserable. Good night, sweet one. Oh how I would be pleased to kiss your sweet lips to night! Let me know how you are. Yours ever more

G.W.P.

P.S. I know I will be proud of my chain of your hair. I wish I had it ready mounted. I will have fine material put on it so that it will chime in with the hair. G.W.P

147

Franklin, Feb. the 21/64[50]

MY PRECIOUS NOBLE LOVE,

As Capt. Spearman is going back to camp on Tuesday and I will be very busy tomorrow preparing your box of provisions, I must write today. I am so pleasantly seated in my easy chair, the gift of your love, ever thoughtful of my comfort. How supremely blest I am to have such noble, handsome, inteligent being to care for me and shelter me from the wide unfeeling world; and if I only know in what way I can render my darling happiest, it will indeed be a great pleasure for me to do so. Honey, I never get weary reading the fond words of affection which you write. They tuch a chord in my heart which echoes back the same melody and makes me so happy. I received another sweet letter from you yestady written on the 16th.[51] I never have even thought for a second that my life would have been happier with any but you. It is just the other way with me. I thought no one but yourself ever could have been so completely loved. I have never seen no being I yet have loved with the deep devotion I do you nor do I expect to if I live a thousand hears. It is pure happiness when the heart's best affections are entwined, and as I said before, I care not for riches when you are not to share it with me. They do not bring happiness no way unless connected with a virtuous life. You shurely did not think I mingled in the giddy throng at the party. It is against my feelings of propriety even were I enclined to such pleasures in your absence. No, I felt more sad than usual, for I missed your presence, and that to me is joy. I detest more than most of persons any thing like marred people flying around. Tell bud Lu Ma says she nor Pa either had any thing to do with this party, and if he coms home, he shall have one if any shugar can be found in the country. Jack Boon & the youngest one of those miss Ships married last week. She is [a] very pritty girl, and he seems to be quite a good looking gentleman, so I hope they will have a pleasant time. Pa says he can tell now why we write so many letters and find so much to write about. I was writing to you the other night and had been reading the piece of poetry you sent me and laid it down. He picked it up, and after reading it, said that revealed to him the secret of all our writing. We filled our letters with poetical quotations and love phrases. Said to tell you the tax bill had passed and we must stop such stuff. What do you think of the tax bill any how? Pa says every thing will go down to nothing. It is creating a great deal of excitement here. People don't

[50]Envelope addressed: "Surgeon G.W. Peddy/Dalton/Ga." and in left bottom corner, "Courtesy of/Capt Spearman"

[51]No. 146.

know what to do. They want to get rid of their money to prevent its being bonded, and then they want enough to pay taxes with. Bud Gily has conlcuded to go to teaching school at this place next week and reading medicine under Dr. Harland. He wants me to give the miss Woods mussic lessons, but I don't think I understand it well enough to teach it correctly. We received a letter from bud Nick last week which was quite humerous. Said he thought some time ago he could turn out to visiting the ladies, but alsas [? for *alas*] for Miss., he found they either chewed tobacko & smoked cob pipes or diped snuff. He would be compelled to go back to Va. His Gen. McCall had been transfered to Ten. and he was very anxious to be also. Said he was tired of Miss. Lt. Cato died yestady. He leaves a devoted wife and little one to mourn for him. No one sympathises more with Brewer than I do, for I know what a loss he has sustained. A tear of regret falls to her memory whenever my thoughts dwell on her. He loved so well, for we were warm friends from childhood and many pleasant hours we used to spend together. I do believe she idolized him, and he can never cease to remember such devotion, which was stronger than death itself. I can't fix up a very nice box now, I fear, for butter is scarce and hard to get.

Monday 22. Honey, I send you 1 ham, some busscuit, pies, sweet cakes, & wafers, and sausuages. I could not get any butter and should have had some light-bread, but the yeast did not rise in time. If I can get any butter, I will try to get some one else to take you some. Every body is scarce of it now. I will write again soon. Laura says a kiss for you. Yours ever more

Kate Peddy

148

Surgeon's Office, 56th Reg. Ga. Vol.
Camp Near Dalton, Ga.
Tuesday night, *Feb. 22nd/64*

HONEY DARLING, Oh how happy I have furthern made by reading your letter of the 19th inst.[52] one of the sweetest and most affectionate ones you have ever written me. Ought I to be proud of one who is so well qualified to render me so happy? A voice from the love chambers of the heart says I ought to be intensely so. No one, my dear, loves so fondly as I do you, and I feel proud that I do, as I

[52]This letter is missing.

have told and written this to you so often that I fear you will get tired of it. You say in your, my love, in yours that in your present condition you like to be made happy by my letters. I intend, my dear, that you shall as I have shown by the number I have written you recently. You[r] condition elisits evry sympathy of my heart, and if I knew what would make you the most happy, I am shure I would exert myself to the utmost to the accomplishing of that object and would feel at the same time that if I were not to do so I would be doing violence to my feelings. I know to[o], my dear, that it takes little exertion to fatigue you. For that reason I donot want you to do anything. I did not espouse you for no such purposes. I done so for my high esteem of your intrinsic worth; also that you might remain handsome; also for the love I had for you for you[r] soft and pliant hands and lo[v]ing face. I do not wish the latter to be prematurely furrowed by phisical labor. Honey, you must not weave the cloth you have the thread spun for. I fear it may impair your health in some way, and I would not have that done for all the jewels of earth. Honey, Uncle Mort promises me as much wool as you might need. You can get it from him as soon as he shears his sheep. Honey, I donot wish any cotton clothes in the Summer, as they would be to[o] cool for me sleeping out at night, and when they get wet, they are very unpleasant. Honey, donot let your Ma know that I said so, but hold on to you shoes if they are nice. I want them to keep your little *sweet foot* small. I suppose little Kitten is very proud of hers. Poor little thing, she did not get them soon enough.

My dear, I wrote to you on the 8th inst. to fix me up a box and send it by Capt. Spearman. Did you not get the letter? I fear you did not, as you have not said anything about it in yours since. In the same one I stated you could get some wheat from Billie Mozeley to make you some flour.[53] I hope he will bring me the box all righ[t], as his time is out on the 24inst, day after tomorrow. Congress has passed a law to allow officers to draw rations as soldiers without paying for them. If the President approves it, I will be enable to save a great deal more money. I hope he will do so. Honey, always let me know when you receive my letters and their dates. Then I will know wheather you get them all. I hope you, my love, will pardon this, for I have a slight headache to night. I do wish I was wtih you so that I might lay it on your lap and get it easy. I donot have it often here like I do at home. Kiss Laur[a] for poppie. My love to all. Yours ever more fondly

G.W. Peddy

[53]The box to be sent by Capt Spearman is mentioned in No. 144 (dated 9 February 1864) and the wheat from Mozeley in that one and in No. 143 (dated 7 February 1864).

149

Franklin, Feb. 26/64[54]

MY DARLING,

I have recieved your letter and watch by Mr. Wood. I was so much delighted to read a long letter filled with such words of melting tenderness whose meaning finds an answering melody in the inner temple of my heart, filling it with such deep tones of music such as no heart but those that are truly happy can appreciate. I would not exchange exquisit feelings of intense joy I experience while reading your fond letters for the wealth of Solomon, for then I know that my undying devotion to such a noble being (one more worthy of the most gifted being that ever lived) finds that it is not in vain, and is more than repaid. Honey, I never doubt your love for me although you are fond of the admiration of all ladies. Yet I have never been so ungrateful as to doubt your affection for one so unworthy of you. I have often feared since you have been in the service & received the smiles and admiration of so many gifted woman of refinement that I would only share the heart whose every throb of love I miserly hoard up and cherish as my fountain of happiness. Hony, perhaps I often test your patience and forbearance to the fulest extent by reciting all the little complaints to which I am subject, no doubt as all in my situation are, but I will only tell you this once, for perhaps you can suggest some remedy which will relieve me. All this week I have suffered by a strange headache. When I get up to walk, I come very near fainting, and when I lie down to go to sleep, I feel just as though I had taken laudanum. I get into a kind of stupor, my bowels are inclined to diareah, and my mouth has such a bitter taste I can't get any thing to taste right. I am affraid when Spring comes I will take some kind of fever, and if I could get something simple now, perhaps I should feel well. Laura got hold of the bottle of turpentine this evening and took some in her mouth and blistered it very badly. I fear she cannot be propperly while with so many who are allowed to do as they please. I am sorry you had your watch broke. It will never, I fear, be as good time piece. I will send it by Pa to be mended. I am told that mountain for jewelry cannot be had at any price now. I have been uneasy all day, for the news has come that a fight was going on near Dalton. I am in hopes that it is not so. Remember, darling, not to expose your dear self in any more fights, and if possible, keep bud Lu out. He has taken up a whim that i don't love him as a brother. I want you to talk him out of it, for you know I always said that he was just as kind as a brother could be to me. Brother John is here on

---

[54]Envelope addressed: "Surgeon G. W. Peddy/Dalton/Ga. Courtesy of/Col. Watkins"

his way to camps. He is not married and says tell you he don't know that he ever will marry. Hony, [do write] for my sake; and I know you won't refuse to write to your father. He says he loves you as a father ought to love a son, but he fears you don't care for him. Now say you will write to him and I will be so well pleased.

Honey, I can buy the meat that I was to pay the government for 2.50. Now would you buy it or not and risk selling it for the same price in this new currency? I have just about $200 dollars now, and the bonds, if any, will be small amounts, and in my oppinion, but of course that is not much. The bonds will not pay but a small sum. I shall need some mony after the mony is all bonded, and how must I get it? I can't get any five dollar bills to keep as a good many is doing. Pa says this tax law is not so bad after all. He insist[s] that every thing will go down when all the mony is bonded, but no one can tell, I know, what will be the result. I will stop now, Hony. Write soon, my love, and advise me, for that is such a relief to me.

Laura sends a hug & kiss [from her] Ma & one from her.

Yours ever more

Kate Peddy

150

Camp Above Dalton 4 miles, Feb. 27th/64[55]

MY PRECIOUS KITTIE, I rec'd your sweet letter yesterday.[56] How glad I was to read it! We had a an engagement all along our lines on the 25th inst. The enemy were repulsed at evry point. Yesterday they fell back toward Chattanooga. I donot suppose they will come again. I am safe. So is Lou and all the Company from our county. No member of it is hurt. I have not got my box yet. I fear that Capt. Spearman lost it. We are still in line of battle. Donot think we will fight here again. I am sorry to hear of the death of Lt. Cato. Honey, this is not a reply to yours. I will answer it, my love, at lingth as early as I can. Write me often, my sweet one. I love you so much. I would give anything to see you. Kiss Laura for me. Yours ever more. G.W.P.

---

[55]Envelope addressed: "Mrs Dr Peddy/Franklin/Ga"

[56]No. 147.

151

Surgeon's Office, 56th Regt. Ga. Vol.
Camp Near Dalton, Ga.
Feb. 28th/64

MY OWN SWEET PRECIOUS KITTIE, I wrote you a short note yesterday on the battlefield with pencil. I now attempt to answer your sweet letter of the 21st inst.[57] You have no idea what a thrill of joy it sent to my heart, being situated as I was. Honey, but the nice box you prepaired for me with your lovely little hands I never got the benefit of. How sorry I am of it. I would not have lost if for no money. Brewer got his safely. I suppose some poor hungry soldier satiated his appetite on its contents. I am going to prefer charges against the Lt. in charge of the depot where it was left. The enemy have all left our front and gone back to Chattanooga. I don't think they will come again soon. We are now in our Winter quarters again. I was truly glad to get back safely. Say to Giles I rec'd his letter; will reply in a few days. Their is no chance for him to get the position he wrote to me about because it is filled. My advice to him is so stay at home as long as he can. Honey, I would give all I possess to see you to night, to kiss those sweet lips and clasp your lovely form in my arms. Would to God that I could realize that greatest of all pleasures! You would know how well I love you. Honey, you are dearer to me than all this world. Would that it was in my power to lay before you in this letter evry feeling of love that's in my bosom for you! If such a thing would make you happy, I am sure you would be the happyest angel that's on earth. Bless you sweet heart, I know not what to write you that will make you most delighted. If I did, I would most assuredly write it. Honey, I feel so badly about he loss of my box. I had rather lost almost anything I had that was worth no more than it was. To think of the care and diligence you used and the pleasing thought in your mind that your was preparing it for one you love and how much he will prize it. It's to[o] bad for me not to have got it and enjoyed its delicious contents. Honey, if I should live to get home, I will pay you for all your troubles about me. Honey, you know I love more than all others, but you have no idea how much. When I see you I will try to tell you, but think even then you will not realize its influence so much as I do. Honey, you must get us up a nice little boy. Then we will have another link in our unseperable chain that if possible will bind our hearts and affections closer. Honey, do not censure me for the above expression. At least, I beg you to pardon me for this inroad on your modesty. Capt. Spearman was trying to tease me about it to day. I told him I love you more when you was in that

---

[57]No. 147.

condition. Bless your heart, I could kiss you always, it seem to me. Honey, you had better burn this letter for fear some one gets hold of it. I think I will send Foster home before long after another box. I suppose I will have to eat the poor beef and cornbread for awhile longer. We got the little box that Brewer's Ma fixed up for him containing some pies and cakes and a side of meat. All that his Ma put[58] in the box with yours was lost, alas.

Tell little sweet Laura a heap of good things for me. I want to see her so much. Yours ever more,

G.W.P.

152

Surgeon's Office, 56th Regt. Ga. Vol.
Camp Near Dalton, Ga.
Feb. 29th/64

MY OWN SWEET DARLING KITTIE, With great pleasure I write you a few lines this eve as I am going to send Foster home after something to eat. I lost the box you sent me. As I have already written to you about [it], I will not tell you the circumstances again. You will get this before the last two letters I wrote reached you. I want you to send him back as soon as you fix up a box for me, which he will bring back. I will send your trunk home with my stove in it. Perhaps you had better send it back packed with provisions if you cannot get a box to put them in. Jim Caswell is here. Will start home in a few days. He will carry the trunk home from Hoganville for me. On his return, if you wish to send the trunk back, it might be left at Hoganville until he starts back. Carry what you want to send me in a bag that far, then put them in the trunk and come on back with it well nailed up. If you think best to send a box, you can start him back at once and keep the trunk. I want him to get back by Fryday. Send me, my love, a ham and a sholdier of meat, also some flour if you have it, and any thing else you may wish to send. Honey, I expect you will think this an extravagant step of mine, but my love, I must have something to eat. My mess will pay their part of the expenses of the trip.

Thom Miller wants Foster to bring him a box back. You will send his father word about it. If anyone of Wm. Miller's family will come as far as Atlanta with

---

[58]Remainder of letter written across the top of the page.

him he can easily bring it. Honey, let him start back Thursday & I will meet him as the depot Fryday. I am sorry to put you to so much trouble, my dear, but hope I will live to pay you for all your cares and trial about me. If you donot have time enough to fix up the box as you wish to, keep him a day longer. Honey, you can form no idea how much I want to see you. I would sacrifice, it seems to me, anything reasonable to be with you just a few days to hear your sweet voice and to behold those lovely eyes of yours. Honey, I have not time to write you but a short letter as its nearly time for F________ to start. Lou is very well. I did not let him go into the last fight, as he was unable to carry a gun. I hear that Dr. Lane & John Hopson will be up in a few days. Try and let F_________ come back with them if he can get ready in time.

Yours ever more

G.W. Peddy

P.S. Kiss Kitten for pappie.

153

Surgeon's Office, 56th Regt. Ga.
Camp Near Dalton
March 2nd, ⌊1864⌋

DEAREST IDOL OF MY HEART KITTIE, Having just moved my tent to a chimney that stood closely by, being now very comfortably situated, the next pleasure I look to naturally is that of responding to your unusually sweet and interesting letter of the 26th intime.[59] Such pathos as yours contained I imagine is rearly felt, to say nothing to expressing it, by but few individuals, and among those few, I find in my bosom a feeling which echoes back evry sentiment of pure love which can possib[l]y arise in your genuine heart. Hearts so united as ours in one eternal bond of love it seems to me should be never seperated so long. It appears to me that it is crewalty on the part of the fates so to treat us. I hope, my love, that the day is not far distant when I and you will be permited to hold sweet converse around our own sweet family alter, their to enjoy that greatest of blessings in listning at the pleasant pratting of our little cherubs. Such felicity I

[59]No. 149.

fear is vain to contemplate, but such happy thoughts often rush pleasantly to my imagination.

Honey, I do desire to see you more and more each day. I scarcely know how to content myself about it. I build thousand of castles about what I would do could I but see you, but alas, they all fall to the ground when I reflect about the impossibility of my getting a leave of absence. Such a thing is almost out of the question. Rest assured that I will seize the first opportunity that presents itself.

Honey, if you continue to feel as you described in yours, I would take a small blue pill at night. No doubt but it would releave you to some extent. Tell Laura she must never taste anything she sees in a bottle for fear it poisons her. I will write to Father in a short time. I think as much of him as I ever did and am shure but few sons ever loved a Father more than I love him. Honey, I would hold on to what money I have and pay the Goverment in meat. I fear if I have to pay any tax we will not have enough money to do it with. You had better invest the money you have in four per cent bonds. I think with the bonds in a short time which you will get you can buy twice as much meat as you can now b[u]y with your $250 dollars. You say you will need some money as soon as it's all bonded. I will send you as much as you want or small bonds, which will answer your purpose as well as money. Uncle Mort has sent me word he would give me cost for my interest in the colt. I donot think I will take it. I know in twelve months or sooner he will bring a thousand. He is working him, and I shall not pay for his food. James Caswell is here. I will send this letter per him. Lee Daniel and Uncle Thos. Shackleford has been to see me. They are perfectly supprised to find the troops in such high spirits and the army in such a fine condition. I hear no talk of our moving soon. I hope we will stay at least until Foster gets back with something to eat for me. The Goverment owes me now $324. I believe I will not draw any until April so I will get my pay in the new issue. Let me hear from [you] often, my love. Your letters render me so happy. Kiss Laura for me. Yours ever more

G W P

154

Surgeon' Office, 56th Regt. Ga. Vol.
Camp Near Dalton, Ga.
Mar. 6th, 1864

I am happy to announce to you the safe arrival of Foster with your sweet letter and delicious box of eatebles. They are doubly sweet to me because they were prepared by your own dear hands. Honey, I know not how to oblige you for your trouble in my behalf. I feel overjoyed often that I was so fortunate as to obtain you as my earthly companion. Hope that you will never have cause to regret your nuptials. Strange to say, Miss Ellen Brewster's Brother is now on a visit to camp. Sits by me while I write this letter. I told him I succeeded in obtaining the hand of one more dear and more lovely than all on earth. He then asked me, *do you think you could have done any better*? I told him frankly none on earth was your equal and I could not have done so well in espousing any one else. So you see that was a knock down argument so far as his sister was concerned, which no doubt he refered to. He in very short order got up and left.

Honey, such a feast as I am having off of the box you so kindly sent me I have not often. How I do wish you could enjoy it with me. I think of you evry time I look at the nice articles sent. You speak of having to buy meat. I hope you will not have to do so. I thought you had more than you could consume or I should not have sent home after it. You must try to make out with what you have. I want to save our money this year so that we will be able to buy us a little home next year, although if you think you need more, of course you must have it. I think it will be lower before long, so I think I would wait before I bought until what I had gave out. Honey, when my eyes began to trace the lines of your letter which spoke of your sickness, I could not keep from sheading tears. Nothing affects me more than to hear of my love and angelic one being in pain when I am away. Honey, if you would get you some Fluid Ext[ract] of Ginger and take it when you get that way, I think it would releave you. I will send you some the first one I see going home, as the Army Regulations entitle all Soldie[r]s' familys to medicines. Honey, I complied with your request in beseaching me to wirte to my Father. I done so with great pleasure and became deeply affected so much I stoped writing to wipe the tears from my eyes. Honey, I am glad you prompted me to do so, as it was a duty that I should have no doubt neglected. I also wrote Chippie, which I insure she has had a sound laugh over. I want you to get it and read it, not that it is anything great, but for the novalty of the effusion. I know not what she will think of it. Learn what she says about it. I hope she will not become offended at it.

Honey, you must hug little Laura, kiss her to[o] evry day for me. I do want to see you and she so much. Foster told me many go[o]d [things] she said while at home. He never saw our hogs, could tell me nothing about them. Hope they look fat and well. Honey, I have eat so much today that my mind will not get up anything good to write you. In reference to what I wrote to your Pa about, asking his advise, I can not go into now from the fact the President Davis vetoed the General Staff Bill, which leaves the Brig. Gens. just as they were with no Surgeon on their staff nor no additional aid.

Honey, it seams like a year since I saw you. I would give anything now, it seams to me, for a short furlough. I donot think we will have another fight here soon. I expect we will have a hard campaign this spring. Evry thing is being gotten in readiness for it. Gen. Hood is now in command of our Corpse. He is a good officer a[nd] the finest looking man I think I ever saw.

Honey, I wish this could reach you by Wenesday, but it will take it until Saturday. I know you will be anxious to know how Foster got through. Lou got beat out for Lt. again. I am very sorry for it. Wily Lee is the Lt. elect. He is to[o] imprudent about giving offence is the cause of being beat out. Do not let any of the family know I write this, for they will be shure to write to him something about it. Tell Eddie I would be pleased to hear from him again. He is beginning to write very well. I think he might afford to come up to see us some time when he is at leasure.

Honey, I do hope you will get along well after that last spell. I am so sorry for you, my love. I do wish I was their to console and caress you when you are well or sick. Let me hear from you soon, my own sweet one.

Good night, my darling. Kiss Laura for me often. Yours ever true and always

G.W. Peddy

155

Surgeon's Office, 56th Reg. Ga.
Camp Near Dalton, Ga.
Thursday Night, Mar. 10th/64

MY LOVELY ANGELIC ONE,

It is my good pleasure to agin address you in the bloom of health and youth. My deepest gloom and grief is that I am forced to pass these haylcion days of my life afar off from one who is doubly dear to me on account of her lovliness, goodness of heart, and whose grandeure surpasses in my humble estimation all others that live. I ask not high position or the honors of this life with all their allurement and charms. What I humbly desire more than all else is your pure love and to realize the fact that their throbs in your noble bosoms a heart which k[n]ows no affection only the reciprocal to mine.

Honey, no doubt that you will think from the variety of sentiment of my letters that I love you only by impulses momentarially, but I assure you that such is not the case. I love you with an ardor that is constant and as true as the fact that we live.

Honey, would that I could see you now! I imagine that I could give you undying evidence of my heart's purest love. If it were in my power, dear, you know I would be happy by your side, enjoyin the sweet music of your voice and the melting kindness of those eyes which ever burn brightly to me! Often do the days rush to my memory when I enjoyed that, the most choice of all earthly blessings. Now I am sorry to add that I am deprived of those joys and allurements which haunts me dayly and nightly with happyness.

Honey, I have no war news to write you. I can form no idea of the future operations that is now known to our Gen. I suppose our army is rapidly recruiting and in better condition, I suppose, than ever. The tented field has but few charms for me. My strongest desire is alway to be with you and our little Laura. I hope with our noble leader that our arms will be victorious wheanever it may be assailed. I have not rec'd any letter from you since Foster came back. He is quite well; so is Lou. I think he is now a blank so far as a sweetheart is concerned. Honey, let me hear often how you are progressing. I hope you are doing well in your critical situation. Honey, I hope you will be good humored until I see you. The duty I owe you now is greater than I owe my native South. Therefore I think I ought to be permited to stay with you for awhile at least. Honey, please let me hear from you often. I am always proud of your letters.

Kiss Laura for me. Learn her all you can.

Good night, my love. May heaven's best blessings rest with my little family. Yours ever more

G W Peddy

156

Surgeon's Office, 56th Regt. Ga. Vol.
Camp Near Dalton, Ga.
Fryday Night, Mar. 11th/64

MY DEAREST DEVOTED WIFE KITTIE, I wrote you last night, conclude I would do myself justice not to do likewise to night on account of having received your more than welcomed letter of the 8th inst.[60] My first effort will be to notice minutely the contents of your sweet letter.

You speak of wanting to see me. Honey, no joy could exceed that to me. Happyness is only mine when I am in your presence. Streames of limpid pleasure flow then only. I am sorry indeed to learn of your low spirits. I hope, my love, you will cheer up if your bodily condition will admit of it. I would exhaust evry effort to make you happy and do so with great pleasure. Honey, always write me anything you desire to. I will let no idea drop that will betray you. I am glad to know, my love, that it is your great effort to make me happy in your letters. Inclosed you will find an advirtisment f[r]om Mr. Duncan, who is the funding agent in Atlanta. If you cannot get anyone to carry your money to have it funded, follow out the instruction which he gives. If you can do no better, send it to him per mail, letting Mr. Watts see you mail it and put the money in it. You will see from the scrip I send you that Your Pa is mistaken in the denomination of the notes to be funded. Honey, I hope you will get my wach in time to send it back by Morrow Wood. Honey, buy you some syrup if you wish to and let Laura have as much of it and butter as she wants. So far as her imprudence in eating so much is concerned, while things are so scarce I donot object to. She shall eat as much as she wants to, for it is for your and her pleasure and enjoyment that I am willing to sacrifice my evry effort. Bless her little heart, she only takes after he Pa in that besetting evil habit. Honey, you must make her eat politely, but let her have evrything she wants that you have to eat. I suppose your Pa was joking when he said he had no corn to feed to cows, but perhaps he ment to tant you for so doing. If he has none thus to dispose of, I am shure if he will reflect upon his losses in stock, he will be sorry that he had not bought a little to save their lives. I think it would have be[en] a proffitiable business. Honey, I donot know what you will do about the soda. I can send you some, but not enough for the whole family. Honey, you must not let our cow die if it takes all the corn you have. Honey, I am shure I enjoyed the contents so nice and delicious of the box you kindly sent me. Darling, I do wish I could come after the next one. I am fully aware that you could not be prouder

[60]This letter is missing.

than myself. I suppose that some one's wicked whims are satiated after having broken open my letter to you. I will say this much to you, that the bearer of it to you[r] town will bear close watching. I do not think our place holds her equal. This, of course, you will keep sacred, for letting anyone know my opinion of the character above refered to could only redound to my injury. I imagine she found nothing indecent in it or that was shocking to one's finer feeling. If I were with you, my love, I am shure I would take a lively intreest in our stock. I admire your plan of feeding them. You must keep them perfectly fat. Let me know how my favorite shoat is doing. Honey, we must save all the money we can this year. I supose you want to live to yourself next year if I cannot be with you, and you are aware that it will take a great deal to set up to housekeeping again. I will save all I can. I donot mean by this that you must not buy anything you need. I went to se Dr. Lane yesterday. He seemed to be getting on quite well. I wish he was in our Regt., but perhaps he will do better where he is. Honey, I wish you could see Andy now. He is nice, slick, and fat. I intend to keep him if I can until the war is over and bring him home to his Ma's, where he can get better treatment and more to eat. If you can send your money out to some one to pay taxes with, I would do so. If I could find a responsible pearson that wished to borrow, you must do so quickly what you are going to or the first of April will be on us before we know it. Then we loose 33 1/3 per cent. My dearest idol, please write me evry mail. I am always proud of your interesting letters. I will always respond at once on receiving yours. Tell Laura all the good things you can think of for me. I am very anxious to see her. I can get her some shoes made up here if you think she needs any. Darling one, Uncle Mort faithfully promised to let me have all the wool that I would need this year. Hope you will get it and have it carded in the hot days of Summer. Then it will not nap. My love to all yours. Ever more proudly

G.W. Peddy

157

Surgeon's Office, 56th Ga. Vol.
Camp Near Dalton, Ga.
Monday, March 14th/64

MY DEAREST DARLING, Once more I have been rendered happy at the reception of you sweet letter f the 11th inst.[61] What a genuine pleasure it is for

[61]This letter is missing.

me to tender you my heart's deepest love through my pen! How much distress would I be in if I were whare I could not hold sweet converse with you. We should both praise the powers that be for the postal advantages we have. I am so much greaved, my love, on account of your recend and unxpected accident. I do hope by this time you have gotten over it. I do wish I could have been there to have arrested, if possible, your pain. I would have caressed and handled the injured part so gently that I imagine you would have to some extent forgotten your pain. I do hope that no other accident will befall my dearest one in my absence. You ask in yours what are you to be so idolized for. I frankly confess I am unable to write an elaborate discription of you[r] superior qualification as a lady of generating in my bosom such heart felt love as never man knew befor the day of our nuptials. Honey, I am unwilling to confess that I am, as you say, in the habit of corresponding with young ladies. I cannot think by that reference that you refer to the letter I wrote Chippie. Were I to ferret for one who is more intelligible and more gifted in wealding the pen in tracing lines whose superburb stile, meaning, and beauty surpass yours in redounding to my happyness, I am shure that none such could be found. I hope, my love, you will dispell such thoughts from your bright and hallowed intilect. I hope that if our meat and cows are impressed, you will make them pay as dear for what they get as they cause me to do. Honey, I send you the box Foster brought (per express) with the following articles in it: 1 Bott Blackbury Brandy in a sack of grits (not labeled), 1 Bottle of Caster Oil, Some Soda, a peace of Castile Soap, Some Mustard, Some books, Some grits for your pigs and Brewer's share, which you will please send to his mother. My love, keep the above articles which I send you in the way of Medicine for the use of our little family. The Brandy you must keep for that memorable event which comes in June. It is a very fine article. I cannot get any here to send for Puss. Hope she is getting on well. I can send you at any time such small quantities of Medicine as you may need, as the Army regulations gives me that privilege. Honey, constant I am made happy by receiving your letter. I hope they will continue to come. Lou and Foster are quite well. I am sorry that I have nothing nice to send to little Kitten. I know, bless her little heart, she will expect something. Say to her that pappie will recollect his darling when he sees anything he thinks will suit her. Honey, I will send you some pins if you need them. Honey, I have been quite unwell for two nights, did not sleep but little, but am happy to say that I feel quite well to night. I send the box per express to Hoganvill. Honey, anything you need, let me know, and I will get it up for you if it's in this region. Always remember, my love, that my happyest moments are when I am meditating of your genuineness and how happily you are adapted to my evry comfort and pleasure. My love to all. Your ever mour truly

G W. Peddy

158

Surgeon's Office, 56th Ga. Vol.
Camp Near Dalton, Ga.
Monday Night, Mar. 21st/864

MY DEAREST IDOL KITTIE,

I hope you will not sensure me for the above expression, for I do idolize you, but by doing so I think I commit no sin nor mean no disrespect towards God. You, my love, occupy a place in my affections far superior to all earthly beings. I love you with a pride and zeal that acknowledges no equal in this life. I feel proud that I have one so supreamly great to bestow my love upon. Your letter of the 18th inst.[62] stired up evry latent feeling of love in my bosom for you. I clasped it when handed to me like it was something of life that could realize the fond emotions of genuine love that passed pleasantly through my heart. Such beautiful and soul stiring sentences of love as its pages contained, I assure you is not often found in letters. Were I to attempt to give you the discription of my fondness in having you as my own, I would fall far short. I want to write you, my love, how dear you are to me, but I cannot. No pleasure would be more gratifying to me than to know that you are aware of my exalted opinion of you in evry particular. My emotion of love for you is more easily felt than expressed. Honey, I will just conclude that you are satisfied with me as a true admirer and hope the subject is one I am incompatent to do full justice to.

Honey, as to trying my patents with your details of affliction, I am sure you cannot do so, for I know if any one ought to know them, it's me, for no one is so well qualified to sympathise with you as myself. You must reccollect, my love, that upon your safty and happyness in this life depends mine. You must therefore give me all particulars about your health. I am happy to know, my dear, that you love me more than anyone on earth. I confidently assure you that evry throb of love for me, wheather feeble or warm, is and will be at all times hastily reciprocated, at the same time give you full confidence that their is no one truer husband on earth to a *fond affectionate wife* than to you. Honey, let me know who asked you what you would do if I was not so fortunate to get home about the time you got sick. I do hope I will have that gratification, although should I not, my love, you must get Dr. Harlan. I know he will give you all the assistance he can.

Honey, I think their is a pretty good chance for me to get a fifteen days' leave of absence as soon as Col. Watkins gets back, but if I get one then, I cannot get

[62]This letter is missing.

one at a time you would most need me. What must I do about it? Must I come while I can get a chance or wait until June and risk the chances of getting of[f] then? The Col.['s] leave will be out on my birthday, the 10th of April. It seems to me that I cannot do without seeing you longer, though I will submit to your will if I have to wait until June. Honey, you say it is no pleasure for me to think of home now. I cannot imagine what makes you think so. I fear you think that I donot love you on account of your condition, but rest assured, my love, that you are doubly dear to me just on that account. Should I be so fortunate as to get home, I will give you manifestations of my fidelity that will be permanently with you. I am sorry to know that you have such a cold. Hope you are well. Perhaps you had better take something for your cough. If I had thought of it, I could have sent you some Syrup Squells in the box I sent home.

Honey, it is to[o] expensive to send Foster home after a box. The next one you must send per express. It will come more safely that way than any other and cost less.

I am glad to learn that our hogs look so well. I fear they will give you to[o] much trouble, but Honey, I will repay you for all your cares in my behalf in love and kindness or any other thing that will satisfy you.

Honey, you can just say to Puss that I will give her such a lashing when I get home that she will not think of being sold [f]or dishonesty. She must be very careful how she treats you in my absence, or else she will get into a bad snap when I see her. Honey, perhaps you can lend your money to some one to pay tax with. Poor little Laura, she has been without shoes all the winter. Papie will have some made up here. Send me the length of her sweet little foot. Lou is out on picket to night. He is very well.

Tell Laura to hug and kiss her Ma for papie. Say to her also she does not love Ma as good as Pappie does. Honey, please write me often. I do love to read your letters so much. Dr. Lane was to see me a few days ago. He is quite well. I had a nice dinner of ham and buscuit for him. He said he was nearly perished.

Yours ever more

G.W. Peddy

159

Surgeon's Office, 56th Ga. Vol.
Camp Near Dalton
Tuesday, Mar. 22nd/64

MY *OWN LOVE,* I write you a few lines per Edd. Daniel. I send also by him my watch, which will not run. Please, my darling, get it fixed; also get Barnes to put a fly spring in the lid, which will be an additional expense. Honey, do not be uneasy about what money you have on hand. You can exchange it for the new issue by loosing one third of the amt., but if you could borrow enough to make out one hundred, you had better get some one to find it for you. Darling, you ought to begin to complain about the amount of business I put on you. I do hate, my love, to have to trouble you so much. I will never omit no opportunity of doing you any kindness in the world I can. Honey, be of good cheer. I hope I will embrace your lovely form in my arms ere long. If I should be so fortunate, how happy I will be! Then I will give you tokens of my fondness that you will ever remember.

Let me hear from you often, my dear. I wrote you a long letter, which you will get Saturday. It contains a host of my true sentiments of love for you. We have the finest snow you ever saw. It's four inches deep on the ground. Good by, my love. Kiss Laura for pappie.

Yours ever more G.W.P.

Tuesday morning, Mar. 22nd/64

Honey, such a snow as we have here this morn is rearly seen in this country. Oh how I wish I could be with you to enjoy it! I fear it will kill all the fruit. Honey, for fear I weary you to[o] much, I will stop writing. I would give all I have this morn to be with you in your lovely and sweet condition. Ladies are more lovely when in your fix than at any other time. I think it is very crewel for me to be exsiled away from you in such a lovly condition. You are lovely to me at any time, but I thought you was more beautiful when I was at home last than I ever saw you.

Except a hug & sweet Kiss from one who loves you more than all else. G W P

160

Surgeon's Office, 56th Ga. Vol.
Camp Near Dalton, Ga.
Fryday, Mar. 25th/864

MY DEAREST SWEET KITTIE,

Agan it is my great pleasure to announce the reception of your l[ov]ing letter of the 22nd inst.,[63] evry paragraph filled with sweet and solacing sentiments of true love, which to me lends enchantment to all the monotony with which I am surrounded. Such noble and heart gratifying letters I imagine are rearly receved by only those who love as we do. It is my great pleasure to record that evry sentiment of affection that is yours for me finds a responsive chord in my nature.

Honey, I *do love you be*[y]*ond the* conseption of human reason. If I can get home I can better act the sentiments of my heart than write them to you. It seems to me if I were with you to night, I could give you a livid manifestation of my profound admiration for you. Honey, I am incompetent to do justice to my heartfelt for you. I will dismiss the subject not half satisfied. Honey, I am so scared about your being sick with cold independent of your sickness and had feelings like a super kind compassion ever ready to sacrafice your comfort for my selfish gratification. The gratitude I owe you already I fear is more than I can pay, although I give you my word that if I do not liquidate the debt, it will not be for the like of exertion on my part. I will ever work to the accomplish that my strongest design. I am sorry that you have no shoes adap[t]ed to your present and lovely condition. Darling, do not go out of the house so as to catch cold. Take special care of yourself, my love, for my sake and my future happyness. Without out [*sic*] you as a stimulant to action, I am shure I would be a blank in this life. I am sorry to hear of Eddie's illness. I am shure if I were at home I would do all in my feeble power to releave his suffering. Tell your Pa to give him a large dose of Sodide Potassium as his system will bear.

Honey, I suppose that Jim and Lou are very much disappointed. If so, I pitty them. I shall not be, but will be proud and perfectly satisfied if you come out safely and have no doubt but what you will. The sex of your progeny makes no difference with me. I am proud of any from you. All I desire is that they will be like their *dear Ma*. Honey, it is disagreeable to think about any animal dying from hunger as our cow did. It is sinfull to treat stock in that way. I do not sensure you for the crime. You no doubt done all that was in your power to put

---

[63]This letter is missing.

a stop to the cravings of her appetite. I should have made arrangements for forage for them when at home in the Summer. Nothing else of mine shall ever perish to death if I can prevent it.

I am glad to hear that you are going to fund all your money. Honey, how I do wish you could realize you[r] dream! I assure you I would be the happyest of the two if you could. Dear, I am sorry to think that you are in a disponding mood, as the last sentence of your letter expressed when you said if Ma cou[l]d not get to Kiss Pappie again, somebody more worthy would. Now Honey, no one in the world is so worthy of me as you, and if those sweet lips are lost to me, be assured that mine is for no one but the survivors of your body. If you were gone, I would caress our little one fondly in memory of one who is dearer to me than life itself. Honey, I now draw my rations, do not have to pay for them, which will enable me to save a good deal of money, should I live for you and Laura. Tell Laura Pappie will bring her a nice pair of shoes when he comes home.

Write me often, my love. Kiss Laura for me.

Yours ever more

G.W. Peddy

161

Surgeon's Office, 56th Ga. Vol.
Camp Near Dalton, Ga.
Tuesday, Mar. 29th/64

MY PRECIOUS KITTIE,

This dreary windy day closes upon me, whos[e] heart is again made glad at the reception of your kind and sweet letter of the 26th inst.[64] Honey, I am glad and indeed proud to know that I have one at home in my absence who is so well constituted to rear and direct the minds of our children in the way they should to. Wish I could share a part of that responsible, but under the circumstance existing, I cordially yield it up to one whom I know is better qualified to that task than myself. You teach them that which in after years will be an imperishable monument for them to behold upon, whereas I could only teach them mischief, as that is the predominant faculty in my nature (except that of

---

[64]This letter is missing.

love). I consider myself more fitly qualified for the latter purpose than almost any other. I am satisfied that our natures are perfectly congenial and am happy in reflecting about the undying purity of our true affection for each other and our lovely charming little daughter. Honey, I suppose their is very little doubt but what I will come home sometime next month, if Col. W[atkins] gets back and Capt. Stoke, who is now absent without leave. Should the enemy move on us about the time they get back or we are moving around, of course I could not come, for when the army begins to move, all furloughs are stoped for the time being. Honey, I am shure you would not be prouder than I could we see each other. I am so sorry, my love, to hear of your sickness. I think after June you will be all right again. Then oh! how happy I will be when I think of my love. Honey, you must not suffer yourself to get low spirited. Cheer up for the sake of one who loves you better than you love yourself. Honey, you know I will come home if I can, but should I not, you must not get sick on that account. I am glad your Pa & Ma went to see the Col. You must get acquainted with him. He is one of the best men. I hope Eddie will be well in a short time, as his rising is about to supurate. I assure you that Nick will have a hard time now and a very expensive one, but it will be a good thing for his health. He will never without an accident get sick in Cavalry Service. Honey, you must watch what you say while in Mrs. W[atkin's] company; if not, she will ring it around, especially if it's about any body. Lou and F[oster] are quite well. Lou wants me to write him an April fool for Miss McPherson to night, but I am shure I feel little like it. I am passing of my time in reading literary books of all kinds that I can get hold of. Let me hear from you often. My love to Eddie, the ballance of the family. Yours ever more

G W Peddy

162

Surgeon's Office, 56th Ga.
Near Dalton, Ga.
Monday, April 4th/64

MY SWEET DARLING,

I have just received you sweet letter of the 2nd inst.[65] I am always so proud when I rec[e]ive one of your letters I fear that I become as source of disgust to

[65]This letter is missing.

my associates here. Dr. Franklin often says that he never saw a man so compleetly infatuated with a Lady as I am with you. I say to him that such infatuation is bliss to me indeed. Honey, you say that you are proud to know that their is one heart who cares so tenderly for you. I am shure that if you could realize that the debth of my hea[r]tfelt tenderness for you, you would have cause to be happy. I esteem and love you as never man loved before, and I am truely sorry that I am so poorly capacitated that I have not ere this been enabled to give you a full and free expression of my admiration.

Honey, I am shure you have a pleasant time with Laura's supburb childlike inteliglegence. If it was not you, I should find myself envying your enjoyment with her. Honey, I do admire your modesty in keeping your own secrets about you[r] antisipated sickness. I am proud to know that I have a modest companion who deals not in the vulgar gossip which is common to, I fear, most of ladies. Hope, my dear, that you will never be one of that class. I hope you will keep your secrets from all but me. I think as one so intimately blended in your wellfare as I should know them all. My curiosity has been hightened to the utmost about the amount of things you have to tell me when I see you. I do wish I could see you for that reason and many others that I will not stop to write of. Honey, I am going to make a powerfull effort to get home. If I fail, it will not be my falt. What a pleasant time we could hav togueather for twelve of fifteen days. I am shure I will enjoy life to the brim if I am permitted to stay with you that long. Honey, if I get home, it seams to me that I cannot be induced to leave you five minutes.

I hope if I am so fortunate that you will let me caress and pett you as much as I wish to. I fear I will weary you with my want to be superhuman kindness. I will try to let you know the day I will get to the Depot if I can, so that you may send their for me. I may not be able to do so.

Let me hear from you as regular as heretifore and much oblige. Yours ever more

G W Peddy

P.S. Kiss Laura for me. Ten thousand kisses for yourself. My love to all
G W P

163

Franklin, Apr. the 5, 1864

MY OWN PRECIOUS ONE,

To day 5 years ago you returned from New Orleans. We had adieu and been parted for many days since we had begun to learn the sweet lesson of love which afterwards was to fill our heart with a world of happiness unknown to our hearts before. What blissful dreams had always filled my imagination when I thought with rapture of our meeting! I thought shurely no one could ever be so happy as I was or loved so well. I love to linger over those days of the past in which I was so supremly happy. I was always overjoyed when you was by my side. Now it is a double joy. I never then dreamed of an intenser joy that I could feel when you returned after being absent from me, but now I know that I then enjoyed a mere shadow to what would be my feeling now if again the mussic of your dear voice could be heard by me in tones of tender greeting. Hony, I have been troubled for two or three days by the rumor of a fight at Dalton. I could not believe it, but was affraid it might be true. Then I knew all chances of your coming would be vain. I have felt better for the last few days than usual. Laura has had a bad cold. The other evening she waked up and coughed violently for some time. At last she found a chance to talk: Ma, she said, I know I am going to have the colic tonight, for I cough so much. She sees me have so many such spells it is natural for her to think there is no sickness but colic. Little Joe is quite sick to night. He has diareha. Several of the negroes have been sick. Pa has lost another fine milch cow. That is 8 or nine cattle he has lost this winter, and another cow to night was found in the mud so she could not get out. I am going to feed mine anyhow to keep them alive untill Summer.
Winsday night, 6.

I thought I would have sent this letter today, but Joe was so sick all night, & this morning had two hard spasms, I could not compose my mind sufficiently to write. He is a great deal better tonight. Dr. Harland gave him some oil which relieved him a great deal. I was so frightened, I shook as if I had a hard ague. It reminded me so much of Laura's spell she had and came so near dying. It think Joe has worms. He is affected that way. I received an other good letter from you today. You can only imagine what pleasure I experience by the emotions you have when you read mine, only yours are more interesting and elegant than mine. I try to school to bear a disappointment if you should not get home, but I find myself buisy weaving bright fancys and beautiful dreams of how I will enjoy your presence. You must not think of leaving home to go down in town many minutes at a time while here, for you know I am a little exacting just now and will need all your company myself (don't get frightened now, honey). I would be glad of it will not be too much trouble and too expensive if you would get me several pounds of *rice*, though, hony, don't do it if you cannot conveniently; also a small quantity assefeodity to give children. That did Joe more good this morning than any thing else. I have not got the trunk & box from Hogansville yet. I can't see any waggon going there, so I shall have to hire some one to go after them. I will send some one out after you on the 17 if I do not hear that you are not coming before then. I have written all the news I can think of, and close with the fonned hope that ere long I can have the sweet privileg of giving those dear lips of yours a hundred good night kisses. Yours with all my heart. Laura sends her pappie a dozen kisses.

Kittie Peddy

164

Surgeon's Office, 56th Ga. Vol.
Camp Near Dalton, Ga.
Saturday, April 9th/64

MY OWN PRECIOUS ONE,

I received no letter from [you] by last mail. I fear that you are unwell is the cause of you not writing. I hope I am mistaken. Honey, I recon you had better send to Hogansville for me next Saturday. If I get my application for leave, I guess I will be there by that time. If not there then, I will get there Sunday, if I can at all soon. If Col. W[atkins] gets back to night, I will start my papers up in the morning. It will take six days to get them through. Honey, I do hope I will get off. I do want to see my love so much and have my ears greeted with the sweet melody of your sirene voice in relating the many things you have to tell me. I will apply for a fifteen days' leave. If I get it granted, what a sweet time I can have with you! Mr. Moore will bring you this letter. I hope you are well and I may find you so when I get home. Kiss Laura for me. My love to all. Yours ever more

G.W. Peddy

165

Surgeon's Office, 56th Ga. Reg.
Camp Near Dalton, Ga.
Friday Night, April 15th/64[66]

MY PRECIOUS DARLING,

It's you that can only imagine how glad I was on the reception of your last sweet letter on the 29th inst.[67] I have no news of importance to write you, only I am here in my tent to night, seated by a fire while the clouds lower and the elements outside are very bostrious. I can imagine how lovely and sweet you look at home, where the wild and furious winds coo by the corner of the house at home. Oh! would I were there with you! No one could k[n]ow how happy I would be but you. I do hope that it will be so that I can get of[f]. If Capt. Stoke and Col. gets back before furloughing ceases by a general order, I will get home by the eve of the 17th inst. Though, honey, if anything should happen that I should not get off, I will come as soon as I can. I am very uneasy for fear that the furloughing will be revoked befor I get a chance to apply. I am so sorry that you suffer so much. It is not colic you have, it is impartial contractions of the womb, which you can ease at any time by taking a little Camp Spirits of Lavender or a small quantity of Paregoric, or if you cannot get the above articles, a small toddy of Brandy & Nutmeg would releave you. Tell Laura she must get through what she intends to do before Pappie comes home, for he wants her whole attention while there. I am glad you sent me her measure, for I was about to have her shoes made to[o] small. Honey, their is so much nonsense being carried on near me that I cannot write with the least interest to night. I hope you will pardon me, my love, this time. I will try to do better next. Lou and Foster are well. I never enjoyed better health in my life. I hate to be so well, it seems to me, while you are in so much pain. I hope you will be all right in a short time, be yourself again. Andy is the prettyest thing you ever saw. I wish you could look at him now. I am shure you would fancy him more than you ever did. If it was not for him in your absence, I donot know what I would do here in this sad old camp. Let me hear from you often. I will write you if I find out their is no chance for me to get home soon.

Your ever more

G W Peddy

---

[66]Letter misdated April 11th, which fell on Tuesday in 1864.

[67]This letter is missing.

166

S.O.,56th Ga. Vol.
Near Dalton, Ga.
Monday, Apr. 18/64

MY DARLING ANGEL, No doubt ere this your pure little heart has relapsed into grief at my failure to get home. My application has not returned yet is the cause of my not coming. It may get back this eve. If it does not, I will renew it and send it up in the morning. I am satisfied it will be approved. I am sorry I have put you to the trouble to send to the Depot for me, but regret more your disappointment when you find out I am not there. I know how you will feel, my dearest. I will sympathise with your lovely tears of regret. I will keep trying, my dearest love, as long as their is an opening untill I get one. What joy I have been thinking and dreaming of I would have with you by this time, but alas, by some one's negligence I have been cut of[f] from your presence, which is the greatest happyness to me. Honey, it appear[s] that I would almost give my life to be with you for a few days to give you all the consolation I have it in my power to do and to hear those many sweet things you have to tell me and talk to me about. Kiss little Laura for Pa, who loves her far more than she will ever realize.

Honey, I think I will be home in a few days.[68] Yours forever truely

G W Peddy

P.S. I send this per Jack Miller.

G W P

[68]There are no further letters until May 1864.

Part IV.

THE ATLANTA CAMPAIGN

17 MAY 1864 - 17 SEPTEMBER 1864
167-197

In December 1863, as a result of public outcry over his defeat at Missionary Ridge, Gen. Braxton Bragg resigned command of the Confederate forces at Dalton, Ga. and was replaced by Gen. Joseph E. Johnston. He had a force of some 62,000 men. Gen. Grant ordered Gen. William T. Sherman to use his army of 100,000 to crush Johnston's army, to penetrate the interior of Georgia, and to devastate the war resources of the Confederacy. Atlanta was the obvious target. Sherman's advance began on 7 May 1864. His strategy was to execute a series of flanking and enveloping movements, forcing Johnston to retreat rather than to accept unfavorable terms for a pitched battle. Johnston's delaying tactics annoyed his government, and on 17 July he was replaced by Gen. John B. Hood. Hood, who was a superb combat commander on the brigade level, was not the man to lead a corps or an army. By the end of July he had withdrawn into the defenses of Atlanta and at 5 P.M. on 1 September evacuated the city. During this campaign Dr. Peddy was attached to the brigade of Gen. Alfred Cumming, which fought at Resaca, New Hope Church, Marietta, and Jonesboro. After the evacuation of Atlanta, Dr. Peddy was at Lovejoy with the rest of Hood's army.

167

Adiersville, [Ga.], May 17th/864

MY PRECIOUS KITTIE,

No doubt ere this you have become very uneasy about me and you have grounds so to do, for I have not written to your sweet self for some time on acco[u]nt our movements. We fought the enemy on the 14th and 15th inst.[1] Our loss was five thousand killed, wounded and missing. That of the enemy's is estimated at twenty thousand. No doubt it's correct. We fought them awhile [we] wer[e] entrenched. The[y] made assault after assault but failed to take our works. After being there one nigh[t] he intrenched himself, and being thought inexpedient to attempt to take their works, we retired from Resica on the night of the fifteenth and are here to day. The enemy are slowly pursuing. I suppose we will make a stand soon, and rest assured, when we do, we will gain a great victory. Our troops are in fine fighting trim and are anxious to meet the enemy. Honey, I would like to be with you to tell you all about the engagement. I have not time to write you any more about it. Darling, I have just received your sweet letter of the 13th inst.[2] How glad I was to hear from you. Honey, I cannot tell how it is that your letters always contain just such information as I like to hear, and sentimental love expressions which they breath[e] alway find a hearty responce in my heart. The Ladies of our section, I am sorry to say, are reduced to very great extreams. I am greaved to think they have to resort to such measures to get along through these trying times. It is the first female raid I have heard of. I hope, sweet, that you will never have to join such a class.

I am sorry to learn of Mr. Mozeley's illness. Hope he is better by this time. Lou, Dr. Lane, & myself are all unhurt, but five of our Regt. got wounded in the two days' fight.

Casville, Ga., May 18th[3] Honey, I had not time last eve to finish my letter. We march to this place last night. I suppose we will fall back still farther. We may make a stand here; if not, we will soon. Andy has gotten well, I am glad to say. Lou is still getting on well.

Their was none of our camp wounded but Jerry Lane. His was not very serious. Honey, you have no idea how much I want to see you. Bless your little heart, I am so glad to learn that you are getting on so well. Gen. Featherston is

---

[1]This refers to the action around Resaca, Ga.

[2]This letter is missing.

[3]The remainder of the letter is written in pencil.

here. I will see him in a short time. I have not time to write you more now. Kiss Kitten for Pappie. Yours ever

G W Peddy

168

Infirmary Steverson's[4] *Divis.*
Near Marietta, time 6 o'clock
P.M., [*May*] *19th, 1864*

DEAREST IDOL OF MY LIFE, I have just received your sweet letter of the 14th inst.[5] You cannot imagine my anxiety to see its contents. I never was so eager to read a letter, as it appeared that I had not gotten one in a month, when rearally it had been put four days since. Honey, never have I read such noble productions. I am led to stop in the middle of your beautifull sentances and wonder how it happened that I was so fortunate in getting a life's companion that is so well qualified to render me more than happy. Bless your little heart and Laura. It will ever be my greatest pleasure to bend evry effort to the advancement of your evry joy. Honey, when I do anything that you dislike and renders you unhappy, let me know it and I will desist at once for your sake. Honey, you say in yours you can never repay me for my kindness. Why, my dearest one, you have already liquedated a thousand fold my debt of that nature. My love, you are worthy of more admiration than I can bestow, although I am shure that no one loves more ardently and zealously than myself. Honey, I cannot write anything that could give your Ma the least inkling of my true love for her worthy daughter. I have never been as kind to you as I intend to be if life last[s]. Out of my mischeif, my love, I have often acted in a maner perhaps that you disliked, but if you will pardon me for that trespass upon you sweet self, I will not do so again. Honey, I am sorry that your dear mind is troubled so much with falts rumors. If it were in my power, you should never by anything else but happy. Honey, I do not think now we will fall back any farther. I think we will make a fight here. If we can compell the enemy to fight us in our trenches, we will be shure of victory. If we cannot, I believe we will beat him at any rate. Our boys are very cheerfull. It seems that the rain will

---

[4]Carter Littlepage Stevenson, Maj Gen CSA

[5]This letter is missing.

never cease. It has been raining incessantly all day and night. I am so sorry for Lou. Poor fellow, he has to be out in it all. I was with him today. He is verry lively, well, an[d] cheerfull. I read your letter to him. It breathed that same pure spirit of sisterly love which is characteristic of your noble heart. You must all write to him often. He loves to get letters from dear ones at home. He is getting plenty to eat, but no vegettables. I gave a handfull of coffee to day which will do him several days. The Regt. drew coffee and sugar to night. I have it all the time and have had not been out of it in a month, I donot think. Honey, I would do anything in the world for him because he has circulating in his veins that pure stream of noble blood. I rearly ever give him any liquor because I donot drink it myself and think it would be an injury to him. I am sorry that such noble fellows as he had to be made a target for the abolition vandals to shoot at. Honey, I suppose by this time you have become acquainted with the little stranger. Honey, you must not treat him coolly as you did Laura, the brightest and lovelyest jewel in a little girl that lives. I feel myself complimented when people say that mine and hers is just alike. They certainly are not, or I would be the most handsome man that ever lived. It is the nob[l]eness of her sweet Ma that shines so beautifully on her lovely face, *only* the *reflection* of you in her that makes her so lovely and dear. Honey, my heart will leap for joy when I learn that you have gotten through safely and well. Never did a heart ache with such dreadful suspense as mine does. My dear, I would give anything reasonable to be with you in that trying hour. It would afford me such unallayed pleasure to smoothe your pillow and kiss your sweet lips and place back the stray hairs that fret your placid brow while sick. Honey, as soon as Foster comes up with mine and Lou's things I will send him back to your Pa imediately as we can get along without him. I have a man cooking and attending to Andy[6] for me. He is now entirely well. I hope your Pa will not sell Leash[?], for if Andy gets killed I cannot get one any where else. I will give your Pa as much for him as any one else will. Got a letter from brother John today. Enclosed please find it.

Honey, kiss Laura for Pappie. Tell her a heap of nice things for me.

Good night, my love, and a pleasant time for you, my sweet, and Oh! that I could caress and entwine my arms around my own and only love. G.W.P.

---

[6]The remainder is written along the top of the page.

169

Camp 40 miles above Atlanta, Ga.
May 21st, 1864[7]

MY LOVE, I write you a few lines which leaves me and Lou quite well. I suppose, Honey, we will fall back farther as the enemy refuses to meet us in battle, divide his forces, one on right, the other on left flank, so far from us that we cannot meet them. They will have to come togueather somewhare. Then I think we will gain a victory that the South will rejoice at. Honey, tell your Pa he had better box our guns and put them in the ground himself. If he lets a negro see him do it and the enemy happen to come there, they will be shure to tell whose they are. My precious darling, notwithstanding all my fatigue and trials, I love you with an ardor that burns brighter and brighter evry day. Sweet one, be cheerful. We will whipt the fight, I think, when it comes off. Take precious care of your sweet self for my [sake], for on your wellfair depends my future happyness. I will write you again soon. My love to all. Kiss Laura for Pappie.

G.W. Peddy

P.S. Col. W[atkins] is well & all right.

170

Camp 56th Ga. Vol. Near
Etowah Station
May 22nd/64

MY OWN SWEET LOVE KITTIE,

My heart has just again been made glad by the reception of your letter of the 16th ad 17th inst.[8]. It was couched, I am happy to say, with those consoleing words of love, those which ever make glad my heart, lively and cheerful my disposition. Honey, I cannot think that any one is so bless[ed] with a companion as myself. I know that nobody loves and worships theirs as I do mine, the dearest and lovelyest of all on earth to me. I am sorry to learn that you

[7]This letter is written in pencil.

[8]This letter is missing.

are occasionally troubled with pains. I am shure that I would cheerfully take (them) all of your afflictions upon myself if I could. Honey, I am glad to say to you that Andy is getting well fast. I have rode him some. Think perhaps I will all the while now. I was not on him when he was wounded. I had him hitched a short distance from me. He looks very well now. I promised him if he got well I would send him to his Mistress, but will not do so for the reason that you could not keep him safely. I do hope that I and he will live to get home togueather. I think he will add to our pleasure no little, should we live to hail the hour with glory of peace when I will be permitted to clasp my dear family to my bosom at will, when I will no longer have a marster to order me and to dictate my outgoing and incoming.

Honey, I know not what direction our army will take from here. We are only stationed here temporarially. I suppose the enemy continues to try to flank us on right and left. We may fall back farther yet. Sharp shooting is now going on across the river about a mile from us at a ford on the Etowah River just above the R.R. bridge, which is now burnt. Lou is quite well and getting on finely. I have not seen Foster in three or four days. I think I will send him home in a short time as he is doing me no good. He stays with the Wagon Train, which is at this time in Marietta, Ga. Honey, I am glad you are going to make me some pants, for mine are nearly worn out. But my darling, you must not work at them, it will fatigue my dear precious one to[o] much of. If I cared nothing for you, you might pine away for want of care and attention. To[o] high an estimate cannot be placed upon you by no one. You are held by me and all your friends in justified reverence. Your parents love you, and no doubt many envy my happyness in possessing your lovely hand. Honey, I will have to close. I will write to you as often as is practacable. Please, dear, if it does not fatigue you to[o] much, write me evry mail.

It seems that your letters are more consolation to me now than ever before. I shall begin to be uneasy about you now, ere long more anxious than uneasy. Honey, try to do the best you can, my darling. The best and purest wishes of my heart are with you ever more.

Direct your letters to me Cuming's Brig., 56th Ga. Vol. Army of Tenn.

Yours ever truely
G.W. Peddy

171

17 miles west of Maretta, May 26th/64[9]

MY SWEET DARLING KITTIE,

I write you a few lines to day which leaves I and Lou well. We had a terrable fight last eve. We repulsed the enemy handsomely. The fight is still going on. None has been hurt in our Regt. as yet, but donot know how soon some one will be. We have our infirmry one mile and a half in the rear of the line of battle. Honey, I will take the best care of myself I can on your account and on account of our sweet little progeney. Honey, Andy has gotten well of his wound, but last nigh[t] from some cause or another he got the worst hurt in the head of any horse you ever saw to be living. I think he will get well. He got tangled in the halter, fell, struck himself just below his good eye against a stob which went in about two inch. He breaths partly through it. He is certainly the most unfortunate horse I ever saw. I expect I will have to send him home to get well. I wish you would speak to your Pa about getting me another down their by some means or other. I cannot by one here for less than my year's wages. I suppose mine will get well in two or three weeks. I have just heard that we are going to advance on the enemy. Foster is with the wagon train between *Decater & Atlanta.* He had as well be at home as their. He is doing me no good and I cannot keep him with me while we are marching. Honey, I hope you are getting on well. Bless your little heart, I would give anything to see you to day. Donot get low spirited, my love, on account of our fall back. I hope it will be for our good. Daer, I am now in sixty five miles of you, but no more chance to see you than if I were five hundred. I think we will drive the enemy back towards Chattanooga. Honey, let me hear from you often as convenient. Kiss Laura for me. Tell her to hug and kiss *Ma* for me. I think I will send Foster home when I get to see him. Your ever more

G.W. Peddy

[9]This letter is written in pencil.

172

In the Field Near Marietta, Ga.
Sunday, May 29th, 1864

MY PRECIOUS KITTIE, As I am going to send Foster home for a few days, I write you per him. I am quite well. Lou has diarrhaea slightly. He is getting better. Heavy skirmishing is going on along our line. Our division is not engaged, nether has been for two day. It is held in reserve a half mile in the rear. It may be called up at any moment. I have no use for Foster until the fight is over. I send some of my clothes home by him to be washed. I will want him to come back in 8 or 10 days. Oh! how I wish I could go as easy as he can. I would be in your lovely embrace in twelve hours. Honey, I think the enemy are as far South as he will come. We are now fairly in his front with a reserve sufficient to check any flank movement he may attempt. They have made several dashes at our works in the last few days resulting to us favorable. We have killed, wounded and captured considerable number, accounts of which you will constantly see in the papers. Honey, I am glad to say that Andy is getting better. I will not send him home unless he gets worse. I am uneasy for him. I fear it will be a permanent injury to him. He rides as well as ever. My love, I have had no letter from you in three or four days. I begin to suspect that something has happened to you. If so, my sweet one, I hope and pray that you are doing well. I am so anxious about you, the purest of the pure and the dearest of all else to me. Bless your pure little heart, I do wish I could see that lovely and enchanting face of your this beautiful Sabbath eve. Nothing could revive my feelings more no[r] be more solace to my heart.

Honey, you must take special care of our little girl. She is so amiable and promising. I want evrything done that can be to keep her so. Ma, you must not through her away for any stranger, for she is Pappie's lovely sweet little girl. I am meditating about the purity and lovelyness of my little family all the while. It often make[s] me happy. Honey, I am satisfied the war will close this year, and if I live, what a happy time we will have! We will make up in joy for all lost time. Honey, take special care of your genuine self. I am anxious for you will fail, if you cannot write me. My love, get some one to do so often when you see a chance to send a letter to the R.R. per hand. Donot wait for the mails. I have not seen Gen. Featherston yet. I will look him up in a few days if he does not get killed. I am in no danger now, my love, nor have not been as yet lately. Dr. Lane is now assisting in the medical department. He is in no danger. Tell Kittie to rest perfectly easy about him. He is doing more good than he would do in a fight. Good buy, my love. Write often as you can, Honey.

Yours ever more fondly G.W. Peddy

P.S. Col. W[atkins] is quite well.

173

Infirmry, 12 Miles West Marietta
June 1st, 1864

MY PRECIOUS IDOL KITTIE, Again it is my happy pleasure to write you and to acknowledge the reseption of your kind letter of the 24th inst.[10] The spirit of yours was quite cheering, instead of being low down about our fall back. You stand up defiantly in your feeling against the enemy and put your trust in a just God who is able to put the legions of the world to flight. Honey, you cannot imagine how proud I felt when I read it. I am willing to undergo any fatigue and disappointmen[t] for your freedom and that of our progeney. Honey, the two armies stand confronting each other, but verry little fighting. Now and then a sharp shooter creaps out from the entrenchments to take a shot or two, then goes back. Our infirmary is two miles back or in rear of the line. Nothing to do but eat, sleep and send a few men to hospital. The major part of my time here is spent in cogitating about you, your condition, the bright prospects set before me for my future happyness whith my little sweet family after this crewel and fratricidal war is over. Let us be hopefull as to the result of the war and look to the day of peace as the dawn of our earthly joys, when our happyness will begin anew and wear brighter and brighter the longer we live. Honey, in contemplating this I am ofter carried of[f] into extatic revalry. Such bliss would be more than earth seems to offer. Honey, I want you send me, if you please, per Foster a bottle of vinegar. I will write to you pretty soon what time to send him back.

Lou is getting on finely. He has had diarrhea, but is getting on finely now. Andy mends verry slowly, though I think he will get well after awhile. I ride him as though their was nothing the matter, a thing which I dislike to do verry much.

Honey, your time of confinement is near at hand. I hope Pa will be with you. If not, you must get Dr. Harlan. I expected Puss would be down ere this. Honey, I am so anxious to be with you, but my dear, it is impossible. I do hope you will get on well. I will pay you in kindness for all your suffering, my love, when I get with you. Let me know how Dr. Northern is. Give him my

---

[10]This letter is missing.

compliments. Write me all the news, honey, about our little town, but donot do so to the exclusion of those pathetic sentances which always render me so happy. Honey, I have to stop as I have to sit on the ground to write and get very tired. Kiss Laura for Pappie. I would give any price that I am able to get to clasp you in her in my arms and caress you as I wish to.

Dr. Lane was well a few days ago. I have not seen him to day.

Give my love to all the family, to Nick and John when you [write them]. I have not heard from John since the fight commenced in *Va.* Dr. Franklin is sick and gone to hospital. Wm Watkins is acting in his place. Bill got very drun[k] the other day. Do not say anything about it.

I think him a very sorry piece of mortality. I sympathise with his Wife. Please keep this to you[r] self.

Yours ever more

G.W. Peddy

174

June 2nd, 1864[11]

I am quite well this morn. So is Lou. Honey please send me per Foster about four pluggs tobacco. Let your Pa select it for me.

Yours ever more G.W. Peddy

Good deal of sharp shooting along our line. We are now three miles in the rear. Bless your little sweet heart, I do love you and want to send a thousand sweet kisses for you and Laura.

175

Infirmry, 5 miles west of
Marietta, June 6th, 1864[12]

MY PRECIOUS SWEET ONE. I received your sweet and well written letter

[11]This note is written in pencil.

[12]This letter is written in pencil.

yesterday.[13] I have not time to reply to it as I wish to. It was such a good one I could not reply to it under an hour. I will reply to it in a short time. I have no news of interest to write, only we are getting on quite well. Lou is well, but I have not seen him in a week. I suppose I will go to the Regt. soon to see the boys.

I am sorry to learn that one of our shoats has died, as we had just enough to do us. Kiss Laura for Pappie. I am waiting anxiously to hear from the stranger. I suppose you have seen him by this time. Yours ever more

G W Peddy

176

Infirmry, 5 miles west of
Marietta, June 7th/64

MY PRECIOUS ANGELIC KITTIE, With deep sense of pleasure I proceed to respond in a semmi respectable manner to you[r] two last sweet and welcomed letters. Honey, I am shure no one was ever so blessed as I with a companion who antisipates my evry want and who by pen is so well calculated to awaken the deepest and profoundest feeling of love that ever burned in the heart of any man. Honey, it seems to me that no one can be so blessed as I am. I am unworthy such a boon. You would be delighted to see my pride on the reception of your letters, if you like to see me happy. My smiles and countenance spoken of in yours is truely bright if they can be made so. Honey, I do not think you need be uneasy about the enemy getting to our home. He is already out generaled in my opinion. I think they will get but a short distance father down in our country, although a sharp look out ought to be ready to burn the bridge at our town in case of their appearance. Then you could be in no danger. As to going to Pa's, I donot know that you would be safer there than you are at home. I have not heard from Nick nor brother John since I left home or at least in a month. Honey, I get plenty to eat on of meat and bread. I want you to sent us a bag of vegetables by Foster of such things as you think will keep you for two days, as it will take him that length of time to get to me. You had better start him back next Sunday. He will find us on the main road west of Marietta, 5 mil[e]s distant. He will have no trouble on that score. Honey, send my new

---

[13]This letter is missing.

[14]These three lines written across the top of the page.

pants per Foster if they are done, also my drawer and another shirt as I will be by that time out of clean cloths. *Honey, your letter* of June the 3rd & 4th was the best letter and the most heart stiring one you have ever written me. It one [*sic*] my very soul good to read it. I am so thankful to Pa coming to see you. Already I owe him a debt of gratitude I will never be able to pay. It is so kind of him to put himself to so much trouble for our benefit. It is an extra favor. I hope he stayed until you got through. If so, I will not be uneasy in the least, for I know he wants to do as much and be as kind to you as I would. I will write him a letter of thanks for his kindness. Honey, I know you miss me worse now than at other times. I am shure that if I were with you I would use all my efforts to make you easy and pleasant and would be perfectly happy in so doing. No pleasure is so great to me as that of making you happy if it is possible to do so. I imagine at times that I am kind to you, but when I think of how easy you are pleased, I become indignant at myself for not trying harder to render you comfortable. Honey, it greaves me to find out the state of morrals spoken of by your Uncle Ben. It only shows the original foulness of the disposition of people who are vulgarly raised. Meanness is original with such people. Honey, it makes me proud to know that no one but you and (I hope by this time our little *ones*) enjoys the best particle of my affections. My heart, mind, sould and body is yours and yours only and it shall ever be yours alone so long as I live. Honey, I would give any fame to know to day how you are and wheather the stranger has come & to know furthermore wheather it is like you. If so, I fear it will supplant Laura in my estimation—not that I will love her the least, but it the more. But you, dear one, in my affections stand above evry creature in worth. Bless your pure heart, I do want to see you so much to day and at all times.

I went to the Regt. to day, saw Lou. He is looking better than I ever saw him. Seems to be enjoying life as well as he ever did. He and Brewer was making a sein out of an old basket to catch fish in a little creek close to the brest works. It's said that the enemy is falling back now in our imediate front. Brewer wants you to send word down to his Ma Saturday eve by some one so that Foster may bring him a pair of drawers. Honey, I can almost see your lovely form as you are laying in bed sick, if you are sick. How lovely, how grand, how sweet you look. If I were with you, I am shure I would be compelled to fall down and worship your dear devoted self. Honey, please send me a pair of gloves. If you can do no better, send me Lou's. You can nit him a pair in the place of them next winter if he needs any. I spoke to him about them, and not knowing he had sent them off, he was willing for me to have them. I am without any. Honey, tell you Ma to send us a mess of English peas if she has them. Good buy, my precious love. I will take good care of myself. Kiss Laura for Pappie. Yours ever more truely

G W Peddy

Andy has gotten well.
My love to all the family.
Honey, am so anxious to hear from you.[14]

177

Infirmry, one mile from Marietta, Ga.
June 9th, [1864][15]

MY LOVE SWEET DARLING,

I drop you a short note this morn which leaves I and Lou well. You need not send per Foster anything but some eshalottts and English peas. We get vinegar and potatoes enouth. Honey, do let me hear from you soon. I am so anxious to know how you are getting on I donot know what to do. Kiss Laura for pappie ten thousand kisses for you. Good by, my only and precious love.

Your truely with delight
G W Peddy

178

Infirmry 1½ Miles North of Marietta
June 13th/64[16]

MY OWN SWEET PRECIOUS KITTIE, I have just received your chaced and elegant letter of the 11th inst.[17] I am shure I never read such a noble production. Evry sentiment of love spoken of so elegantly and so tuchingly in yours chimes in with my profound feeling of admiration for you very accurately. Honey, no one never was more devoted to an individual. No one never idolized and worshiped so fondly as I do you, the handsome of the handsomest, the sweetest of the sweet, tha loveliest of the lovely—*in fact* you are evrything full and

[15]This note is written in pencil.

[16]Envelope addressed: "Mrs Dr Peddy/Franklin/Ga" This letter is written in pencil.

[17]This letter is missing.

complete to fill up the cup of my fancy. Honey, no one short of Deity will ever be able to fathom the profound sentiment of love which constantly burns in my heart for you.

Honey, I think we will fall back on the Atlanta side of the River as soon as the roads will admit of it. The rain has been falling incessantly for eight or ten days and got the roads in such a condition that our Artilery cannot get along. Honey, I think you had better begin to prepare to go father South. Your Pa ought to be ready to move all his essential articles at once. It will not do to get in the enemy's lines. They will distroy evrything. Nothing but devestation, desolation and ruin follows in the wake of the federal army. Theirfore I think it the best policy to keep out of the way. He will have time enough to get away. Honey, donot get frightened at the above opinion. I think it a correct one. Honey, do not render yourself uneasy. You shall not suffer, my love. I will make enough money to take care of you. The Goverment owes me over seven hundred dollars & I have no use for it, only for your benefit. Honey, oh! how I want to see you. I was perfectly supprised to think you had not been confined before the eleventh inst. I expect ere this you have. If so, I do hope and pray you are doing well. Honey, you did not let me know wheather you was going to send Foster up yesterday. I wrote to you about it last week. I suppose you did not get the letter. Honey, I have worn a hole in the seat of my pants and will need the ones you are preparing for me very much. Honey, if it requires your labor to finish them, let them alone. I do not want my sweet Baby to work when she is not in condition to do so. Please quit it, my love, for my sake. You know its my admiration for you that makes me advise you to do so. Lou is well. I was up at the line yesterday. He was on a picket.[18] Kiss Laura for me. she is such a smart little girl to go to Sabbath School and still be sorry for her Ma that she cannot go. My love to all.

Send my sash the first chance.

I am looking for Foster to day.

Your ever more.

G.W. Peddy

[18]The remainder is written along the top of the page.

179

Infirmry, Cumming's Brig.,
One and a half Miles on the R.R. above Marietta, Ga.
Wednesday, June 15th/864

MY SWEET PRECIOUS DARLIN KITTIE, I sit down quietly to night to the sweet task of writing to one whom I love to live for, one upon whom all my affections are concentrated, one without whom my life would be a perfect nuisance. Honey, I am so proud of you I would almost sacrifice my all to see you to night. Bless your little heart, you have no idea how often and how fondly & sweetly I think of you. I have no letter from you, my love, since the eleventh. No one can imagine how anxious I am to hear from you. Honey, I expect ere this you have passed through the antisipated ordeal. I hope you have, my dear, and safe and getting well. I do sympathise with you, my love, in your trials. No doubt ere this you have thought you would have been better off if you had remained in your single blessedness. If you had, I am shure their would have been one sad heart to plod alone in this cold world. Women frequently regret marrying at such times. I hope if you do, you do not love me the less. Honey, I am satisfied that my devotion to you will never grow cold, but think on the contrary it will increase, if possible, in old age. Lou is well & seems to be getting on joyfully. I donot see him often as I am busy in the rear all the time. Honey, I am looking for Foster evry day. I wrote you last week to send him up on Sunday. He has not reached here yet. I have no clean clothes now nor will not get any until he comes.

Honey, do not think I am grumbling at you by writing the above. Far be it from me to object in the least to anything you do or want to do. I suppose you did not yet get my letter is the cause of his failure to come.

Honey, your horse is well again. He is looking finely now. I wish you could see him. I have been offered some fine trades for him, but reject them all because you like him so well. I never will trade him on your account. Anything that you fancy you must have. Honey, I am so sorry that I did not succeed in getting your shoes. I tried verry hard but failed. Honey, send to Atlanta and get you some.

I will send you some money as soon as I can get to draw it. I hope you will get this letter as I will send it by James Stricland, Esq., who is here to see his youngest brother, who is sick, but I have sent him to hospital.

Honey, I cannot give you any idea of what our next move will be. There has been pretty heavy cannonadings to day, some skirmishing. I do not think we will have a gen[eral] engagement here, although we may. If the enemy attacks us, we will gain no doubt a compleat victory. Honey, you need not be uneasy about me. I am now quartered in a nice house which is our division hospital. I never got in here until after the rain. Honey, send Foster on as soon as you can. Let me hear from you, my love, as often as you can.

Kiss Laura for pappie. Tell her how much I love her and you.

Yours ever more

G. W. Peddy

P.S. Col. W[atkins] is here now with me. He is a little sick. Will return to the command, I suppose, tomorrow.

G W P

180

Infirmry in Marietta, Ga.,
Tuesday, June 21st/64

MY [PRECIOUS KITTIE],

I have just received and read you letter of the 18th inst; also one of the sixth inst.[19] You can well imagine how delighted I was with the sweet tenor of both, but they did not bring me the glad tidings of your relief. With yours was one which made my soul happy and my heart leap with joy. Honey, I was perfectly rejoyced and did not sleep but little the night after the glad inteligence of your safe confinement came to hand. My dear, you are the greatest of your race. I love you, if possible, more than ever. I have imagined a thousand times since I received your Pa's letter that I could see you in bed just as you lay, the very personification of loveliness, innocence and beauty with a nice little boy by your side. No sight on this earth could so supremely delight me as to see you just as you are. Would to God I could be around you bed and kiss those sweet lips of yours! Bless your little sweet heart, Honey, I will pay you in kindness and love for all your pain if possible. I fear I cannot, but this belief shall not deter me in trying. My dear, I do hope you are doing well. I am still anxious about you and the little boy's welfare. Suppose you are both still doing well.

---

[19]Both letters are missing.

Honey, let me know how you like him and if he resembles you—hope he does,—what Laura has to say about him, &c.

Poor little Laura must not be treated coolly on her brother's account. Pappie knows her Ma is to[o] good and kind for that. Ma, you must love me and Laura as good as ever. We will love you dearly always. Honey, I am so proud I know not what to write you that's good enough for your sweet eyes to read. Sufice it to say that no one could possible by made happier than I am.

Honey, we can never repay your Pa & Ma for this supreme kindness to us.

Honey I will attend to finding out all about Lee's tale for your Pa as early as I can.

Say to your Pa that if Foster starts through the country with that Mail he will be apt to fall in the hands of the enemy unless he comes through Atlanta and keeps east of the State R.R. from Atlanta to Marietta. I suppose although he will start before this reaches you. Honey, I never wanted to see you as bad as I do now. Evry time I try to sleep I find myself exulting over my good fortune in having such a lovely family. Honey, I know you must be proud indeed. Oh! how I wish we could rejoice togueather if I could be with you. Honey, you must kiss the boy for me. You must also name him. Give him a short name. I named Laura. You must name the boy. Honey, tell me is he pretty, has he nice hair like Laura had?

Lou is well, my love. Good night, love. I will go to my blanketts only to think of you and the little Stranger. I am too proud to sleep.[20] My compliments to Dr. Harlan for his kindness. Honey, I would give almost anything to know how you are tonight. I have not told Lou of my good fortune.

The Doct[ors] of our Brig. congratulate me no little on account of your boy and your safety.

A thousand kisses in store for you.

Write soon as you are able, Sweet one.

G W Peddy

181

Infirmry in Marietta, Ga.
Sunday eve, June 26th/64

MY SWEET ONE, Again it is my sweet privalidge of writing to you, the idol of

[20]The remainder is written across the top of the page.

my heart and the joy of my affections. No one, honey, is so happy in love as my myself. No one has so pure a creature to admire as I. I received you good Ma's letter yesterday. I was so glad to hear that you was doing so well but was greaved to learn that you had suffered so much since the birth of your nice little boy. Honey, I am nearly dead to know if you are proud of him and to know all about what you think of him. If he is nice like Laura and his Ma, I will love him truely. Honey, I am so proud of you I could kiss you almost out of breath were I premitted to be with you. Honey, your Ma wrote me you took a good cry because I was not with you. My love, I am equally as sorry as you could possibly be. I will repay you for all your tears when I see you. You have no idea what strange feelings run over me when I think of the greaf that weighs down your little heart while shedding tears on account of my absence. I often think of how supremely much I admire you when at home and begin to talk about leaving, and the thought weighs so heavily on your little hearth that it melts into tears. Honey, then I love you so much (as all the time) that I want to have wings to waft you away from all annoyances and set you down in some nice and beautifull place, there to rest with our little children forever in peace and in the enjoyment of each other's love. Honey, I do want to see you with your two little sweet birds so much. I know that I love you the full extent of my affections. No one enjoys the thought of loved ones at home so much as I. I am perfectly happy at the though[t] of my little family at home. I ought to be the happyest man in the world a[nd] believe I' am.

Honey, let me know in your next what sort of clothes you sent I and Lou. The boy brought two colored cotton shirts and two pair of drawers, but Bill & Col. W[atkins] said they were sent to them. I expect they were mistaken and got ours. If so, as soon as I hear from you I will get them. We got no clothes per him atall. One of the shirts [I] have just seen. It had a small collar; appeared that it was intended to be worn with a falts collar. I think it was intended for me, although I will not take it until I find out from you about them. Bill Watkins has gone home and wore one of the suits off. Send me a peace of clothe like the shirts and also like the drawers. Lou is well. I have not been to the Regt. in several days. I will go pretty soon. Our Division made a charge on the enemy last Wenesday: two of the Regt. killed, several wounded. You will see in the Inteligence the names of those wounded.[21]

[21]This letter is unfinished.

182

Marietta, June 30th/64

MY SWEET PRECIOUS ANGEL,

You have no idea how much delighted I was to have the pleasure of reading a sweet letter from you[r] lovely hand after the passage of your trying ordeal.[22] I often imagine how sweet and enticing you looked proped upon your elbow writing to me, with your nice little boy laying by our side. Honey, you cannot imagine how proud I would be to see you and him. I think if I could get home now I would get a sweet kiss from you, that is, if you are as proud of your boy as you said you would be. Honey, you ought not whip him before his pappie gets to see him. Poor little Laura, Pappie is afraid she will be thrown away now, but I will not think that Ma loves either of us the less on account of the little stranger. Your Pa writes that he favors the F[eatherston] family. If it is you he favors, I will love him the more. Honey, the Yanks have give us several trials here, enough, I think, to convince them that they cannot break our lines. I think they will let us alone before long. Then perhaps I can get to come home for a few days. Honey, the pants you sent me are the prettyest I have ever worn. They fit me more than I have ever had any fit. Evry one who sees them & knows me wants me to have them a pair made like them. I tell them that they ought to have got such a wife as I had, then they would never be out of nice clothes. Honey, I fear that all my attemps to repay you for your super kindness to me will be futile.

Foster arrived safely with his vegetables. I am having a nice time eating them. You need not be uneasy about Lou's getting something to eat as long as I have anything. Poor fellow, I would be more than glad if I could get him out of the way of the balls if it wer[e] in my power, but I see no chance. If one should present, I assure you & your Pa I will take advantage of it.

Say to your Pa that the Ordenance Sergt. has to stay in the trenches all the time and has often to leave the trenches under a hot fire to get his ordenance & return through the same. So I donot want Lou to have that office. I send you to day per Rev. H. H. Jackson one [hundred] and eight dollars, supposing you will need it. Buy anything you want with it, my love. I want it only for you. I will send you more as soon as I can draw it. I am staying in Marietta. The Regt. is three miles from town. I will not write you anything about the fights as you get accounts in the papers sooner than you can get them from me by letter. Honey, I have been very busy all day making out reports. I took time this eve to take a

[22]This letter is missing.

nice ride on *Andy*. Honey, you have no idea how proud I am of my pants. I will despatch to you at once if Lou should get hurt. Honey, take good care of yourself and the children. I will be at home some day if Dr. Lane donot get out of bed to[o] soon. Foster says our boy is verry pretty. F[oster] says he has as much hair on his head as Laura did when she was little.

Let me know, my love, what the women has to say about him.[23]

Let me hear from you often.

I got a letter from Pa yesterday.

I also rec'd your Pa's letter.

Let me know all about how you get on & the children, which will be of more interest to me than anything you can write.

My love to all.

Yours ever more

G. W. Peddy

183

Infirmry, Six Miles South
Marietta, July 3rd, 1864[24]

MY DEAREST SWEET WIFE KITTIE,

How differently situated I am now to that of last year on this day. Now I am permited to cumunicate per letter to that one whom I hold in higher estimation than all the gems & jewels of this wide world. Then I was invested by our crewel invaders and subject at each moment to be destroyed by their deathly missels and cut off entirely from the sweetness of your letters. I then felt sad and melancholy fearing that I might not be allowed the privalidge of that sweetest of pleasure[s], that of embracing again my two pure creatures at home. Knotwithstanding my far better situation now and less exposure to death, I yet am sorely greaved to say we are faling back to your side of the Chattahoo[c]hee, and the prospect is very good for the enemy to get to those whom I hold dearer than my own life. Such being the case, I feel sadly. I keep well, my love. So does

[23]The remainder of the letter is written across the top of the page.

[24]This letter is written in pencil.

Lou. I do hope you are getting on well with our little lovely family. I feel no interest in nothing but your and our little one's welfare. Honey, we ought to feel immeasurably proud of our little cherubs. If the little boy is as handsome & will be as inteligent as Laura, we ought to be doubly thankfull. Laura has a nice little brother to amuse herself with and be with her, which leave[s] Ma for me & me for Ma if I can claim enough of her affections or share such a part of them as I desire to. Honey, no one here wanted to get home as much as I do. I would give anything to be at home to help you and manifest to you how much I appreciate you for your evry thing which makes you so lovely and grand.

Honey, I cannot help thanking you again for you[r] nice present, the pants. Honey, I was told before marrying that a Wife was a heavy expense, but I find it untrue. You are a helpmate, perenial ally, as well as evry other accomplishment. Write me if you have enough of the cloth left from which my pants were made. I would be glad you would make me a vest. If not, donot trouble yourself about it. Honey, I think your Pa had better be ready to move if the Yankee army crosses the river. I would only if I were him keep out of the way of a rading party, would not move off on that account. I have not got any letter from you since last Saturday was a week, on account, I suppose, of the irregularity of the mails. Think I will get one to day. Honey, should the enemy get between us & I cannot get to see you soon, rest assured that I still love and adore you above all things else & will never cease to do so. I want our names and good characters e'er to remain pure & spotless independent of distance or length of time we may be seperated. Teach Laura all you can, my love, so that we will be proud of her when this crwel war is over and we are permited to sit quietly, peasably and joyfully around our hearthstone. Such a state of being I often ref[l]ect off as being the most delightfull that I could possibly be placed in. How would you like it, Sweet one?

Give my love to all the family, your Ant Kitt. Let me hear from you, sweet Kittie, as often as you are able to write.

Kiss Laura for me. Tell her to kiss [Ma] and her little brother for pappie. Yours ever more devotedly G W Peddy

184

July 4th, 1864[25]

MY LOVE, I have just rec'ed your letter of the 2nd inst.[26] Such intense pleasure it gave me to read it is not often felt. It seemed to embrace evry thing about which I wanted to hear with one exception, that is, are you fat & do you look as pretty as ever? I suppose you have falen off some. I hope not much. Bless your little heart, I see you in my imagination evry moment of my life almost. Would that I could see you & your little boy and Laura! I am glad to learn that he is like you. I will love him more on that account. Hope he is the very image of you both intelectually & phisically. If he is, he will be such a nice & beautifull. I will love him as well as Laura, but not as well as I do Ma. It is natural, I suppose, honey, for you to love the children better than me, but I love you supremely to evry living creature on earth. We have formed another line of battle six miles below Marietta & entrenched. I suppose we will remain here for a few days at least ere we fall be[y]ond the river. Honey, in your next let me know if you are fleshy & all about how you look. I imagine you look sweeter & more lovely if possible, than ever. If you do, my sweet one, I recon it's well that I cannot get to see you, for I am shure if I were at home now, you would want to get rid of my constant caresses & fondlings. Lou is well. I will go to see him to day. Let me hear from you often as you can, my dear. Kiss the children for me. Yours ever more G.W. Peddy

P.S. Honey, should the enemy thretten our little town to[o] strongly, I believe I would load up the two horse wagon with meat & flour and go out to Pa's and live their awhile. If you should determine to do so, you must keep a close watch over Laura, for the children are bad out their. So is society. That's the only objection I have to your going. I believe now that our place is to[o] far from the R.R. for the enemy to ever occupy it. I suppose you will have some watermelons before long. Hope you will have some fine ones. Laura loves them so much, you must let her have plenty.

GWP

[25]This letter is written in pencil.

[26]This letter is missing.

185

Infirmry, two Miles
from Atlanta, Ga.
Tuesday, July 12th, 1864

MY PRECIOUS DARLING KITTIE, Again I have the inestimable pleasure of responding to your two last letters, which were so rich in sentiments of burning love that it did my very soul good.[27] Certainly no one on earth is so blessed as I in a companion so well qualified, *one gifted* in evry particular to render me happy. I owe you a debt of gratitude, my fond one, that I can never pay for y[ou]r unwavering affection for me and your great desire to render me perfectly pleasant in evry particular. Honey, intentions ar[e] pure with regard to your happyness, and if I fail to render you constantly so through life, it will be an error of the head and not of the heart. If any one ever loved an individual more than I do your worthy and endearing self, I donot know nor can I imagine how it is done. Honey, if it was in my power to give you an idea or one indication of my love and unbounded esteem for you, you would be suppriesed and wonder how it so is that man could love with such ardor. I am sorry to learn that you feel so feeble and sick at times. Were I at home in your joyfull presence I would do all in my feeble way to avert those bad feelings which menace your happyness. It is you that I would shield from evry phisical pain and evry m[or]tal anguish and always if possible bear you joyfully from all harm. I often ask myself what it is that I would not do for you to enhance your pleasure. The constant responce is that no sacrefice is to[o] great for me to freely yield to your joy or promote your happyness. God bless your pure heart and briliant mind and evry idea that may arise from its pure fount for the furtherance of your happyness. Honey, I have written more than two pages to try to impart to you an idea of my affection for you but have failed. I hope you will imagine the admiration of my heart for you by stiring up in your own sweet bosom all the tender feelings you have for me. Honey, I scarcely know what to do about your leaving home. I do not know wheather we will give up Atlanta or not. I hope not without a fight. Your Pa can do as he thinks best. I trust to his judgment. He must be shure not to let the enemy get hold of him. The enemy are not interupting Ladies alone through the country they have passed, as letters received here from them to soldiers abundantly show. I do not think they will get to our place. They may pass down the river on the other side if we hold Atlanta. If we donot, you may look out for a raid in our town some day. Honey, you must hide my uniform and all the cloth you have made for me in case you

[27]These two letters are missing.

hear of them coming, for they will be shure to take them from you. You must not let any of the negroes know whare you put them. I think I will perhaps send Foster after them soon. I and Lou get plenty of vegetables now without sending home for them. Your Pa must send the negro men or at least Lin, Lee and also Mary of[f], for should the enemy come, they will have you robed & whiped if they could. I would not keep Marry an other day if I was your Ma & Pa, for they will find her a great annoyance should the enemy get their, as the mules are unable to carry you all of[f]. If you want to go, I would, if I was your Pa, have some boats built and go down the river in them to get out of the way.[28]

Honey, if you pretend to stay at home, stay their, donot run to the woods should the enemy come, but stay at the house. Honey, I think we will whip the enemy should they cross the river here. I think Gen. Joh[n]s[t]on intends having a gen[eral] engagement here.[29]

Honey, has Puss done anything yet? You have said nothing about her in none of your letters in a long time. I hope she has got through ere this.

Honey, my sweet one, I can see your lovely form in my imagination sitting in your rocking chair and hear your sweet talk to your little boy which so compleetly enraptures him as it does me. I almost envy the little fellow in the enjoyment of that bliss which is bliss indeed to me. Bless your sweet voice, which is so joyfully tuned for my ear.

Evrything in your composition, honey, acurately chimes in with my idea of the most perfect and lovely being on earth.

I am glad that you and Laura think so much of your little treasure. I am proud he is fattening. Hope Ma is too. Honey, never in life did I want to see you so much as now. Evry moment that I am away from you seems like years. I am glad, honey, to read that portion of your last letter in which you state you will allow no one to usurp in your affections myself.

Precious one, I hope you will not say anything about those people of whose behavior you wrote. Let them go their own way so they do not trouble you. Say nothing about them to no one but me. They are dangerous people should they become enemys of ours. I think her language to W. Martin was ridiculous in the extreme.[30]

Kiss Laura and the boy for Pappie. What are you going to name him, my love? Give my love to all.

Be sure to have the negroes sent off—those that I have spoken of. Be shure to have my clothes out of the way should the enemy get there. Do not put them in

---

[28]This sentence is written along the top of the page.

[29]During 4-9 July Sherman turned Johnston's position along the Chattahoochee, and Johnston withdrew to Peachtree Creek.

[30]The remainder is written along the tops of the last two pages.

any trunk or any thing about the house, for they will look in evry box & trunk.
Honey, write to me evry mail.
Yours ever more

G.W. Peddy

186

Infirmry near
Atlanta, Ga., July 16th/64

MY OWN PRECIOUS KITTIE, With a heart overflowing with an intense devotion and a far stronger desire to see you than I am permited again to write you. I want to see you so badly it almost makes me sick, and I know, my love, you would receive me with open arms and fond caresses. Oh! that I could taste this morning some of the bliss of your presence. No one could enjoy it more than I.

My precious one, I have had no letter from you since Saturday. Hope I'll have the pleasure of reading one from you to day. I often imagine how sweetly you look now with your little boy. I know you must be very proud of him as you recollect what you used to say about a boy. You may have been justing with me then and no doubt was. Honey, I am getting on finely here. I have sugar and coffee morning and evening and plenty of all kinds of vegetables. Fear that you are not living as well as I am. I wish you was. Honey, I am in fine health now, look as well as you ever saw me. Hope your lovely self is doing as well as I am in that particular. It greaves me to see my love and the fond object of my love look unhealthy.

I am glad to learn that my winter clothes are under way. My dear, you have already done more for me than I can repay you for. No one ever had as good and as kind companion. I am so proud [of] you I know not how to content myself. Lou is getting on finely, gets plenty to eat of vegetables of all kinds, also sugar and coffee.

I hope our two little cherubs are well. Tell Laurie Pappie has not forgot her. He thinks of her often, and how pleased she is of her little brother. I know no more to write you concerning the army or the movement of the enemy. We have had a fine rest spell. All had time to clean up, have washing done & ar[e] ready for another campaign or finishing up this.

Honey, I will have to have some more shirts from some quarter. Mine are tearing all to pieces. I expect you think ere this that I am a great source of trouble. I ought not to look to you for such things, ought I, my sweet one?

Honey, I now imagine I can see you walking about in your majestic beauty and loveliness. You certainly have the most enchanting carriage of any lady on earth. In fact, you are possessed of evry thing that chimes in with my idea of beauty and loveliness. Kiss Kitten. I write in haste, excuse this. Kiss the babies for me. Would give anything in life to see you. I must stop, my love. Let me hear from you soon.

Give my love to all the family.

Yours ever more
G.W. Peddy

P.S. I close but with a sigh to see you and feel the welcomed grasp of your lovely arms.

187

Infirmry, Cumming's
Brig. Near Atlanta
July 17th/864

MY DARLING KITTIE, I read with much pleasure your very sweet letter received yesterday.[31] As I have a chance to send you a reply per Pe Wood in advance of the mail, I proceed to answer it. You have no idea how pleased I was to hear you was well enough to sit at the window with your dress on. I am shure if I had seen you I would have exulted over you more than Laura. Bless her little heart, she is as proud of her Ma as I am. I am greaved that you are so week that you cannot walk without staggering. I'm proud that you look so well in the face. Hope the reduction in size of your extremities is only the result of the natural swelling leaveing after being confined. Honey, no doubt you are wearied no little with extravagant stories of the enemy. You need not, my love, believe only reasonable ones of them. Honey, do not suffer yourself to have the blews so long as we are all living and doing well. It is joy enough to know that we are all well yet and have the glorious pleasure of getting letters from each other. I donot think our communication will be cut off entirely even if you stay whare you are. If you go off, I think you had better take evrything you can, for

[31]This letter is missing.

all you have will be lost. Honey, I wish your Pa would go with you whare ever you go. I donot want you to be away from the family if you could help it. You no doubt would be safer at Pa's, but hate for you to go their unless your Pa would go also. I fear if you get away from them you would be dissatisfied, although should you go there you will be treated as cleaverly as you ever was in your life. Should you go out there, I had rather you would live in the house you spoke of, to yourself. I am afraid Laura would get to[o] bad being with those children out there of Pa's. They are very badly spoiled. Pa will send and get my books and my office furniture if you go out their. I would be glad he had them all. You had better take your stock with you if you go, and as to buying the wheat, I think you should do so by all means. It is a thing that I had not thought of. I am glad you spoke of it. Your watchfull and provident mind is always on the alert for our intrust. Should Pa not send for the Books and medicines, furniture, you had better have them boxed and send them to some one's house who expects to stay and will take the best care off them for me. Uncle Thomas S. is not going away. He would no doubt take care of them. It's true as you say, the hour looks dark to us, but let us, my sweet bride, be as cheerful as we can. Thousands are far worse off than we.

Perhaps this is the darkest one in the history of our existence and that a glorious and lasting peace may break fourth in all its splendor. Then, oh then, my angel of life, what a happy future awaits us! Pleased am I that I have such a solace in this war as you. He who has no one to love him as I imagine you do me must be truely miserable. Life without you would be to[o] sad a thing for me to enjoy. Honey, you need not be guided by Jo Lane's movements, as I have heard he is just leaving on account of the draft. says T. Shackleford. You will please say nothing about the above. You must all be ready to leave in case we fall back from here, which we may do. Cannot tell yet. Rumor says the enemy are falling back. Cannot vouch for the truth of the rumor. Honey, I hope you will not be troubled to[o] much by the confused state of affairs. Hope evrything will work out for the best. I am inclined to the opinion that we will be victorious should we make a stand here. We may be flanked away, but cannot be by a movement in the direction of our home. Hope you will not have to move at all. Honey, should Mobry move, I think you had best start to. Whare ever you go, my love, rest assured that I will not let you suffer for anything you want to eat. If you were living to yourself, you should have anything in the world that I could get. My dear, I suppose you have children enough now to satisfy you, *have you not?* Let me know in your next, my sweet one. If you have, you had better write me not to come home, had you not?

Honey, I would give anything to see you and our little ones now. Bless your little heart, at the time you are in the most trouble, it seems that the fates keep us separated. I imagine I could console you so much if I were with you now. I will try to come, my dear, just as soon as I can.

You know, sweet one, how much I want to be with you. Should I not see you again for months or years, their will ever be burning in my bosom and fond and profound feeling of love that time nor distance can erase or cause to grow feeble or lukewarm. Honey, if the R.R. is cut between here and West Point you will get your letter whare you are through Ala. Kiss Laura and the little boy for me. Tell them that Pappie will always love them. Pappie wants Laura to be a good little girl. She must love her Ma and little brother good while I am gone. I will close this for fear you get tired of reading. Honey, please let me know how Puss gets on. I want her to cut hay if you remain whare you are as soon as she gets well.

Yours ever more
G.W.P.

Thousand kisses for you, my dear idol love & sweet darling.

188

Infirmry in Atlanta, Ga.
July 21st, 1864

MY PRECIOUS SWEET ONE, I write you again this morn after night's hard work. Our regt. had a slight engagement with the enemy in which we had four Lieut. & two privates wounded; none killed nor none of which you know. On our left yesterday we drove the enemy.[32] Think we will gain the victory over them if we can get them to engage us in an open field. I am sorry to announce to you that Gen. Johns[t]on has been removed and Gen. Hood placed in command. All regret the removal of the former but are perfectly satisfied with the latter. A few shells were thrown into Atlanta yesterday, but our men soon run the battery off. We will hold the City, I suppose, at all hazards. I am in hopes, Honey, that you will not have to move. Think we will drive the enemy from here. Honey, before I forget it, let me tell you to keep your gold watch hid so that in case the enemy comes to our town they may not get it. They take all the jewelry they can find on their raids.

---

[32]This refers to the battle of Peachtree Creek, where Gen. John B. Hood, who had replaced Gen. Joseph E. Johnston on 17 July, suffered heavy casualties and failed to defeat the army of Gen. George H. Thomas. Hood withdrew into the defenses of Atlanta.

Sweet one, I have had no letter from you this week. Hope I will get one soon, perhaps today.

Sweet darling, our little, or shall I say, your little boy (for rearly I donot know wheather I have any part in his composition) is just thirty two days old to day. How I want to see him no one can tell, but want far more to see his dear sweet mother, who is more precious to me than all the jems and jewals of the earth, as I have often said. How much I want to kiss again your sweet little lips and have them lisp again those sweet consoleing word[s] of love, which are far sweeter to me than all the melodies of this earth, which sink delightfully in the heart and bewilders the brain with such rimenecenes of joy. Bless your little sweet tongue, I can almost hear the sweet warble it gives to your enchanting voice as you talk to your prattling little boy. Ma, you must not deprive little sweet Laura of the joys which have made her little heart glad so often. Your words bread [? for *break*] upon her little ear with a pleasantness that makes her little bright eyes sparkle with inteligence and joy.

Honey, your letter last is so sweet I cannot destroy it. I must keep it to read evry day. It is enough to make an angel proud I am of your affection, sweet idol of my daily and nightly joys. Honey, I cannot express the secret emotions of my heart to you. I will leave you to conjecture how fondly I love you. Honey, I have just got up from a nice briefast of coffee and sugar and fried Irish Potatoes. I done full justice to the repast. Liked one thing of enjoying it propperly, and that was to have the presence of my loved little family. Honey, it will be another pleasure for me to labor for you all when the war is over. Lou is yet safe and well, Foster also. Good by, my sweet love. I do sincerely hope that I will get to see you before long. If we we[re] to gain a victory, I could get to embrace your lovely form again in my arms. Col. Watkins is quite unwell. He is staying at the infirmry with me. Let me hear from you often, my dear

Yours ever more G W P

Kiss our little cherubs for me; ten thousand kisses in store for you.[33]

[33]Written across the top of the page.

189

Infirmry, Cumming's
Brig., 3 miles East of Atlanta
Aug. 2nd/864

MY OWN PRECIOUS DARLING KITTIE, Not having heard from you in a long time & being very anxious to do so, I have concluded to send Foster home to carry you a letter and bring me a sweet one from your hand in return. Honey, you can form no idea of what a sorce of pleasure I am cut of[f] from, partially that of reading your letters. I cannot imagine why the mail is not brought on the trains, as they run regular. I suppose they are afraid it might be captured. Honey, I have sent up an application for four days leave of absence, but have no idea it will be granted, as it was disapproved by the Brig. Gen. Nothing would be so joyfull to me as to get home with you if it is only for a few days. I never wanted to see you half so badly in my life. You are all that I think about, and our little children. It seems to me I cannot do without seeing you longer. I am in fine health, as good as I ever was in my life. Lou, poor fellow, gets a little sick occasionally, but does not come to whare I am. He came and stayed all night with me a few nights ago. You never saw a boy in finer spirits than he is. He is the best boy in the world. He has some of the amiable qualities of his sister, whom I love with all my heart and soul. I am getting on finely. Sometimes I donot see the Regt. in a month. I have to stay at the Infirmry all the while. Honey, should I be so fortunate as to get my leave, I am shure you will get worried with me before I leave you. I will not stop kissing you only to hear the sound of that sweet voice, which sound[s] far more melodious to me than all the rich music of earth.

Honey, I do hope I will live through the war so that I can pay my love for all her trouble and help her to rear those lovely little cherubs which delights our hearts so much to think of and love. Honey, I am so proud of you all, when I think of you I scarcely know how to content myself. All my desire is to be with you. I do hope the war will close this year at least so that I can get home with you. All I desire is the privaledge of working for you. I would be perfectly willing to grub or plow and hoe from day's end to day's end for you. If I can get through with my sweet little family and Andy I will be perfectly happy.

Honey, we, I think, will hold Atlanta in despite of all the enemy can do. We have got a reinforcement of twenty thousand in the last few days. They still keep coming in.[34] Col. Watkins is here with me sick and has been for several

[34]Hood was holding Atlanta with 37,000 infantry reinforced by 5,000 Georgia State Militia under Maj. Gen. G.W. Smith.

days. He has been looking for his Lady up for some time. I have just give[n] him permission to go out to Thomas Stokeses to stay a few days, which is just one mile from here. Almost all the citizens has left Atlanta. It is now a dreary looking place and is greeted occasionally by a shell from the enemy, but I am glad to say that they do no harm. I have heard of but one being injured by them, and that was a lady. Honey, I want you, if you please, to send Foster back next Saturday. Send us some light bread and butter if you can, some vegetables. Send two or three pons of light bread. Honey, you must keep my uniform and all the cloth you have closely hid, for if the enemy get there they will take it all from you. I donot think you will be molested by raiders whare you live, for all that have been sent to our rear have been almost all killed and captured.[35] The enemy are now mo[v]eing down on our left. Our forces are so disposed that it is very difficult for them to flank us again. I wish your Pa, if he has not already, [would] send Mary and Lin off the place. I would not like to see their actions in case the enemy were to go to our place. If your Pa is afraid to keep any of his horses at home, if he will send me one, I will take care of it for him. Honey, I wish you would borrow about twenty-five dollars from your Pa and send it to me, for I cannot draw any. Lou needs some also. I hope you will buy wheat with what you have on hand. Save a little in case you have to leave home. If you cannot move you[r] things, I would advise you to stay with them. The enemy has not interupted families in their rear. They require them to take the oath. The raders were badly defeated at Newnan a few days ago, as you have no doubt already heard.[36]

Honey, you have a hard time, I know, but I will always do my utmost to repay you. I send Laura per Foster a little tin cup and a confederate knife and fork that will just suit her little hands. I wish I had something more valuable to send her. Ma, I have nothing to send the little boy. He's too little to have any thing yet. I will get him and Laura a Shutland Pony when I see some. Honey, take time when you write to send back by Foster and give me all the news about our town. Honey, please send me some vinegar and fix me up a nice Bottle of Catsup. Foster must bring what you send in a bag. He must bring nothing for no one but Lou & myself unless it is a little something for Brewer. I suppose you have by this time some nice watermelons out of our little patch. I suppose you have also some peaches. I have had none this year. I have seen a few melons, but they asked ten dollars a peace for them. Honey, please send me a canteen of vinegar. I expect you will think my bill of fare is quite lengthy if I add some fried chicken also. I hope Puss has got through by this time and is able to go to

[35]This is probably a reference to Gen Joseph Weeler's defeats of Gen. George Stoneman at Hillsboro and Gen. E.M. McCook at Brown's Mill, near Newnan, 26-31 July.

[36]See the preceding footnote.

mowing the grass. You must send to Newnan for one of those mowing blades, & your Pa can show her how to use it. I will meet Foster at the Cars Saturday if the R.R. is not cut. I have not seen Gen. Featherston yet. There is one of your cousins by the name of Black staying close by me. I wish your Pa could come to see us, but I am willing to forego the pleasure of seeing him to get him to stay at home, but he must be carefully not to let the enemy get hold of him. They would not shoot or hang him, but they would give him a great deal of trouble.[37] I will stop a short time to eat a little beef, the flesh you so much detest. We have plenty of bacon, have eaten it until we are tired of it. We get no flower, but plenty of meal. I have thought of another vegetable, onions & beets we would like to have (we get sugar and coffee) also.

I have just seen a man from Carroll Co. who says that Capt. Martin had a squad of men picking up the Yankees that was scattered at Newnan. He stated that he met Capt. M. & his father with two driving them along. Hope if any came down our way, the citizens will do likewise. Honey, our cause look gloomy now, but I am perfectly confident we will be successful in the end. Honey, do not despair, but be cheerfull & hopefull. I will see you again, I hope, ere long. Honey, I may be kept away from you a long time & be deprived of the privalidge of writing to you, but I will never cease to love & idolize you. I love and adore you be[y]ond all human conception. Such love as I cheerish for you rearly enters the bosom of human being. Bless your little heart, how sweet, how lovely, & how evrything that's calculated to make me happy. I do hope you have gotten quite well and recovered your strength. Hope also that our little cherubs keep well. Hope the family are all well, also your Ant Kit & children. Dr. Lane has been gone to Hosp[i]t[al] for some time. I donot know what was the matter with him when he went off. I hope he was not sick mutch. Honey, this time last year I was at home but sick. I am unable to tell what bliss I enjoyed while with you at home. Would to God that I were with you again now, although I am doing a great deal of good here. I have had since we left Dalton a great many operations to perform, & I am glad to say so far as I have heard have all done well. Honey, while I am writing the air is listing me the sweet

---

[37]As a sidelight on Judge Featherston, the following piece from *The Southern Literary Companion*, Newnan, Ga., June 1, 1864 (Vol. V, No. 21, p. 2, col. 5) is of interest: "We had the pleasure of meeting in our town a few days since, Gen. L. H. FEATHERSTON, the able and upright Judge of the Tallapoosa Circuit. He was on his way home from Atlanta, where he had been to lend his aid in defence of the city, in the event that it was likely to be besieged. Having satisfied himself from the best information to be had, that, there was no probability of an early attack, Judge FEATHERSTON justly felt, that, the civil administration of law demanded his presence at home. He is a patriot in the true sense of the word, all his feelings being enlisted in the welfare of his country. After having given all his sons to the service, we find him feeble in health and emaciated from sickness repairing to the 'Gate City' at the first note of alarm, to pour out his life blood if need be, in its defence. Such an example we pronounce worthy of all imitation."

music from our brass bands, but none of it would chime me so much as the sound of your enchanting voice. My Darling, night has come now and visions of your unsurpassed beauty & loveliness hants me. I am glad that I yet live to love my darling while so many of our brave men a[re] wraped in their blankets and occupy a soldier's grave. I begin to think like Morgan that I owe my safty and health to the prayers of that dear one at home who told me in tears that she prayed for me evry day. Crewel am I for being so wicked, at the same time having a lovely little sweet Wife in whos piety and religion I haven't the least doubt. Proud am I of such a sweet one to rear our little children. Honey, you have not written me what you intend to name your little boy. Anything you want to name him he must be named, for I named Laura. Hope you will give him as sweet a name as I think I gave Laura. Honey, if you need anything I can get for you, let me know and I will get it if their is any chance. I hope you will have my winter suit done in time or at least by the time winter comes. Let me know who all in town has gone into the malitia. I hope your Pa is still out, for I donot see how he can possibly leave home. Let me know what Doct[ors] are left by the Inferior Court in our county. Brewer is getting along pretty well. Honey, oh! if I can just get to come home in a short time, how happy I will be. Do not be disappointed, my love, if I donot come, for it is quite uncertain. Honey, I am so proud that I have the privalidge of writing to you it seems I can never stop. I fear I will weary you in reading this. I keep your last letter along all the time and read it evry day. It is the sweetest letter you have ever written me. One sentiment in it I will always think of with a happy heart—that was that nothing in the world could usurp my place in your affections. Honey, that ought to make me happy as long as I live and will.

Honey, my uniform would be safer here with me, but I would ruin it. I want to keep it so nice so I can look neat while I am at home with my darling to keep her loveing me. You need not put it in a trunk or wardrobe and think you have it hid, for if the enemy come whare you are they will make you open evry trunk to see if their is any Pistols or arms of any kind in them. At least, that is their pretence. They will also break my gun if they get their hands on it, as I have already written you. Foster can bring letters back to the men in the Regt. None of them are getting letters nor haven't in some time. I learn that the Army Office will be brought up in a few days. Then we will all get letters, I hope. Honey, let me know if Nick Brickell is at home. If so, I want to get him to make me a saddle or the wood work of one. I will send him ere long the patterns if he is. I send you my old Pants for you to fix if you can. If you undertake to remodle them, you must put in a new seat entire. Honey, I will love to have a new vest when you make my suit. Honey, you must hire your work done. Please, my love, donot do it yourself. You know, my love, if I wer[e] there I could not think of letting you do so much labor. Honey, you must let Mrs. W[atkins] know when Foster is going to return, for the Col. is pretty low down because he cannot hear from home, and sick also. He is a good fellow and I feel for him, being similarly situated in reference to hearing from home, but not quite so low down about as he. I have learned that Andrew Daniel is eather killed or captured. I donot know wheather it true or not. It was on the 22nd inst. that the fight occured in which it was said he was lost. Lance Roggers was wounded at the same time. I have not heard wheather Jno. Shack was hurt or not. I look on the Hospital register of that Regt. and did not see his name among the wounded. I visit their Hospital or the hospit[al] of the Brig. they are in evry time they are in a fight. Honey, I will soon need some shirts. If you had something to make me two colored shirts it would be better for me, but as you have not any good[s] of that kind, I will make out with such as your good judgement may fix up. Some with colored bosoms would do very well. Three at a time is as many as I ever want. Honey, let me know about how you get on, how the children are, how they look etc. Honey, I will have to stop for to night. Will write you more before Foster starts in the morning. It is painfull for me to quit writing to one I *do* love so much. Honey, I will take good care of myself on your account and on account of our little one[s] who I hope to be able to bring up propperly that they may be an ornament to their good, sweet mother, who is dearer to me than all the honors and treasures of this earth.

Aug. 3rd/64. Sweet one, I write you again this morn, which leaves me well and able to eat my rations, and thankfull indeed am I that I have the privaledge of writing to one whom I love so well and so devotedly as I do you. I can imagine your disappointment to day when you send down to the office & find no mail for [you] nor no letter from me for those bright eyes to feast upon. This will reach you by five o'clock. Then how much I would give to see your sweet face light up with joy. Would that I could be there to increase your exstacy by a flood of fond Kisses. It seems that if I could behold your lovely self now, I would be overwhelmed with delight, but dearest one, let us cheer up and not despare. Perhaps some proud occurence will waft us toguether ere long. Then what joy we will have is not often experienced by two so fondly mated and weded as we are. It seems that if t[w]o souls ever did exactly chimed that ours does, in one grand river of love uninteruptedly, and increases as it goes. Each look, each interview, each sight, each letter, and each fond caress, like the tributary branch as it flows peacefully along only increases it[s] purity. Would to heaven that my imagination was vivid enought to portray to you the intencity of my undying and everlasting love for you! Sweet one, I have not had such a feast of writing in a long time. I stop reluctantly and fear the happy feeling will leave me low spirited but cheer up at the idea of getting a sweet letter from you, which I had rather read now than any composition that could be written by the most gifted of earth. Sweet one, give my love to all the family, to your Aunt Kit &c., but Honey, the love you are to give our relations is no part of that unexaustable faucet which is ever gusing fresh in my heart for you. Good by, my own sweet one. Kiss our little cherubs for me & pleas[e] occasionally remind them of one that they[38] not forget me or one who loves them more fondly than their little hearts can possibly conceive of.

I have had no letter from Brother John or Pa. Hope you will give me all the news you have from them.

Yours evermore fondly
G.W.P________

Honey, I have just received your letter of the 17th July.[39] I was so proud to read it. I am sorry you all suffer yourselves so much excited about falts rumors. Honey, I am sorry to learn that you are not well. I do hope you will not have a spell of fever. Write me often, my love. Good by again. Yours fondly.

I send you some Essence of Ginger for the baby when he has the colic. Three drops is a dose for him given in brest milk.

190

Infirmry, Cumming's
Brig., 2 Miles West of Atlanta
Aug. 9th/64

MY DEAR LITTLE SWEET ANGEL,

Again I write you, bless your sweet little heart, which gives me more pleasure than anything except seeing you, which would render me happier now than anything in life. Honey, I made an application for leave of absence but am grieved to inform you that it was not granted. You cannot imagine how much I hated to give up the idea of being kept away from you longer. I never want to see you as badly in my life. I have got to that point I would give evrything I have to see you. I am in such good health, better than ever before, it seems to me. Bless my sweet darling, I wish she was so too. Honey, such inteligence as your last letter contained, such tender and heart tuching sentiments I never read before in my life. I am so proud of your evry accomplishment I scarcely know how to content myself. I suppose that Giles thinks I am the closet quiser he ever

[38]The remainder is written along the tops of the first and twelfth pages.

[39]This letter is missing.

met. I fear that I worried him with my many enquiries about your darling self. Honey sweet one, I get freted with my inability to tell you the pure sentiments of my heart towards you. Honey, I do love you better than evry thing that exist now or ner can. I am glad to learn that our little boy is growing & becoming so interesting. I do wish I could see him, but, my love, the thought of seeing you would do me more good than all else, although I would like to see them both.

Honey, enclosed you will find a part of your letter that I want you to keep for me. I think it the best peace of composition I ever read. It does make me so happy, sweetest, dearest, most precious one. Honey, all the time I am writing I see your lovely form in my vision. How sweet to dwell upon how you look as you sit at home with your little boy, and then I can imagine your gracefull form and movements as you walk out the yard thinking of one who you know loves you better then he does himself. Sweet one, I think of you and our little ones in such emotion of love that I am forced to quit with a sigh, then a tear, that you are not more favorably situated in life. Honey, if our little boy is as pretty as Laura, I assure you that no parunt has more cause to be happy. Bless the hour that my heart was impressed with your superior charms and grace! With you as a lifetime companion no one has more or better prospects for future bliss than I. If this crewel war would end, *how happy, how happy* I would be. Lou is here. So is Giles. Both will stay with me to night. What a pleasant night I will have. Lou look[s] better than you ever saw him and is a good boy. Lou and Giles now sit under the fly togueather. How glad I am that they are with me. Col. Watkins has just gone to the Hosp[i]t[al] at Macon. Honey, kiss our two sweet cherubs for me evry day. I hope sweet little little Kitten was proud of her knife and fork & cup. Giles will start home to morrow. I am so sorry to see him leave. I like his company. I am truly glad that he is again out of survice. I feel now that you have a protector in my absence. He has promised to take care of you while I am away. He can help with your Pa's family. I am afraid for you to go to Coosa Co., my love, you would be to[o] far west then. I rather you would go to S.W. Ga. if you go anywhare. I do hope we will hold Atlanta. If we do, you need not move. Should we fall back twenty or thirty miles below this, then will be time for you all to get away. I would have evrything in readiness to go, should I be forced to do so. I will finish this letter tomorrow as Giles will not leave until then. A thousand kisses for you this eve, sweet one. After sitting for two hours in pleasant conversation with Lou & Giles, I & Lou getting Giles to tell us how and whare you sit at night and what you all say, I will go on to write you more. Their is no news here of interest. Our army is in fine spirits and the boys all seem lively, anxious for the war to close, but rather fight on indefinitely rather than sacrifice any of the grand principles for which we are contending. Honey, I have been looking anxiously for Foster on evry train since Saturday last. I fear should you keep him at home to[o] long the R.R. might be cut again. Then he would have great difficulty in getting back. My sweetest one, I yet cannot tell how to advise you as to leaving home. Perhaps it would be best to remain there, perhaps not. I am sorry I am unable to advise you propperly and for the best. Gen. Featherston told Lou to write you to not leave home from no cause. His idea is you all had best stay whare you are. I am perfectly satisfied, my love, that the enemy will not occupy our county permanently. It is no strattegic point, and from that cause they will be only occasional visitors.

My precious one, it makes no difference whare you are when I get a leave of absence, I will see you at all hazards. Honey, all the Drs. in our Brig. save one have their wives in the Yankee lines, and scouts bring letters from them. They say they are doing very well and seem to fear the distruction of our Cavalry more than that of the enemy. Good by to night, love, I will write you more in the morning. Honey, you had better get Brickell to make you and Laura some shoes before winter sets in and he gets crouded with business. Ma, I recon our little boy will not need any this winter, will he? His foot is to[o] little. Honey, their is but few shops in Atlanta. None of them have Indigo. Giles will try to get you some as he comes home. Hope he will succeed. Honey, you must teach our little Boy that his Pa loves him if he has not seen him. Poor little sweet Laura knows that Pappie loves her dearly.

Wednesday, Aug. 10th. I proceed this morning, my precious one, to finish up this letter as Giles is going to start home today. I hope Foster will come to day and bring me a good letter from [your] lilly white hand. I would give a fortune to kiss it now. Honey, take good care of yourself for my sake. I attribute your health to your clenly habits and constant bathing. No doubt you would have had a spell of sickness this summer had you not kept up your bathing. Honey, as it is raining I will have to stop writing. Honey, I want to say ten thousand good things for you, but I have not time. Write often. Your evermore

G W P

191

Infirmry, Cumming's
Brig., Aug. 12th, 1864

MY HOLY PURE AND PRECIOUS DOVE, I take this the first opportunity of tendering to you my heartfelt thanks for the nice favors sent me per Foster and the long sweet letter which sends a thrill of joy through the remotest avenues of my heart,[40] which knows no love and entertains no pure feelings of it only for you, the sweetest and most endeared of all things to me. Honey, the delicacies sent me are doubly delicious because they were prepaired by your dear little hand. Bless them, how I long to feel them grasp me in affection & feel their gentle presure as they pass in velvet softness over my brow, smoothing evry wrinkle that time, absence, and evrything that's calculated to develop them. I cencerly thank God for such a glorious inheritance of my affections. Such a boon as I regard you, my dear, in earthly perfections was ne'r given to man before me. Would that I could give you justice or do myself justice in portraying with my pen the proufound admiration of my heart for you. Honey, could I see you, such overtures of burning I have for you I could make manifest, short of which I could not be satisfied. Bless *again* the day that my heart was taught to love you, the purest and sweetest object that it could have possibly consentered upon. Honey, how I long for the war to close and restore me again to the bosom of her whom I regard with more fondness, more tenderly attachment, more love than *all else*. Proud and lovely little sweet bird, whould that I could this night he[a]r the enrapturous cooing of that sweet voice, which has so often smothed my evry care and wraped my soul in bliss. Sweet one, forgive my mischief. I am perfectly willing to hear that nice little scolding you have in store for me. Bless your pure little heart, you do have such a lovely way of reprooching me for my badness. My light is about to go out, my love. Oh! how I hate to break this sweet converse with her *who I do love* so supremly, dear. Kind little love, good night. Will write you more in the morning. May guardian angels whatch over the slumbers of my *beautifull* while her little *cherubs* breath inocently by her side, only awating a few more years to reflect credit on their parents with their inteligence and beauty.

Aug. 13th. Bright star of my future hopes and happyness, you have no idea of my anxiety to see you. Nothing could give me such unalloyed pleasure. I do hope, my dear, that you are well and will remain so always. I would cheerfully be sick for you at any time and take all your pain upon myself. Lou is well and seems to be as cheerfull as you have seen him. I am unusually so. I am in as good health as you ever saw me. Honey, I will come home as soon as I can get off, but cannot tell when that will be. I hope not long. Tell Giles to attend to what I requested him. I feel much better satisfied about you since he got permission to stay at home. Let me hear from you often, my sweet one.[41]

Kiss the little sweet one for me.

Yours ever more

G.W.P________

[40]This letter is missing.

[41]The remainder is written along the top of the fourth page.

Some thief stole my halter off of Andy night before last. Foster lost my old pants and several other things I sent home by him. He brought all you sent me safely. Honey,[42] you & your Pa had better quit wearing your Gold watches. Put them away so that if the enemy come to whare you are that they may not get them. The negroes will tell them that you have the watches. Then they will have them at all hazards. You had better create the impression of the negroes' mind that you have sent them to me. I have just heard of them awhile on the last raid hanging a man twice nearly to death because the negroes told them that he had a watch when he never had possessed one.

Good by, sweet one, my hearts joy. G.W.P.

192

Infirmry, Cumming
Brig., Aug. 15th/64[43]

MY DEAREST LITTLE DARLING LOVE KITTIE, as I have an opportunity of sending you a letter per Lou, I avail myself of the pleasure of so doing. I have no news, my love, to write. Their has been no material change in the aspect of affairs in several days. Lou is well. As to myself, I am unusually so. Never did I in my life want to see any one so much as I do you now. I want to see your bright eyes flash that pleasant beam of love and see again that same enchanting little smile of affection which haunts me even in my dreams as well as in my diurnal rounds. It does seem that I cannot stay away from you longer. Would to God that I could be with my hearts treasure this morn! It does seem so crewel for me to be kept away from those I love so devotedly, dear. Honey, I often reflect of how sweet you look in your personal relations with little sweet Laura dangling around your dress. I do hope, my love, that you and the little interesting boy are well and will stay so until I get home. It greaves me so much to be away from my love and she in pain all the time. I do pray the day is not far distant when I will return home and be again allowed to follow the common avocations of life uninterupedly with my precious ones around my happy hearthstone. Honey, the Cars run regular. You must write me evry mail. I am always s[o] happy when I get a sweet letter from you. You said in yours that you feared I would not be content to stay at home when I get their. I assure you, my love, that I will

---

[42]The remainder is written on a separate page.

[43]The envelope is addressed: "Mrs. Dr. Peddy/Franklin/Georgia"

never leave you again to stay any length of time. In peaceable times I will always carry you with me so that I will be in a happy and blissful condition all the time, as happyness genuine is not in store for me only by your side, sweet birdie of my whole life. Oh! how I do want to be at home to pet my darling & see her bright sweet face as she walls back her beautiful hair, showing in all its pleasantness and loveliness that bewitching co[u]ntenance which first taught my heart to pay homage at the shrine of her who engrosses wholy my affections. My dear, I cannot say enough to you about how tenderly and devoutly I love and worship you. I will leave you to infer and to judge and appreciate them by the passions which ly so ca[l]mly in your own dear heart.

Kiss the sweet little cherubs for pappie. Remind them often of me. Get them to kiss your sweet little lips for me and imagine at the time, my love, how happy I would be to perform that delightful task.

Good by, my sweet one, take special care of yourself, love.

Wholy and devotedly thine

G.W.P.

193

Infirmry, Cumming
Brig., Sept. 6th, 1864[44]

MY SWEET DARLING, In a great hurry I write you a few lines per John McLendon of Coweta Co., who is about to start home and will start back here from home by next Sunday morning. So if you wish, you can send me a letter by him if you can get it up their by that time. Honey, I am quite well. So is Lou. We are now at Lovejoy's Station on the Macon & Western R.R. Have given up Atlanta. The enemy left our front last night. They may have gone back to Atlanta. Hope they have.

Precious one, I have just received your letter per Col. W[atkins].[45] I have not time to read it before I write this. I hope you are well, my own sweet one, also our precious little cherubs. Honey, you have no idea how much I want to see you and the children. I would give all I have for one hour's sweet converse with

[44]Enveloped addressed: "Mrs Dr Peddy/Franklin/Georgia"

[45]This letter is missing.

you, whom I love and worship more than all else in this world. I will send Foster home in a short time to see how you all come on & to get mine & uncle Mort's horse. I fear the enemy will get him if he remains there. I am sorry I have no money to send you. I cannot get any from the Q.M because he has none on hand.

Good by, sweet one. I love you, if possible, more fondly than ever. Honey, you can have part of your boy's name Charlie for yo[u]r Brother Nick. Anything else you may suggest will suit me. I want you pleased with the name. Give my love to all. Kiss the cherubs for me often.

Thine only G W P

194

Infirmry, Cumming's
Brig., Sept. 10th, 1864

MISS LAURA, Pappie was about to forget to write to his little daughter of whom he is so proud. You must be a nice good little girl while I am gone from home. Do, my little darling, as your good Mama wants you to, and Pappie will love you better. You must not let your little Buddie be a bad boy. You tell him it is ugly for him to cry, that by so doing he troubles his Ma, who tryes to make him a good little boy. Laura, you must make haste and learn to write, so that Pappie may have the pleasure of reading one of your letters. Good by, my sweet little Laura. Pappie will come to see you as soon as he can. Kiss Ma & little Buddie for me. Yours ever, G.W. Peddy

---

195

Lovejoy's Station, M. & W. R.R.,
Ga., Sept. 10th/864

DEAREST AND MOST PRECIOUS IDOL OF MY HEART, KITTIE, Again I send Foster home to see for me that one in whom is concentred all my earthly joys and future happyness, one on whom memory ever dwells fondly as being the most lovely, the best adapted to my present and future delight, and the brightest and purest jem in the galaxy of my affections. Honey, I was truely proud to receive your precious letter of the 31st untimo[*sic*] bearing tidings and sentiment of tender affection, which never fails to give my heart a bright tuch of intense joy even in the saddest hour of my existence.[46] If it were not for you, my dearest one, and the sweet little cherubs which prattle around your knees so fondly, life would be for me nothing but a concatenation of sad events, to be increased in proportion to the rapid march of time.

The deceptive dreams spoken in yours of my coolness towards you when I return home should not be entertained, for I assure you the rapid march of time only increases my genuine affection for you. No circumstance can ever change my adoration for you so long as you remain constant, and even then I could not forego the joy of your love. The only genuine happyness I have ever experienced in life has been since you gave me your fair hand, which I pledge you my word shall never be dishonored, or any act of mine bring a blush of shame to that lovely face which I had rather see now than anything in life; but my dear, I cannot get to see you until this campaign is over. I hope that McLelland will be elected, which will bring to us peace with all its soothing elements.[47] We will leave here in a few days for East Point or near there to confront the enemy again. I hope they will not be able to hold Atlanta long. I will hail the day with joy when they are forced from the Gate City. Our army is in fine spirits knotwithstanding we had to evacuate the City.

Dearest one, I wish not to pro[s]cribe you in the least in any association you like, but my dear, I would suggest for your safety that you donot call on or have anything to do with Mrs. W[atkins], for I learn from reliable authority that she is a regular *Prostitute*. For that reason, *my pure little angel*, donot keep her company in the least, as people are oftened judged by the company they *keep*. Do not cut her, but let her alone entirely. *The above, my love, keep sacred.* I would not object to you renting land, but I wish it not to be close to her. As for going west with her, for my precious one to have such an associate, I could never think of such an idea and wish you, my dearest, to be as pure and as lovely and as free from contamination by bad society as you was the day I married you. I sincerely hope, my darling, you will *appreciate the above hints* and *conduct your pure* self accordingly, without saying one word about what I have written you. Honey, I would like to know what you think of the above in your next. My love, you have no idea how I would like to see you and the little cherubs. Col. says our boy is the prettyest baby he ever saw. I would give any thing to get to see him. Honey, I do hope your health has improved: nothing greaves me more than to think that you are in bad health. I will come to see

[46]This letter is missing.

[47]Gen. George B. McClellan was an unsuccessful presidential candidate in 1864.

about it as soon as I can get off. Honey, the Government owes me a thousand dollars, which I will send you as soon as they will pay me. You can buy corn from Lee Daniel, for which I will pay him when I draw some money. I would keep my hoggs fat if I had to pay ten dollars per bushel for corn. Dearest, I want you to send Foster back as soon as you can. We need him all the time, but we are so anxious to hear from home and to know how you all get on that we will spair him for a few days. I expect he will want to go to see his Wife again, but you must not let him go. Lou has gone on a scout. It will be several days before he get[s] back. Honey, please let Foster have your bridle so he can bring mine & Uncle Mort['s] horse back if their is danger of his being taken by the enemy or our cavalry. No doubt he would be safer here than there. I think Aunt Lancy had best let Foster bring him back until the danger is over, if uncle Mort has not brought him away. If you cannot furnish a saddle for him to ride the horse back, he must bring Capt. Spearman's that he captured, as he is very anxious for him to bring it. I would rather your Pa would let him have one, as he will need one to ride the horse with all the time I keep him. Honey, please, sweet one, send back per Foster my net shirts and also my over shirts as I will need them soon. Honey, no one has any idea how much I want to see you. It seems I would give evrything but my & your honor to have that pleasure. I often spend hours in contemplating the unallayed pleasure we could now have togueather. Bless your little sweet heart, I do hope I will see you sometime before long. Honey, your Pa can give in my tax. My old books are worth about three hundred dollars. The Gov[ernment] owes me $1000. My horse is worth two thousand. My interest in the horse which Mort has is about $1000. Anything else I have at home you give in at your discression. Good by, my precious one. Write to me often as you can. Thine Only G.W. Peddy

Kiss the sweet little cherubs for me. Tell them Pappie wants to see them very badly.[48]

196

Infirmry, Cumming's
Brig., Near Lovejoy's Station, Ga.
Sept. 11th, 1864

MY PRECIOUS KITTIE, As I have a good chance to send you a letter per the hand of Judge Stricland's negro Buy, who is going home & to return next

[48]The postscript is written at the top of the page. He has used pages 759-60 of a ledger as stationery.

Tuesday week, I do so with pleasure. Honey, you know not how happy I feel while writing to one I love so devotedly and fondly. Since Foster left, we have got up an armistice for ten days until all the Citizens of Atlanta can be removed eather north or south. Such crewalty on the part of the Yankee Gen[eral] in thus driving women and children from their homes is unprecendented. The armistice begins tomorrow, which is Monday. All our wagons and ambulances are ordered to Rough & Ready, the point to which they are to be delivered to us. So tomorrow will be a strange day with soldier[s], to see a train of wagons ten or fifteen miles long laden with helpless women and children who have been forced from home by a crewel invader. Not one is to remain in the City. I suppose their property will be confiscated. Honey, I suppose you had as well remain whare you are. You will not be driven from you home on account of living so far from the R.R. Honey, should ten thousand come to your home, maintain your unsulied dignity as a lady and the cowards will crouch before your steady gaze. You must do the best you can if they come, for the sake of one who loves you dearly & who expect[s] more happyness in [the] future in your presence and with you than the human mind can conceive off. Honey, be constant and faithfull in your love for me, and I assure you that I will do my utmost to render you as completely happy in [the] future as I am capable of rendering one so noble, sweet, and lovely as yourself. Hearts so warmly and fervently united in love as ours can shurely never grow lukewarm or entirtain the least idea of ever a wave upon the smooth ocean of our love. Honey, I think I will try again to come home toward the last of next week, but I have no idea that the authorities will let me off. If I cannot get home, I wish you and Giles would come to see me. You can come on the Cars by Clombus and Macon if you think you are able to travail this far in a buggy with your little boy. You and your Pa might come some time this week, as their will be no danger now for ten days commencing Sept. 11th, ending Sept. 21st. Darling, if you think the trip will fatigue you to[o] much, donot come. I would forego the exquisite joy of seeing you and our little boy rather than have you jepardize your or his health in the least. It is but little more than a day's drive from home here. Let all the people about Franklin [know?] the chance to come now, and perhaps they will take advantage of the fine opportunity.

Honey, I sent you a nice towel and comb by Foster that I failed to mention in my last.

Honey, should you conclude to come, you must bring plenty to eat with you. I want your Pa to come at any rate. Now is his best time. I wrote you that Lou might come home soon, but I was mistakened. He has gone scouting in the direction of Stone Mountain instead of towards home. He will be back in a few days. If your Pa comes, perhaps Foster had better return with him if he likes.

Honey, I never wanted to see you and our little cherubs so badly in my life.

Each day's absence increases my anxiety to have that, the greatest of pleasure to me. Honey, you must remind our little cherubs often of me, for you nor they have no conc[e]ption of my fathomless and unbounded adoration and love for you & they.

Dearest one, I never felt so well in my life. I am not ever sunburnt in the least. Bless your pure little heart, I wish you could be in as good health. If their was any chance for me to get off, I would do so. I would even start home on a 48 hours leave of absence if I could get it. I could ride home in one day.

Andy is doing tolerable well only. He is not as fat as he has been. Let me hear from you often. An Officer has just received an application for leave of absence for four days, w[h]ich was disapproved. Maj[or] Generals cannot even get off. So you see, my love, their is no chance for me to get off ever the latter part of next week.

Honey, let us bear our separation with the best fortitude we can, hoping that the day is not far distant when we can be embraced in each other's arms, not to seperate again until death shall lay his icy hands upon us.

Good by, sweet little terestrial angel. Honey, should you want to farm, perhaps you and your Aunt Kit could form a league in that business.

Give my love to her and her children. Your ever more

Thine only
G.W. Peddy

197

Infirmry, Cumming Brig., Sept. 17th/64

MY PRECIOUS KITTIE, I received you[r] sweet letter of the 12th inst per Wm Gorden.[49] I have an opportunity to respond by the hand of Capt. Potts, who is going to Newnan today. Honey, I have never seen such an improvement in the handwriting of any one as their is in yours. Would give no little to write as well as you do. How happy am I often made in my private reveries in possessing one who is so well qualified in evry respect to rear our lovely cherubs. Honey, no one knows but myself how much I want to get home to see you and our lovely little children. I would gladly come at any time if I could and am sadly greaved

[49]This letter is missing.

that I cannot do so, but my own dear one, rest assured that I will do so at the first opportunity. Honey, do not censure me for not comeing. I assure you it is not my fault that I donot do so. Honey, you spoke in yours of my getting wearied by your repitition of tender words of love to me. I am at a loss to know, my love, how you got up such an idea. Suppose I donot write or make a repitition of, of those tender emotions of love which ever hang with delight on my mind, I am shure I would do my feelings great injustice. I cannot think for a moment that you want me to cease writing such things to you, but perhaps you do. Hope not. Should I be mistaken in the kind of letter you like, I am shure I have mistaken your character and have for a long time been doing you gross injustice. Honey, I can but repeat that I love you more devotedly and ardently than ever before. My heart leaps with joy at the thought of having one that I can ever press to my bosom fondly and give her evry assurance of my heartfelt devotion. Honey, I know not what to say about your farming, nor will I know until I see which way the enemy will go. They may go down towards West Point. I know not which R.R. they will travel down. Rumor say[s] that we will move tomorrow down on the Atlanta & West Point R.R. If so, it will be to pre[ve]nt the enemy from going down their. If you want to go in with your Pa and rent Uncle Jack's place, I have no objection. If you get land further off from a main road, it would be much better for you. If you and your Aunt Kit could farm togueather, it would be far better. Your crops would not be so liable to be distroyed by the army of eather side. I can buy you a nice little horse for six hundred dollars that will make a fine horse for farming purposes. The Goverment owes me over a thousand dollars now. That will be enough to commence on. I think you had better live to yourself next year. Should you go over to live with your Aunt, you can live in the Bortpean houses, fix yourself up neatly their. If your Aunt cannot spair the land for you to cultivate, you perhaps can rent some from your Grand Ma. If you cannot get suited or think the undertaking to[o] great for you, you had better get a house as near your Pa's as you can & live to your self. You shall not suffer, my love, for anything as long as I am able to do. Bless your little heart, I will never be able to do you kindness enough to remunerate you for your cares on my account. A constancy to you and a fervend love is all I have to offer you at this time. Will pay you more as soon as I am permited to see you. Honey, should you live to yourself, you had better get Eddie to live with you. Make him take his books and learn him all you can. I heard of Foster's, poor old fellow, illness in Newnan. Hope he is better by this time. I do not expect him back so early on account of it.

Honey, I will come home just as soon as I can get off to assist you in your many cares. I hope Lou has gone home. Ten thousand kisses for you, my sweet one. I shall expect to see when I come home a most beautiful and inteligent little boy. If he resembles you, I would not take a dozzen worlds for him. Kiss he and

Laura for me. Tell Laura she must let Puss dig all the grass she can. Entirely thine.

G.W.P.

Part V.

HOOD'S INVASION OF TENNESSEE SURRENDER IN CAROLINA

23 SEPTEMBER 1864 - 17 APRIL 1865
198-216

After the evacuation of Atlanta in September 1864 Gen. John B. Hood's plan was to move north and to attack Gen. W.T. Sherman's line of communications to Chattanooga, thus forcing him to abandon Atlanta. In this he was unsuccessful, and Sherman, leaving Gen. George H. Thomas to cope with Hood's subsequent movements, on 15 November began his famous March to the Sea. Hood launched a counter-offensive into Tennessee, where two disastrous battles at Franklin (30 November) and Nashville (15-16 December) brought his casualties to about 7,700, not counting some 5,000 captured. His shattered army reached Tupelo, Miss. on 10 January 1865, where he was relieved of command at his own request. Dr. Peddy wrote: "Our campaign has been the most disastrous of the war. Hood is a compleet (sic) failure." On 23 February Gen. Joseph E. Johnston was reassigned to command the Army of Tennessee and led it through the Carolina campaign. Realizing that the situation was hopeless, Johnston signed an armistice with Sherman on 18 April. Hostilities were never resumed, and on 26 April, despite President Davis's insistence that he continue to fight, Johnston surrendered. Since Lee had surrendered to Grant seventeen days earlier, the Civil War was virtually over.

198

Infirmry, Cumming's
Brig. Sept. 23rd/64[1]

MY OWN SWEET ANGEL KITTIE, As it will cost me ten dollars to buy a basket of potatoes, I have concluded to send Foster home after a few [things] it is impossible for me to get here. My love, I have no news to write you a[nd I am] quite well except for a slight headache [this morn]. I suppose we will remain here several days. We are strongly entrenched [here. There is] no enemy nearer us than Atlanta. Col. Watkins has wrote for his wife to [come and] see him. I suppose she will do [so] in a few days. I would like for you to [co]me also, but not with her. Perhaps it w[ou]ld trouble you to[o] much to come as you are feeble and perhaps the baby wo[u]ld be to[o] much trouble to you. So Honey, perhaps you had better remain at home until I get a chance to come, which I hope will be soon. Mrs. Leander Watkins, Mrs. Boyd & E[li]za Hardegree are here—will go home this eve. I called to see Mr. Bond and and family today. They think of going back to Franklin if the army should remain here any length of time. Honey, you had better send Foster back Sunday. Kiss the Babies for Pappie. Tell Laura to kiss Ma often for me. Entirely thine

G.W. Peddy, Surg.

Please send me some good biscuit, my love[2]

199

Franklin, Sept. 28, 1864

MY PRECIOUS ONE,

As Dick is going up to carry uncle Joe some provisions and we were all sick when Foster left, you might be uneasy if I did not write again soon. We are all better. I feel much better than I thought it possible after such severe suffering. Honey, I received your letter of the 17th by Capt. Potts today.[3] Am sorry it did

[1]This letter is badly stained.

[2]Written on the back

[3]No. 197.

not come sooner, for I want to tell you that you are the most mistaken you ever was to even think for a moment that your letters, which are filled with tender words and loving expressions, fail to interest me. You know that my heart thrills and my whole existance is enrap[t]ured when you talk to me when at home in such loving words. While you are crewelly kept away, nothing gives me so much joy as to read words of burning affections traced by a dear hand which none have any right to but myself.

Aunt Kit will be here directly. She received a letter from uncle Joe telling her to rent me some land. She told Eddy she was coming over here today a purpose to beg and persuade me to go over there and live. She will do any way, she says, to get me over there. I shall not conclude what to do untill you come. Then you can deside yourself. Any where you think best for me to go, just say so and I am willing to do it. You know, honey, it is to[o] expensive to buy corn at present prices when Puss could make it, and to hire her out, the money wonn't buy one half what we need. I know Pa will object to my having him buy it. I think it best, though I may be mistaken.

Mrs. Dr. Northern has gone to her father's untill after her confinement. She will then live near him. Mrs. Dr. Grimes is going to move to Macon next Chrismast, so we will have a new set of inhabitants in our town.

I had bad luck in having any wool carded, honey, again, but I am now carding it over on hand cards and then spinning it. It will be a great deal of trouble, but then, my love, you like a any thing nice so much, I like to make them. Evry one says they would not do it for no pay, but I don't think about trouble when I am working to please you. Puss is cutting grass now. I fear she will not do much at it as it has been cloudy and raining for the last week untill the last two days. Ma says she would make Puss card for me, but then I am afraid she would not do it as nice as I like.

Honey, I am glad you like my writing, This paper, bud Gily says, is enough to ruin anybody's hand, it is so rough and catches the pen so often. We have just heard the army had moved up to FairBurn. If I cold only send you some flour. But Dick will have such a load, he can't carry any. You must come home, honey, then you can get any thing to eat, or if you can't come, send Foster on the Cars and I will try to get some flour. If I was just keeping house, I could send you some chickens' eggs and butter, but I won't think about it.

I must close now, as ant Kit will start soon and your boy has just opened his bright blue eyes and is crying untill the tears are running down his cheeks. Ain't that too bad, papie? He tries to put his little thumb in his little mouth with his *jug*. That is a nice baby trick. Come home, papie, and you shall have some sweet little arms around your neck, and you will think you are in the seventh heaven of delight. Laura is well and talks continually of you. Good by darling, I am looking for you every day. Yours ever more Kate Peddy

200

Four Miles above Cedartown, Ga.
Oct. 9th, 1864[4]

MY DEAREST LITTLE SWEET KITTIE, I write you a short note this morning as it is the first opportunity I have had, which leaves me quite well bud sad that I cannot be with you; whom I love with greater admiration than ever before. Honey, I do love you more devotedly than anyone ever loved before. I got back to the command safely, and all is right with me. We are on our way to middle Tenn[essee]. We are tearing up the R.R. as we go. I believe that the disaster to the enemy will be as great as that represented by President Davis in his speach at Macon, Ga. I know that he meant something when he said that the seen of defeat and retreat from Macon would be reenacted by the enemy by this move. Honey, I am so proud that this move relieves our country from the enemy. If they have not left Atlanta yet, so much the worse for them. They will do so in a short time. You can now make your arrangements for farming next year & living to your self if you wish to. You will not be interupted. I will send you a horse or mule if you need one. Perhaps you can keep Andy, if Mr. Daniel lets me keep his horse. I have no doubt but what he will. His horse is doing finely. I expect I will see Nick in a short time if he is about Blue Mountain, & no doubt he is. Honey, I am so glad that I went by home to see you and the sweet little cherubs. Ma, you have no idea how I love the little Boy, not better than you & Laura though. Honey, I hope to be able to come to see you again sometime this winter. If we succeed in this move, the Federal army will be completely ruined, after which I hope to realize peace with all its glory. I hope Andy is getting on well, also that the leather is rapidly being prepared for the completion of my saddle. Foster will have to be very carefull when he starts with it that someone does not steel it from him. Perhaps if he does not come horseback he will have to come around by Celma, Ala., from thence to Talladega Town. Well, my love, I leave to go. Good by, sweet one, kiss the babies for Pappie, Yours forever & thine only

G.W. Peddy

Direct your letter to me 56th Ga. Regt., Cumming's Brig., Army Tenn.

---

[4]This letter is written in pencil.

201

Gadsden, Ala., Oct. 21st/64[5]

MY DEAREST SWEET LITTLE ANGEL, I love you so much and idolize our sweet little cherubs that I scarcely know what or how to write you. We will start in the morning, my love, to middle Tenn[essee]. I know not when I will see you again. May guardian angels watch over you & keep you and our little sweet cherubs from all harm until I return! My dearest, you know not how much I love you & our sweet ones. I am so proud of our little sweet boy Charlie. I love him for myself and his mother. no one will ever know how devotedly I love you. I wish you knew, my love. Honey, remember that I will ever love and be constant to you under any and all circumstances. Bless your sweet little heart, would that I could see you to day! Nothing would render me so happy. My dear, I hope you will get Andy fat and keep him so until I return home or send for him. When Lou takes a notion to come, Foster, I recon, better come with him and bring the leather to fix my saddle with. I think I can do without the raw hide, but will want the side of leather to cover it with. You need not send him to Newnan to see the man about making the saddle, for he has left there and is now up here. I will write to you often as I can. My precious little angel, you must write me once or twice per week. I will get your letter if directed to the army East Tenn. Honey, I would be glad that you would send my winter clothing by Lou & Foster. When they start, they had better come to Blue Mountain by way of Montgomer[y] and Selma. Honey, I hope the war will close this winter so that, should we both live and our little petts, we will have a happy future before us when the war ends. Honey, take good care of your health in my absence & recollect that I love you more than all else in this troublesome world. I learn that the enemy have all left Atlanta. I hope it's so. If correct, our country will not be interupted again during the war. Our move so far has been a compleet success. You will learn from the papers what we have done on our trip. Honey, I believe if I was Lou and was well, I would come on back, though he can do as your Pa thinks best. Give my love to all the family. Kiss the Babies, bless their little hearts, for me.

Good by, sweet one, I will write you again soon. Mr. Daniel's Horse is fatning evry day and has since I first got him.

Yours ever more only G.W. Peddy

P.S. Send my clothes by Foster if you possibly [can][6]

---

[5]This letter is written in pencil.

[6]A line is obliterated where the letter is folded.

202

Florance, Ala.
Nov. 7th, [1864]

MY PRECIOUS SWEET KITTIE, It is my sweet pleasure to write you this eve for the first [time] since Tommie Watkins left. No one but myself, sweet one, knows how much real pleasure it gives me to write to one whom I love so devotedly and dearly. We are now in the beautifull little town of Florance, situated on the north bank of the Tenn[essee] river, a lovely vilage. It is one in which I would delight to live. Honey, the Tenn[essee] valley in Ala[bama] through which we have just passed is a spretty country as you ever saw. It is scarcely second to K[entuck]y. Evrything beautiful, sublime and lovely loses all its charm for me because you are not here to witness it with me. bless your little heart, I would rather see you now than evry body else. I am sorry that their is no pleasure on earth for me only with your lovely self. You are dearer to me, my love, far [more] than life itself. My love, I hope you are not disturbed any by the enemy. If not, I imagine you are doing very well. I hope so at least.

Honey, I have received no letter from your lovely hand since I left home. I have written you four with pencil. I hope you have got them ere this.[7]

I am happy to state, my precious darling, that I am quite well. Honey, you need not trouble yourself, as I have before written, to get the leather for the saddle. I have one now that I made myself which cost me only eighty dollars. That is as pretty [a] one as you have seen. I am all fixed up now for riding. I do wish you could see the saddle. I will think it very handsome if you could see it and say that it was pretty. Honey, I need nothing from home now but my clothes. I need these very much. My boots and gloves I will be ob[l]iged to have some way. You will have to send them by the first one passing. If Giles expects to carry Nick's to him, I would be glad he would bring mine to me also. I fear if you start Foster with them he will loose them. You will have to borrow the money from Giles to pay for the books. I have drawn no money sence I came back from home. The Government owes me now $1400.00. Should you go to keeping house, you will need it. If I cannot get any opportunity to send it to you, you will have to borrow and give my note payable in confederate issue. Honey, I do want to see your little cherubs so much, but cannot tell when I can come. Good by, sweet darling, in great hurry or I would write more.[8]

Keep Andy out of the way of the rogues and Yankees. Ten thousand kisses for you and the sweet little cherubs.

Forever thine
G.W. Peddy

---

[7]Two of these letters are missing.

[8]The remainder is written at the top of the page.

203

Florance, Ala., Nov. 14th, 1864[9]

MY SWEET ONE KITTIE, I write you a short note this eve as I have an opportunity of sending it the most of the way per hand. I am well, my love. Hope you and our precious sweet children are also. I would be happy to see you indeed. I never think of you, the little boy, and Laura only with the proudest feeling of delight. I can see and hear you talk in my imagination so sweetly to our little cherubs and see their beautifull countenances light up with joy at the sound of your sweet voice, which always haunts me so pleasantly. I have heard that Lou left home on the 28th ultimo. He has not come up yet. We will start for middle Tenn[essee] in the morning. I regret that I have to go so far from you. I have heard that we will be gone there six weeks, after which we will perhaps go into winter quarters on the South side of the Tenn[essee] River. Kiss the babies often for me. I would be glad I could get my clothes before very cold weather sets in. Good by, sweet Kittie. Tell the little cherubs to kiss their Ma for me each day that I am absent.

Good by, my sweet one. I do hope I will see you and spend a few days in your lovely presence.

Give my love to all the family.

Mr. Daniel's horse is doing very well. Hope Andy is. Write often, my love, write me of your affection for me, of which I feel prouder than all else can make me. Again good by, my sweetest angel.

Thine only
G. W. Peddy

P.S. Perhaps, dearest, our division will remain here to garrison this place. Madam rumor says we will. If so, we will have a comparatively good time, escape many hardships. You will be glad of that, will you not? Honey, me thinks I hear you say in a sweet voice, Yes. Honey, oh! how I wish I could feel this eve the lovely pressure of your fond embrace. Nothng would give me so much rearl happyness.

Good by, sweetest one
G.W. Peddy[10]

---

[9]This letter is written in pencil.

[10]Added immediately following is a series of lyrical sentences termed "References." These are written in another hand, and the hand is not Mrs. Peddy's.

204

Tenn. River, South Side, five
miles above Florance, Ala.
Dec. 27th, 1864

MY OWN SWEET ANGEL KITTIE, I will ever fondly remember how much unalloyed pleasure I experienced in reading your very sweet letter of the 30th ult.,[11] which reached me on the north band of the Tenn[essee] river when it was doubtful wheather we would cross before the enemy came upon us, & with Gun Boats in front to dispute our crossing an[d] the enemy in our rear flush with a briliant victory. You can imagine our suspense until we crossed to the south side whare we are now safely encamped for a few days, after which we will march, it's said, to Abberdeen, Miss., a distance of one hundred miles. Suppose it will take us to the middle of Jan[uary] to make it. Our Campaign has been the most disastrous of the war. Hood is a compleet failure. We have lost about 8000 prisoners at Nashville and about five hundred killed dead at Franklin, Tenn. charging brest works of a very formidable construction.[12] Honey I am sorry to add we have nothing left but a remnant of a demoralized army. I am happy to add that our division saved the army by their unparallelled valor. Among the captured of ourRegt. that you know is Wm Garrison, Ed Daniel, Louis Glanton. Abb Kelly of the 34th Ga. was severely wounded and captured. Joseph Shackleford was of the 41st Ga. was captured also. Mort Lane is safe. Dr. Lane is safe and doing finely. Nick, I suppose, is safe. His command is bring[ing] up the rear. I am getting on finely. My health is quite good. And sweet one, I am so proud of you I feel perfectly delighted even if I am away from you. I feel inexpresably gratefull to you for writing me the sweet letter before spoken of in this. Honey, have no fear that my love will wane in old age. I love you more fondly now if possible than ever before. Honey, do not let a doubt cross your mind with regard to the purity of my affections. I assure you in all candor that I love you more *dearly* than ever *man loved before* and *pledge you my sacred honor* that it will *never degenerate* in the *least* so *long* as your character remains as pure and spotless as it is.

Honey, I am sorry that you[r] dream troubled you in the least. Such an act of injustice to you I will never will be guilty off. As to the Ladies of Florance giving parties, they did so, but I never attended them or anyone of them. I have not

[11]This letter is missing.

[12]It is claimed that this charge, on 30 November 1864, was more dramatic than Pickett's charge at Gettysburg. Confederate losses amounted to 6,252 (including five generals), of whom 702 were missing, and 22 battle flags.

spoken to a half dozzen Ladies since I left you. Have eat one meal in a house only on the campaign.

Darling, I will come home as soon as I can. Cannot tell you exactly when. I am nearly dead to see you and our sweet little cherubs. Your Pa is mistaken about my not loving little Charlie. I love him dearly as I do Laura, the sweetest little girl in the world. I will bring you all something nice when I come. Will get your Ma & Pa some shirts if I find any to sell.

Honey, Kiss the babies for me often. Don't let them forget me, for I know I love them more than ever they will find out.

I would give anything to see you riding Andy. I am happy that you like him so well. He is a noble animal. Mr. Daniel's horse is getting on well, is fatter than he was when I brought him from home.

Sweetest one, orders have just come to start, I fear, on a more arduous march than we have ever made this winter. I do hope that we will get to a stoping place before the winter is over. I will have to stopt this very pleasant task. May guardian angels watch over you and our two little sweet cherubs in my absence! Honey, if kindness on my part and true love will prevent you from saying what the old Lady Parker did, I am shure you will never say it, for evry effort shall be put forth to render you happy as long as I live.

Good by to one I love dearer than I do my own heart. Will write you again as soon as I can. Ten thousand kisses for your sweet lips. Yours only

G.W. Peddy

Ieuka, Ala., Dec. 30th, 1864.[13] My dear, I have seen Lou. Got my drawers. He is well, will join us in a few days. Saw Nick yesterday. He is well. Lou left his clothes at Maredian. He will send for them in a few day[s]. he needs them badly. Honey, no one knows but myself how much I love you and how anxious I am to see you and our sweet little ones. I will try to come home for my clothes. I do not need them at present. I have the nicest saddle you have seen. Will not need the leather now to make it, as I written you before. We are going on towards Corrinth. Cannot tell whare we will stop. Kiss the babies for me often. Honey, have Andy fat by the time I come home.[14]

You must keep Andy locked evry night. I am very uneasy that some one will steal him.

Honey, I will bring you all something nice when I come home if I can draw some money. Have not drawn any since I left home.

Honey, you must get me up some nice boots if you can. Mine are nearly gone.

Dearest, if you do not farm next year, you had better hire Puss out. You get

---

[13]Iuka is in Mississippi, not in Alabama.

[14]The remainder is written along the tops of the fourth and first pages.

$25 per month for her by hiring her to cook and wash in Hospital in Lagrange.

Write me often, my own dear.

I have not said anything to Lou about his case, but will in a few days.

Will write to your Pa in a few days. I want to try to get a detail to go home and practice medicine if the law passes to take in all exemps and details. Then detail Dr. Millers, Tanner &c, giving the power to make such details to the Department commander.

I want him to notice specially all the acts pass[ed] by Congress in reference to the army.

Good by, dear idol. Do hope I will see you soon.

G.W.P.

205

Tupelo, Miss., Jan. 12th/865

MY *OWN SWEET DARLING ANGEL KITTIE,*

As my good old friend, Col. Watkins, is going to start home in a few days on a sixty days' sick leave, I conclude to writing you a letter, hoping you will get it sooner than by mail. I have no news to write you, my love, only we are here encamped, I hope, but for a few days in this misearble poor country. Think we will leave here in a short time for Columbus, Miss. From there rumor says we will go to Opalaca, Ala. I hope its true. I have no desire to soldier it in this section of country. You have heard and read no little ab[o]ut Tupelo. Well Honey, you have no idea what a miserable plae it is—no end to the mud; but two houses in the place and one of them blew down yesterday, which leaves but one. I have had no letter from you recently. Hope I will get one when the mail comes. We have had no mail in some time. Sweet one, I cannot tell you when I will be at home. I hope some time this winter. Gen. Hood says he will soon adopt a liberal system of furloughing, after which I hope to get of[f] to see those I love far dearer than life. Bless your pure and true little heart, I know you love me, yet by the conviction in my own heart that I love you more dearly, if possible, than ever before. You, my love, are the brightest jewel that earth has any idea of how I love more than the human imagination can fathom. I love to, my darling, [think of] our little ones, who if we can keep as pure and untarnished as their sweet Mother, I will be more than satisfied. They take their extraordinary inteligence from their mother. Bless your sweet heart, I ought to pray and be thankfull to God for such a blessing as you are to me. You are my sweetest solace in this life. Honey, I cannot tell you how doubly dear to me. I will leave you to infer from my former course towards you. If the war would clos[e], I would devote my entire life to the completion of your earthly happyness. Of all things in the world I desire your please more than all things else. If I only could keep you hapy, I would be more than pleased all my life. Honey, I wrote you in my last that you had better take up Giles' propostition, but think now perhaps it would be better for you to remain with your Pa. If you would like to live down on the plantation, raise your own poltry and meet, I have no objections. Honey, I would rather you would get our children off to themselves and begin Laura's education. Honey, you ought to soon begin to pay regular attention to her learning. I have a nice book I will send or bring there soon as an opportunity presents. Honey, if you cannot rent any land, I want you to hire Puss out next year. It will not do to keep her at home doing nothing. I would hire her out with understanding that she is to be paid for in corn. I will get Andy away from home as soon as I can in order to stop the expence of feeding him. Mr. Daniel's horse is fat and doing well, with the exception of the worst scratches you ever saw. I am getting him well of them now. He is a splendid little horse and easy kept. Honey, I do hope you will not let Andy get stolen before I get him again. If I can get him here, I will keep him. If I can get home, I will ride him back. I will finish this letter with ink and pen, as Lou has just lent me one. He is doing very well, in fine health, is acting Sergt. Maj. of our Regt. Hope he will continue to do so. Honey, I would like to have Foster to bring Andy to me, but fear some one would take him away from him. If he can, I will wait until we get settled down, then I will send for him. If Col. Watkins comes back by dirt road, I will get him to bring my horse, or Foster can come with him. Dearest, I hope you will get me the boots I wrote for from Brickell. he said he would make me a pair for $150.00. You must hold him to his promise. Honey, you must excuse the writing of this letter, for I am hunkered down of my blanket writing. I would like to have my clothing, but cannot take care of them unless I can get a chance to send some of my old ones home. I am afraid for Foster to start with them. Some rogue might steal them from him. I will try very hard to come home for them. If their is any virtue in a thorough trial to come home, I assure you I will come. Honey, I think if some of my friends would get up a very strong petition with the sanction of the inferior Court for me to come home to practice Med[icine] and present it to or send to Gen. Beauregard, he would detail me for that purpose. If such men as Uncle Tom. Houson Jackson, Sanders Favor &c. would take hold of it, I think they could succeed in getting me off for twelve months at least. Perhaps Charlie Mabry would get it up, as I and he have got in the same line of policy now.

Brewer sends his compliments. Honey Sweet one, I will close. Hope to hear from you twice per week.

Good by, dear Sweet Angel. Will send you some money as soon as I can draw it.

Yours ever more

Kiss the sweet little *cherubs* for me often.

G. W. Peddy

206

Franklin, Jan. the 20, 1865[15]

MY DEAREST LOVE,

My whole heart was made supremely happy when the last mail arrived and brought me one of the best letters and one that would win the coldest hearts and bid them hop with joy. It had been so long since one of those messengers had come to tell in fond words and eloquent language that the hand of Providence had still permitted one hearth to throb with life which will ever stand me and a cold unsympathizing world, and where I am shure to find a tender resting place when weary with toil or care. How thankful I am and proud that you have come through so many dangers since last we met safti. Honey, while I write it does seem to me I would give almost anything to lay my head in its resting place on your bossom and tell you how *dear you* are to me. I am very low down now. We are shurely on the verge of ruin. I cannot see one glimmering ray of hope that we will ever have any peace. Every body is whipped now. Uncle Leevi received a letter from John a few days ago, and he wrote that Richmond would be evacuated in a short time and the troups sent to meet Sherman at Branchville in S. Carolina. We have heard that Hood's army also will be sent around to that place. I hope you will come home to stay a long time with us. Honey, if you can get detailed, by all means do so. I would be so glad I would almost go crazy. Pa will do all he can to get you home. Honey, I do feel so low down to night I ought not to write while feeling so, but hope you too will not catch the infection. The children are both well and as prettie as ever. Laura never will forget you in the

---

[15]Misdated 1855. The envelope is stamped "PAID 10" and bears a faded postmark. It is addressed: "G.W. Peddy,/Surgeon 56th Ga Regiment/ Cummins Brigade/ Army of Tennessee"

world, she loves you so well. Poor little Charlie has never known much of a father's love, but I do hope will ere long. He is one of the finest most sensible children I ever saw. I know you would love him so much. Every one says he is so much like Laura was, and she, of course, is her Pappie['s] own child. Several have told me of late that you & I ought to be two of the happiest, proudest people in [the] world, for we had two of the finest looking children that ever lived. You know I felt complimented, for I knew it was because it was their father's resemblance in that made them lovely. I had to stop and undress Charlie and put on his night dress. You ought to have seen him dancing in my lap and looking at himself in the glass. I believe that he has more life and activity about him than any child of his age I ever saw.

You did not tell me what has become of Uncle Winfield, if he got home. We heard he was wounded and supposed he had gone home. Mrs. Watkins is looking for the Col. to come home as he wrote his health was very bad now. I fear yours is not so good. I can't see how it can be after so much exposuure. We have heard that Capt. Spearman is dead, but you did not mention it in your letter. Suppose it is not so. We had a good deal of excitement here at the election of judges. Such electioneering never was done before. Messrs. Pace, Ware, Phar, Grimes, & Shackelford was elected. I wish you could fix up some way to keep out, for I think you have served long enough. Be shure to bring me a good deal of money, for I owe some for corn that will have to be paid soon. Don't buy any for us. I only told you to get some things while up where good, I imagined, is cheap. I will close now. Come home, love, and you don't know how glad I will be. Yours ever more Katie Peddy

Andy is not as fat as you would wish him, but hope he will be soon.[16]

207

Tupelo. Miss., Jan. 20th, 1865

DEAREST SWEET KITTIE,

I write you with pleasure this morning, giving you the inteligence of the return of our corps to Ga. I will come no nearer home, I suppose, my love, than Opolacca, Ala. I think my application for leave will fail and I will be deprived of the pleasure and exceeding joy of seeing you and our sweet little cherubs of

[16]Written upside down at the top of the first page.

whom I am so fond. If you wish to, you can come down to Opolacca, Ala. and remain there at the Hotel until I come. If you cannot come, your Pa had better come or send Foster with my clothes. I send my Saddle by Ben, Your Grandma's Boy, to go on Andy that he may be brought to me. Bill Gorden & Andrew Daniel will come through the country with the horses [that] belong to some of the Officers of our Brig., Mr. Daniel's horse among the No., the one I have been useing. We will go on the Cars and will get to Opolacca next Teuesday or Wendesday, perhaps not so soon as that; but at any rate, we will get to the above mentioned place before Gorden & Daniel get home. I want them or Daniel at least to bring my horse with him when he returns to camps. If you or your Pa or Foster comes to meet me, you must be shure not to let any one steal them. I am affraid if Foster comes, someone will take the clothes away from him. That is the reason I want some white person to come with them. Who ever comes will have to come on the train. Take the cars at Hoganville. Honey, just as soon as you get this, send someone up to Wm Crosby's and buy me one of the hats he has on hand. Lou says he has some nice ones at forty or fifty dollars. Size 7¼ fits me. Then delay no time in getting someone to Opolacca with my things to meet me. Ben will go ahead of us two or three days. I will try to get to stay at Opolacca twelve hours. Capt. Spearman's father may come to meet us, perhaps Col. Lane. Also Brewer's mother, as she has some kin at Opolacca. As soon as you get this,you must send the ballance of the letters which Ben brings to those to whom they are directed, so that they may have time to meet us. Bless your little heart, I do regret so much that I cannot get to stay with you some this winter. I would give a world almost to spend a month with you or even a few days. But the powers that be refuse me this joy. I do hope the day is not far distant when I will be allowed to stay with you all the time. Darling, it is a happy thought to me that I have such a noble one to love. You have no idea, my love, how devotedly I love you and our dear little sweet one.

Honey, if we should pass Opolacca before you get there, I will have a notice or note at the hotel for you, so that you may know that we have gone on.

Darling, I have had no letter from you since the 13th Dec. I am getting very anxious for one, I assure you. I will send my old clothes back home by the one that brings my new ones. If you should send them by any one to me when I get down about Augusta, I will have to throw my old ones away. You can have my clothes brough[t] to meet me in your Pa's Valeece, which I will return by the one who brings them. Kiss the babies for me often. If you should conclude to meet me and can get Brewer['s] mother to come with you, you can have no trouble. She has relatives in Opolacca.

I want you to caution Andrew Daniel not to brake my saddle when he starts with Andy. I told him to call for him when he goes to start back. You must be certain that he brings him when he comes back.

I suppose from what I hear from Dr. Lane's letter that you and Giles have put up togueather. If so, I wish you a happy time. You must promise me, my love, that you will not do more than you did at your Pa's. You must not cook or do anything of that kind, my precious one. When I come home, I would be greaved to see your face burnt in the least or to see it care worn. I donot want to see that lovely face only as I left it, beautifull, bright, and lovely. Honey, wear your Bonnet and keep yourself sweet as ever to me.

I will stop now, dear.

Yours ever more
fondly
G. W. Peddy

P.S. Give my love to all.

GWP

Say to Joseph Lane that I have his Boy George with me. If he wants to see him, meet me at Opolacca. I will keep him until further notice.

Kittie, I have drawn no money yet. Lou sends a note in my letter.[17]

208

Franklin, Jan. the 24, 1865

MY BELOVED,

Although I am much fatigued by a day's hard work, yet I could not close my acheing eyes untill I had told you, although it will be but imperfectly, the delicious pleasure I felt sweeping like a resisless torrent through my heart to day while reading your more than usual tender letter brought by Col. Watkins.[18] How I wish I was every way worthy [of] that love which your noble heart lavishes on me. I often wonder and think why do you love me at all, and perhaps others equaly surprised that you should love one so plain in personal appearance and equally as deficient in those qualifications of mind and disposition which draw the heart as if by magic to them; and I am surprised still father when I remember your intense love for the beautiful of every thing. but as long as life last[s], my every effort will be to render you as happy by every

[17]These two sentences are written in pencil at the top of the first page of the letter.

[18]No. 205.

exertion on my part as it is possible for me to do. I had such a sweet dream a few [nights ago]. I thought that again we wander as we used to in our garden in the early days of our married life. I felt again the thrilling preshur of loving arms folded around me, and saw the tender smile of love kindle in those eyes, ever beaming with inteligence. Oh! I was so happy by your side, where the earth seemed clothed with bea[u]ty and the sky appeared bluer than ever to me with a few rosy clouds floating through the air like cars of happy spirits, but I awoke. It was a dream. I could har[d]ly believe the stern reality that you was absent. I found little Charlie's head nestled close to my side. I could not help thinking for a long time of the crewel necesity of your being gone and, my love, will we ever live again togeth[er]. I fear often times we will not. I think *Peace* has folded her lovely wings on some other shore where she can find better enjoyment than in our country, where we find brother against brother. Honey, I have killed my hogs to day and I am so tired I will go to sleep and in the morning will tell you all the news. Sweet dreams for you, my precious one. Again after a good night's rest sit down to finish my letter. I killed my hogs yestaday. They weighted more than I thought they could be made to do, being so young. Pa and myself had quite a debate about the way we raised our hogs. Mine outweighted his by a good deal and were four or five months younger. Yet because I gave mine while raising them two ears of corn a day and his got *none*, he says the corn I gave them would buy more meat than I will get off of them. Andy is getting on finely now. I give him as many peavines a day as he can eat so he will be fat by the time you want him. Honey, I do wish you could come home. So many things trouble me that you can rectify. Honey, you wrote about my sending your letters back. I did not know it and thought I read every piece of paper you send in your letters. Pa is going to stay at the plantation and says he wants me to stay here, so as Bud Gily is going to teach here, I will remain here also. Charlie is one of the brightest boys in the Confedracy. Every one who sees him remark[s] what an intelligent pretty boy. He has two little teeth, papie, the sweetest little ivory pegs you ever saw. I am the happiest wife and mother ever lived and think how supremly blest I am every day. You asked me to tell you how the children looked. I could not begin to do them justice. I would take the most gifted to describe their beauty & loveliness. You can tell how they loo[k] by seeing your self in a mirror, for they have their father's features on a baby face with all the innocent charms of childhood. Honey, bud Gily says send him his French grammar by the first one who will be reliable. Honey, I know you are just like you was when you came from Kentucky. Your health will be gone if you have to take many more such trips. The place you are at now, I have been told, is very unhealthy. I shall be uneasy untill you get away.[19] Laura has spun two little

[19]The remainder is written at the top of the first page.

broaches & thinks she is getting to be so large. Give my kindest respects to Brewer. Tell bud Lu to write often. Yours ever more, Kate Peddy.

209

Abbyville C.H. [*S.C.*]
Feb. 26th, 1865

MY PRECIOUS LOVE KITTIE,

I arrived at this place after a march of forty-two miles which wearied me no little on account of the four day's rain which we have had. I will have to walk about one hundred miles father yet to get to my command. I am now absent without leave, but hope it will all be right when I reach my command. I suppose I will remain here three or four days.

This is the sorryest country I have seen in all my travails over the Confederacy. I passed the residence of John C. Calhoun of S.C. The people of this State reverence him yet. Honey, I can see in my imagination you, Charlie, and Laura as you sit so cosily around the fire. I can see sweet little Charlie with his little arms stretched jumping up and down. How I wish I could be with you all, no one knows but myself. I often think how sweetly you and Laura kissed me when I was with you. Bless her little heart, she is as affectionate as her *noble* Ma and I hope will make as good a woman. Honey, tell Giles to rest easy. I hope I will be able to send him his money soon. The prospect for sending it in a week or ten day[s] looks very gloomy, but will send it at the first opportunity.

I suppose by this you are snugly sot up in your new home, but perhaps not, for I think your chances for leaving your Pa's house is quite slim if their persuations will affect anything. Honey, you have a hard time now, but if life is spaired to us to live togueather, I assure my evry effort will be bent to promote your happyness and that of our precious one[s] who I hold in my affections far dearer than all on earth except you, who I love better than I do my own self. I am anxious to learn, my love, how you come on with the petition I left with you. You can write me a letter by Hue Houston as he returns, as he can at all times on his rout to Va. see some of our Corps.

The Enemy are between me and my command. I cannot tell when I will get to them. I do hope my horse will come up before I leave here, for I am so weary of walking and carrying my baggage. Had I known what I do now, I would not have carried Dr. Lane's things for five hundred dollars. It is the last time I will carry anything for anyone (but donot let Kit k[n]ow *this*). Honey, it appears an age since I saw you. I am more anxious to see you now than ever before. Bless your dear little self, I will ever fondly remember what a pleasant time I spent with you while at home. It seemed[20] to me while there that I had entered a paradise. Would to God I could stay with you always! Kiss the sweet cherubs for me. Good by, dear idol. Forever thine[21]

210

Franklin, March the 2, 1865

MY DEAREST ONE,

With a heart overflowing with the most delicious feelings of love for you, my darling, I sit me down to night by the same hearth stone where so lately we sat side by side whiling away the hours in sweet converse or sweeter caresses untill the hours seemed to pass with the speed of lightening. To night I find myself alone, the vacant chair & no loved one near tells me that I have no one to to love, no one to carress me to night. Honey, I do miss the mussical voice of yours whose tones have the power to make the sweetest melody in my heart of all others. I feel so sad to night, my love, and have felt so ever since you left. The change from suprem happiness to cheerless solitude is too much. It presses heavily on my heart, although I am daily surround[ed] by noise and confussion, it seems to render me more gloomy. Honey, I am not moved yet. I went down and planted my Irish Potatoes and a few seed. Mr. Watts says now he will not give much towards having the place repaired. He will try to get Mr. Baker. If he will not do so, he had rather not rent it, so I don't know what to do about. I am so sorry I did not get Mrs. Rollins' place. That is the cheapest place I know of. I can't stay here. The house is so crowd[ed] there is no satisfaction to be here. There are 7 or eight music scholars who keep a continual banging on the piano from morning till night. This evening bud Gily brought the whole school here to hear mussic, and you never saw such a scene. I came in here and found four girls up on the railing of my bed-sted, others leaning back against the beauraugh. Bud Gily is lecturing to night on Astronomy, so a good crowd had to stay and eat supper. If it is to continue so much longer, we will eat out, and I think it best to get away as soon as I can. Then the music teacher, I fear, will not

[20]The remainder is written around the edges of the page.

[21]There is no signature.

prove so amible all the while. She has already taken several mad spells. Jimmie Jackson is at home now. He belongs to the board and is taught by Chase of La Grange, one of the best musicians in [the] country. He sings all the new pieces and has a good voice too. He is going to learn the class two new pieces which I think is very pretty, "Kitty Wells & Wait till the war love is over."[22] I asked him to sing "Hard times"[23] for me this evening, which he did finely. I think the old scrape between him and bud Lu's girl is about to be made up. No[w] if bud Lu will do right, he can get out and still be friendly. Tobe Hall has been here too and spent several days with his old love, and I am enclined to think they have made up too, and after all the current of love may glide on smoothly. I never see others love each other but what I think [of] our lives. If you will only love me on to the end as you do now is all I ask of fate to give. It has been raining for over a week and the river has been but a few inches below where it was swolen to the other time. I saw Hugh Houston yestady. He told me he met you wading in the mud & it raining. I was so grieved to hear how you have to do. Pa & Ma is so distressed because you are not with bud Lu. They fear you will not get to him if he is wounded. I got Pete Wood to take your petition ot Carroll to get the officers there to sign it so you can get located here as an army surgeon to give extension of furloughs. Every body is so anxious for you to come back. Dr. Harland has a school of 25 schollars and has been teaching several days. I must stop now. Charlie is not well, has been fretful several days. Yours ever more, Kate Peddy

Andy has been gone a week and three days. I feel lost without him, he was so gentle.

Bud Gily is anxious to hear from the hat.[24]

---

[22]"Kitty Wells" is attributed to Thomas Sloan, Jr. "Wait Till the War, Love Is Over": words by A.J. Andrews, music by C.W. Burton, published by West & Johnston, Richmond, Va. in 1864. There is a copy in the Emory University Woodruff Library.

[23]By Stephen Collins Foster.

[24]The postscripts are written at the tops of the pages.

211

Goldsburroug, N.C.
March 12th, 1865

MY DEAREST SWEET ANGEL KITTIE,

With pleasure, my sweet one, I write you this eve. I have not got to my command yet. I have come up with part of our division, and the judicial director of the Corps was several days behind my time, but it is all right, as the railroad was cut and I was delayed on that account. Have seen Dr. Lane. He is well. Gave him his book back and his shirts. He did not want his shirts. Was sorry I brought them. Will send them back by the first one that passes. Lou is well, I suppose. Heard from him a few days ago. Will see him in a short time. I am on duty with Ala. Brig. but will go back to mine in a few days. I suppose we will remain here for a few days, then will get after Sherman again. We had a fight day before yesterday at a place twenty miles below here.[25] Captured fifteen hundred prisoners and three pieces of Artilery. Honey, say to Giles I have not yet got to any place that I could get any music. I will as soon as I can find some. I will send him his money as early as I can get it and see some one passing. Suppose I will get it as soon as I get to my Brig. Honey, our wagon train has not come up yet. Am having a fine time walking. I am a little uneasy about my trunk. An officer has been sent back to bring up the horses and to order the wagons to stop. I fear the baggage in it with my trunk will be deposited some whare and get lost. The wagoner is a good friend of mine. For that reason I hope he will look specially after it. Honey, suppose you are ere this snugly fixed up in your new home. If so, hope you are happy. Bless your little heart, you have no idea how devotedly I love you and want to be with you. No pleasure is so sweet as your presence. How much and how well I love you, you can form but a meager idea; and our little sweet cherubs are second to none in my affections but yourself. Bless there sweet little hearts, I can see them now in all their beauty and loveliness. Remember well evry motion and action and gesture: all seem supremely sweet to me. Honey, I try to give you some idea with my pen of the extent of my admiration for your precious self and our sweet cherubs, but fall so far short of it that I almost dispair. Honey, you must speak to the little ones often for me. Tell them how I love them and how exceedingley proud of them I am. I do wish I could get to my trunk to send home my little presents for them. I will send George by the place whare the wagon train is and let him bring them home. Give my love to all. Good by, my sweetest one. Ever thine G.W.P.

[25]This refers to a series of actions at Kinston, 7-10 March.

212

Smithfield, N.C.
March 23rd, 1865

MY SWEET CHERUB KITTIE, With the greatest pleasure, my love, I write you a short letter this eve. I do wish I had time to tell you how devotedly I love you and how much I miss you since I left home [and] your dear presence. No one, it seems to me, my dearest, ever loved so fondly as I do you. Bless your sweet soul, it greavs me to think that you will never find out how dearly and devotedly I love you, and as for the passion of love which is in my soul for our lesser cherubs, they, bless their little hearts, like you will never be able to find it out. Dearest, it seems to me that I never missed you and our cherubs so much as I do now. I think of nothing else but you all and how dearly I love you. In sadness and in joy I always reflect how happy I ought to be while I am well, even if away from you. Honey, you have no idea how proud indeed I feel when I think of your beauty, inteligence and one in evry way so well fited to discharge the very responsible duty we owe to our dear ones. Honey, we have been fighting for the last two days with no very desided result. Both army are now on the move. Shearman, I think, will be after flanking us again. That is the reason we are on the march to meet him again. Gen. Johns[t]on is in command. Evry face looks bright and cheerfull. You need not doubt our ability now to whip Shearman. We will have in a short time a splendid army, better if possible than we have had before. My horse has not come up yet. I am looking for him evry day. Be assured that I should like to see him, for I am very tired of walking. say to uncle Jeo I will send George home as soon as I think it safe. He is very well and seems to be well pleased. Lou cam out of the fight safely and is in good health. Jake Hawk was killed. His brother Jerry is seriously wounded. So is James Scroggins. Poor fellows, I am so sorry for them. They acted gallantly and nobbly, killed and wounded at their post. I deeply sympathise with their familys in their sad state of mind. Honey, I suppose ere this you are happyly situated at your new home. I have some money for you now, if I could send it to you. I will send Giles' hat to him by George, also Charlie's and Laura's little book. The wagon has not come up with them yet, but will in a short time. Honey, when you write, give me all the news about home. Tell me how our little cherubs look. Honey, please get Laura to say a lesson evry day. I am very anxious about her learning. I want her to know how to read by the time she is six years old.

Honey, I have received no letter from you since I left your dear presence. Honey, Kiss our sweet little cherubs for Pappie often.

Good by, my precious one. Think of me often and always remember that I will ever love you fondly.

Thine only
G.W. Peddy

To his Dear Wife
Kittie

213

Near Smithfield, N.C.
March 27th, 1865

MY DEAR SWEET CHERUB KITTIE, I wrote you last night,[26] write you again to day to let you know that their will arrive at Hoganville for you ere long per express four hundred dollars. It will be express to you from Columbus, Ga. It's all I can send you now. Will send you more before a great while. Lou has just come to see me. He is not very well. Hope he will be in a few days. My love to all at home. Kiss the sweet cherubs for their Pa.

Ever Thine
G. W. Peddy

214

Camp Near Smithfield, N.C.
March 30th, 1865

MY SWEET CHERUB KITTIE,

In sadness and in joy I like to have some one to console me, but alas, I am far away from that one who is best calculated to console me. I feel sad to night, as all the horses have up, but Andy, poor fellow, he gave out in the foot that he was

[26]This letter is missing.

lame in and was left at Millidgeville, Ga. with Mr. Edwards. I do hope the poor fellow will get on well—a friend of mine, a soldier whose Father lives in Millidgeville. I rather he was at home. I am here now a foot. I will try to borrow a horse until I can hear from him. My saddle, I learn, is coming on in the wagon. I suppose I will make out so as not to buy another. I am not able to do so and do you and our little sweet cherubs justice. I will walk the balance of the war before I will deprive you and our sweet ones the least comfort. I hear that the young man will bring my horse to me if he gets well soon. If he does not, he will leave him at his father's until he get[s] well. I suppose if he does not get well soon, I will have to try and get him home. Poor fellow, I donot want to loose him because you like him so well. Honey, I am glad to say my trunk is safe and will be up in a few days. I will then start George home. I donot want uncle Jeo to find out that I am detaining him for that purpose. Dearest, our army will be consolidated in a few days. I donot know what will become of me. I may be thrown out of my position. If so, I will come home if the powers that be allow it; if not, I will join some Cavalry command if I can get a horse. If I am droped from the roll, I will be allowed sixty day[s] to choose my command. In the mean time I will come home, but perhaps I will be assigned to some Regt. after it is consolidated. A great many medical officers who are exemped will go home and rem[a]in in their. Honey, do not forget to think of how dearly I love you and our little cherubs. Honey, donot lament over my misfortune in regard to our favorite Andy and my present condition. I will get along doubtless well. Have not yet received any letter from you. Am quite anxious to see again some lines pened by your beautifull hand.

Good by, sweet one. Be cheerfull and buoyant. There is yet, I hope, much happyness in store for us togueather. Bless our sweet little idols. Kiss them for me. Will write you again soon.

Ever thine
G.W. Peddy

P.S. My complement to friends. Love to our family. Lou is now quiet well.

215

Camp Near Smithfield, N.C.
April 2nd, 1865

MY DARLING CHERUB KITTIE, I am glad indeed to announce the safe arrival of your sweet letter of the 2nd ult, to which I now hasten to reply.[27] I was perfectly happy while reading it; such tender, sweet and welcome message of love as it breaths in evry word and line chaces away from my soul evry feeling of gloom and dispondency, and their nestles deep in my heart (*as your sweet hand oft does in my own while strolling* with *you*) responsive feengings [*sic*] of true love, which will be as unwavoring as time and which is the panacea to all my sad feeling and diffidence. I always, Honey, feel far more manly and a greater desire to survive this struggle that I may contribute to your happyness in future, after a paroosal of your sweet and heart cheering letter. You, my *Cherub,* have a peculiar tact in your communications of making me feel delightfully pleasent. For this reason, my love, your letter cannot come to[o] often. I sympathise truely with you, my own, in your lonely condition. I do wish it was so that I could now occupy the vacant chair and feel the sweet sensation of the fond caresses spoken of in yours. You canot possibly miss nor desire more fondly than myself a constant repitition of these delightfull tokens of love.

Oh! how nice it would be to taste the nectar of the lips of little Charlie and Laura. Now imagine I see in your dear eyes the feelings of responsive joy it would produce in your heart. God bless you and our Cherubs in my absence and presence. Honey, donot give your *dear self* to[o] much concern about your situation. If it is not to[o] unpleasent, I would not leave whare you are. Better stay. Perhaps if you are to have so many cares, I fear you would have to[o] much to look after. If so, I would not move, but my *dearest*, if you wish to go to the plase and Mr. Watts does not object, I am more than willing you should do so. Honey, I wish you to act in the move as you wish to and do *without hesitation* that which you think will conduce most to your comfort and happyness and the wellfare of our cherubs. I *will be satisfied* and *happy at any course you take in the changes.* I suppose ere this you have desided what you will do and have acted as your good discression prompted. I will send Giles' hat in a short time if the enemy has not captured it with my trunk and saddle. If my saddle and uniform is gone I will feel mortified greatly. I learn that their is a raid going in the direction of the train. I do hope it is not true. I hope Andy will be well in a short time. I learn that he is at a good place and in good hands. Honey, if you have not moved I should not let my Bureau remain in the parlor. I am glad you all tried to interest Jimmie Jackson while at home. Am pleased to learn his efficiency in music.

Their is great excitement among the officers of the army about the consolidation bill. We will be consolidated in a short time, which will necessarially throw out many officer. All of them seem to be anxious to get out,

---

[27]No. 210.

with the privalege (as the law allows) of joining any other branch of the survice they wish. All want to join Cavalry. Its getting late, my love. Must close. Goodby, my sweetest and dearest of all on earth. Hope to hear from you soon. Kiss our Sweet Cherubs for me. Will start George home as soon as the raid gets out of the way. Lou & Dr. Lane were both at my quarters this eve; are quite well. Give my love to all, to Chippie when you see her.

Ever thine only
G.W. Peddy

216

Saulisbury, N.C. April 17th/865

MY OWN PRECIOUS CHERUB KITTIE,

Again it is my sweet pleasure to write you a few lines. We came to this place a few days ago to repell a raid that succeeded in burning a large amount of stores and distroying a large quantey of Goverment machinery. Suppose we will remain here until the main army falls back to this point. I suppose that ere this reaches you, you will learn that the proud army of the old Dominion has been all captured by the enemy except a large number of straglers that ran out.[28] Our army has been consolidated. I am not certain as yet that I will be retained as a medical officer. If I am not, I will come home and remain for sixty days and perhaps all the time. I could be thrown out at my own request and perhaps remain at home during the war, but am almost afraid to ask it for fear I am taken in, in a different capacity. I do wish, my love, I could have an hour's talk with you on the subject. I would then know exactly what to do. Honey, I am almost in the notion to be droped from the roll and take the chances hereafter. *What* must I do, my dearest? Of course I will know my fate ere this reaches you. I am so sorry I am deprived of your advise in this very important matter. Honey, I think our army will come back to Ga. in a short time and perhaps go again to Miss. Now, my love, is far the darkest hour in our history that I have ever seen, but hope we will yet achieve our independence. Our troops yet seem hopefull.

Honey, bless you and our little ones. How much I wish to see you no one

---

[28]Gen. Robert E. Lee surrendered to Gen. U.S. Grant on 9 April at Appomattox Courthouse, Va.

knows but myself. I often think of you and our sweet cherubs as you sit at night around your little hearthstone. I would give all it seems to me just to have the pleasure of seeing you quietly at home. Give my love to all. Hope I will hear from you soon. Kiss our sweet cherubs for me. (Excuse haste)

G.W.P.

(Lou is well)[29]

* * *

On 14 April 1865 Gen. Joseph E. Johnston, realizing that his situation was hopeless, requested an armistic. Hostilities were never resumed, and Johnston surrendered to Gen. William T. Sherman on 26 April 1865.

---

[29]Written across the top of the first page.

PEDDY GENEALOGY
(Abbreviated)

Alexander George PEDDY m. Celina D. H. Shackleford
1803-1878 1828 1814-1867

Lamantha Orange m. Thomas Jefferson BECKHAM
1829-1887 1849 1826-1875

- Frances Emeline (b. 1850)
- Nancy Ann Minerva (b. 1851)
- Mary Celina (b. 1853)
- Margaret Elizabeth (b. 1854)
- James Buchanan (b. 1856)
- Alice (b. 1858)
- Lamantha Orange (b. 1859)

William J.
b. 1831

George Washington m. *Zerlina Catherine Featherston*
1834-1913 1859 1838-1927

- Annie Laurie ("Laura"), b. 1860
- Charlie Featherston (1864-1865)

Frances M.
b. 1836

John Taylor
1838-1910

Susan
b. 1844

Andrew T.
b. 1848

FEATHERSTON GENEALOGY
(Abbreviated)

Lucius Horace FEATHERSTON m. Maria Ann Tompkins
1814-1886 1836 1819-1898

- *Zerlina Catherine* ("Kate," "Kitty"), *see* PEDDY
- Charles Nicholas ("Nick"), b. 1839
- Giles Winfield ("Giley"), b. 1842
- Lucius Horace ("Lou"), b. 1844
- Edward Pitts ("Eddie"), b. 1846
- John Henry, b. 1849
- Sarah Maria ("Sally"), b. 1851
- William Steagall ("Will"), b. 1853
- Mary Emma ("May"), b. 1856
- Thomas Middleton ("Tommy"), b. 1858
- Annie Elizabeth, b. 1860
- Joseph Ernest ("Joe"), b. 1863

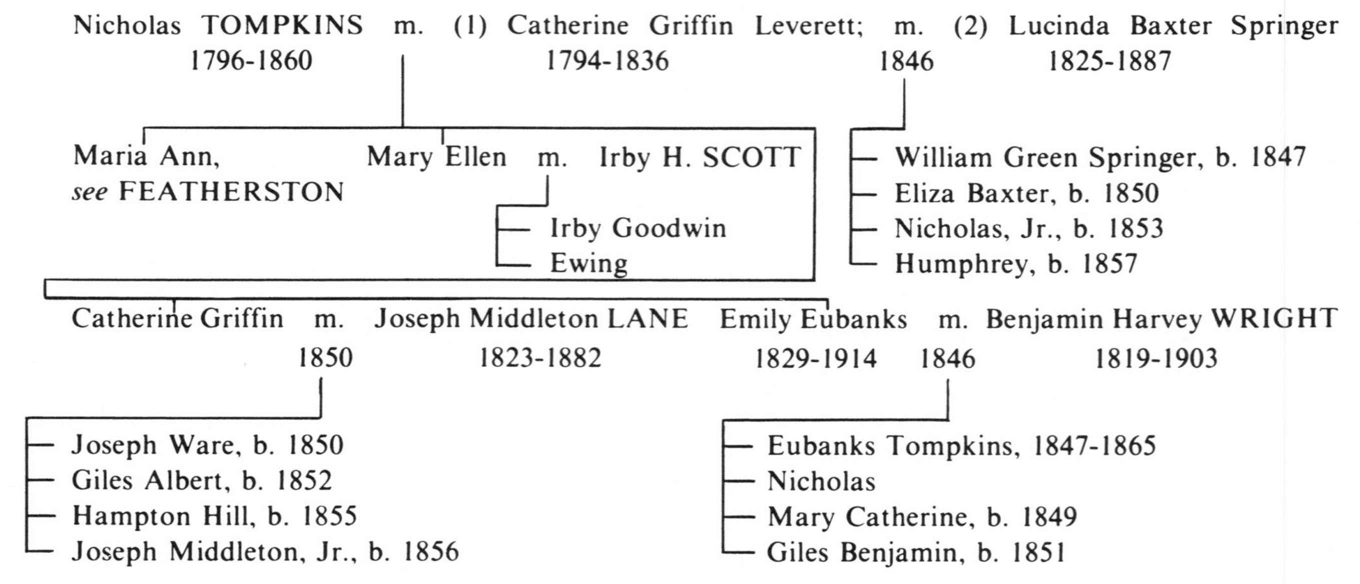

TOMPKINS GENEALOGY
(Abbreviated)

INDEX

References to letter numbers, not page numbers